The unknown Virginia Woolf

Roger Poole

Reader in Literary Theory,
University of Nottingham

HUMANITIES PRESS INTERNATIONAL, INC.
New Jersey • London

First published 1978 by the Syndics of the Cambridge University Press

Third edition reprinted with new preface 1990 by
Humanities Press International, Inc.,
171 First Avenue, Atlantic Highlands, NJ 07716
and 3 Henrietta Street, London WC2E 8LU.

Library of Congress Cataloging-in-Publication Data
Poole, Roger, 1939–
    The unknown Virginia Woolf / Roger Poole.—3rd ed.
      p. cm.
    Includes bibliographical references.
    ISBN 0–391–03666–1
    1. Woolf, Virginia, 1882–1941. 2. Authors, English—20th
century—Biography. 3. Psychoanalysis and literature. I. Title.
PR6045.072Z862 1990
823'.912—dc20
[B]   89–29976
                                    CIP

British Cataloguing in Publication Data

A CIP record for this book is available from the British Library.

Appendices 1 and 2 which develop lines of thought implicit in
The Unknown Virginia Woolf, originally appeared in *Charleston Newsletter*
No. 13 (December 1985): 19–37, and No. 16 (September 1986): 16–32,
and are reproduced here by kind permission of the Editor, Mr. Hugh
Lee. Professor Quentin Bell has kindly given permission for his
comments, which followed the essay on Virginia Woolf's *Diary*, to be
reproduced in this edition of the book.

Printed in the United States of America

CONTENTS

ACKNOWLEDGMENTS

The excerpts from the writings of Virginia Woolf and Leonard Woolf, from *Moments of Being*, edited by Jeanne Schulkind and *The Letters of Virginia Woolf*, edited by Nigel Nicolson assisted by Joanne Trautmann, are reprinted by permission of the Literary Estates of Virginia Woolf and Leonard Woolf, the Hogarth Press and Harcourt Brace, Jovanovich, Inc.; copyright, 1920, by George H. Doran and Company; copyright 1925, 1927, 1931, 1938, 1941 by Harcourt Brace, Jovanovich, Inc.; copyright, 1948, 1953, 1954, 1955, 1959, 1966, 1969, © 1963, 1964, 1969 by Leonard Woolf, copyright © 1975, 1976 by Quentin Bell and Angelica Garnett.

Preface to the Third Edition

The Unknown Virginia Woolf has had a riotous and exciting reception, and a great deal has happened since it first appeared in 1978. Through letters from psychiatrists, historians of medicine and people acquainted with some of the original *dramatis personae*, I have come to learn a great deal more about the medical and psychiatric background to the book, and everything tends to confirm its central contention.

It has been gratifying, too, to see a certain amount of expert opinion coming around to a point of view which was, in 1978, regarded as more or less heretical. Mr Nigel Nicolson, for instance, in editing the sixth and final volume of Virginia Woolf's *Letters*, considers the implications and chronology of the three suicide notes, and, after long and careful weighing of the evidence, finally opts for a decision identical with mine:

Was this insanity? No, it was a combination of fantasy and fear. She would have recovered, as she had before. She was not mad when she died. . . . Virginia Woolf chose to die. It was not an insane or impulsive act, but premeditated. She died courageously on her own terms.[1]

In 1978, that view was irreceivable.

One of the most interesting result of the publication of this book has been the opening up of a discussion of the way Virginia Woolf herself uses the words mad and madness in her writings. It was pointed out that she does indeed write of herself as having been 'mad', and that on one occasion she even implies that 'madness' had been beneficial to her work.[2]

This, I am afraid, solves nothing. The matter is indeed largely linguistic (or 'semantic') but it is so in a subtle way. I understand these uses of the words mad and madness as follows. Her specialists would have referred to her as 'mad', and for them 'madness' was equivalent to 'moral insanity', and that in its turn was virtually indistinguishable from social malingering. The language of description was morally laden, and the cures meted out were intended, at least partly, to be punitive. The judgment passed upon Virginia Woolf, in 1913–15, that she was 'mad' was one which she had no alternative but to accept and to learn to live with.

So inevitably, I think, she came to adopt this term. But I feel she did it at one remove. When she refers to her own 'madness' she is using the terminology of the doctors, somebody else's diagnostic phrase.[3]

That this is true even of the suicide letters, indeed especially true of them, reinforces my belief that these last letters were written in Leonard's language in order that Leonard should comprehend her decision.

But she also uses the word 'mad' in her last letter to Vanessa. I have argued in this book that Leonard's view of Virginia's 'madness' was derived from Vanessa's, and consequently it comes as no surprise to me to find that Virginia uses the same terminology to Vanessa, in her letter to her of 23 March 1941, as she does to Leonard.

'Madness' in both cases is used as an equivalent term for 'hearing voices', and 'hearing voices' is the ultimate small change for what is obviously an enormously inward and subjective problem. Whose voices? No one has stopped to ask. So the outer phrase is offered for the inner reality, the dominant language is used in order that Virginia, faced with the inexpressible, the terrifying and the unanalysed, can quietly defect.

But a great deal more ought to be said about the actual project of *The Unknown Virginia Woolf*, as opposed to the project many of the earlier reviewers took it to have.

Quentin Bell and Leonard Woolf may well have been using the terms mad and insane without any clear medical or analytical notion of what they were affirming, but it is certainly true that in deploying the language of madness in the way they did, they were both perfectly in tune with the dominant psychiatric discourse of their day. The psychiatric divisions of the psychoses did not differ significantly, when Bell was writing his biography and Leonard Woolf was telling the story of his life with Virginia, from the original analysis of 'manic depressive insanity' as laid out by Kraepelin at the beginning of this century.

It is remarkable how little the understanding and categorisation of the psychoses have differed since that time. One of today's teaching textbooks in psychiatry, *Clinical Psychiatry* by Mayer-Gross, Slater and Roth, which first appeared in 1954, had a third edition in 1969, was reprinted in 1974, since when it has been constantly reprinted, simply sets out from where Kraepelin left off.[4] The chapter 'Affective Disorders' names him in its third sentence:

The term affective disorders is used for a group of mental diseases with a primary disturbance of affect from which all the other symptoms seem more or less directly derived. The affect is of a special kind, varying between the poles of *cheerfulness and sadness*. This is clearly expressed in Kraepelin's term 'manic depressive insanity.'[5]

Mayer-Gross, Slater and Roth obviously see nothing incongruous in starting a mid-twentieth-century account of the 'affective disorders' by basing it on a late nineteenth-century theorist. Indeed, they cheerfully cite mid-nineteenth-century theorists in the following paragraph:

Around the nucleus of the periodic manic-depressive illness, first described by Falret (1854, 1864) and Baillarger (1853/4) under the name of *'folie circulaire'*, other French psychiatrists grouped many variants of periodic disorders containing depressive or manic phases only, with longer or shorter lucid intervals, and gave each variant its special name.[6]

The continuity of psychiatric doctrine is impressive. This mid-nineteenth-century French phase of the subject is only modified, it would appear, by the superior insight of the late nineteenth-century theorist, Kraepelin:

It was Kraepelin who saw that the different forms belong to one nosological entity; he included isolated attacks of mania and depression and, after some hesitation, also the depressions of later life (involutional melancholia) into his manic depressive insanity.[7]

Three pages later Kraepelin is cited again as the theorist from whom we still have to start:

If Kraepelin's conception of the manic-depressive constitution is adopted, four types may be distinguished (see the accompanying table). They have been considered the *'basic states'* from which the psychoses rise like mountain peaks from a structurally similar level plain.[8]

'*If* Kraepelin's conception of the manic depressive constitution is adopted'! But it *has* been adopted. What transpires is that the received textbook in psychiatry today simply lays out the divisions of 'manic depressive insanity' as Kraepelin laid them out at the turn of the century.

Thus one of R. D. Laing's 'placing remarks' in *The Divided Self* (1960) takes on a quite new resonance. Preparing to cite a particularly barbaric passage (which I quote below) about Kraepelin's use of his patient in front of an audience, Laing observes:

That the classical clinical psychiatric attitude has not changed in principle since Kraepelin can be seen by comparing the following with the similar attitude of any recent British textbook of psychiatry (e.g. Mayer-Gross, Slater and Roth).[9]

That judgment itself dates from 1960. Thus the period in which Leonard Woolf was writing his *Autobiography*, and when Quentin Bell was writing his biography of Virginia Woolf, would still have been under the undisputed sway of Kraepelin's account of the affective disorders.

The psychiatric assumption that the psychotic 'affective disorders' (such as mania, depression, manic-depression) could correctly and technically be called madness would have been as much a part of the discourse of psychiatric power in the 1960s as it would have been in 1913–15. Both Leonard Woolf and Quentin Bell, in using the words mad and insane, were merely conforming with current linguistic usage.

But that assumption about the nature and reality of psychosis carries with it the further assumption that the patient's discourse is itself unintelligible. That is the sticking point. It is at that point that *The Unknown Virginia Woolf* attempted to do some new investigations. Taking the novels, and as much of the life as was then available, in double harness, it seemed to me when I published this book originally in 1978 that the speeches of Virginia Woolf herself (preserved for us by Vanessa Bell, for instance, or glimpsed through the decently veiled accounts of Leonard Woolf) were far from unintelligible, were in fact extremely intelligible. If a certain kind of psychiatry be conceived of as a theoretical and deliberate training in insensitivity, it trains itself first and foremost not to hear what the patient is saying. The psychiatrist wants to analyse, perhaps to treat, but he does not want to hear. The patient desires above all to be heard. While the psychiatrist is working on the assumption that the patient's discourse is unintelligible, I suspected that the patient's discourse is intelligible if there is anyone around in whose interest it is that it should be intelligible.

Here, however, the trouble arose. The hostile reception which *The Unknown Virginia Woolf* received in some quarters showed that certain interest groups did not want to read off these legible aspects of the 'madness'. It was not, it clearly transpired upon publication, a question of the intellect, it was a question of the will.

It had been decided that Virginia Woolf had been mad and insane. Leonard Woolf had said so. Leonard Woolf was the most intelligent member of his brilliant generation at Cambridge; if Leonard Woolf could not see any rationality in his wife's behaviour, then there was none. There were no forms of rational discourse which Leonard Woolf could not have recognised *as* forms of rational discourse.

Leaning upon Leonard Woolf's first-hand account in his *Autobiography* for the details, Quentin Bell seemed to imply that Virginia Woolf at her 'maddest', especially at her 'maddest', made no sense, was unintelligible. But if one uses the assumptions of received psychiatry to imply that the discourse of the patient is unintelligible, these assumptions have to be examined and, if necessary, opposed. However accurate they may be at the technical level, these assumptions and terms imply something about the alleged insanity which may not be quite so innocent.

A great deal of the early criticism of *The Unknown Virginia Woolf* seemed to miss this very elementary distinction, and consequently very few reviewers actually understood what the book was about. It was not concerned with some nominalism—whether this or that behaviour should or should not be called mad—but was concerned with our almost complete ignorance of what 'insanity' is, coupled with a certain impatience at the lack of humility with which damaging and unhelpful terms can be deployed. The book was concerned, finally, with the conditions under which psychotic discourse could, in spite of the psychiatrists, be capable of coherent interpretation.

cf,
Kristeva

So far as Quentin Bell could see, when he came to write his famous biography, if Leonard Woolf could perceive no rationality in his wife's behaviour, the behaviour must indeed have been truly mad and insane.

There was thus a received version of Virginia Woolf's illness, one which set up, accepted as a premise and vigorously defended a certain kind of reasonableness, a certain kind of Reason, as a paradigm which one could not seriously question. I have tried to define the forms that this Reason took in my book. Here it must suffice to say that the rationality that Leonard Woolf and after him Quentin Bell were assuming was one in which meaning was made verbally explicit, and in which there were no ambiguities, no symbolisms and no 'hidden' psychological referents.

For an outsider, particularly for someone who had not known Virginia Woolf personally, to meddle with these decisions about 'family' reputation and prestige was perceived as little short of outrageous. To those who held the received version of Virginia Woolf's madness, *The Unknown Virginia Woolf* appeared as an offence, as an impropriety, an iconoclasm, even as a sacrilege. (I am citing the gist of early reviews.) Above all, why should anyone meddle with this matter at all? Had not Leonard Woolf and Quentin Bell said (and tactfully) all that needed to be said? Had not the matter been *decided* by the competent authorities?

That was the real reason for some of the more ecstatic reviewing: the matter had been decided by the competent authorities. I had naively been assuming that my book would open up a theme of intrinsic interest, a subject which could be discussed 'in the common pursuit of true judgment'. Nothing so fruitful as that was allowed to become possible. My book had to be opposed at any cost and at any level, simply because it refused to recognise two sorts of authority. And with the realisation that what was at issue was the mere challenging of authority, the shadow of Michel Foucault fell across the stage a second time.

I had recognised the importance of his *Folie et Déraison, Histoire de la Folie à l'âge classique*, not long after it came out in 1961. It had played a part in my thinking ever since, and I was aware while writing *The Unknown Virginia Woolf* that her case fitted into his general contention, and that she would have been one of his prohetic *'fulgurations'*, as I noted in the preface to the second edition in 1982.

But I had not realised the *extent* to which any given discourse is itself an aspect of power relations. This was one of the basic connections Foucault was himself slowest to make, as he admitted in an interview of 1977:

On the contrary, I am struck by the difficulty I had formulating it. When I think about it now I ask myself what I could have been talking about, in *Histoire de la folie*, for example, or *Naissance de la clinique*, if not power? Yet I am perfectly well aware that I practically never used the word and did not have that field of analysis at my disposal. This inability was certainly bound up with the political situation in which we found ourselves.[10]

In his inaugural lecture at the Collège de France in 1970, drawing on the experience gathered during the 'events' of May 1968, Foucault once again hinted at the power structure underlying the fact that some people simply cannot be heard:

But our society possesses yet another principle of exclusion; not another prohibition, but a division and a rejection. I have in mind the opposition: reason and folly. From the depths of the Middle Ages, a man was mad if his speech could not be said to form part of the common discourse of men. His words were considered null and void, without truth or significance . . . the madman's speech did not strictly exist. . . . No doctor before the end of the eighteenth century had ever thought of listening to the content—how it was said and why—of these words; and yet it was these which signalled the difference between reason and madness. Whatever a madman said, it was taken for mere noise.[11]

But in 1975, Foucault admitted straight out that his master of thought had come to be Nietzsche, Nietzsche who had allowed him to pull the two sides of his thought-project into focus:

It was Nietzsche who specified the power relation as the general focus, shall we say, of philosophical discourse—whereas for Marx it was the production relation. Nietzsche is the philosopher of power, but he managed to think power without confining himself within a political theory to do so.[12]

To suggest otherwise, to suggest that the madman's words might not just be 'mere noise' was the most daring contention of *The Unknown Virginia Woolf*. The reactions to it in 1978 could not have been a clearer proof of the rightness of Foucault's analyses of the psychiatric and social 'discourse of power'. The amount of loyal, offended, stridently defensive reviews was impressive. But it was also noticeable that none of the offended reviewers actually had any counter evidence. No one seriously questioned my case: in fact, that was left respectfully alone. In the academic journals a new form of investment was noticeable. My book would be held up to derision, then exculpated on some rather major ground, and finally its general argument and contention would be silently added into the next book or essay of the reviewer. But it would very rarely be *named* in those later uses. The essential contention of *The Unknown Virginia Woolf* was accepted into the body of scholarly expertise, but few of those drawing on its conclusions would admit to the origin of their new insight. In terms of 'reception theory' alone, *The Unknown*

Virginia Woolf is worthy of consequent documentation.

In questioning Quentin Bell's biography of Virginia Woolf and Leonard Woolf's *Autobiography*, I had implicitly questioned the reach, adequacy and completeness of a certain Cambridge rationalism which is still dominant in parts of English academic life today. To question Leonard Woolf was to question that whole rationality—to question G. E. Moore, Bertrand Russell, Maynard Keynes, even the positivist Wittgenstein, and that whole manner of doing things and talking to people. Secondly, I realised that *The Unknown Virginia Woolf* was itself an uncovering of a discourse of power that Virginia Woolf had been submitted to in 1913–15 and on later occasions. She herself had been the victim of a certain discourse of power which reigned unquestioned and unquestionable in her own day. She had been the victim of stereotyped 'medical' prejudices of that time, been seen by what Foucault calls 'le regard médical'. She had been asked questions, the answers to which allowed the specialists to 'place' her within existing medical categories, into which she was slotted as just another 'case'. What was *non*-typical about her would have been systematically ignored by 'le regard médical'.[13]

These mental specialists—whose primitively physical-reductive-moralistic view of things is mercilessly revenged in the portrait of Sir William Bradshaw in *Mrs Dalloway*—were full of *theories*: theories that artistic females were decadent and ought not to have children; theories about the degeneration of the race and the necessity of preserving its vigour by certain decisions in eugenics; the social deviancy of all artists and intellectuals.

Two central assumptions of the discourse of power in psychiatry in Virginia Woolf's day would have been that the patient is talking unconnected gibberish and, as a corollary to that, that he or she does not have to be listened to. Stephen Trombley has set out the reductive and doctrinaire views of some of these specialists in his book, *'All That Summer She was Mad'*. Their hostility to any show of an artistic temperament would be funny or grotesque if had not led to such grim suffering on the part of those who fell into their power. T. B. Hyslop, in particular, gives

vent to an animosity towards artistic expression which must
have cost Virginia Woolf dear in her time:

Many of the greatest painters, sculptors, and engravers, whose names
live in their works, have their names inscribed in the case-books of our
asylums . . . Giorgione, Tintoretto, Paul Veronese, Botticelli, Leonardo
da Vinci, Rubens, Raphael, Albert Durer, Claude Lorraine, Salvator
Rosa, Benvenuto Cellini, van Dyck and Watteau, all suffered from
some form of neurosis. . . . We are told Molière, Petrarch,
Charles V, Handel, St. Paul, and Peter the Great were epileptics.
Paganini, Mozart, Schiller, Alfieri, Pascal, Richelieu, Newton and Swift
were victims of diseases, epileptoid in character. . . .[14]

And so it goes on.

Evidence of the actual power of the nerve specialists of the
early twentieth century continues to come to light. Elaine Showalter's *The Female Malady: Woman, Madness and English Culture
1830–1980* has a chapter which illustrates the authority that
nerve specialists could exercise around the time of Virginia
Woolf's 1913 breakdown.[15] Although she calls her book 'The
Female Malady' and obviously intends her work to bear mainly
on the problems of women, she is forced, by the very reality and
urgency of her materials to present at one point the suffering of
men. Her book thus turns out to be fairer and more generous
than (to judge by her title) she seems to have intended.

The chapter called 'Male Hysteria: W. H. R. Rivers and the
Lessons of Shell Shock' contrasts the applied psychiatric
methods of two specialists operating during World War I. The
more frightening of the two is Dr Lewis Yealland, who was
treating men suffering from 'shell shock' in the trenches. His
methods included the use of 'very strong faradic shocks' which
were applied over a period of hours to patients strapped into a
chair. The more gentle, but equally determined, W. H. R.
Rivers, who treated the poet Siegfried Sassoon at Craiglockhart
Military Hospital near Edinburgh, brought all the powers of
dialectic and suggestion to bear on members of the officer class
who had succumbed to the moral and psychological effects of
the war. The contrast between the two men, and the two
methods, is neatly established by Elaine Showalter. She sug-

gests that from these two men and these two methods may flow the two major forms of modern psychiatric practice:

The crude faradic battery of the military hospital became the electric-shock machine of modern psychiatry. In this era, psychiatric descendants of both Yealland and Rivers would come to fullest power.[16]

The violence brought to bear by Dr Lewis Yealland must be understood, of course, in the context of a war still in progress, where the aim was a practical one: to get men psychologically disabled back into a condition to fight. Showalter writes:

Attitudes towards hysteria and neurasthenia also influenced treatment. Disciplinary therapy provided for soldiers took a harsh moral view of hysteria as within the conscious control of the patient; they stressed quick cures, shaming, and physical re-education, which often involved the infliction of pain. Therapeutic treatments provided for officers took a situational view of neurasthenia, saw its source in unconscious conflict beyond the patient's control, and stressed the examination of repressed traumatic experience through conversation, hypnosis or psychoanalysis. But though they were strategically different, both of these treatments were essentially coercive. The goal of wartime psychiatry was to keep men fighting, and thus the handling of male hysterics and neurasthenics was more urgently purposeful than the treatments Harley Street specialists had offered their nervous women patients. Nevertheless the two kinds of treatment suggest parallels to the hostile therapies and silencings that English doctors had recommended for hysterical women, on the one hand, and the talking cures developed in Europe, on the other. The two psychiatrists most identified with each treatment, Lewis Yealland and W. H. R. Rivers, represent the two poles of psychiatric modernism.[17]

The point is an important one. There were two praxes, two approaches, two sorts of discipline. Yet one has to wonder whether all of the '114,600 neurasthenic ex-servicemen who applied for pensions for shell-shock-related disorders between 1919 and 1929'[18] were treated, were they to have applied for therapy as well as for money, with the same slow-paced and elegant courtesy which W. H. R. Rivers had shown to Siegfried Sassoon in Craiglockhart Military Hospital. The strong implication of Elaine Showalter's study is that they were not: that the gentlemanly, Socratic, mutually investigative manner practised by Rivers was reserved for the officer class. Let us assume so with her for a moment. What would have been the experience of the 114,600 ordinary privates who applied for, or got, psychiatric attention between 1919 and 1929? Virginia Woolf, in her description of her fictional Septimus Smith, made a suggestion so instinct with verisimilitude and probability that, pending further evidence, we could well accept her description as being largely the truth. In fact, though it might appear paradoxical, I think a case could be made out for Virginia Woolf's *Mrs Dalloway* being the best 'war-novel' that the 1914–18 war produced.

What emerges from the section on the praxis of Dr Lewis Yealland, however, is one of the most striking continuities of psychiatric practice from Kraepelin to today. It is the refusal of the psychiatrist to *listen*. Not just the inability to hear or to attend, but the actual methodological decision *not to listen*. Perhaps the best way to grasp this is to look at Dr Lewis Yealland's own account of the treatment of one soldier of the war. Showalter introduces him thus:

In 1917, he had treated an unnamed twenty-four-year-old private who had fought in the worst campaigns of the war—the Mons retreat, the battle of the Marne, Ypres, Hill 60, Neuve Chapelle, Loos and Armentières.[19]

Given war experiences of this ferocity and this continuity, a loss of the desire to speak would have seemed natural enough. But not for Dr Yealland. Not to speak was subversive, insubordinate, threatening. This young man had to be treated for his 'illness':

The soldier was fastened down in a chair, his mouth was propped open with a tongue depressor, and strong electric currents were applied to his pharynx, causing him to start backwards so that the wires were pulled out of the battery. . . . For four hours the shocks continued. After the first hour the patient could whisper 'ah'. . . . Eventually [Dr Yealland] returned to the battery, administering shocks until the patient began to stammer and cry. Even then Yealland was not satisfied, and 'very strong faradic shocks were applied' until this young man spoke without stutter or tremor. He was required to say 'thank you' at the end.[20]

It is on Yealland's own admission that we have the fact that he did not want to listen to what the patient had to say:

When he did not make satisfactory progress, I increased the strength of the current, refusing to listen to anything he had to say.[21]

Showalter goes on:

Symptoms of emotional disturbance—nightmares, terrible memories, anxieties, depression—were harshly rejected as irrelevant, and Yealland would not listen to any description of them. One of his patients, a twenty-three-year-old who had spent six months in the trenches near the Somme, choked and twitched continually, and dreamed of blood and being near an exploding mine. 'It makes very little difference to me what you think of your condition,' Yealland told him. 'I do not want to hear about your views on the subject'. After ten minutes of strong electric shocks he had stopped what Yealland called his 'silly noises'. That night he dreamed no more of blood and mines. He 'dreamt that he was having electrical treatment in the trenches'. Yealland considered the therapy a success.[22]

The fact that the psychiatrists of that period insisted on not listening to what the patient had to say is a very interesting comment on psychiatry's investigative model. Ironically enough, that discourse of power operated through a deafness: its insistence that it did not want to listen to what the patient had to say was an indirect or occluded admission that what the patient had to say *would* be significant in the patient's own context. But to deny the context is to deny the significance.

It was with this recognition that R. D. Laing began his work nearly three decades ago. In *The Divided Self*, he starts out from a critique of the lecturing practice of the famed mental specialist Kraepelin:

That the classical clinical psychiatric attitude has not changed in principle since Kraepelin can be seen by comparing the following with the similar attitude of any recent British textbook of psychiatry (e.g. Mayer-Gross, Slater and Roth).

Here is Kraepelin's (1905) account to a lecture-room of his students of a patient showing the signs of catatonic excitement:

The patient I will show you today has almost to be carried into the rooms, as he walks in a straddling fashion on the outside of his feet. On coming in, he throws off his slippers, sings a hymn loudly, and then cries twice (in English), 'My father, my real father'. He is eighteen years old, and a pupil of the Oberrealschule [higher-grade modern-side school], tall, and rather strongly built, but with a pale complexion, on which there is very often a transient flush. The patient sits with his eyes shut and pays no attention to his surroundings. He does not look up even when he is spoken to, but he answers beginning in a low voice, and gradually screaming louder and louder. When asked where he is, he says, 'You want to know that too? I tell you who is being measured and is measured and shall be measured. I know all that, and could tell you, but I do not want to'. When asked his name, he screams, 'What is your name? What does he shut? He shuts his eyes. What does he hear? He does not understand; he understands not. How? Who? Where? When? What does he mean? When I tell him to look he does not look properly. You there, just look! What is it? What is the matter? Attend; he attends not. I say, what is it, then? Why do you give me no answer? Are you getting impudent again? How can you be so impudent? I'm coming! I'll show you! You don't whore for me. You mustn't be smart either; you're an impudent, lousy fellow, such an impudent, lousy fellow I've never met with. Is he beginning again? You understand nothing at all, nothing at all; nothing at all does he understand. If you follow now, he won't follow, will not follow. Are you getting still more impudent? Are you getting impudent still more? How they attend, they do attend', and so on. At the end, he scolds in quite inarticulate sounds.[23]

I feel myself constrained to cite this passage at length because it is so painful, because it rings so true and because it is so eloquent about the discourse of power in the hands of the nerve specialists of the early part of this century. Laing goes straight on to make the explicit connection between the right to speak and the refusal of the right to remain silent, or to reply in other terms than those required by the mental specialist. Almost at the same moment as Foucault, Laing is demonstrating the relation of power and servitude between those who are allowed to speak and those who desperately and vainly try to make themselves heard:

Kraepelin notes here among other things the patient's 'inaccessibility':

Although he undoubtedly understood all the questions, *he has not given us a single piece of useful information.* His talk was . . . *only a series of disconnected sentences having no relation whatever to the general situation* (1905, pp. 79–80, italics my own).

Now there is no question that this patient is showing the 'signs' of catatonic excitement. This construction we put on this behaviour will, however, depend on the relationship we establish with the patient, and we are indebted to Kraepelin's vivid description which enables the patient to come, it seems, alive to us across fifty years and through his pages as though he were before us. What does this patient seem to be doing? Surely he is carrying on a dialogue between his own parodied version of Kraepelin, and his own defiant rebelling self. 'You want to know that too? I tell you who is being measured and is measured and shall be measured. I know all that, and I could tell you, but I do not want to'. This seems to be plain enough talk. Presumably he deeply resents this form of interrogation which is being carried out before a lecture room of students. He probably does not see what it has to do with the things that must be deeply distressing him. But these things would not be 'useful information' to Kraepelin except as further 'signs' of a 'disease'.

Kraepelin asks him his name. The patient replies by an exasperated outburst in which he is now saying what he feels is the attitude implicit in Kraepelin's approach to him: What is your name? What does he shut? He shuts his eyes. . . . Why do you give me no answer? Are you getting impudent again? You don't whore for me? (i.e. he feels that Kraepelin is objecting because he is not prepared to prostitute himself before the whole classroom of students), and so on . . . such an impudent, shameless, miserable, lousy fellow I've never met with . . . etc.

Now it seems clear that this patient's behaviour can be seen in at least two ways, analogous to the ways of seeing vase or face. One may see his behaviour as 'signs' of a 'disease'; one may see his behaviour as expressive of his existence. The existential-phenomenological construction is an inference about the way the other is feeling and acting. What is the boy's experience of Kraepelin? He seems to be tormented and desperate. What is he 'about' in speaking and acting in this way? He is objecting to being measured and tested. He wants to be heard.[24]

It does not seem as if we have advanced much since Kraepelin's day. The alternative which R. D. Laing was suggesting— that the psychiatrist should actually listen to what his patient had to say—has been erased from the psychiatry textbooks with

Stalinist efficiency. The discourse of power against which Laing waged his lonely and courageous war has won twice over: by refusing to listen to what he was saying while he was saying it, and then by erasing all trace of what it was he said after he fell silent. The explanatory power of a book like *The Divided Self* remains a conceptual possibility which psychiatry has refused to listen to.

Consequently, *The Unknown Virginia Woolf* was describing a Foucaultian discourse of power which was at work during the lifetime of Virginia Woolf, but which had come to be doubled by the discourse of power of a Cambridge rationalism that had buried the first discourse of power under a second. Everything that Leonard Woolf and Quentin Bell said about the madness of Virginia Woolf being 'unintelligible' would have fitted in admirably with the assumptions made by psychiatrists in the period about which they were writing.

The Unknown Virginia Woolf inherited the hostility, then, of no less than two impacted discourses of power, and indeed there was a third. Ever since the New Criticism of the 1940s and 1950s had propounded the so-called intentionalist fallacy, all attempts, within the literary critical enterprise, to expand the intelligibility of a literary work by reference to its historical or biographical background had been laid under a strong taboo. Many of the first hostile critics of my book believed that I genuinely could not tell the difference between 'fact' and 'fiction', and deplored any attempt to increase the intelligibility of the fiction by introducing any facts. That fiction, in the case of Virginia Woolf, was a very strong representation *of* fact was dismissed either as irrelevant to the literary enterprise or as offensive to finer sensibilities.

If I had to surmise in what ways *The Unknown Virginia Woolf* could be re-read and re-deployed for the second decade of its life, I would suggest that it be seen as an extension of Foucaultian practice and a retrieval of one particular strand of phenomenology. This might seem an unlikely combination. Yet the ways in which Foucault's own analyses of the discourse of power allow of an analysis of the relation of speech and silence within any given social context could only be enriched, I would suppose, by a phenomenological account of the 'lived project' which an individual may set up within that social context. A Foucaultian analysis of speech and silence could only be successful if one decides in advance that individuals in their utterance are socially intelligible.

The model set up by William Cain in *The Crisis in Criticism*, for instance, seems the most promising project on the horizon.[25] In an extended conclusion, and himself drawing on Michel Foucault, Cain sets out a programme for reading which makes sense of a whole tradition by making one text central to a reading of that tradition.[26] That text may not necessarily be the most successful *literary* work within that tradition, either; it just proves to be an ideal reference point for a whole fan of readings, from whose combined inferences one can finally build up a sense of the meaning of that particular project. Cain gives one work as an illustration of one project, but the method is generalisable.

Like *The Unknown Virginia Woolf*, that conclusion to *The Crisis in Criticism* tries to conceive of a form of literary theory and practice that would take account both of social context (discourse of power) and of individual project (phenomenological reconstitution). Now that deconstruction is nearing the limits of its credibility, and that Neo-Historicism has insisted on our taking a new account of the insertion of a text within history, this particular combination of approaches seems the most hopeful one for the next decade.

The kind of phenomenology I have in mind has, though, been abandoned in mid-development: the phenomenology which descends not through the idealism and essentialism of Edmund Husserl, but through the tradition of Jean-Paul Sartre, Simone de Beauvoir, Maurice Merleau-Ponty and Paul Ricoeur. That tradition gave rise, in time, to the tradition of existential psychiatry developed by R. D. Laing and Aaron Esterson, which itself gave rise to the existential psychotherapy of Peter Lomas and David Smail.[27]

This tradition is very rich in possibility, but, as I say, it has been abandoned half-way through its development. Other, materialist and chemico-reductivist streams of thought have proved too overwhelmingly powerful for it. Yet it did contain the basic premises according to which enormously interesting work could be done, starting from the concept of embodiment. Sartre's own accounts of Beaudelaire, of Genet and of Flaubert have made themselves basic to any future understanding of those three writers.[28] Nor is Sartre's work 'psychobiography'. It is an engagement with the embodied subject in the context of his relations to his parents, environing social reality and life project, but it is the 'intentional' layer, the direction of a life along 'intentional' arcs which form a project, that gives Sartre his edge over psychobiography. His is no Husserlian essentialism. That Baudelaire, Genet, Flaubert inhabit an all too real world of resistance and danger is never for a moment forgotten. Sartre is Foucaultian before Foucault. He shows that one can phenomenologise within a historical context, and that the kinds of understanding derived from this unlikely combination of theoretical models are richer than the results of either method taken alone.

It may well be true that Husserlian phenomenology, which rests upon idealist principles, has come to the end of its usefulness. Paul Ricoeur, one of the able expositors of the Husserlian cause within French philosophy ever since he published his translation of Husserl's *Ideas I* in 1950, has recently come to the conclusion that particular phenomenological direction can no longer be followed, indeed that the Husserlian tradition of idealist, transcendental phenomenology has been 'ruined' by the new importance of hermeneutics.[29]

Paul Ricoeur is now of the opinion that Husserlian phenomenology has to be abandoned because it can hardly be distinguished from 'transcendental subjectivism', and that the perilous sense that the Husserlian problem leads directly to a solipsistic impasse is difficult to resist in so historicist an age as ours:

Phenomenology is always in danger of reducing itself to a transcendental subjectivism. The radical way of putting an end to this constantly recurring confusion is to shift the axis of interpretation from the problem of subjectivity to that of the world. That is what the theory of the text attempts to do, by subordinating the question of the author's intention to that of the matter of the text.[30]

Nevertheless, shifting attention from 'the problem of subjectivity' to that of 'the world', shifting attention from 'the author's intention' to 'the matter of the text' carries with it its own brand of difficulties. Hermeneutics may well have 'ruined' Husserlian phenomenology because hermeneutics is, of its very nature, historical, while the 'idealist' form of phenomenology attempts to 'bracket out' the world of history altogether. Nevertheless, to pay total attention to the problems of 'the matter of the text' can also lead us into the sterile impasse in which deconstruction, for example, now finds itself. What we obviously need is a kind of literary and philosophical enquiry which preserves *both* 'the problem of subjectivity' and 'the matter of the text'.

There are forms of phenomenology which are *not* Husserlian and essentialist, *not* idealist and transcendental. Those forms of phenomenology which admit historical data, indeed thrive upon them, are *not* 'ruined' in this expensive, Ricoeuresque sense. The most outstanding example of such a historically oriented phenomenology is that of Maurice Merleau-Ponty.

The phenomenological bequest of Maurice Merleau-Ponty is capable of a historical, social and textual deployment, even though Merleau-Ponty himself hesitated so to deploy it. But pointers abound to the effect that Merleau-Ponty thought his work could easily be adapted to the needs of social historical analysis.

Merleau-Ponty was a 'committed' (*engagé*) intellectual of the Left during and after World War II, and was co-founder, with Jean-Paul Sartre, of the radical Left review, *Les Temps Modernes*. His early essay on the problems associated with the Stalinist phase of Russian communism, *Humanisme et Terreur: Essai sur le problème communiste* (1947), was followed, after the experiences of 1950–52—the discovery of the Russian camps, the disillusion of having to realise that the Russians were capable of participating in the Korean War—by *Les Aventures de la Dialectique*, (1955). An essay so authentic and so austere in its moral self-denial makes clear why Merleau-Ponty had felt himself forced to break off from his collaboration on *Les Temps Modernes*. And the essays collected in the twelfth section of *Signs* (1960) make it clear that his commitment to an authentic vision of the Left after the collapse of the Soviet model of communism had driven him to a position of drastic yet admirable isolation.

All of this 'stream' of his writing indicates that in Maurice Merleau-Ponty, phenomenology has a theorist of the most historically committed kind. It is an immense waste that his work has been left derelict for so many years. It seems to demand development in every direction. It is, among other things, the answer that Paul Ricoeur is implicitly seeking in his turn to hermeneutics. And yet, in spite of the astounding richness of his analyses of the human body in *Phenomenology of Perception*, Merleau-Ponty never wrote an ethics.[31]

Outside astronomy, logic and mathematics, Merleau-Ponty suggests, there is no objective truth to be had. In the world of lived experience, what is taken as objectively true depends upon what 'the lived body' (*le corps vécu*) decides is true.[32] What the lived body decides is true is a function of that embodiment itself—how it perceives the world, in terms of what inner obsessions, hopes and fears it registers certain aspects of the world. There is no way that perception can be pure, just as there is no way in which perception can be objective. Perception and judgment have to go through embodiment. Thus embodiment is perception itself. As the body perceives, so will the world be.

This is a profoundly unsettling conclusion for traditional philosophy. It rules out, not as unnecessary but as unavailable, that 'objectivity' about the world which traditional philosophy constantly seeks to arrive at. In one sense it is profoundly empirical—Merleau-Ponty simply notes the fact that our versions of the world do not agree. Paradoxically enough, he derives this extreme empiricism from the old master of Idealism himself, Husserl, who realised (in the fifth *Cartesian Meditation*, for instance) that there can be no 'pure' communication, no pure transmission of information between two subjects who happen to be embodied subjects in a shared social space.[33] Husserl did not dare take it further, but clutched it to him as some dreadful mystery. Merleau-Ponty most courageously accepts the implications of Husserl's discovery, and pushes on to see where it would lead. It led him to *Phenomenology of Perception* (1945) and to the task of examining the world 'out there' as a function of the embodied intentional 'constituting' consciousness which every individual is.

Such truth as there is, then, will be a function of the perceptions of the perceiver, and can have no greater truth than this. In a way, it is a re-activation of the old debate between Plato and Protagoras, though much more sophisticated because of the concept of 'intentionality' drawn from Husserlian phenomenology. But, and this is a second debt to Husserl, such truth as there is available to the perceiver will have a *necessary* (eidetic) status. An embodied subject *can* only perceive the world in the various ways allowed by his embodiment, and consequently what he perceives cannot be false for him.[34] Of course it can be 'false' for others. And that is where the immense usefulness of Merleau-Ponty's form of phenomenology begins to be seen: not only within psychiatry and psychology, but also within literary theory.

For what the 'patient', for what the man or woman who is called 'mad' or 'insane' has to say must be true for him or her. Just because we can have no perception of the world which is not eidetically true, i.e., necessarily true, for that very reason a man or woman who speaks from within 'madness' is incapable of telling a lie.

And this is where I started from. And this is the problem.

Notes

1. *The Letters of Virginia Woolf*, edited by Nigel Nicolson and Joanne Trautman (Hogarth Press 1975–80), Vol 6, p. xvii.
2. *The Diary of Virginia Woolf*, edited by Anne Oliver Bell (Hogarth Press 1977–84), Vol 2, p. 283; *Letters*, Vol 4, p. 180.
3. *Letters*, Vol 3, p. 180.

4. W. Mayer-Gross, E. Slater and M. Roth, *Clinical Psychiatry*, (Baillière, Tindall and Cassell 1954; 3rd ed. 1969; rptd. 1974).
5. Ibid., p. 188.
6. Ibid., p. 188.
7. Ibid., p. 188.
8. Ibid., p. 191–2.
9. R. D. Laing, *The Divided Self* (Penguin Books 1965), p. 29.
10. Alan Sheridan, *Michel Foucault: The Will to Truth* (Tavistock 1980), p. 115.
11. Michel Foucault's inaugural lecture at the Collège de France was published in 1971 as *L'ordre du discours* (Paris, Gallimard, 1971). It was added as an appendix to the American edition of *The Archaeology of Knowledge* (New York, Pantheon, 1972). I cite from pp. 216–7.
12. Sheridan, *Michel Foucault*, p. 116.
13. Michel Foucault, *Naissance de la Clinique* (Presses Universitaires de France 1972), Preface.
14. Stephen Trombley, *'All That Summer She was Mad'* (Continuum 1982), p. 234. Trombley is citing from a work of T. B. Hyslop's dated 1918.
15. Elaine Showalter, *The Female Malady: Women, Madness and English Culture 1830–1980* (Virago Press 1987).
16. Ibid., p. 194.
17. Ibid., p. 176.
18. Ibid., p. 190.
19. Ibid., p. 176.
20. Ibid., pp. 176–7.
21. Ibid., p. 177–8.
22. Ibid., p. 178.
23. Laing, *Divided Self*, pp. 29–30.
24. Ibid., pp. 30–1.
25. William Cain, *The Crisis in Criticism: Theory, Literature and Reform in English Studies* (The Johns Hopkins University Press 1984).
26. Ibid. pp. 247–74.
27. Remarkable successes in this tradition are: R. D. Laing and Aaron Esterson, *Sanity, Madness and the Family*, Vol 1: *Families of Schizophrenics* (Tavistock 1964); R. D. Laing and David Cooper, *Reason and Violence: A Decade of Sartre's Philosophy 1950–1960* (Tavistock 1964); R. D. Laing, *The Politics of the Family and Other Essays* (Tavistock 1971); Aaron Esterson, *The Leaves of Spring: Schizophrenia, Family and Sacrifice* (Pelican Books 1972); Peter Lomas, *True and False Experience* (Allen Lane 1973); Peter Lomas, *The Case for a Personal Psychotherapy* (Oxford U. P. 1981); Peter Lomas, *The Limits of Interpretation* (Penguin Books 1987); David Smail, *Psychotherapy: A Personal Approach* (Dent 1978); David Smail, *Illusion and Reality: The Meaning of Anxiety* (Dent 1984); David Smail, *Taking Care: An Alternative to Therapy* (Dent 1987).
28. Jean-Paul Sartre, *Baudelaire* (Gallimard 1947); *Saint Genet, Actor and Martyr*, trans. B. Frechtman (Braziller 1963); *L'Idiot de la Famille:*

Gustave Flaubert de 1821 à 1857 (Gallimard 1971, 1972).

29. Paul Ricoeur, 'Phenomenology and the Human Sciences', in John B. Thompson (ed.), *Paul Ricoeur: Hermeneutics and the Human Sciences* (Cambridge U. P. 1981), p. 101.
30. Ricoeur, 'Phenemenology', p. 112.
31. Roger Poole, 'Indirect Communication' (Part 2), in *New Blackfriars* (August 1966), pp. 594–604.
32. Maurice Merleau-Ponty, *Phenomenology of Perception*, trans. Colin Smith (Routledge and Kegan Paul 1962). See, in particular, Part I, Chapter 6, 'The Body as Expression, and Speech', p. 174ff.
33. For a clear description of the problems attached in Husserl's *Ideas II*, see Paul Ricoeur, *Husserl: An Analysis of his Phenomenology*, trans. E. G. Ballard and L. E. Embree (Northwestern University Press 1967), Chapter 3; and Chapter 5, on Husserl's fifth *Cartesian Meditation*. For a precise definition of Husserl's problem, from quite another angle, see also Jacques Derrida, 'Speech and Phenomena: Introduction to the Problem of Signs in Husserl's Phenomenology', in *Speech and Phenomena and Other Essays on Husserl's Theory of Signs*, trans. David B. Allison (Northwestern University Press 1973).
34. Roger Poole, 'The Bond of Human Embodiment', in *Universities Quarterly* 28, No 4 (Autumn 1974); and 'From Phenomenology to Subjective Method', in *Universities Quarterly* 29, No 4 (Autumn 1975), pp. 412–440.

The unknown Virginia Woolf

Was Virginia Woolf 'insane'? Was Virginia Woolf 'mad'?

Leonard Woolf, in the course of his *Autobiography*, constantly speaks of his wife in terms of her 'insanity', and Quentin Bell in his widely read *Virginia Woolf: A Biography* repeatedly uses the word 'mad'.

As Virginia Woolf's letters and diaries appear, the editors, Nigel Nicolson, Joanne Trautmann and Anne Olivier Bell, implicitly accepting the view of Virginia put forward by Leonard Woolf and Quentin Bell, refer again and again, in their commentaries and apparatus, to Virginia's 'madness'. Quentin Bell's interpretation is used as if it were canonical. In the first volume of the letters, the editors write '[Professor Bell's] biography of Virginia Woolf has formed the basis of our chronology and our interpretation of her character.'

The present work is the result of a sense of unease in face of all this undefined assertion. When I read Professor Bell's biography, I was puzzled by the failure to offer any evidence for the alleged 'madness' of his subject, and I was offended by the looseness and crudity of the word 'mad' as applied to one of the subtlest writers of this century.

Professor Bell's acknowledged source was Leonard Woolf, and I therefore read through the five volumes of his *Autobiography* looking for evidence of what he consistently calls 'insanity'. Again I could not find any, though Leonard Woolf is more worried by the terms he uses than is Professor Bell.

True, there were, here and there, both in Quentin Bell and in Leonard Woolf, some passing descriptions of what Virginia *did* during the course of what were obviously very distressed periods. But there was never any enquiry into why she did what she did. There was never any enquiry into what she might have meant by what she said. There was never any enquiry into whether there might not be a reasonable explanation for the states from which she suffered. There was never, in fact, any attention paid to what Virginia herself thought, felt, or meant. She was seen from the outside, as someone suffering from 'madness'.

The present work is the result, then, of the puzzlement and unease I felt in the face of this failure to regard Virginia Woolf as a subjectivity. She was the author of some of the most remarkable analyses of inter-subjectivity in the language: why had no-one done her the compliment of examining her own subjectivity in a way which attempted to come up to her own very high standards?

There was, of course, the literary criticism, and I read much of this hoping for some help. But almost without exception, the writers of literary criticism chose to create an abyss between the 'life' and the 'work'. They concentrated on various perceptible literary qualities in the novels, and obviously left all biographical matters to Professor Bell and his successors. The 'New Critical' embargoes especially on biographical interpretation were all still faithfully in place, after thirty years of unquestioned domination.

There was therefore no possible recourse except to the novels themselves. I had to re-read the novels to see if Virginia Woolf herself had offered us the key to what she suffered from in her bouts of so-called 'insanity'. Perhaps she had taken her precautions? Perhaps she had tried to tell us, in another way, more subtle than direct self-analysis, what she suffered during her life and what she thought the causes of it might be?

I looked at the novels anew. I looked at them, not as the literary critics insisted I should – as 'fiction', 'art', as something utterly different from 'life' – but as records of a life, Virginia's own life precisely. And the novels began to speak.

I read the novels through in order, from *The Voyage Out* to *Between the Acts*, comparing what I knew of the alleged 'madness' and 'insanity' at the dates where these were recorded, with the act of continuous reflection going on in the fiction. With a few slight variations in time, which were due to merely empirical factors, I found that Virginia had herself documented the reasons for her own mental distress, and very intelligently 'exorcised' certain key persons and passages from her conscious or unconscious life by writing them fully out. The novels were an account of the mental distress: how it had been caused, how it manifested itself, and how it was overcome.

Each novel spoke of the obsessive themes of the period of life to which it refers or in which it was conceived, with some lapses of time to take up extremely difficult material. It took ten years after the events described in it, for instance, for Virginia to write *Mrs Dalloway*, and nearly thirty years to master the material in *To the Lighthouse* and *The Waves*. *Orlando* spoke for its moment, but *Between the Acts* referred itself retrospectively back to the time when Virginia had married Leonard Woolf. The inner time of the novelist was absolutely consistent. The novels were written to master people and states of mind and states of embodiment which had previously mastered her. She had a proud spirit, and did not like defeat.

I had formed my theory when, in 1976, Jeanne Schulkind's collection, *Moments of Being*, came to confirm a part of it. In the three pieces in that collection, *A Sketch of the Past*, *22 Hyde Park Gate*, and *Old Bloomsbury*, I found the confirmation, in Virginia's own hand, for the theory that I had myself derived from reading the novels, the theory about the influence in the 'madness' of 1913 and 1915 of Gerald and George Duckworth. This theory was now given explicit documentation by the only person who could ever have confirmed it.

This book does not risk a theory of what Virginia positively did suffer from, in some medical or psycho-medical terminology. First, the evidence is missing, and we are too far from the events. Second, such terminology itself is only in a very crude sense applicable to the lived experience; and finally, my concern has been to show that the words 'mad', 'insane', 'lunacy' must be withdrawn, since Virginia's behaviour throughout her life is, given the subjective factor, explicable in terms of cause and effect. Given the subjective problems of her childhood and adolescence, given the problems she inherited when she married Leonard in 1912, everything that happened thereafter happened by necessity. Once the causes have been seen, the words 'mad', 'insane' and 'lunatic' seem not only crude and offensive, but also peculiarly inappropriate.

They would be so anyway, even if we were discussing Mrs Brown. But to use these words about a writer who analysed her own problems with such courageous percipience, and who in doing so created works of art which stand amongst the most brilliant of our century, seems indefensible.

It will be easily perceived that this book represents an innovation in literary research. While taking account of works of art, it allows itself reference to the life. While referring itself to the life, it does not attempt biography. By approaching the writer as subject, it allows of a psychological understanding, while remaining independent of any school of 'psycho-analytical' theory.

The major theoretical premise is the one I sketched out, in a chapter called 'The Perspectival World and Subjective Method', in my book *Towards Deep Subjectivity* in 1972. The method consists in permutating perspectives. No single perspective is privileged, and all are examined in the light of all the others. The perspectives are 'subjective' ones, that is to say, the meaning attributed to them is the meaning which the person himself or herself attributed to them, not the meaning which other people attributed to them. The book is thus proposing a new departure in literary studies.

The study avails itself of valuable insights from phenomenology. It is however, post-phenomenological, in that its aim is to apply phenomenological method to a life and to a series of novels. Husserl's concept of a world of constantly changing horizonal validities has been part of my approach, and Merleau-Ponty's concept of the embodied subject, 'le corps vécu', has been equally important to me. Those interested in the theory could consult Husserl's *Cartesian Meditations* and his *Crisis of European Sciences* (paras. 47, 48 and 49), and Merleau-Ponty's *Phenomenology of Perception*.

On the question, whether or not a novel is 'art' or a part of 'life' or whether there is any permissible literary intercourse between the two, I would like to be quite explicit. The novels of Virginia Woolf are works of art. Many of them rank, in my view, amongst the finest works of literary art in the language.

They are also works which treat of the lived experience of Virginia Woolf. Richard Lovelace contends that:

> Stone walls do not a prison make,
> Nor iron bars a cage;

yet a modern wit has observed:

> But they make an excellent imitation.

In the same way one could risk the aphorism that novels are not exact copies of, or transcripts from, a life, but there is a sense in which they are perilously like them. All the more perilously like them, for straining not to be like them. In the strain away from the lived particular, there is the symbolic substitution, shift or displacement, which tells more, if that were possible, about the lived particular than that particular could itself have offered.

It is the lived reality, in the case of Virginia Woolf, which interests me. For this purpose, the life and the novels are equally important and cannot be separated.

This study is offered as a hypothesis. Its aim is to illuminate a whole series of connections which have not been made before, such that a coherent pattern emerges from what have been, up to now, dispersed particulars and missed clues. If it does illuminate these connections, the aim of the work will have been achieved.

If it does not illuminate these connections, and there are those who express disagreement, then I should be interested to see their alternative reconstructions. I do not conceive in a matter as profoundly difficult as this that there could be any sort of 'refutation' offered, from whomever it might come, which would have some kind of undeniable 'objective' superiority. There is no one person whose view on this matter could be definitive, or be (in some factual sense of the word) 'right'. In literary research of this kind, where one is dealing with hypothetical reconstructions at each point, there are no 'facts'. There are only opinions. And each person has a right to his own, provided he does not claim that his is the only 'right' one.

A final word of explanation about a point of detail. I frequently write in this study 'Virginia', not 'Virginia Woolf', and 'Leonard' not 'Leonard Woolf'. This is not mere affectation, but represents a decision taken in the face of a real problem. Anyone who reads widely in the literature about Virginia Woolf will become aware, after a while, that the convention of writing the full name 'Virginia Woolf' every time a reference is to be made to the author, irks everyone who writes about her. It is not merely the length of the name which irks, but rather that there is a felt incongruity in the name itself. There is a sense, discernible in the writing of many critics, that the appellation 'Virginia Woolf' represents some kind of existential oxymoron, a sense that there is an act of force involved in constantly and consistently linking these two parts of the name together. 'Mrs Woolf' is sometimes tried as an alternative, but that obviously militates against something important. 'Woolf' is occasionally tried too, but that looks very odd indeed. There are those who have tried to cut the knot by writing 'VW', but this, while it undoubtedly saves printer's ink, does not solve the incongruity.

So I have had recourse to using simply 'Virginia' and simply 'Leonard'. It may be that the difficulty we experience in trying to find a correct nominal designation for this author is due to a deeply buried, but real, lived fact, which is, that the two names did in life stand for two antithetical realities, and that these two realities never could, and never did, fuse.

CHAPTER 1

'Rosy-flowered fruit tree and beak of brass'

And then to want and not to have – to want and want – how that wrung the heart, and wrung it again and again! Oh Mrs. Ramsay! she called out silently, to that essence. . . Ghost, air, nothingness, a thing you could play with easily and safely at any time of day or night, she had been that, and then suddenly she put her hand out and wrung the heart thus.

(*To the Lighthouse* (*TTL*) p. 275)

The pressures of living in the household of Leslie and Julia Stephen must have been enormous. Tremendous currents of energy flowed between Virginia's father and mother. Virginia felt herself powerfully attracted to her mother in face of the demands made by Leslie Stephen on his wife and all his womenfolk. And yet Leslie Stephen too was a powerful, dominant, compelling, figure. To Virginia, it must have seemed as if her mother were all gift, her father all demand. In order to understand her first two 'madnesses' as Quentin Bell calls them, it is necessary to study the relation of Virginia to each of her symbolic parents.

First, Virginia's relation to her mother. The novels describe the adoring trust and limitless admiration for the intuitive and healing talents of Julia Stephen at such length that there is no need to attempt any kind of summary. Mrs Hilbery in *Night and Day* has something of Julia, and Helen of *The Voyage Out*, and of course Mrs Ramsay of *To the Lighthouse*. She was, by all accounts, immensely beautiful, she had presence and style, she was sympathetic, understanding, intuitive, flowing, all the things that the angular, intellectual, conceptual father was not. Above all, she had the power of seeing where human problems were likely to arise, and delicately averted them if she could. The family adored her, as did all those who knew her. It is hardly too much to say, in the light of the last section of *To the Lighthouse*, that Virginia worshipped her.

Her main function in the Stephen household was to soothe the violent self-distrust and self-disappointment of Sir Leslie. Virginia noted this structure of their relationship, and made it central (I believe) to her whole view of men and women in relationship. That the brilliant, dominant, intellectual Leslie Stephen needed support, encouragement, relief from his own sterility and male arrogance, Virginia saw; and she transformed this from a structure she observed in her own parents to a structure observable in any couple.

for that was true of Mrs. Ramsay – she pitied men always as if they lacked something – women never, as if they had something.

(*TTL* p. 133)

That single observation by Lily of Mrs Ramsay sorting out, arranging, directing and manoeuvring her dinner table of fractious male children in *To the Lighthouse*, stands for many remarks dropped here and there through the novels. Never more so than in *The Voyage Out*, where the endless flow of male arrogant intellectual conversation is suddenly interrupted by the quiet voice of Helen saying:

'You've all been sitting here,' she said, 'for almost an hour, and you haven't noticed my figs, or my flowers, or the way the light comes through, or anything.'

(*The Voyage Out* (*VO*) p. 379)

Earlier, there is Helen's quick vision of Hirst, the intellectual:

She pitied him, for she suspected that he suffered . . .

(*VO* p. 244)

and immediately after that, after having listened to Hirst the aspiring philosopher (Leslie–Mr Ramsay is also a philosopher, we recall, stuck at Q and unable to advance to R in his conceptual career), there follows a further insight into Helen's way of looking at the world:

She looked at him against the background of flowering magnolia. There was something curious in the sight. Perhaps it was that the heavy

wax-like flowers were so smooth and inarticulate, and his face – he had
thrown his hat away, his hair was rumpled, he held his eye-glasses in his
hand, so that a red mark appeared on either side of his nose – was so
worried and garrulous. It was a beautiful bush, spreading very widely,
and all the time he had sat there talking she had been noticing the
patches of shade and the shape of the leaves, and the way the great white
flowers sat in the midst of the green. She had noticed it half-consciously,
nevertheless the pattern had become part of their talk.

(VO p. 247)

Helen is Nature: calm, reposeful, wise, beyond wordy definitions and combats, pitying men because they lack something.
What they lack is a kind of inner balance, a repose in the created
world, a trust in the way things are, a respect for beauty. They
never look at the world, but past it, as if it, in its manifold colour
and variety, had nothing to teach them, were a mere impediment
to the flow of their ideas. Their arrogant talk goes on and on,
verbal refutation following verbal refutation, and all the while the
world is there, unnoticed by men in their egoistic self-absorption,
there, unobserved, unloved, unappreciated, unaccounted for.
That is partly why Mrs Ramsay–Helen–Mrs Hilbery pities men:
because they never look at the beauty of the created world of
shape and colour, they look through it with the hard stare of
abstraction.

The same device, the woman noticing the natural world while
the man drones on, is given quintessential expression in the
scene where Mr and Mrs Ramsay are wandering through the
garden:

He did not look at the flowers, which his wife was considering, but at a
spot about a foot or so above them. There was no harm in him, he added,
and was just about to say that anyhow he was the only young man in
England who admired his – when he choked it back. He would not
bother her again about his books. These flowers seemed creditable, Mr
Ramsay said, lowering his gaze and noticing something red, something
brown. Yes, but then these she had put in with her own hands, said Mrs
Ramsay.

(TTL p. 106)

The whole scene is marvellous in establishing this continual and
fruitless dialectic between the male mind caught in its conceptual
advance at Q and unable to advance to R, and the observing,

loving, sensitive female intuition hovering in the space between natural beauty and intuitive knowledge.

Virginia is constantly sharpening her indictment of the 'intellectual'. The figure is endlessly repeated, and is obviously an amalgam of all the self-opinionated and arrogantly cocksure young intellectuals she met at Cambridge and in London. But her father, Sir Leslie, was a special case. He did not deserve, and he did not get, the treatment meted out to such irredeemably 'intellectual' figures as St John Hirst, in *The Voyage Out*, and to Charles Tansley, in *To the Lighthouse*. For under his arrogant, hard, conceptualising, nature-denying absorption, there was another, softer layer. This layer was not in itself good, for it did not correspond to any real ability to let things be, to love and admire the natural created beauty of things, but it was at least a chink in the covering of the Tansley–Hirst armadillo. It was, in fact, self-pity.

It is here that the dialectic between Leslie and Julia Stephen takes on its special quality, the quality that fascinated Virginia as a girl when she must have observed it many times. It is given its classic expression, as so much of the distilled childhood experience is, in *To the Lighthouse*, in the image of the 'beak of brass':

Nothing would make Mr. Ramsay move on. There he stood, demanding sympathy.

Mrs. Ramsay, who had been sitting loosely, folding her son in her arm, braced herself, and, half turning, seemed to raise herself with an effort, and at once to pour erect into the air a rain of energy, a column of spray, looking at the same time animated and alive as if all her energies were being fused into force, burning and illuminating (quietly though she sat, taking up her stocking again), and into this delicious fecundity, this fountain and spray of life, the fatal sterility of the male plunged itself, like a beak of brass, barren and bare. He wanted sympathy. He was a failure, he said.

(*TTL* pp. 61–2)

The female qualities are energy, force, life, spray; and the male qualities are sterility, barrenness, bareness, the plunge of violent demand upon the female, like a 'beak of brass'.

As Virginia must have observed them time and time again in her childhood, the sudden demand, and the sympathy and understanding which rushes out to meet it, are here given in highly symbolic form. Sir Leslie Stephen, intellectual, mountain-climber, editor of the *Dictionary of National Biography*, writer, scholar, is struck by one of those sudden inner failures of confidence which makes him run to his wife like a child afraid. He is struck with the conviction that all he has done, all he has written, is as straw. He is a failure, he says, and he goes to his wife, not asking, but demanding, sympathy. Indeed, he will not go away until he has been soothed. Mrs Ramsay alone is capable of this magical act, from the depths of 'what she has', to help the man 'who lacks something'.

She arches in a kind of life-curve, emitting energy, belief, positiveness into the air. She is fluid, magic, fecund. She responds to the demand by the self-pitying male.

He was a failure, he said. Mrs. Ramsay flashed her needles. Mr. Ramsay repeated, never taking his eyes from her face, that he was a failure. She blew the words back at him. 'Charles Tansley . . .' she said. But he must have more than that. It was sympathy he wanted, to be assured of his genius, first of all, and then to be taken within the circle of life, warmed and soothed, to have his senses restored to him, his barrenness made fertile, and all the rooms of the house made full of life – the drawing room; behind the drawing-room the kitchen; above the kitchen the bedrooms; and beyond them the nurseries; they must be furnished, they must be filled with life.

(*TTL* p. 62)

It is not a request. It is a demand for the renewal of life. And it comes from what Virginia certainly sees as a form of death. Because Mrs Ramsay is life itself. What then can he be, 'the beak of brass, the arid scimitar of the male', but death?

Charles Tansley thought him the greatest metaphysician of the time, she said. But he must have more than that. He must have sympathy. He must be assured that he too lived in the heart of life; was needed; not here only, but all over the world. Flashing her needles, confident, upright, she created drawing-room and kitchen, set them all aglow; bade him take his ease there, go in and out, enjoy himself. She laughed, she knitted. Standing between her knees, very stiff, James[1] felt all her strength flaring up to be drunk and quenched by the beak of brass, the arid scimitar of the male, which smote mercilessly, again and again, demanding sympathy.

(*TTL* pp. 62–3)

---

[1] Read: Virginia. The sexes of the combatants are often inverted, to preserve the semblance of fictional 'distance'.

One might think the job done. Life is brought into being by the magic woman, who 'creates' drawing-room and kitchen, restores a living world to the man who can see only stretches of sand and waste; life is converted into strength which 'flares up' only to be 'drunk and quenched' by the 'beak of brass'. He absorbs enormous quantities of it before he goes away assuaged. But Virginia wishes to be even more precise:

He was a failure, he repeated. Well, look then, feel then. Flashing her needles, glancing round about her, out of the window, into the room, at James himself, she assured him, beyond a shadow of doubt, by her laugh, her poise, her competence (as a nurse carrying a light across a dark room assures a fractious child), that it was real; the house was full; the garden blowing. If he put implicit faith in her, nothing should hurt him; however deep he buried himself or climbed high, not for a second should he find himself without her. So boasting of her capacity to surround and protect, there was scarcely a shell of herself left for her to know herself by; all was so lavished and spent; and James, as he stood stiff between her knees, felt her rise in a rosy-flowered fruit tree laid with leaves and dancing boughs into which the beak of brass, the arid scimitar of his father, the egotistical man, plunged and smote, demanding sympathy.

Filled with her words, like a child who drops off satisfied, he said, at last, looking at her with humble gratitude, restored, renewed, that he would take a turn; he would watch the children playing cricket. He went.

(*TTL* pp. 63–4)

The constant references to the reassuring of a child are not meant merely metaphorically. The great scholar and philosopher, the 'genius' who is stuck at Q and cannot advance to R, has to be calmed like a child in a fit of the terrors. Mrs Ramsay is mother and 'nurse' to him. She gives and gives. Finally, lulled by the wife–mother's consoling reassurances, he goes off for a walk, healed.

And the cost?

Immediately, Mrs. Ramsay seemed to fold herself together, one petal closed in another, and the whole fabric fell in exhaustion upon itself, so that she had only strength enough to move her finger, in exquisite abandonment to exhaustion, across the page of Grimm's fairy story,[1]

---

[1] She is reading to a child, and reassures the big child in the course of the fairy story. She is surrounded by children, some little, some big, some the leading intellectuals of her time.

while there throbbed through her, like the pulse in a spring which has expanded to its full width and now gently ceases to beat, the rapture of successful creation.

(*TTL* p. 64)

It is common to both Quentin Bell's and Noel Annan's accounts of Sir Leslie Stephen that his presence was simply exhausting. He was, according to both of them, a tiresome, petulant, demanding, querulous, self-pitying old man, leaning heavily upon his womenfolk for his continued daily dose of self-confidence and life. When Julia died, he leant on his daughter by his first marriage, Stella Duckworth, bitterly resenting her wanting to leave him to marry Jack Hills, and when Stella died, he leant with equal weight upon Vanessa, crying and beating his breast when the weekly accounts were presented to him, complaining of the hardness of life and demanding sympathy of all the female members of his household. This show of self-pity so alienated Virginia that she found it hard or impossible to forgive him for it, even at the end of her life. He groaned out loud in public at the boredom and tiresomeness of his guests. When finally Vanessa, obdurately refusing sympathy to the old man and simply holding her peace in face of his tantrums, finally failed to come up to expectations, the heavy weight of his demand fell upon Virginia. As he died, slowly and painfully, it was Virginia who had to shoulder the weight under which Julia, Stella and Vanessa had laboured before her.

In the exchange between Mr and Mrs Ramsay, the elements of the dialectic are presented with great care for their essential structure. From this passage alone (though there are many others) it is quite clear what their relationship must have been like. And it is not surprising that Julia, although twenty years younger than Sir Leslie, succumbed, exhausted, to the after-effects of influenza and died in 1895. Quentin Bell writes:

Beautiful still, but increasingly worn and harassed, Julia became more and more obsessed by time. She was always in a hurry, ever more anxious to save time by doing things herself, ever more anxious that others should be spared. And so she exhausted herself. Still young in years, she had raced through a lifetime in altruistic work and at length her physical resistance burnt out.

(I, 39)

Virginia idolised her mother. Julia represented for her everything that was beautiful, life-giving, spontaneous, intuitive, loving and natural. She watched her father impose upon her mother again and again, smiting mercilessly down at her again and again with his 'beak of brass, the arid scimitar of the male'. We have every reason to suppose, from a variety of other sources, that on occasion Virginia hated her father in the same way as little James does in the novel which describes their family life together, *To the Lighthouse*.

But also, of course, she loved him and admired him profoundly. This ambiguous swing between admiration for his immense human and intellectual abilities, and contempt for his unmanly and despotic impositions upon his womenfolk, marked Virginia's view of her father to her dying day. It also, I believe, formed a kind of ground plan on which she built her interpretations of men in general. Men, however brilliant their intellectual plumage, were, she suspected, petty tyrants at home, running to their wives or mistresses or daughters for comfort.

To those who came to visit Leslie Stephen in his last months, for instance, he was still the great man: indomitable, independent, the same man who had trod the Alps and edited the *Dictionary of National Biography*. It was only when the general public was not there that Sir Leslie indulged himself in self-pity. And the whole weight of this fell on the daughters. Vanessa refused on many occasions to humour him, and, at the end, as he lay and died of cancer, the task of looking after him fell to Virginia.

In fact, Virginia had to exorcise her father from her imaginings, by writing him out in a novel. She succeeded. In 1928, a year after *To the Lighthouse* had appeared, she wrote in her diary:

Wednesday, November 28th

Father's birthday. He would have been 96, 96, yes, today; and could have been 96, like other people one has known: but mercifully was not. His life would have entirely ended mine. What would have happened? No writing, no books; – inconceivable.

I used to think of him and mother daily; but writing the *Lighthouse* laid them in my mind. And now he comes back sometimes, but differently. (I believe this to be true – that I was obsessed by them both, unhealthily;

and writing of them was a necessary act.) He comes back now more as a contemporary. I must read him some day. I wonder if I can feel again, I hear his voice, I know this by heart?

(A Writer's Diary p. 138)

The passage at the end of *To the Lighthouse* gives the impression of the man exactly as Virginia must have experienced it in 1903–4, when her father lay dying at Hyde Park Gate:

'But I beneath a rougher sea,' Mr. Ramsay murmured . . . he seemed to himself very old, and bowed. Sitting in the boat he bowed, he crouched himself, acting instantly his part – the part of a desolate man, widowed, bereft; and so called up before him in hosts people sympathising with him; staged for himself as he sat in the boat, a little drama; which required of him decrepitude and exhaustion and sorrow (he raised his hands and looked at the thinness of them, to confirm his dream) and then there was given him in abundance women's sympathy, and he imagined how they would soothe him and sympathise with him, and so getting in his dream some reflection of the exquisite pleasure women's sympathy was to him, he sighed and said gently and mournfully,

> But I beneath a rougher sea
> Was whelmed in deeper gulfs than he,

so that the mournful words were heard quite clearly by them all. Cam half started on her seat. It shocked her – it outraged her.

(TTL pp. 256–7)

The two children in the boat with him are outraged at his self-pity and his tyranny, and are determined 'to resist tyranny to the death'. James and Cam have a pact about this. But their father is so very pitiful they cannot help but relent. He sits there in the boat sighing under his breath

> But I beneath a rougher sea

and

> We perished, each alone,

and the two children are torn in the grip of an immense struggle between love and admiration for this great old man, so famous and so esteemed, and fury and resentment at his self-pity and his shameless demands for 'the exquisite pleasure women's sympathy was to him'.

James (the Virginia *persona*, partly) feels, as his father reads a book in the boat 'that each page was turned with a peculiar gesture aimed at him: now assertively, now commandingly; now with the intention of making people pity him' (*TTL* p. 282). James has a recurrent fantasy that he will seize a knife or a pair of scissors and strike his father to the heart, his hatred and resentment are so intense:

He had always kept this old symbol of taking a knife and striking his father to the heart. Only now, as he grew older, and sat staring at his father in an impotent rage, it was not him, that old man reading, whom he wanted to kill, but it was the thing that descended on him – without his knowing it perhaps: that fierce sudden black-winged harpy, with its talons and its beak all cold and hard, that struck and struck at you (he could feel the beak on his bare legs, where it had struck when he was a child) and then made off, and there he was again, an old man, very sad, reading his book. That he would kill, that he would strike to the heart.

(*TTL* pp. 282–3)

James recalls 'the beak of brass, the arid scimitar of his father' from earlier in childhood. And this tormenting ambivalence, for a man old, weary and pitiful, whose other *persona* is the tyrant, is obviously Virginia's. There is a point in regarding any 'character' in Virginia Woolf's fiction as in some way a facet of an experience which has been significant to her personally.

James experiences his father in terms of 'the beak of brass, the arid scimitar', but Cam, the female child, is subject to a more distressing split in her experience of him. By splitting her experience of her father so equally between a male child, who is impervious to the attractiveness of his father, and a female child, who while attracted to him physically cannot forgive his brutality, Virginia manages to achieve maximum precision in her indictment of her father's own dual nature:

For she thought, looking at James who kept his eyes dispassionately on the sail, or glanced now and then for a second at the horizon, you're not exposed to it, to this pressure and division of feeling, this extraordinary temptation.

(*TTL* pp. 261–2)

The temptation is felt as a physical one, between herself and her father:

For no one attracted her more; his hands were beautiful to her and his feet, and his voice, and his words, and his haste, and his temper, and his oddity, and his passion, and his saying straight out before every one, we perish, each alone, and his remoteness . . . But what remained intolerable, she thought, sitting upright . . . was that crass blindness and tyranny of his which had poisoned her childhood and raised bitter storms, so that even now she woke in the night trembling with rage and remembered some command of his; some insolence: 'Do this', 'Do that'; his dominance: his 'Submit to me'.

(*TTL* p. 262)

When Mr Ramsay is told that three men were drowned just where their own boat is now:

Mr. Ramsay taking a look at the spot was about, James and Cam were afraid, to burst out:

But I beneath a rougher sea,

and if he did, they could not bear it; they would shriek aloud; they could not endure another explosion of the passion that boiled in him. . .

(*TTL* pp. 315–16)

It was a tense business, living with Sir Leslie Stephen. Virginia still felt the strain nearly a quarter of a century later, and had to exorcise it in a work of fiction which, as she writes in her diary in 1928, laid him in her mind.

In 1903–4, Sir Leslie lay dying.

of the children none, I think, suffered so much as Virginia [writes Quentin Bell] . . . Virginia, although she had felt hatred, rage and indignation at Leslie's conduct to Vanessa, felt also very deep love for him. She saw that he was reluctant to die because his children had at last got to an age at which he could know them, and knowing, love them. He wanted to see what would become of them. In his present state he could no longer be a tyrant and his tyranny might be forgotten. Between him and Virginia a special bond had been established.

(I, 84)

That he could no longer be a tyrant is the essential point to note. In his last years and months of life, when he was weak and helpless and the ground for self-pity was more valid than it had ever been before, Virginia could forgive. But in her mind's eye she could still see the tyrannical old Lear who had run her mother into an early grave, leant heavily upon Stella and rejected Vanessa because she would not sympathise enough. Only Virginia was left, and she was torn by conflicting emotions.

One of the most fundamental of these was due to a difference of intellectual kind which existed between her father and herself. Leslie Stephen was a rationalist, an agnostic, and more or less (he admits in one place) a positivist. Religion was not for him an option, and only what could be stated clearly and without self-contradiction was intellectually respectable. His rage and impatience with people who made silly, or even fanciful, remarks, is documented many times. He was a man whose yea was yea and whose nay was nay. The reasons for his loss of faith may be read in Lord Annan's biography[1] and his intellectual position generally is given lapidary statement there, so I do not need to attempt a portrait. The man was typical of the best of mid-Victorian thinking. Darwin had shattered his faith, and his temper was rationalist and agnostic. He was basically in sympathy with the utilitarians about most things, and believed in muscular ethics and no-nonsense social morality, trimmed with high social respectability and prestige which nevertheless took no pains to avoid eccentricity.

He was, moreover, steeped in the spirit and mood of the eighteenth century. His *History of English Thought in the Eighteenth Century* (1902) had become an authoritative work and is still today one of the best accounts. His massive and scrupulous, if boring and pedestrian *The English Utilitarians* (1900) presents Bentham and Mill in a fashion which implicitly endorses the essential rationality of the intellectual transitions he is concerned to describe. He was at home in the eighteenth century; he was very much at home with the utilitarians. With certain currents in his own century he was very much at variance, and would not have understood at all much of the literature of the twentieth.

All this has its bearing on the reasons for Virginia's ambiguous and torn emotional relationship to her father. For we know (we have the novels to prove it abundantly) that her own temper was not logical, deductive, or analytical in the straightforward meaning of that term; neither was it in any way analogous to nor

---

[1] Noel Gilroy Annan, *Leslie Stephen: His Thought and Character in Relation to his Time* (MacGibbon & Kee 1951).

compatible with the thought of Locke, Hume, Bentham, Mill, Spencer, Comte or Darwin. She was, as thinker, competent in other modes of apprehension: adept in intuition, analogy, and perceptions of spiritual significance at the interface of inner and outer worlds. Intellectually, there could not have been a greater distance between her father's mind and her own. If one is to attempt a distinction between her mind and her father's, one could do worse than to consider John Stuart Mill's two essays on Bentham and Coleridge. According to Mill, Bentham and Coleridge divide the thought of the nineteenth century between them, and as he wrote these essays before the century was half over, that judgment had a certain prophetic quality. Certainly it held true to the end of that century, and it is still very largely true today. Virginia's position vis-à-vis her father was very much Coleridge's position vis-à-vis Bentham.

The radical difference between types of mind did not of course have time to make itself seriously felt before Sir Leslie died. And Virginia admired much about her father's frankness and intellectual integrity, which has much in common with his mountain climbing. In her retrospective account *Leslie Stephen*, written in 1932, she acknowledges that her father gave her free run of the library, forbidding her nothing:

It was the same with the perhaps more difficult problem of literature. Even today there may be parents who would doubt the wisdom of allowing a girl of fifteen the free run of a large and quite unexpurgated library. But my father allowed it. There were certain facts – very briefly, very shyly he referred to them. Yet 'Read what you like,' he said, and all his books, 'mangy and worthless', as he called them, but certainly they were many and various, were to be had without asking. To read what one liked because one liked it, never to pretend to admire what one did not – that was his only lesson in the art of reading. To write in the fewest possible words, as clearly as possible, exactly what one meant – that was his only lesson in the art of writing.

(*Collected Essays* IV, 79–80)

Very different from the education of John Stuart Mill, admittedly, except for that ominous last sentence. 'To write in the fewest possible words, as clearly as possible, exactly what one meant – that was his only lesson in the art of writing' is authentically in the spirit of Bentham. To the future author of *To the*

Lighthouse, *The Waves*, and *Between the Acts*, 'as clearly as possible' involved parameters of style which Sir Leslie would have regarded (had he lived to see them) as sheer self-indulgence, sheer poppycock, sheer nonsense. For the 'clarity', the ability to say 'exactly what one meant' had to be fought for by Virginia along paths and byways which Sir Leslie had never trodden, indeed the very existence of which he would have either denied or condemned.

There was, then, a deep split between the rationality of Sir Leslie, historian and utilitarian, editor and compiler, and his daughter, who was to write fiction utterly opposed to the utilitarian canvases of Bennett, Galsworthy and Wells. Part of the impotent fury which Virginia must have felt for her father was due, no doubt, to his tyranny, his self-pity, his remorseless leaning on his womenfolk in order to assuage his own deep sense of failure. She refers to this self-pity in the last page of her essay on her father. But part of the frustration must have been due to the fact that her father represented a model of thinking and writing which was antithetical to hers: one which deliberately and as a matter of principle excluded feeling, poetry, intuition, suggestion, overtone, subjectivity. Virginia had to break away from her father's model of thinking, in exactly the same way, and with exactly the same urgency, as John Stuart Mill had to break away from the model of thinking of Bentham and James Mill.

CHAPTER 2

The body, the mirror,
Gerald and George

In estimating the claims that Virginia was 'mad' or 'insane' in her younger years, then, we have to hold in mind this family set-up and its powerful influence on her developing consciousness. She adored her mother, who was the centre of the family, its soother and refresher. Lily Briscoe, at the end of *To the Lighthouse*, crying out to the departed spirit of Mrs Ramsay, gives us the kind of level at which the mother Julia was missed after she died.

And her father was loved and admired, too, and yet he was also despised. His heavy, tyrannical impositions did not escape without penalty. On occasions, he must have appeared directly inimical to Virginia's subjective world which she shared with her mother. He was the 'beak of brass' plunging and smiting:

Had there been an axe handy, a poker, or any weapon that would have gashed a hole in his father's breast and killed him, there and then, James would have seized it. Such were the extremes of emotion that Mr. Ramsay excited in his children's breasts by his mere presence; standing, as now, lean as a knife, narrow as the blade of one, grinning sarcastically, not only with the pleasure of disillusioning his son and casting ridicule upon his wife, who was ten thousand times better in every way than he was (James thought), but also with some secret conceit at his own accuracy of judgment. What he said was true. It was always true. He was incapable of untruth; never tampered with a fact; never altered a disagreeable word to suit the pleasure or convenience of any mortal being, least of all of his own children, who, sprung from his loins, should be aware from childhood that life is difficult; facts uncompromising: . . .
(*TTL* pp. 12–13)

'Such were the extremes of emotion that Mr Ramsay excited in his children's breasts by his mere presence. . .' The recurrent desire to plunge a knife, scissors or an axe into the father is directly presented. Perhaps in the very directness of the statement lay some of the restoring and soothing influence of 'laying him to rest' in the novel. Now she had told the world what he had been like, now she could let him be.

Quentin Bell says that Virginia was 'mad' in the summer of 1895, and in the spring of 1904. But the obvious thing to note about the two alleged 'madnesses' of 1895 and 1904 is that they both follow the death of one of the parents. Julia Stephen died on 5 May 1895, and Quentin Bell contends that Virginia went 'mad' during the summer of that year (I, 44). Sir Leslie Stephen died, after a long drawn-out illness in which Virginia had had to nurse him all the time, on 22 February 1904. Quentin Bell asserts that in May of that year, Virginia went 'mad' again (I, 89–90): 'All that summer she was mad'.

Now, given that Virginia adored her mother and regarded her as a nonpareil among women, was it not likely that her mother's death should have stirred her profoundly, and that she should have had a nervous collapse? But that is not 'madness'.

And given that she admired and loved her father, yet also despised him; and that she had watched his tyranny over Julia, Stella and Vanessa before her; then that she had to nurse him through his terminal illness for six months herself – is it not likely that she should have been so upset and disturbed by the conflict of feeling that in the early summer of 1904 she should have had some sort of nervous collapse? But that is not 'madness' either. In neither case does Quentin Bell give any supporting aetiology.

No evidence has been offered to support the remark that Virginia was 'mad' on either occasion. It is fairly evident that the extreme nervous strain which resulted from the death of her two parents caused a temporary lack of control, or some kind of breakdown. But until some sort of solid evidence is produced, there is no reason to suppose or to state that Virginia was 'mad' on either occasion.

Quentin Bell uses the word 'mad' to cover anything that is in any way abnormal. He even uses it to cover the case of the wretched J. K. Stephen:

In 1886, while paying a visit to Felixstowe, the young man had an accident†; he damaged his head, and although the hurt did not appear to be serious it was, in fact, fatal and he began to go mad.

† The nature of the accident is not certainly known; in the Stephen family it was said that he was struck by some projection from a moving train.

(I, 35)

If you are prepared to use the word 'mad' to denote the after-effects of damage to the brain or brain haemorrhage, then obviously you are using the word loosely and do not intend any serious kind of definition with it. For instance, on the same page, Bell uses the word again in an even more peculiar way:

Whether there was, in those early years, any seed of madness within her, if those 'purple rages' were the symptom of some psychic malady, we do not know; neither probably did she; but madness walked the streets.

It is peculiar because the 'madness' referred to is apparently the 'madness' of a sexual exhibitionist, whose frightening effect is described in *The Years*, rather than anything to do with Virginia.

Quentin Bell describes the first breakdown as 'madness':

the first 'breakdown' or whatever we are to call it, must have come very soon after her mother's death. . . From now on she knew that she had been mad and might be mad again.

To know that you have had cancer in your body and to know that it may return must be very horrible; but a cancer of the mind, a corruption of the spirit striking one at the age of thirteen and for the rest of one's life always working away somewhere, always in suspense, a Dionysian sword above one's head – this must be almost unendurable.

(I, 44)

Quentin Bell equates a 'breakdown' with 'madness', 'madness' with a 'corruption of the spirit', and a 'corruption of the spirit' with a kind of life-long servitude to unknown factors in one's brain, external to one's inner life, which await their destined moment with a kind of tragic necessity. To call a thirteen-year-old girl's desperate mental distress at the death of her beloved mother 'a corruption of the spirit' is to use words in a very arbitrary way indeed.

The same insouciant use of language appears again in the context of Sir Leslie's death. For six months and more she had nursed her father through his terminal illness. To see how this wore her down one only has to consult Virginia's letters to Violet Dickinson for late 1903 and early 1904. She lived between the sickroom, the dining-room and her bedroom, on duty all the time. She leant on Violet Dickinson for help, as she was carrying a burden too big for her. The deep resentment she felt against her father was in conflict with pity at the sight of him as he lay dying. After the months of strain, she collapsed. But Quentin Bell chooses to put the matter like this:

In the breakdown that followed she entered into a period of nightmare in which the symptoms of the preceding months attained frantic intensity. Her mistrust of Vanessa, her grief for her father became maniacal, her nurses – she had three – became fiends. She heard voices urging her to acts of folly; she believed that they came from overeating and that she must starve herself. In this emergency the main burden fell upon Vanessa; but Vanessa was enormously helped by Violet Dickinson. She took Virginia to her house at Burnham Wood and it was there that she made her first attempt to commit suicide. She threw herself from a window, which, however, was not high enough from the ground to cause her serious harm. It was here too that she lay in bed, listening to the birds singing in Greek and imagining that King Edward VII lurked in the azaleas using the foulest possible language.

All that summer she was mad.

(I, 89–90)

The recent publication of the autobiographical papers under the title *Moments of Being*[1] has allowed a new insight into some of the factors which might have led to intolerable nervous stress on at least one of the occasions Bell calls 'mad', the period in 1904. There is also evidence of a continuous sort of stress which we had no means of knowing about until the publication of these papers. And this stress is set up by her two half-brothers Gerald and George Duckworth.

When he wrote his biography, Professor Bell, even if he had read the materials now newly published, had not seen their significance, for he does not distinguish between the activities of Gerald Duckworth and George Duckworth. Both, at different times of Virginia's life, had a very great effect upon her, as both

[1] *Virginia Woolf: Moments of Being, Unpublished autobiographical writings of Virginia Woolf*, edited with an introduction and notes by Jeanne Schulkind (Sussex University Press 1976). References in the text are given as 'Schulkind'. Quoted by permission of Harcourt Brace, Jovanovich, Inc. and Sussex University Press.

interfered with her sexually. For this we have the irrefutable evidence of Virginia's own memoirs.

For the new evidence on Gerald Duckworth, we have only to look at *A Sketch of the Past* in *Moments of Being*. Virginia is explaining her relationship to the mirror in Talland House at St Ives.

There was a small looking-glass in the hall at Talland House. It had, I remember, a ledge with a brush on it. By standing on tiptoe I could see my face in the glass. When I was six or seven perhaps, I got into the habit of looking at my face in the glass. But I only did this if I was sure that I was alone. I was ashamed of it. A strong feeling of guilt seemed naturally attached to it. But why was this so?

(Schulkind pp. 67–8)

There follows a fascinating self-analysis in terms of 'the mirror stage' of identity. But Virginia emphasises that looking at herself in a mirror produced a feeling of shame in her.

At any rate, the looking-glass shame has lasted all my life, long after the tomboy phase was over. I cannot now powder my nose in public. Everything to do with dress – to be fitted, to come into a room wearing a new dress – still frightens me; at least it makes me shy, self-conscious, uncomfortable. 'Oh to be able to run, like Julian Morrell, all over the garden in a new dress', I thought not many years ago at Garsington; when Julian undid a parcel and put on a new dress and scampered round and round like a hare.

(p. 68)

Here is the origin of Rhoda's sentiments of envy towards Jinny in *The Waves*, clearly. But there was something very precise about the connection between mirror and dress which Virginia now bravely tackles in her memoir:

Yet this did not prevent me from feeling ecstasies and raptures spontaneously and intensely and without any shame or the least sense of guilt, so long as they were disconnected with my own body. I thus detect another element in the shame which I had in being caught looking at myself in the glass in the hall. I must have been ashamed or afraid of my own body. Another memory, also of the hall, may help to explain this. There was a slab outside the dining room door for standing dishes upon. Once when I was very small Gerald Duckworth lifted me onto this, and as I sat there he began to explore my body. I can remember the feel of his hand going under my clothes; going firmly and steadily lower and lower. I remember how I hoped that he would stop; how I stiffened and wriggled as his hand approached my private parts. But it did not stop. His hand explored my private parts too. I remember resenting, disliking it – what is the word for so dumb and mixed a feeling? It must have been strong, since I still recall it. This seems to show that a feeling about certain parts of the body; how they must not be touched; how it is wrong to allow them to be touched; must be instinctive.

(pp. 68–9)

This connection of the feeling of shame in her own body with both the mirror and with Gerald Duckworth was to affect Virginia's whole emotional and sexual life, was to affect her marriage with Leonard, and would have a great deal to do with the causes of her several breakdowns. We shall see how all this fits together. For the moment, though, this evidence about Gerald, the mirror in the hall and the shame attached to touching certain parts of the body must be noted as part of my case that the breakdowns always had an explicable cause, part of which lies in this precise connection of experiences. In this early sensitisation of a young girl (about six years old?) to the feeling that certain parts of the body must not be touched, lies much of the problem that Virginia was later to struggle with in silence, if she could never (as we assume) bear to tell Leonard about the matter.

Virginia was nearly sixty when she wrote *A Sketch of the Past*. Much earlier, in 1920–1 she had presented her piece *22 Hyde Park Gate* to the Memoir Club. In this paper she gives an extremely caustic account of George Duckworth, which we shall turn to in a moment. But it is interesting to note, before we leave the question of Gerald Duckworth, one connection which Virginia is to make again and again with reference to George: the connection between sexual lust and a horrible animal face. Writing then of Gerald, the mirror, the body and the shame she still feels about her body, Virginia makes a very striking connection which seems to unite the two Duckworths in a common image: the horrible face of animal lust.

Let me add a dream; for it may refer to the incident of the looking-glass. I dreamt that I was looking in a glass when a horrible face – the face of an animal – suddenly showed over my shoulder. I cannot be sure if this was a dream, or if it happened. Was I looking in the glass one day when something in the background moved, and seemed to me alive? I cannot be sure. But I have always remembered the other face in the glass, whether it was a dream or a fact, and that it frightened me.

(p. 69)

It seems that in these pages of *A Sketch of the Past*, there is enough evidence to solve most of the mysteries which Leonard Woolf and after him Quentin Bell have presented as insoluble. It may well be that Virginia never summoned courage to tell Leonard about the interference from Gerald Duckworth when she was very young, nor the interference from George when she was much older. But it explains a lot of the feelings of 'guilt' of which Virginia talked when she was supposedly 'insane', and which Leonard insisted were quite unfounded. It explains a lot too about the reasons why Virginia had the nervous collapses when she did; above all it explains the problem of why one of the most serious ones immediately followed her honeymoon with Leonard in 1912. We shall come to that. But for the moment, this evidence about Gerald must be noted for its multiple significance. The chain of signifiers in Virginia's unconscious:

Body:shame:mirror:Gerald–George:not touch:Greek:animal:no

will weave its way all through the fiction and explain most of the apparent mysteries of the life.

Virginia cannot even be sure whether the 'horrible face – the face of an animal –' was a dream, or whether it happened. It has some reality for her which is so strong that she always makes this connection (feeling private parts:horrible face in the mirror: shame:fright) because of the memory of the mirror at Talland House, and because of Gerald. How this gets integrated into the history of George, Greek, and other animal faces we shall see.

Yes, the old ladies of Kensington and Belgravia never knew that George Duckworth was not only father and mother, brother and sister to those poor Stephen girls; he was their lover also.

Where does *that* come from? It is the punch-line from a paper given by Virginia to the Memoir Club sometime between March 1920 and May 1921. It has recently been published for the first time in the Schulkind collection, and comes from Monks House papers MH/A 14 and MH/A 15.

22 Hyde Park Gate is a full-length and detailed description of the effect of George Duckworth on Virginia as an adolescent and as a young woman. Quentin Bell had already summed up his own impressions as follows:

His public face was amiable. But to his half-sisters he stood for something horrible and obscene, the final element of foulness in what was already an appalling situation. More than that, he came to pollute the most sacred of springs, to defile their very dreams. A first experience of loving or being loved may be enchanting, desolating, embarrassing or even boring; but it should not be disgusting. Eros came with a commotion of leathern wings, a figure of mawkish incestuous sexuality. Virginia felt that George had spoilt her life before it had fairly begun. Naturally shy in sexual matters, she was from this time terrified back into a posture of frozen and defensive panic.

(I, 44)

Quentin Bell refers to the Monks House papers in a footnote. At the time when he wrote, these were unpublished. Now they are given to us in full. Bell's footnote reads:

Statements by Leonard Woolf and the late Dr Noel Richards suggest that George's advances were made shortly after his mother's death; on the other hand unpublished memoirs (MH/A 14, 15 and 16) by Virginia make it almost certain that his activities began at, or were continued to, a much later date, i.e. 1903 or 1904. There is some reason to think that George's interest in Virginia was from the first peculiar: 'I still shiver with shame at the memory of my half-brother, standing me on a ledge, aged about 6 or so, exploring my private parts.' (VW to Ethel Smyth, 12 January 1941). Unusual behaviour for a young man in his twenties.

(I, 44)

Given the complexity of the situation, it is not surprising that Professor Bell has made the mistake of conflating the two half-brothers in these remarks. Bell suggests that 'George's advances were made shortly after his mother's death', which means shortly after 1895. But these advances were surely Gerald's, not George's, since Virginia writes in *A Sketch of the Past* that Gerald's sexual exploration of her body in front of the mirror at Talland House took place 'once when I was very small'. When Julia Stephen died in 1895, Virginia would have been thirteen. But since we know that Talland House was sold just after Julia's death, the incident with Gerald must precede 1895. Therefore,

Gerald's interference must lie somewhere between the time when Virginia was 'very small' and her thirteenth year.

Professor Bell is right to note, however, that the interferences from George, which are recounted in MH 14, 15 and 16, were 'continued to a much later date', since we know that George was caressing and fondling Virginia while her father lay dying, that is to say as late as 1904.

Or it may be that Professor Bell is right to say that George's activities began 'shortly after his mother's death' in which case Bell would not have taken any account of the interference by Gerald, which took place before that.

There was, then, definitely, sexual interference from both half-brothers. Gerald's took place when Virginia 'was very small' and may or may not have continued in some form or other up to 1895. But some form of interference was begun by George, either as early as 1895, or soon thereafter, and continued until 1904.

However one finally interprets the evidence, there is now no doubt that from some early and impressionable age, Virginia was sexually interfered with by first Gerald, and later George Duckworth. The time-span is extremely wide. It stretches from a possible sixth year up to and including a definite twenty-second year. The interference from Gerald must have lain somewhere between the sixth and the thirteenth year, and the interference from George must have begun somewhere after the thirteenth year. The sheer length and continuity of these interferences must give one reason to pause before one starts to apply the word 'insane' to Virginia.

In *22 Hyde Park Gate*, Virginia is explicit in her indictment of George Duckworth:

. . . George Duckworth had become after my mother's death, for all practical purposes, the head of the family . . . George had made up his mind to rise in the social scale . . . 'Kiss me, kiss me, you beloved', he would vociferate; and the argument was drowned in kisses. Everything was drowned in kisses. He lived in the thickest emotional haze, and as his passions increased and his desires became more vehement – he lived, Jack Hills assured me, in complete chastity until his marriage – one felt like an unfortunate minnow shut up in the same tank with an unwieldy and turbulent whale.

(Schulkind pp. 146–7)

The irony of that last parenthesis must have been available only to Virginia herself as she gave the talk. But she goes on to subvert her own irony in her talk.

Nothing stood in the way of his advancement. He was a bachelor of pre-possessing appearance though inclined to fat, aged about thirty years, with an independent income of something over a thousand a year... George's mind swam and steamed like a cauldron of rich Irish stew... But poor George was no psychologist. His perceptions were obtuse. He never saw within . . . His face was sallow and scored with innumerable wrinkles, for his skin was as loose and flexible as a pug dog's, and he would express his anguish in the most poignant manner by puckering lines, folds, and creases from forehead to chin.

(pp. 147–150)

This last series of notations will recur as a coded reference to the situation of terror in the face of sexual desire, in the novels.

There follow some references to George and Greek, which will be more appropriately examined for their significance later. But the whole description of George ends in the most dramatic man-ner, which should leave no doubt at all as to the closeness of the relationship George had established with Virginia:

Sleep had almost come to me. The room was dark. The house silent. Then, creaking stealthily, the door opened; treading gingerly, someone entered. 'Who?' I cried. 'Don't be frightened', George whispered. 'And don't turn on the light, oh beloved. Beloved –' and he flung himself on my bed, and took me in his arms.

Yes, the old ladies of Kensington and Belgravia never knew that George Duckworth was not only father and mother, brother and sister to those poor Stephen girls; he was their lover also.

(Schulkind p. 155)

In a further communication to the Memoir Club, called *Old Bloomsbury*, which was delivered near the end of 1921 or in 1922, Virginia was even more precise about when these nocturnal visits of George's took place. It was during the period when her father was dying of cancer:

It was long past midnight that I got into bed and sat reading a page or two of *Marius the Epicurean* for which I had then a passion. There would be a tap at the door; the light would be turned out and George would fling himself on my bed, cuddling and kissing and otherwise embracing me in order, as he told Dr Savage later, to comfort me for the fatal illness of my father – who was dying three or four storeys lower down of cancer.

(p. 160)

The conflict of emotions brought about as the result of the concurrence of her father's terminal illness and George's repeated embraces, can well be imagined. It takes us a long way, surely, towards understanding why Virginia's collapse of 1904 took place. But Virginia, in the same paper, is quite explicit about the immense tensions which the attentions of George and the death of her father engendered:

When I look back upon that house it seems to me so crowded with scenes of family life, grotesque, comic and tragic; with the violent emotions of youth, revolt, despair, intoxicating happiness, immense boredom, with parties of the famous and the dull; with rages again, George and Gerald; with love scenes with Jack Hills; with passionate affection for my father alternating with passionate hatred of him, all tingling and vibrating in an atmosphere of youthful bewilderment and curiosity – that I feel suffocated by the recollection. The place seemed tangled and matted with emotion. . .

When I recovered from the illness which was not unnaturally the result of all these emotions and complications, 22 Hyde Park Gate no longer existed. While I had lain in bed at the Dickinsons' house at Welwyn thinking that the birds were singing Greek choruses and that King Edward was using the foulest possible language among Ozzie Dickinson's azaleas, Vanessa had wound up Hyde Park Gate once and for all.

(pp. 161–2)

George Duckworth's rôle in 1903–4, then, is clear: he complicates with irrelevant and hypocritical assertions of affection, and unwanted nocturnal visits, a situation which was already unbearable. His insistence that he was 'comforting' Virginia 'for the fatal illness of her father' must have produced an immense strain, given that Virginia's 'passionate affection' for her father was alternating with 'passionate hatred' of him. After what must have been years of emotional and sexual disturbance at the hands both of Gerald and of George Duckworth, the collapse of 1904 seems more or less inevitable.

In a letter to Vanessa (dated 25? July 1911) Virginia gives a very precise clue about George, in the context of a discussion she had been having with Janet Case, her old Greek teacher.

She has a calm interest in copulation (having got over her dislike of naming it by the need of discussing Emphies symptoms with a male doctor) and this led us to the revelation of all Georges malefactions. To my surprise, she has always had an intense dislike of him; and used to say 'Whew – you nasty creature', when he came in and began fondling me over my Greek. When I got to the bedroom scenes, she dropped her lace, and gasped like a benevolent gudgeon. By bedtime she said she was feeling quite sick, and did go to the W.C., which, needless to say, had no water in it.

(Letters i, 472)

Given that the subject Virginia and Janet Case were discussing was 'copulation' and that it was this which 'led us to the revelation of all George's malefactions' and that 'when I got to the bedroom scenes, she dropped her lace and gasped like a benevolent gudgeon', I think it is not unreasonable to assume that George had been involved in some form of physical intercourse with Virginia, which she does not mention here, as indeed she does not mention it anywhere. She refers only to 'all George's malefactions'. No-one can know what sort of physical intercourse was involved, and doubtless the technicalities do not matter. What does matter is the unbearable strain this physical relationship must have put on Virginia as her father lay 'dying three or four storeys lower down of cancer'. It goes a long way to explaining a possible cause for the nervous distress of 1904, and a long way too to explaining why that distress led to a temporary loss of control of some kind. It goes a long way too, to making quite untenable the theory of 'madness'. 'All that summer she was mad' writes Professor Bell. In the light of the evidence about Gerald and George Duckworth, that easy assurance is no longer credible.

vvvvvvvvvvvvvvvvvvvvvvvvvvvvvvvvvvvvvvvvvvvvvvvvvvvvvvvvvvvvvvvvvvvvvvvvv

The terrors of engagement

The effect of George Duckworth's attentions was, I believe, to traumatise Virginia, and to provoke in her a sexual anaesthesia. She could not feel any normal sexual feeling, and sexual matters were attended in her mind with fantasies of horror and dread. The first two novels she wrote, *The Voyage Out* and *Night and Day*, are both explicitly about the problem of getting engaged, and the attendant problem of how to feel something emotionally as well as sexually for the preferred or prospective partner. In the years before her engagement to Leonard Woolf, she was writing and re-writing *The Voyage Out* and she continued to work on it after their honeymoon and their return to London. It is thus a palimpsest. The early forms of the novel were written by a young woman who was not yet married, and the novel was finished by a woman whose honeymoon was just over and whose so-called 'madness' was about to recur. In *The Voyage Out*, Virginia was engaged in the analytic enterprise of trying to discover, through the use of fiction, what her own attitude towards engagement and marriage could be.

The sexual side of it is negated and refused. The heroine, Rachel Vinrace, dies before the engagement can lead to marriage, and her prospective husband Terence Hewet sits by her deathbed in a trance, thinking (in effect) what a relief it is that the marriage will not now have to be consummated. The sexual problem has been avoided, and for Hewet it is a sheer relief:

and then he listened again; no, she had ceased to breathe. So much the better – this was death. It was nothing; it was to cease to breathe. It was happiness, it was perfect happiness. They had now what they had always wanted to have, the union which had been impossible while they lived. Unconscious whether he thought the words or spoke them aloud, he said 'No two people have ever been so happy as we have been. No one has ever loved as we have loved.'

(TVO p. 431)

For the connoisseurs of coincidence, there is a very strong verbal assonance here with the suicide letter that Virginia was to leave Leonard in 1941. The evasions of certain physical issues in the one and the other are the same. The sense of relief, as if a catastrophe has been averted, is tremendous. 'They had now what they had always wanted to have, the union which had been impossible while they lived.' In other words they had the form of love without its physical reality, without the crumpled sheets of a real marriage. They had a marriage in the spirit. This was one way out, one sort of 'voyage out': it ended in *Liebestod* and renunciation.

> Entsagen sollst du, sollst entsagen!

It could not be in a richer, more overripe Romantic tradition of high chivalric love. The lady dies, and the knight retires to his club to spend his days dreaming of a happiness which he was too happy ever to have possessed.

The reason why *The Voyage Out* ends as it does is surely clear enough. Virginia has built into the novel a description of the loathing and terror she feels at sexual contact of any sort. It happens in an early scene, in which Richard Dalloway, a prototype of the effete diplomat of the later novel, has been showing off in the usual arrogant male manner about the superiority of men's brains to women's when he is suddenly struck by some errant desire to kiss the heroine, the Virginia *persona*, Rachel Vinrace. This he does with a good deal of violence. 'He kissed her passionately':

'You tempt me,' he said. The tone of his voice was terrifying. He seemed choked in fight. They were both trembling. Rachel stood up and went. Her head was cold, her knees shaking, and the physical pain of the emotion was so great that she could only keep herself moving above the great leaps of her heart. She leant upon the rail of the ship, and gradually ceased to feel, for a chill of body and mind crept over her. Far out between the waves little black and white sea-birds were rid-ing. Rising and falling with smooth and graceful movements in the hollows of the waves they seemed singularly detached and unconcerned.

'You're peaceful,' she said. She became peaceful too.

(*TVO* p. 85)

There is the tell-tale 'code' notation: the sea, the waves. It is always there, as resolution, as peace, when the heroine feels attacked by male arrogance and threatened by male desire. The sea, the waves, dissolution, escape, fluidity, forgetfulness, away from all this violence of kissing and fornicating. Rachel falls into a trance. But the important thing to notice is her physical and emotional reaction to the violence offered her: she 'gradually ceased to feel, for a chill of body and mind crept over her'. That is the authentic Virginia-reaction we get to know so well in the novels. The approach of male desire numbs her. She ceases to feel. She falls into a trance. Rachel Vinrace does it a dozen times in this novel, and Katharine Hilbery does it a dozen times in *Night and Day*. Whenever it is a question of responding to male desire, she switches off. There is a sudden access of inability to feel. George's work had been all too thoroughly done.

But what is fascinating about this gauche lunge at Rachel by Dalloway is the sequel, the dream which follows it during the night. Rachel had been more frightened by Dalloway's kiss than excited or pleased. Nightmare comes to haunt her:

Helen advised bed, and she went, not seeing Richard again. She must have been very tired for she fell asleep at once, but after an hour or two of dreamless sleep, she dreamt. She dreamt that she was walking down a long tunnel, which grew so narrow by degrees that she could touch the damp bricks on either side. At length the tunnel opened and became a vault; she found herself trapped in it, bricks meeting her wherever she turned, alone with a little deformed man who squatted on the floor gibbering, with long nails. His face was pitted and like the face of an animal. The wall behind him oozed with damp, which collected into drops and slid down. Still and cold as death she lay, not daring to move, until she broke the agony by tossing herself across the bed, and woke crying 'Oh!'

Light showed her the familiar things: her clothes fallen off the chair; the water jug gleaming white; but the horror did not go at once. She felt herself pursued, so that she got up and actually locked her door. A voice moaned for her; eyes desired her. All night long barbarian men harassed the ship; they came scuffling down the passages, and stopped to snuffle at her door. She could not sleep again.

(*TVO* p. 86)

The references to George Duckworth are very clear, and Virginia is obviously allowing only a very intermittent or lenient repression of unconscious associations. Indeed in this early passage, the *Leitmotifs* for George are clearly established, and they will run through Virginia's writing until her death. The 'little deformed man' whose face was pitted like the face of an animal, is a symbol of the terror the heroine feels for male desire as such. For her it is 'deformed' – and understandably so. It is squatting on the floor, gibbering. The walls behind ooze with damp. Barbarian men harass the ship and snuffle at her door. She is lusted after. She is in the grip of complex terrors, and the kiss of Richard Dalloway has unclicked the mechanism which swings open the door into the horror which sex and desire will always provoke in her.

There is another passage which must be cited in this context. It comes from a much later novel, but since the experience is the same, I insert it here for the purposes of comparison. It comes from *The Years* (1937):

As she ran past the pillar-box the figure of a man suddenly emerged under the gas lamp.

'The enemy!' Rose cried to herself. 'The enemy! Bang!' she cried, pulling the trigger of her pistol and looking him full in the face as she passed him. It was a horrid face: white, peeled, pock-marked; he leered at her. He put out his arm as if to stop her. He almost caught her. She dashed past him. The game was over.

She was herself again, a little girl who had disobeyed her sister, in her house shoes, flying for safety to Lamley's shop. . .

There was the long stretch of bare street in front of her. The trees were trembling their shadows over the pavement. The lamps stood at great distances apart, and there were pools of darkness between. She began to trot. Suddenly, as she passed the lamp-post, she saw the man again. He was leaning with his back against the lamp-post, and the light from the gas lamp flickered over his face. As she passed, he sucked his lips in and out. He made a mewing noise. But he did not stretch his hands out at her; they were unbuttoning his clothes.

She fled past him. She thought that she heard him coming after her. She heard his feet padding on the pavement. Everything shook as she ran; pink and black spots danced before her eyes as she ran up the door-steps, fitted her key in the latch and opened the hall door. She did not care whether she made a noise or not. She hoped somebody would come out and speak to her. But nobody heard her. The hall was empty. The dog was asleep on the mat. Voices still murmured in the drawing room.

(The Years pp. 28–30)

This experience has the authentic ring, and Quentin Bell tells us that it really happened:

madness walked the streets. I write advisedly; the scene in *The Years* where the child Rose sees a man exposing himself by a lamp-post is based on experience; there was such a man who hung around Hyde Park Gate and was seen by both Vanessa and Virginia. And of course there was madness in the home. . .

(I, 35)

It would appear from this that having been the victim of a deranged man's sexual exposure points to *Virginia*'s madness.

This traumatic experience, like the one in *The Voyage Out*, is followed by a desperate dream, a nightmare:

Rose lay asleep in the night nursery. For some time she slept profoundly, curled round with the blankets tight twisted over her head. Then she stirred and stretched her arms out. Something had swum up on top of the blackness. An oval white shape hung in front of her dangling, as if it hung from a string. She half opened her eyes and looked at it. It bubbled with grey spots that went in and out. She woke completely. A face was hanging close to her as if it dangled on a bit of string. She shut her eyes; but the face was still there, bubbling in and out, grey, white, purplish and pock-marked. She put out her hand to touch the big bed next hers. But it was empty. She listened. She heard the clatter of knives and the chatter of voices in the day nursery across the passage. But she could not sleep.

She made herself think of a flock of sheep penned up in a hurdle in a field. She made one of the sheep jump the hurdle; then another. She counted them as they jumped. One, two, three, four – they jumped over the hurdle. But the fifth sheep would not jump. It turned round and looked at her. Its long narrow face was grey; its lips moved; it was the face of the man at the pillar-box, and she was alone with it. If she shut her eyes there it was; if she opened them, there it was still.

She sat up in bed and cried out, 'Nurse! Nurse!'

There was dead silence everywhere. The clatter of knives and forks in the next room had ceased. She was alone with something horrible. Then

she heard a shuffling in the passage. It came closer and closer. It was the
man himself. His hand was on the door. The door opened. An angle of
light fell across the wash-stand. The jug and basin were lit up. The man
was actually in the room with her . . . but it was Eleanor.

(*The Years* pp. 41–2)

This has certain elements in common with the autobiographical
fragment recently published, and quoted on p. 30. In both passages the girl is alone, almost asleep in a silent house. There is the
sound of an intruder, the door opens, a man enters. In the
autobiographical fragment it was George who 'flung himself on
my bed, and took me in his arms'.

In *The Voyage Out* and *The Years* the faces of the monstrous men
have a similarity. One has a 'pitted' face which is 'like the face of
an animal'. The other has 'a horrid face: white, peeled, pock-
marked'.

It is striking that it is the condition and nature of the facial skin,
observed from very close, which links the approach of male lust
and panic terror in Virginia's mind. She had obviously observed
George Duckworth's facial skin from close up on many occasions, and she writes this of it:

His face was sallow and scored with innumerable wrinkles, for his skin
was as loose and flexible as a pug dog's, and he would express his
anguish in the most poignant manner by puckering lines, folds, and
creases from forehead to chin.

(Schulkind p. 150)

It is a face very like that which haunts the dreams of the two
girls in the novels, and it is no great associative step to perceive in
this face of horror a close resemblance to George's. His entry into
her room, perhaps repeated over several years, and under conditions that were already extremely tense, must have a great deal to
do with the trauma she expresses in her novels as a response to
male desire.

When sex manifested itself, Virginia repeatedly went into a
state of inner shock. In the case of the heroine of *The Voyage Out*,
the reaction is clearly typical of Virginia's own: Rachel goes out to
stare at the sea, the waves, the green water, which stands as a
promise of a future state where all this distress will be remedied.

One has to face the possibility that by the time Leonard Woolf and Virginia were engaged, the damage had been so extensive that what both he and she inherited was an insoluble situation in and with the other. Leonard himself had had traumatising experiences at his school, which he recounts in his autobiography. He and Virginia were in a similar state. Neither of them could relate to the other physically. This made their marriage of a very special kind, and this would not be a proper matter to investigate further were it not that, because of their physical non-communication, their mental opposition – their mental non-communication – was aggravated, and a physical incompatibility was reinforced by a mental incompatibility which put such pressure on Virginia that several times she found the strain too great to bear.

This hypothesis is not meant to be impertinent. At a certain level, the discussion of the physical basis of a marriage is, of course, improper. It is only because it is largely in the conditions of the marriage itself that the causes lay for Virginia's 1913 and 1915 breakdowns, that it seems permissible to make certain connections. After all, it is Leonard who called his wife 'insane' in his autobiography, and Quentin Bell followed suit in using the word 'mad'. It seems only fair, then, to enquire into the conditions of the marriage itself (which neither Leonard nor Quentin Bell discuss) such that the insulting words 'insane' and 'mad' can be examined for their validity.

The most menacing document I know of in all this arsenal of deadly material, is the letter in which Virginia agrees to marry Leonard. The recipient of this letter (which purports to be a letter of acceptance) might reasonably have taken the first ship back to Ceylon. The relevant passage reads:

Then, of course, I feel angry sometimes at the strength of your desire. Possibly, your being a Jew comes in also at this point. You seem so foreign. And then I am fearfully unstable. I pass from hot to cold in an instant, without any reason; except that I believe sheer physical effort and exhaustion influence me . . . So I go from being half in love with you, and wanting you to be with me always, and know everything about me, to the extreme of wildness and aloofness. I sometimes think that if I married you, I could have everything – and then – is it the sexual side of it that comes between us? As I told you brutally the other day, I feel no physical attraction in you. There are moments – when you kissed me the other day was one – when I feel no more than a rock. And yet your caring for me as you do almost overwhelms me. It is so real, and so strange. Why should you?

(To Leonard Woolf, 1 May 1912, *Letters* i, 496–7)

This letter is of an extreme frankness and honesty, and one can only admire a woman who could analyse herself and her lover so fearlessly. Yet every word in the letter contains a menace. Every phrase, every implication, points to their entering a situation which neither of them would be able to control. The kiss of 'the other day' was the Dalloway–Vinrace kiss, obviously, the one that Virginia was most afraid of. And yet it could have been a very gentle, a very decorous one. But we have Virginia's own explicit testimony to the fact that the contact of Leonard's lips turned her to rock.

'Possibly, your being a Jew comes in also at this point. You seem so foreign.' This, though it should not be overemphasised, was undoubtedly an element in the situation of non-attraction. In an early letter to Violet Dickinson dated 5 April 1905, 'Somewhere off the Coast of Spain' (the original sea-trip which underlies *The Voyage Out*), Virginia lets slip the sort of remark in the easy fashionable snobbish way of a certain class of that time, that shows that she was really a quite frank anti-semite: 'There are a great many Portuguese Jews on board, and other repulsive objects, but we keep clear of them' (*Letters* i, 184). Doubtless this is a mere slip into bad taste, and regrettable. But we have the evidence of Leonard's own *The Wise Virgins* to show how easily the slip, and the assumption, were made, and how they hurt.

Then there is that notation about Leonard in the newly published MH/A 16, dating from the end of 1921 or early 1922, in any case long after she had married him, which mentions the first things she heard about Leonard from her Cambridge friends:

And then Thoby, leaving me enormously impressed and rather dazed, would switch off to tell me about another astonishing fellow – a man who trembled perpetually all over. He was as eccentric, as remarkable in his way as Bell and Strachey in theirs. He was a Jew. When I asked why he trembled, Thoby somehow made me feel that it was part of his nature – he was so violent, so savage; he so despised the whole human race . . . I was of course inspired with the deepest interest in that violent trembling misanthropic Jew who had already shaken his fist at civilisation and was about to disappear into the tropics so that we should none of us ever see him again.

(Schulkind, p. 166)

The accent on Woolf's Jewishness is heavy. When she came to write the letters in which she informed her friends of her engagement to Leonard, she emphasised the Jewishness of her fiancé with excessive crudity. It was obviously essential to defend herself by attacking violently before she could be attacked. To Violet Dickinson she wrote, for instance:

My Violet,
    I've got a confession to make. I'm going to marry Leonard Wolf [sic]. He's a penniless Jew. I'm more happy than anyone ever said was possible – but I *insist* upon your liking him too.

(4 June 1912, *Letters* i, 500)

And in the letter to Janet Case, her old teacher of Greek, she pokes a good deal of cruel fun at Leonard's home and family. This passage in the letter is obviously the germ of that fictional tea party in *Night and Day* where Katharine Hilbery is submitted to the *peine forte et dure* of middle-class tea at 'Highgate':

My dear Janet,
    . . . relations have begun, and such a tea-party at Putney.
    'A sandwich, Miss Stephen – or may I call you Virginia?'
    'What? Ham sandwiches for tea?'
    'Not *Ham*: potted meat. We don't eat Ham or bacon or Shellfish in this house.'
    'Not Shellfish? Why not shellfish?'
    'Because it says in the Scriptures that they are unclean creatures, and our Mr Josephs at the Synagogue – and –
    It was queer –

Yrs. aff.
VS
(June 1912, *Letters* i, 502–3)

The editors of the *Letters* tell us in a footnote that 'Leonard had taken Virginia to meet his widowed mother, who lived in Colinette Road, Putney, with several of her children.' In *Night and Day*, Virginia has moved the setting of this ordeal from Putney to Highgate (both socially inferior places) and Katharine Hilbery thinks to herself:

The unsparing light revealed more ugliness than Katharine had seen in one room for a very long time . . . Katharine decided that Ralph Denham's family was commonplace, unshapely, lacking in charm, and fitly expressed by the hideous nature of their furniture and decorations. She glanced along a mantelpiece ranged with bronze chariots, silver vases, and china ornaments that were either facetious or eccentric.

She did not apply her judgment consciously to Ralph, but when she looked at him, a moment later, she rated him lower than at any other time of their acquaintanceship.

(Night and Day (N&D) pp. 396–8)

In this passage, it is clear that Virginia did not hesitate to take the risk of hurting Leonard's feelings. But then he had not hesitated to take that risk with regard to Virginia's feelings when he portrayed her so candidly in *The Wise Virgins*. Virginia recalls the visit to Leonard's home in fictional form with remorseless accuracy.

Two major elements in Virginia's thinking about Leonard as future husband stand out clearly, then. The explicitly sexual element in marriage showed every sign of turning out to be disgusting, lustful, 'deformed', nightmarish, intolerable. She admits to Leonard frankly in her letter of acceptance that she feels no physical attraction in him. Secondly, Leonard was Jewish, foreign, the product of milieu of striking tastelessness, and sufficiently 'foreign' in himself for her to realise from the start that a great deal of adaptation on her part was going to be called for.

These two major elements by no means represent the whole problem of engagement and marriage. There was, above all, the problem of affectivity as such, the problem of how to feel any emotion at all, the problem of how to relate to another person at all. And this is the major problem of both the first novels, *The Voyage Out* and *Night and Day*.

In the first novel, *The Voyage Out*, it is evident that this difficulty in finding out the nature of one's own feelings is fundamental to the design of the whole enterprise. In encountering the possibility of loving each other, Rachel and Terence are baffled. The difficulties of bringing feelings and words together are appalling. In fact, the two lovers can come to an agreement only by means of the most primitive offers of good will:

'Does this frighten you?' Terence asked when the sound of the fruit
falling had completely died away.

'No' she answered. 'I like it.'

She repeated 'I like it'. She was walking fast, and holding herself more
erect than usual. There was another pause.

'You like being with me?' Terence asked.

'Yes, with you,' she replied.

He was silent for a moment. Silence seemed to have fallen upon the
world.

'That is what I have felt ever since I knew you' he replied. 'We are
happy together.' He did not seem to be speaking, or she to be hearing.

'Very happy,' she answered.

They continued to walk for some time in silence. Their steps unconsciously quickened.

'We love each other,' Terence said.

'We love each other,' she repeated.

(TVO pp. 331–2)

It is as if one is present at the most primitive stammerings and
gropings for acceptable words, between two people who are
utterly unused to being allowed to express, or even to possess,
their own feelings. It has to be examined carefully and slowly,
this new feeling. Neither lover wishes to make any quick move,
in case the evanescent thing slips away.

'What's happened?' he began. 'Why did I ask you to marry me? How
did it happen?'

'Did you ask me to marry you?' she wondered. They faded far away
from each other, and neither of them could remember what had been
said.

'We sat upon the ground,' he recollected.

'We sat upon the ground,' she confirmed him. . .

Rachel became conscious of a new feeling within her. She wondered
for a moment what it was, and then said to herself, with a little surprise at
recognizing in her own person so famous a thing:

'This is happiness, I suppose.' And aloud to Terence she spoke, 'This
is happiness.'

On the heels of her words he answered, 'This is happiness,' upon
which they guessed that the feeling had sprung in both of them at the
same time.

(TVO pp. 345–6)

The alienation of the lovers, both from their own bodies, and
from their own feelings, would be absurd if it were not so obviously sincere and painful. Happiness is something they turn up,

like a pebble in the way, and ask of it: What is that? So tenuous is the grasp of the lovers upon their own emotions. Their bodies they have put into almost permanent abeyance.

But, in these two first novels, no such sweet primitive feeling is allowed to remain unchallenged for long. Doubt, isolation, words, intervene to make the situation intolerable. What agonises the male partner is that his fiancée keeps on slipping away into a dream, a trance. She is caught, but she will not be caged. She does not want to advance into the relationship. Really, she wishes to withdraw from it:

. . . Terence had ceased to stare contentedly in front of him, and was looking at her keenly and with dissatisfaction. She seemed to be able to cut herself adrift from him, and to pass away to unknown places where she had no need of him. The thought roused his jealousy.
'I sometimes think you're not in love with me and never will be,' he said energetically. She started and turned round at his words.
'I don't satisfy you in the way you satisfy me,' he continued. 'There's something I can't get hold of in you. You don't want me as I want you – you're always wanting something else.'
He began pacing up and down the room.
'Perhaps I ask too much,' he went on. 'Perhaps it isn't really possible to have what I want. Men and women are too different. You can't understand – you don't understand –'
He came up to where she stood looking at him in silence.
It seemed to her now that what he was saying was perfectly true, and that she wanted many more things than the love of one human being – the sea, the sky. She turned again and looked at the distant blue, which was so smooth and serene where the sky met the sea; she could not possibly want only one human being.
'Or is it only this damnable engagement?' he continued. 'Let's be married here, before we go back – or is it too great a risk? Are we sure we want to marry each other?'
They began pacing up and down the room, but although they came very near each other in their pacing, they took care not to touch each other. The hopelessness of their position overcame them both. They were impotent; they could never love each other sufficiently to overcome all these barriers, and they could never be satisfied with less. Realising this with intolerable keenness she stopped in front of him and exclaimed:
'Let's break it off, then.'

(*TVO* pp. 370–1)

It is *she* who makes the suggestion, just as it is *she* who 'wanted many more things than the love of one human being – the sea, the sky'. She may long for the love of one human being, but when that thought involves the body and the joining of bodies, she remembers the 'little deformed man who squatted on the floor gibbering' in his dank constricting cave. Every time her lover approaches her with desire ('You don't want me as I want you – you're always wanting something else') she remembers the nightmare, the terror, the shame, the ugliness. And so they pace up and down the room, but 'they took care not to touch each other'. For, in the problem which they are actually discussing, physical contact would solve it instantly. And she cannot bear the problem to be resolved by physical contact.

And so the novel moves to the only close it could have: the death of the heroine. The alternative would be too gross.

That was the strange thing, that one did not know where one was going, or what one wanted, and followed blindly, suffering so much in secret, always unprepared and amazed and knowing nothing; but one thing led to another and by degrees something had formed itself out of nothing, and so one reached at last this calm, this quiet, this certainty, and it was this process that people called living. . . 'Love,' St John had said, 'that seems to explain it all.' Yes, but it was not the love of man for woman, of Terence for Rachel. Although they sat so close together, they had ceased to be little separate bodies; they had ceased to struggle and desire one another. There seemed to be peace between them. It might be love, but it was not the love of man for woman.

(*TVO* pp. 384–5)

The woman has had her way. There will be no marriage, no honeymoon, no breeding, no children, no desire. A *pax romana* has been imposed. Desire has been suppressed, and only peace remains. *Fear no more the heat o' the sun*. The Shakespearean motif which haunts Mrs Dalloway all through her day, has found its first symbolic placing as early as 1913.

Therefore, necessarily, this novel ends with the death of Rachel. And when her spirit is represented as passing away over the bay as the lightning of the great storm crashes down round the hotel, there is no doubt that this is meant to represent a tremendous romantic victory of the spirit over the body.

Virginia began writing *The Voyage Out* before her marriage to Leonard, and continued to rewrite it after their honeymoon. It represents, therefore, very much a thought-process. The thought-process was to be continued in *Night and Day*, and indeed in every novel up to and including the last one. *The Voyage Out* does not represent so much a conclusion, as an abrupt breaking-off of an argument too difficult to sustain. The conclusion is permitted to be so 'Romantic' only because the lived existential problem of Virginia and Leonard had only just begun.

Leonard and Virginia were settling down to married life. And therefore a further study was required, a study in depth of the actual relationship of a woman who lived in fear of physical contact, as well as in fear of her own emotions, and a man who himself was dreadfully isolated within the same problem. Leonard and Virginia certainly shared, after their marriage, the same problem, which was how to achieve this 'peace' with which the first novel ends, without engaging in the low commerce of embodiment or of emotion. They had to work out a *modus vivendi* together.

Therefore *Night and Day* was written. It is a meta-study of *The Voyage Out*. The theme is the same, but some years on, so to speak. The problem has matured in form, and it does end in a kind of uneasy recognition that the man and woman will have to live together under the same roof, even if they don't at first wish to get married. So the body is re-admitted by proxy, as it were. But before that precarious balance is reached, the same dialectic of advance, trance, withdrawal and recrimination is gone through a dozen times between the two characters who most resemble Virginia and Leonard – Katharine Hilbery and William Rodney, who is later transformed into Ralph Denham.

Katharine Hilbery agrees to marry William Rodney out of a weary sense that it is inevitable. This sort of thing has to be:

She felt certain that she would marry Rodney. How could one avoid it? How could one find fault with it? . . .

'William,' she said, speaking rather faintly at first, like one sending a voice from sleep to reach the living. 'William,' she repeated firmly, 'if you still want me to marry you, I will.'

Perhaps it was that no man could expect to have the most momentous question of his life settled in a voice so level, so toneless, so devoid of joy or energy. At any rate William made no answer. She waited stoically. A moment later he stepped briskly from his dressing-room, and observed that if she wanted to buy more oysters he thought he knew where they could find a fishmonger's shop still open. She breathed deeply a sigh of relief.

(*N&D* pp. 144–6)

She breathes deeply a sigh of relief because the necessity of showing or receiving or processing emotion has been obviated. William Rodney is as unable to respond to her toneless offer of marriage as she is to show any pleasure in making it. They act for all the world like two zombies. Their highest hope is that neither will betray the other by breaking into a strong, and recognisable, emotion. So afraid are they both of their own feelings.

Later on, in a passage which tells its own story, Virginia lets us know how her heroine thinks about her forthcoming marriage:

she took up her knitting again and listened, chiefly with a view to confirming herself in the belief that to be engaged to marry some one with whom you are not in love is an inevitable step in a world where the existence of passion is only a traveller's story brought from the heart of deep forests and told so rarely that wise people doubt whether the story can be true.

(*N&D* p. 226)

Inevitably, the old dialectic of withdrawal and recrimination is set up. Rodney takes her moody silence, reserve and refusal to show him even an elementary sign of affection with understandable pique:

Thus to lose touch with her, for he had no idea what she was thinking, was so unpleasant to him that he began to talk about his grievances again, without, however, much conviction in his voice.

'If you have no feeling for me, wouldn't it be kinder to say so to me in private?'

'Oh, William,' she burst out, as if he had interrupted some absorbing train of thought, 'how you go on about feelings! Isn't it better not to talk so much, not to be worrying always about small things that don't really matter?'

'That's the question precisely,' he exclaimed. 'I only want you to tell me that they don't matter. There are times when you seem indifferent to everything. I'm vain, I have a thousand faults; but you know they're not everything; you know I care for you.'

'And if I say that I care for you, don't you believe me?'

'Say it, Katharine! Say it as if you meant it! Make me feel that you care for me!'

She could not force herself to speak a word.

(*N&D* pp. 252–3)

Say it, say it, say you love me, begs the man. 'She could not force herself to speak a word.' The judgment is terrible. Her emotions are completely sealed off inside her. She cannot express anything. Moreover, she does not feel anything either. And suddenly she determines to make this clear:

> Why should she not simply tell him the truth – which was that she had accepted him in a misty state of mind when nothing had its right shape or size? that it was deplorable, but that with clearer eyesight marriage was out of the question? She did not want to marry anyone. She wanted to go away by herself, preferably to some bleak northern moor, and there study mathematics and the science of astronomy.[1] Twenty words would explain the whole situation to him. He had ceased to speak; he had told her once more how he loved her and why. She summoned her courage, fixed her eyes upon a lightning-splintered ash-tree, and, almost as if she were reading a writing fixed to the trunk, began:
> 'I was wrong to get engaged to you. I shall never make you happy. I have never loved you.'
> 'Katharine!' he protested.
> 'No, never,' she repeated obstinately. 'Not rightly. Don't you see, I didn't know what I was doing?'
>
> (*N&D* p. 254)

The historical origin of this is doubtless the abortive engagement between Virginia and Lytton Strachey. But it is the recurrent situation which is significant, the situation that Virginia feels compelled to describe again and again. It is exactly the same situation as the one in the previous novel between Rachel and Hewet. The man complains he is not loved and that the woman does not show any feeling for him, any affection. After a moment's hesitation, the woman suggests breaking it all off: it was a mistake in the first place. Rather than face the question of love, sex and physical exchange, the heroine suddenly tears up the contract and revokes her agreement. She cannot bear to go further into what she finds herself trapped in, so she struggles desperately to withdraw. Such is the terrified refusal brought upon her by any show of passion or desire. It is the continual failure of the ability to feel anything:

[1] In the novel, Katharine's clandestine absorption in mathematics, geometry and astronomy, which reads so bizarrely, must surely stand for some desperate desire to escape flesh and commitment and to retreat into an abstract world where she would be protected from male pursuit and lust.

And she thought of them and looked at the faces passing, and thought how much alike they were, and how distant, nobody feeling anything as she felt nothing, and distance, she thought, lay inevitably between the closest, and their intimacy was the worst pretence of all. For, 'Oh dear,' she thought, looking into a tobacconist's window, 'I don't care for any of them, and I don't care for William, and people say this is the thing that matters most, and I can't see what they mean by it.'

(*N&D* pp. 283–4)

And so inevitably, inexorably, the situation moves to its pre-destined end:

'I think it's a little odd, don't you?' he said, in a voice of detached reflection. 'Most people, I mean, would be seriously upset if their marriage was put off for six months or so. But we aren't; now how do you account for that?'

She looked at him and observed his judicial attitude as of one holding far aloof from emotion.

'I attribute it,' he went on, without waiting for her to answer, 'to the fact that neither of us is in the least romantic about the other. That may be partly, no doubt, because we've known each other so long; but I'm inclined to think there's more in it than that. There's something temperamental. I think you're a trifle cold, and I suspect I'm a trifle self-absorbed.'

(*N&D* pp. 301–2)

With courageous accuracy, Virginia traces the disintegration of a relationship which is informed by no desire, and which is limited by the fear of self-expression. The fact that the engagement to William Rodney is probably based on the lightning engagement of Virginia and Strachey is not structurally significant, since the problems which Katharine and her new lover Ralph Denham inherit are more or less identical to those which Katharine had with Rodney. The characters may change, but the base situation cannot change. The idea of introducing the substitution figure of Ralph Denham, who can, in expressing his own emotions slightly more freely somehow manage to unlock Katharine's, was a happy one. Whether or not it corresponded to any real mutation in the relationship between Virginia and Leonard seems unlikely. But at least it serves as a technical aid which intervenes in time to prevent this novel ending in exactly the same way as the previous novel did: with the death of the heroine and the marriage once again unconsummated. That would have been a technical blunder and would also virtually have amounted to a public declaration of her problem. Virginia cannily avoids a second *Liebestod* by introducing the passionate and romantic Ralph Denham, who so much resembles Leonard Woolf, even down to the detail of his family background. But the expression of feeling was as difficult in Bloomsbury as it was either in Putney or in Highgate. In the autobiographical writings, Virginia gives us a sudden insight into a group, and an atmosphere, which must have been as utterly disconcerting for Ralph–Leonard as it was for Katharine–Virginia:

> Now I had begun to be puzzled. Those long sittings, those long silences, those long arguments – they still went on in Fitzroy Square as they had done in Gordon Square. But now I found them of the most perplexing nature. They still excited me much more than any men I met with in the outer world of dinners and dances – and yet I was, dared I say it or think it even? – intolerably bored. Why, I asked, had we nothing to say to each other? Why were the most gifted of people also the most barren? Why were the most stimulating of friendships also the most deadening? Why was it all so negative? Why did these young men make one feel that one could not honestly be anything? The answer to all my questions was, obviously – as you will have guessed – that there was no physical attraction between us.
>
> (Schulkind p. 172)

It is true that Virginia here, in writing of 'Old Bloomsbury' is discussing the company of homosexuals – 'buggers' as she frankly calls them. The problem is given in this passage with a forceful precision. Whether homosexual or heterosexual, feeling, emotion was difficult, because 'there was no physical attraction between us'. It would be perfectly legitimate to read this passage as meaning, as well, that even if 'physical attraction' existed among men, it was of a peculiar kind which may have done little to break down the difficulties of expressing emotions, one for the other, and the passage might well be indicating that, in a highly intellectual and repressed society, feeling between men and women (and with that, 'physical attraction') was not made any easier when the basic relationship was, symbolically enough, homosexual.

That is the problem given, examined, probed, and never solved, in the two first novels.

In August 1926, Vita Sackville-West, writing to her husband Harold Nicolson, and very much taken with Virginia, makes the following illuminating comment:

Also – since I have embarked on telling you about Virginia – I am scared to death of arousing physical feelings in her, because of the madness. I don't know what effect it would have, you see: it is a fire with which I have no wish to play. I have too much real affection and respect for her. Also she has never lived with anyone except Leonard, which was a terrible failure, and was abandoned quite soon.

(Nigel Nicolson, *Portrait of a Marriage* p. 204)

The fact that 'it was a terrible failure, and was abandoned quite soon' we can easily gather from the novels. That is what *The Voyage Out* and *Night and Day* actually tell us. That is what the novels are about. Vita Sackville-West's testimony was scarcely needed, but it is interesting as inside evidence that the sexual basis of the marriage between Leonard and Virginia was very soon discontinued. Virginia's sensibility developed consistently towards women, such as Violet Dickinson and Vita herself, largely because they were not perceived as abrasive, arrogant or demanding, or even, disgusting. The anaesthesia in sexual matters was proportionately relieved in the context of beautiful and talented women. The whole of *Orlando* is there to prove how passionately she could feel love for a woman. Both Harold Nicolson and Quentin Bell are very cautious when they come to describing what degree of physical intimacy existed between Vita Sackville-West and Virginia. Nigel Nicolson quotes Bell: 'There may have been – on balance I think [that] there probably was – some caressing, some bedding together' (Nicolson p. 202; in Bell II, 119). And Vita, in the letter to Harold Nicolson cited above, writes calmly: 'I *have* gone to bed with her (twice), but that's all' (Nicolson p. 204).

So, on Vita's own admission, she slept with Virginia. The relationship with Leonard 'was a terrible failure, and was abandoned quite soon'. Nobody would have better reason to say that than Vita, if she were the intimate, the confidante and the bedfellow of Virginia, as well as being the object of that most passionate and sustained erotic poem *Orlando*.

Leonard's own account of the marriage and the honeymoon, as

told in his autobiography, takes exactly forty-two lines (*Beginning Again* pp. 82–3). There are several significances in his account. First, there is no mention at all of the fact that, in the first few days of the honeymoon, they went to the Plough Inn at Holford, the place where, almost exactly a year later, Virginia's endurance gave out and from where she was taken back to London, under the supervision of 'Ka' Cox and Leonard himself, to see the psychiatrist.

Second, his refusal to regard the honeymoon as in any way a matter on which he owes the public a description is, in the circumstances, significant. He talks about anything and everything rather than the relationship with his new wife. He makes the whole thing sound like a boy-scout outing. He talks of his life in Ceylon, lonely tracks in Spain, mulecarts, 'a Hungarian ship on the point of sailing to Marseille'. He represses any reference to the new relation to Virginia and, typically, with almost parodic energy, describes what they ate. If it were not so ominous, the following account of a honeymoon at sea would be funny:

At 7.30 in the morning I staggered up on to the deck and found the Third Officer who spoke English. I explained to him that I was very hungry and why. He took me up on to the bridge and had breakfast sent to me there; the first course was an enormous gherkin swimming in oil and vinegar. One of the bravest things I have ever done, I think, was to eat this, followed by two fried eggs and bacon, coffee and rolls, with the boat, the sea, and the coast of France going up and down all round me.

(*Beginning Again* p. 83)

Where was Virginia? He does not mention her. But this introduction of the question of food on the honeymoon is of some importance if one is to explain why Virginia had her third collapse on their return from the honeymoon to London.

Virginia makes some fictional reference to that same morning of the honeymoon in chapter 5 of *The Voyage Out*, where a massive storm hits the ship. Mrs Dalloway and Richard may be taken to be Virginia and Leonard:

. . . Clarissa owned that she would be better off in bed, and went, smiling bravely.

Next morning, the storm was on them, and no politeness could ignore it. Mrs. Dalloway stayed in her room. Richard faced three meals, eating valiantly at each; but at the third, certain glazed asparagus swimming in oil finally conquered him.

'That beats me' he said, and withdrew.

(*TVO* p. 77)

The 'glazed asparagus swimming in oil' is certainly related to the 'enormous gherkin swimming in oil and vinegar' which Leonard took as his solitary breakfast.

The point raised here is important. Food was symbolic, and food was to divide Virginia and Leonard till the end. Leonard was determined never to recognise the validity of his wife's claim that she didn't like food, feared it, and hated eating it. Virginia felt, wrongly according to Leonard, but nevertheless with an inner conviction which was perfectly real to her, that to eat led to being fat, gross, absurd, ridiculous, and the butt of everyone's scorn.

CHAPTER 4

Full bellies, dull minds

At this point one has to consider quite seriously the relation between Virginia and food. This relation is quite distinct from the relation which Leonard saw between them. It is obvious, if one reads with more subjective and less rationalist eyes than Leonard used, that Virginia feared food. It was a fear which Leonard never chose to acknowledge. Indeed in endorsing certain 'psychiatric' 'treatments' (milk, food, rest) which caused Virginia to put on weight, he acted in despite of, and in refusal of, what was clearly a neurosis of some kind, which Virginia felt about her body image. But Quentin Bell clearly states:

It is perhaps worth noting that Virginia was always critical of her friends' behaviour at table. Her sensitivity on this point was perhaps connected with her own phobias about eating, phobias which, when she was ill, could make her starve herself and, at ordinary times, made her always very reluctant to take a second helping of anything.

(II, 170)

The problem was certainly present on the honeymoon. The 'food' theme always points to a 'displacement', of some kind, in the 'sex' theme. It is significant that the problem should arise on the honeymoon. Even if Leonard had had many opportunities to observe her attitude to food before their marriage, he had chosen to ignore the meaning of that attitude. The reasons why she felt her body to be absurd, ridiculous, gross, fat and the butt of everyone's scorn, may have been partly the result of the years of having her body mistreated by Gerald and by George. But also there would have been other reasons. Her body represented for her the area of her greatest vulnerability. At any rate, it may have seemed to her that everyone looking at her could see how help-less, how undefended, she felt. When one considers the morbid obsession with food, eating, fatness and weight in the first novel, the one written over the honeymoon period, one is made aware of the presence of a very great suppressed anxiety.

Consider this, for sheer virulence:

'Astonishing!' she exclaimed at last. 'What sort of shape can she think her body is?' This remark was called forth by a lady who came past them, waddling rather than walking, and leaning on the arm of a stout man with globular green eyes set in a fat white face. Some support was necessary, for she was very stout, and so compressed that the upper part of her body hung considerably in advance of her feet, which could only trip in tiny steps, owing to the tightness of the skirt round her ankles. The dress itself consisted of a small piece of shiny yellow satin, adorned here and there indiscriminately with round shields of blue and green beads made to imitate the hues of a peacock's breast. On the summit of a frothy castle of hair a purple plume stood erect, while her short neck was encircled by a black velvet ribbon knobbed with gems, and golden bracelets were tightly wedged into the flesh of her fat gloved arms. She had the face of an impertinent but jolly little pig, mottled red under a dusting of powder.

St. John could not join in Helen's laughter.

'It makes me sick,' he declared. 'The whole thing makes me sick. . . Consider the minds of those people – their feelings. Don't you agree?'

(*TVO* pp. 187–8)

The picture conjured up here, the caricature, represents quite obviously a bodily possibility which Virginia deeply feared. This woman, with 'golden bracelets tightly wedged into the flesh of her fat gloved arms', represents the kind of absence of self-consciousness which Virginia feared above all. She was terrified of becoming gross. This fictional creation is done with the savage and morbid hate of a picture by Edvard Munch. Although she was in fact very thin, if not underweight, all her life (except when subjected to her 'rest cures' when she was forced to eat more than she could endure), she always feared that she might become overweight, fat, obese, ridiculous, stupid.

The fictional character St John makes, at the end of this passage, the connection which Virginia herself doubtless made all the time. Obesity increases the possibility of dull minds, sluggish spirits and insensitive souls.

' "Astonishing!" she exclaimed at last. "What sort of shape can she think her body is?" ' This makes a very important connection. It is not so much a question of how one's body appears to other people, as of what kind of shape one conceives one's own body to have. Leonard and Virginia entered a life-long struggle about food, presumably from this early point in their relationship. He himself, though thin, and able to eat as much as he liked without ever putting on weight, apparently never wished to understand that his wife, equally thin, might in fact be suffering about the possibility of becoming fat, obese, gross and therefore . . . stupid. Leonard either could not conceive, or else refused, this thought.

Virginia gives several descriptions which are turbulent with hate, of the inmates of the hotel in terms of their eating habits. The guests have just dined, and are trying to kill the hours between dinner and bedtime by sitting reading their 'plump' letters from England:

[This] prompted Hirst to make the caustic remark that the animals had been fed. Their silence, he said, reminded him of the silence in the lion-house when each beast holds a lump of raw meat in its paws. He went on, stimulated by this comparison, to liken some to hippopotamuses, some to canary birds, some to swine, some to parrots, and some to loathsome reptiles curled round the half-decayed bodies of sheep. The intermittent sounds – now a cough, now a horrible wheezing or throat-clearing, now a little patter of conversation – were just, he declared, what you hear if you stand in the lion-house when the bones are being mauled.

(TVO pp. 208–9)

This description, with all its savage and violent fury, belongs to expressionist art. And its very intensity requires of the reader that he take seriously the possibility that, for Virginia, eating, digesting, and sitting still, were loathsome activities which led directly to visual ugliness, as well as to spiritual and intellectual decadence. She sees these disgusting animals digesting and absorbing their huge quantities of food as a direct attack upon intelligence, fineness, response, intuition, mind. The sheer grossness of such eating makes her fear for her own weight, and for herself.

In order that the reader should not have any possibility of escape from the seriousness of her belief, she repeats her theme again within a few pages. The 'loathsome reptiles' now become 'crocodiles . . . fully gorged'.

The clock, which had been wheezing for some minutes like an old man preparing to cough, now struck nine. The sound slightly disturbed certain somnolent merchants, government officials, and men of independent means who were lying back in their chairs, chatting, smoking, ruminating about their affairs, with their eyes half shut; they raised their lids for an instant at the sound and then closed them again. They had the appearance of crocodiles so fully gorged by their last meal that the future of the world gives them no anxiety whatever.

(TVO p. 216)

Again, it is Hirst who makes Virginia's comment for her:

'Ah, the creatures begin to stir. . .' He watched them raise themselves, look about them, and settle down again. 'What I abhor most of all,' he concluded, 'is the female breast. Imagine being Venning and having to get into bed with Susan! But the really repulsive thing is that they feel nothing at all – about what I do when I have a hot bath. They're gross, they're absurd, they're utterly intolerable!'

(TVO p. 216)

Virginia's mind lies open to us here in some of the complexity of its symbolic inter-relationships. Fat, reptile-like creatures, gorged, are gross, absurd and intolerable. But so is any sexual contact. The female breast is repulsive. Venning is to be pitied when he gets into bed with Susan. Both eating and sex are absurd. And absurdity is the negation of intelligence, mind, intellection, freedom. Threading its way through that complex series of assertions is the basic one, the serpent in the garden: 'the really repulsive thing is that they feel nothing at all'. They feel nothing when they eat, they feel nothing when they 'fall in love' and they feel nothing when they copulate. Gorged, fat, obese, somnolent, they doze in the sun from meal to meal; 'they're gross, they're absurd, they're utterly intolerable!'

And what do these gorged animals eat? What goes on behind the scenes to feed them at feeding-time? Another expressionist vignette of extraordinary power:

'They kill hens down there,' said Evelyn. 'They cut their heads off with a knife – disgusting! . . .'

[Rachel] looked down at the kitchen premises, the wrong side of hotel life, which was cut off from the right side by a maze of small bushes. The

ground was bare, old tins were scattered about, and the bushes wore
towels and aprons upon their heads to dry. Every now and then a waiter
came out in a white apron and threw rubbish on to a heap. Two large
women in cotton dresses were sitting on a bench with blood-smeared tin
trays in front of them and yellow bodies across their knees. They were
plucking the birds, and talking as they plucked. Suddenly a chicken
came floundering, half flying, half running into the space, pursued by a
third woman whose age could hardly be under eighty. Although
wizened and unsteady on her legs she kept up the chase, egged on by the
laughter of the others; her face was expressive of furious rage, and as she
ran she swore in Spanish. Frightened by hand-clapping here, a napkin
there, the bird ran this way and that in sharp angles, and finally fluttered
straight at the old woman, who opened her scanty grey skirts to enclose
it, dropped upon it in a bundle, and then holding it out cut its head off
with an expression of vindictive energy and triumph combined.

(*TVO* pp. 307–8)

These fluttering wretched birds who are decapitated for tonight's
dinner are only going to gorge the already over-gorged, to fatten
the already over-fat, to dull the already over-dull. The scene is
cruel in itself. But Virginia, in forcing the attention of the reader to
this senseless waste of life, wishes to emphasise the lowness of
the forms of life which are to be nourished by this wasted life.
Seen in this absurd context, the killing becomes both menacing
and disgusting at once, intolerable and unendurable. The
menace consists in the 'food' being presented as strictly *unnecessary*.

CHAPTER 5

'What exactly do you mean *by* that?'

When Virginia returned to London with Leonard from the honeymoon at the beginning of October 1912, huge existential issues lay unresolved between them, which became focused as the question of sex, the question of the expression of feeling, and the question of food. Her gradual disorientation after their return to London, which moved Leonard to go and consult psychiatrists as early as January the following year, 1913, had its roots in real, lived problems. There were problems she could not solve by herself, and being married to Leonard made the matter, if anything, worse because he was equally distrustful of his own emotions and equally anaesthetised with regard to sex. The only difference between them was that Leonard had a primitive, witch-doctor attitude to sanity and health, which led him to do a thing which Virginia herself would never have done – consult 'experts' – who knew nothing of Virginia's inner life at all, nor indeed of her past.

But there was a worse problem lying between them than even these three, and that was that Virginia and Leonard had quite different kinds of intelligence, quite different kinds of perception, quite different kinds of thought-process. They regarded quite different things as elucidation and clarification, and had quite different ideas about what constituted evidence.

To marry Leonard, in view of known and admitted physical incompatibility, was a dangerous enterprise. Virginia's motives for actually getting married are fairly clear – marriage seems to have been seen as a means of having or achieving 'a room of one's own', a status in society, a social identity. Katharine Hilbery, the

Virginia *persona* in *Night and Day*, reflects as follows on one occasion:

'To begin with, I'm very fond of William. You can't deny that. I know him better than any one, almost. But why I'm marrying him is, partly, I admit – I'm being quite honest with you, and you mustn't tell any one – partly because I want to get married. I want to have a house of my own. It isn't possible at home. It's all very well for you, Henry; you can go your own way. I have to be there always. Besides, you know what our house is. You wouldn't be happy either, if you didn't do something. It isn't that I haven't the time at home – it's the atmosphere.'

(*N&D* pp. 202–3)

This sentiment doubtless played a major part in Virginia's decision to marry Leonard. Her social status ('one of those poor Stephen girls' as she puts it) was second-order. She wasn't a real social entity, without getting married. She was a problem, a person to be 'matched up' or, simply, a negligible quantity.

Respect increased immediately one got engaged. People changed their attitude to one instantly. There is a very wry acknowledgment of this in *The Voyage Out*:

Directly she became engaged, Mrs Paley behaved with instinctive respect, positively protested when Susan as usual knelt down to lace her shoes, and appeared really grateful for an hour of Susan's company where she had been used to exact two or three as her right. She therefore foresaw a life of far greater comfort than she had been used to, and the change had already produced a great increase of warmth in her feelings towards other people.

(*TVO* p. 212)

Virginia must, surely, have felt in some such way about getting engaged to Leonard. It was a bid for freedom from what was becoming a drifting, impermanent, makeshift and perhaps threatening existence.

But the fact that it was Leonard she chose carried within it premonitions of disaster. Just as Virginia had analysed the probable kinds of difficulty in *The Voyage Out*, so Leonard too had expressed his pessimism in his two novels of 1913 and 1915. It was evident to both of them that they were marrying, in a sense, against the grain of their separate characters. It was not that Leonard was not a good man, a kind man, an intelligent and a tolerant man, a man of infinite good will – he was all these things.

What was more to the point was this simple but irreducible difficulty: Leonard had the mind of a rationalist, and his wife did not.

For the purposes of this analysis, I shall not define what I intend by rationalist, but rather let Gerald Brenan, who knew the Bloomsbury group well, do the job for me:

I was always divided in my loyalty to 'Bloomsbury', considered as a group. There could be no doubt about the high level of their intelligence, while their cult of good conversation made them very stimulating people to know. But I thought that Maynard Keynes' description of them as 'water spiders swimming gracefully on the surface of the stream' contained a good deal of truth. Civilized, liberal, agnostic or atheist like their parents before them, they had always stood too far above the life of their day, had been too little exposed to its rough-and-tumble really to belong to it. Thus, though they thought of themselves as new brooms and innovators, they quickly found they were playing the part of a literary establishment. What I chiefly got from them was their respect for the truth. Yet this – they gave the word a capital letter – was defined in a narrow and exclusive way so that anyone who held views that could not be justified rationally was regarded as a wilful cultivator of illusions and therefore as a person who could not be taken seriously. Religion in particular was anathema. The subject was finished, closed, or existed merely as a personal weakness or as a hangover from early associations, like not washing or continuing to play with dolls or tin soldiers. That psychological pressures could drive people to believe things that could not be proved rationally or scientifically was something that they refused to allow. Scepticism was a moral duty. They thus found themselves out of touch both with large areas of the world they lived in and with most of the past. For if history showed, as they thought, a slow progress from superstition to enlightenment, why bother to understand the impulses that drove people to religious belief, much less to communism or Nazism? By saying 'they're so stupid', they imagined that they had disposed of them.

(Brenan, *Personal Record* pp. 156–7)

If one considers that Virginia was living in that group, and that Virginia was the author of *Mrs Dalloway*, *To the Lighthouse* and *The Waves*, then this judgment by Gerald Brenan suggests the direst consequences. It suggests the setting for a tragedy. The description of the general attitude of the group is so concisely put, and one can grasp so clearly its intellectual stance that Virginia's place in it becomes instantly a matter of grave doubt. Far from being the 'queen' of Bloomsbury, was she not going to be its Antigone? Was not this illuminated, narrow, affectedly logical group going to surround her, punish her and drive her to desperation?

Brenan writes: 'anyone who held views that could not be justified rationally was regarded as a wilful cultivator of illusions and therefore as a person who could not be taken seriously'. That was to be, literally and in a pure state, Leonard's attitude to Virginia's 'insanity' and her 'illness' from the beginning to the end; and long after her death he reiterates his belief that his wife was 'insane' in his autobiography. What she asserted, Leonard says again and again, could not be justified rationally, and therefore, since she was in Brenan's sense 'a wilful cultivator of illusions', she could not (in *that* sense, in the sense in which what she was talking about might have some other meaning than the obvious literal or logical one) 'be taken seriously'. This belief, that Virginia was talking nonsense, led him to consult one specialist after another. For what Virginia asserted on occasion, could not be 'justified rationally'.

Brenan writes again: 'That psychological pressures could drive people to believe things that could not be proved rationally or scientifically was something that they refused to allow.' That refusal was going to cost Virginia dear, because she was advancing a model of intellection which, while not being opposed to rationalist thought-processes, sets out rather to complement them in a fundamental way. Virginia was proposing, in her novels, a form of thinking which would be informed by feeling, and intuitively adequate to what was being discussed. This was something to which Bloomsbury was opposed. What we have then, is a paradox. Far from being the most brilliant adornment of Bloomsbury, Virginia Stephen, later Virginia Woolf, was working like an undercover agent in enemy-occupied country. The strain on her was terrific. She was surrounded on all sides by people who not only knew better than she did because they were men, but simply knew better. They could define what they meant, 'rationally', and an attempt at definition like *Kew Gardens* or *The Mark on the Wall* they regarded as charmingly eccentric. And when Virginia, after years of mauling by George Duckworth, lay in a fit in bed saying the nightingales were singing in

Greek and that 'King Edward VII lurked in the azaleas using the foulest possible language', she was, in Brenan's formulation, holding views that 'could not be justified rationally' and she was therefore 'a wilful cultivator of illusions' and 'could not be taken seriously'.

To read Leonard Woolf's volumes of autobiography is to breathe in the aroma of the very fine flower of the Bloomsbury rationalist–reductive consciousness. He was its very exemplar, its paragon, its nonpareil. It would be tedious and indeed unnecessary to document this: a reading of the volumes will turn up case after case where the reader is struck by the actual naïveté of what is being asserted, a naïveté which is the conscious and chosen result of excluding all parameters of thinking which are not strictly logical or deductive. And nowhere is this self-imposed set of limitations more evident than in those pages of his autobiography where he writes of his wife's 'insanity'. It very often looks as if the rationalist mind, because of its very presuppositions about views which 'could not be justified rationally', deliberately refuses to see what, to a less blinkered intelligence, is strikingly obvious.

It is Gerald Brenan again who gives us the clearest indication of the clue to Leonard's exclusiveness of intellection, his vanity:

'As for intelligence,' said Leonard, 'I would back myself against all of them.'

(Personal Record p. 79)

That really is pretty staggering. Leonard, looking round the room at the assembled company, finds himself simply the best man. Brenan continues:

Leonard, I thought to myself, will always be, wherever he is, the most intelligent person in the room, even when Roger Fry or Bertie Russell are present. And this is because, having a head so clear that no one could have a clearer, he has energy to spare for watching and comparing the speakers and their psychological motives: that is to say, he is detached and this gives him a feeling of superiority, of being in some sense more intelligent than even people like B[ertrand] R[ussell], whose mental capacity he sums up under the rather disparaging word 'brilliant'.

(p. 79)

Russell, in Leonard's eyes is merely 'brilliant', but he, Leonard, is the most intelligent of all. 'As for intelligence,' said Leonard, 'I would back myself against all of them.'

He has mastered the argument going on (whatever it is) so quickly and so intelligently, that he has time over 'for watching and comparing the speakers and their psychological motives: that is to say, he is detached and this gives him a feeling of superiority'. Leonard follows an argument detachedly, and believes that in analysing the motives of the speaker, he is defending himself from emotional contagion. Yet the motives behind what the speaker says are the motives which Leonard is imputing to him. And insofar as the speaker's motives are in any way subject to illusion, what the speaker is saying will be discounted. Hence Leonard's mode of attention is in fact split and self-contradictory. It enters the subjectivity of the speaker's motives, only to refuse any truth value to what the speaker says if either motives or statements fail to measure up to what Leonard himself takes to be reasonable.

Now this is the man Virginia had married. Sexually disturbed from years of interference from her half-brothers, terrified of her own body, and deeply distrusting food, it began to dawn on her, on their return from their honeymoon, that she had married an adversary in the mind *too*. Not only were she and Leonard physically incompatible, but they were going to be mentally incompatible, and above all else, were going to be mentally incompatible on this matter of their physical incompatibility.

It must be for some such reasons that her 'insanity' sets in so soon after the honeymoon. Her behaviour must have begun to be strained, strange, even desperate. One can see clearly why. But Leonard, as he himself says several times in his autobiography, has no patience with, and no understanding of, 'insanity'. Since Virginia doubtless did not express most of what was preoccupying her upon the return from the honeymoon, Leonard found his natural inclination to observe 'insanity' from the outside, as a detached observer, reinforced.

What Virginia was claiming could not be 'justified rationally' and therefore it would have followed that she was 'a wilful cultivator of illusions'. For these reasons, Leonard's natural recourse was to take advice from people who were pre-eminently 'sane', and who, moreover, shared his own view about Virginia's mental balance. Leonard became convinced that he had married a sick woman, that she was 'ill'.

But 'ill' as used by Henry Head and by Leonard was an entirely external appellation, which made no attempt to discover verbally what the origin of apparently 'insane' talk or action might be. Leonard was, in any case, the last man who would be able to judge the matter in terms of its real causes, since he was himself part of the problem, and suffered from it doubtless as much as Virginia did.

But Virginia was being observed in a world in which even the basic insights of Freud still had to gain acceptance, and the idea of symbolic referents in the unconscious discourse obviously was not available.

So when Virginia returned to London in 1912, she may well have realised that she had married into a far greater isolation than any she had known before. She had been able to live previously in this atmosphere of Moorean rationalism without reaching the end of her resources to cope, but when physical problems with Leonard emerged and appeared insoluble, she may well have had the feeling that she was not going to be able to cope much longer.

She may have realised that she had married a man who was, at a deep and unconscious level, intellectually hostile to her. One has only to read *The Wise Virgins* to see how hostile Leonard really felt towards the privileged, well-off, bourgeois, gentile family into which he had married.

And certainly, Virginia had expressed *her* contempt for the male intellectual in that long line of pedants and brilliant young Cambridge men who pass through her novels, all of whom have much of Leonard in them. Leonard is recognisable in both St John and Hewet in *The Voyage Out*, in William Rodney in *Night and Day*, and in Tansley in *To the Lighthouse*. As late as *Between the Acts*, Mrs Swithin is always being reproached, corrected or deflated by a recognisably Leonard-like Bartholomew, who, moreover, even looks like Leonard. Some of Mr Ramsay in *To the Lighthouse* is a comment on Leonard too. In fact, there is a logical connection between Sir Leslie and Leonard, who may have had a great deal to do with each other in Virginia's mind. In both, the highest standards of logical rationalism were present and required, and both were, in a sense, inimical to what Virginia's talent was trying to become. To both Leonard, and had he been alive, to her father, many of Virginia's actions in 1913 and 1915 would have been seen, from the rationalist point of view, as mere self-indulgence. Anything that was not rationally explicable, would have been seen, as Brenan puts it, as a wilful cultivation of illusions. Eventually, Virginia succumbed.

It is not for nothing that the presiding influence in Virginia's group was G. E. Moore, the killer of Idealisms and spooks of all sorts, the chaser of fairies and fays. His influence was apparently all-pervasive. Leonard recalls 'the ghostly echoes of *Principia Ethica*, the catechism which always begins with the terrifying words: "What exactly do you *mean* by *that*?" ' (*Beginning Again* p. 138). Note the word 'catechism', for the person employing this triumphant formula was aware of putting his interlocutor on the spot, making him face up to 'reality', depriving him of the comforting presence of illusion or self-deception. 'What exactly do you *mean* by *that*?' was the rationalist verbal device which exposed nonsense at once, uncovered the hypocrite and put the sloppy thinker to flight.

Words, in the world of G. E. Moore very especially, were logical counters in a world of public logical discourse, and must have a clear and precise, not a merely personal, meaning. 'What exactly do you *mean* by *that*?' is a demand for a publicly available and checkable meaning. The mere force of this insistence ran the opposite way to any openness to the idea of an unconscious process.

Now, the call for greater precision in expression is admirable provided that the maximum of expressibility has not already been passed and left behind, in which case the question is shot across the bows as a warning not to speak in terms that the group will not accept. If a person has merely been unclear, 'What exactly do you *mean* by *that*?' will be a welcome invitation to further exposition. But the question was most often used to bring conversation to a halt whenever anything was said that was not, in Brenan's phrase, capable of being 'justified rationally'. It was used as a weapon. The person was required to stand and deliver an alternative verbal proposition, when and if the initial one had not pleased or not been accepted. 'What exactly do you *mean* by *that?' meant*: conform to our verbal conventions, or prepare to be ridiculed.

It was of the essence of Virginia's genius that what she had to say, to show, was not capable of being further verbally reduced from the expression she had already given it. If anything, her mind led her to describe *inclusively*, and to expand upon certain aspects of what was described, rather than to *exclude* more and more from the description. The description and the intelligibility had to belong together. It might take fifteen pages to describe a mark on the wall. The Moorean attitude had no patience with such descriptions. Its question was, so to speak, 'Is it a stain or is it a nail?' Virginia was trying to draw attention, however, not to what the mark in fact empirically *was*, so much as to the process of human vision which allows such enormous and radical imprecisions. In doing so, she was working in the opposite direction to Moore. She was not so much interested in what such and such a thing *is*, as in how many different ways it could be seen or experienced. Thus Virginia was trying to explain, not so much what was seen, as how we see. And this involved the opposite of the Moorean 'stand and deliver'. It was not shorter and clearer definitions that were required, but rather longer and more complex ones.

The demand for verbal definitions of what should be states or experiences, can be quite comic, and Virginia gives a parody of one when Katharine and William Rodney face each other over the abyss of lovelessness in *Night and Day*. 'I think you're a trifle cold,' says Rodney, 'and I suspect I'm a trifle self-absorbed.' They stare at each other glumly, trying to decide what it is they don't have. And, obeying the 'catechism' of Moore, they fall into trying to do it verbally:

'What is this romance?' she mused.

'Ah, that's the question. I've never come across a definition that satisfied me, though there are some very good ones' – he glanced in the direction of his books.

'It's not altogether knowing the other person, perhaps – it's ignorance,' she hazarded.

'Some authorities say it's a question of distance – romance in literature, that is – '

'Possibly, in the case of art. But in the case of people it may be – ' she
hesitated.

'Have you no personal experience of it?' he asked, letting his eyes rest
upon her swiftly for a moment.

'I believe it's influenced me enormously,' she said . . . She sighed,
teased by desires so incoherent, so incommunicable.

'But isn't it curious,' William resumed, 'that you should neither feel it
for me, nor I for you?'

Katharine agreed that it was curious – very . . .

(N&D pp. 302–3)

This is so painful that I do not know whether it is meant to be a
parody or not. Two young people, strapped into their bodies by
moral strait-jackets indulge in a kind of verbal post-mortem
which is utterly inappropriate to the situation, which should be
one of feeling and exchange. Yet they feel themselves obliged to
go through this verbal rigmarole of books, definitions, authorities
and words. 'What exactly do you *mean* by *that*?' had done its work
all too well. Neither has the courage to take the other's hand and
say simply: this is it. For the first casualty of the Moorean catechism is spontaneity.

And it was to this circle that Virginia returned after the honeymoon in 1912. It was, of course, the same circle that she had
recently left, but I think it must now, returning to it, have seemed
different, more menacing, more malign than before. Her need for
emotional contact being what it now was, the refusal of it was all
the more painful. The body made its demands, and they were
refused. And the minds (of others) were there to show that any
relenting towards the demands of the body was illegitimate,
self-indulgent, weak. At first, she wrote and rewrote her manu-
script, *The Voyage Out*. Leonard writes 'Virginia was rewriting the
last chapters of *The Voyage Out* for the tenth or, it may have been,
the twentieth time' *(Beginning Again* p. 87). Or it may have been
the thirtieth time for all Leonard knew. That she was in travail he
did not allow to occur to his conscious mind, and he goes on to
discuss the sales of *The Voyage Out* and compare them with his
own literary production of that time, *The Village in the Jungle*.

But she must have been trying to stave off a growing panic. She had begun to see the full implications of the position she had got herself into. With her husband, she had (it would appear, from their mutual testimony) no physical relationship and only a very strained intellectual one, the marriage having been turned into a civilised agreement based, no doubt, on affection and respect. He did not understand her fear of food, her sexual traumatisation by George and her resultant frigidity, nor her feeling that her body was ridiculous and that everyone laughed at her. What she said about her own 'body image' could not be justified rationally, and not to be able to justify something rationally was the equivalent of wilful self-deception, or to put it another way, unless experience could be justified rationally in words, it might as well be considered as not having any reality, and had to be discounted as illusion.

And it would have been impossible for Virginia to explain about Gerald and George, the 'deformed little men', her sexual anxiety, her fear of her body, and her intense fear of making herself ridiculous by an open appeal for emotional response. She must gradually have become aware that she was inhabiting a state of being which Kierkegaard called *Indesluttedhed*, 'self-immuration'. What was worrying Virginia to the point of agony, she could not express to Leonard. Did she fear that he would ridicule her, as her whole family had done, and as the whole circle traditionally did when someone said something that was not rationally justifiable? She must have had reason to fear so. Although *Night and Day* did not appear until some years later, it contains a sustained analysis of the themes of *The Voyage Out*, and many of the discussions Virginia and Leonard actually had must have been very like the agonised verbalisations and mutual incomprehensions between Katharine Hilbery and William Rodney, and later Ralph Denham – useless, pointless, ending in some mute impasse. Even there, in the last chapters of *Night and Day*, when Rodney has been rejected for the much more compatible Ralph Denham, the woman and the man are still unsure whether they are in love, and begin to speak of each other's 'lapses':

'Katharine,' he added, his assumption of reason broken up by his agitation, 'I assure you that we are in love – what other people call love.

Remember that night. We had no doubts whatever then. We were
absolutely happy for half an hour. You had no lapse until the day after; I
had no lapse until yesterday morning.

(*N&D* p. 500)

Rodney has to reassure Katharine that they *are* in love – 'what
other people call love'. It is a verbal matter, though: they have to
check the experience to see if it fits the word, not the other way
about. And they were happy for . . . half an hour! Then began the
'lapses'. What are these lapses? The novel is there to tell us, but it
does not. It refers to the 'lapses' in shorthand, the usual Virginia
code which means she retreats into herself at the slightest
advance of emotion:

. . . Ralph expressed vehemently in his turn the conviction that he only
loved her shadow and cared nothing for her reality. If the lapse was on
her side it took the form of gradual detachment until she became completely absorbed in her own thoughts, which carried her away with such
intensity that she sharply resented any recall to her companion's side. It
was useless to assert that these trances were always originated by Ralph
himself, however little in their later stages they had to do with him. The
fact remained that she had no need of him and was very loath to be
reminded of him. How then, could they be in love? The fragmentary
nature of their relationship was but too apparent.

(*N&D* p. 501)

'The fact remained that she had no need of him and was very
loath to be reminded of him.' The situation is patched up, more or
less, within the novel, and the situation is saved by another Julia
figure, Mrs Hilbery, who manages to extract the various men
from their limited and narrow tangles by the use of a kind of
sublime empathy for everyone's feelings. Nevertheless, in the
real situation between Virginia and Leonard in 1912–13, this
impasse must have been all too common. Virginia retreats into
herself, Leonard tries to recall her, she resents this, and after a
verbal exchange of some sort, they both sit mute, unhappy,
suffering their own private inward agonies.

He turned sharply to implore her help, when again he was struck cold by
her look of distance, her expression of intentness upon some far object . . . their physical closeness was to him a bitter enough comment
upon the distance between their minds.

(*N&D* p. 502)

They cannot communicate. They cannot resolve their problems, even their disagreements, as most lovers do, through the body, for both are too afraid of their bodies to make the attempt that way. So they sit, perfect products of the murderous ethic of muscular Victorian prudery, which has effectively cut them both off from free access to their own bodies and their own emotions.

Leonard could bear this better than Virginia could. There is no trace in his autobiography that he found the deprivation of normal warm emotional and physical exchange between man and wife oppressive or in any way punishing. He put the whole matter aside, and thought of his political work. He became very fond of dogs. And there is no hint there that the origin of his wife's successive disturbances and 'insanity' after 1912 might have been due to the fact that she found it much harder to bear than he did. Or, if this did occur to him, he found he could not afford to recognise it. It would have been more than he could have borne, to have had to admit that the deprivation of emotional and physical exchange at the very beginning of a marriage was harsh: it was to be regarded as something which two rational beings could cope with, by the adroit use of their minds. He managed it, Virginia did not.

It seems to me then, given all this evidence about Virginia's past and upbringing, given all the evidence of the novels, that Virginia's third collapse was no more 'insane' than the first two had been. In the first case, her nerves gave out after the death of her mother – and she had been disturbed by Gerald. In the second case, her nerves gave out after nursing her father through his terminal illness – and she had been disturbed by George. The third collapse followed the honeymoon. Given the realisation that Virginia may have come to on the honeymoon, about the impossibility of ever explaining herself to Leonard in any satisfying way, she may have felt more alone than ever.

In a *bon mot* which is worthy of La Rochefoucauld, Virginia writes in *The Voyage Out*: 'When two people have been married for years they seem to become unconscious of each other's bodily presence so that they move as if alone, speak aloud things which they do not expect to be answered, and in general seem to experience all the comfort of solitude without its loneliness' (p. 230).

That may have suited Leonard, though obviously he too would have wished things to be other than they were. But it was an intensification of solitude which Virginia, sealed off in her body, could not bear. Not able to bear the strain, she collapsed. From 1913, the year after their marriage, Leonard took on his rôle as nurse of a sick woman, visited doctors and specialists, made arrangements and took on the responsibility of nursing the mentally unbalanced.

And yet, scarcely six months had elapsed since Leonard and Virginia had been married and gone off on their honeymoon. Virginia showed stress in early 1913, collapsed in July, and again in August. Leonard's account in his autobiography does not give the impression that he considered that the 1913 collapse could have been a direct result of the conditions of the honeymoon and of the realisation of incompatibility, physical and mental, which sprang from it. He tells us he read *The Voyage Out* in early March of 1913 and that he took it to 'Gerald Duckworth, her half-brother' on 9 March. He must have decided to close his eyes to what is open to every reader: the novel is about the tragedy of an engagement which cannot be consummated.

It is at least highly possible that Virginia did not go 'mad' on the third occasion any more than she had been 'mad' on the first two. But, when she could not endure the existential situation of being married to a man with whom emotional and sexual commerce was difficult to the point of impossibility, she collapsed. And the world closed round her.

Once you fall, Septimus repeated to himself, human nature is on you. Holmes and Bradshaw are on you. They scour the desert. They fly screaming into the wilderness. The rack and the thumbscrew are applied. Human nature is remorseless.

(*Mrs Dalloway* p. 108)

But Virginia had reached the end of her ability to hold out alone. That passionate piece comes from *Mrs Dalloway*, which was written nearly a decade after the events described in it; so does this, the moment Virginia must have remembered clearly:

At last, with a melodramatic gesture which he assumed mechanically and with complete consciousness of its insincerity, he dropped his head on his hands. Now he had surrendered; now other people must help him. People must be sent for. He gave in.

(*Mrs Dalloway* p. 100)

vʊʊ

Leonard's three problems

Leonard Woolf's two novels, *The Village in the Jungle* (1913) and *The Wise Virgins* (1914) are little known. Yet they throw a very interesting light over the way he was thinking in the years which preceded his marriage to Virginia Stephen in 1912, and the way he came to think of his new wife in the breakdown which so closely followed their honeymoon.

They allow us, indeed, to reconstruct the presuppositions in Leonard's mind, which led him so easily to consult psychiatrists in 1913, and so easily to endorse the 'cures' which Virginia underwent at their hands.

But they also allow us an insight directly into Leonard's anxious attitude towards his marriage itself. In a way which is totally unexpected in such a nuanced and subtle mind, Leonard has written out his own fears and hopes as a young suitor, with a candour and a wealth of local detail which is disconcerting. He has also expressed himself directly and repeatedly (through the most flimsy of fictional disguises) on the question of his Jewish race, and his reactions to what he clearly perceived as gentile scorn.

The first novel, *The Village in the Jungle*, reflects the experience of the years spent in Ceylon. It is an excellently constructed narrative, and it shows a complete grasp of Ceylonese social and racial structure. Leonard has familiarised himself, not only with the way his characters think and speak, but also the unconscious assumptions they make. In this context, it is interesting that Leonard constructs a story which has as its main impulse the desire of two young people to marry across their caste system, and in defiance of that system.

The Headman's wife's brother, Babun Appu, who is a lusty young bachelor of twenty-one, comes to join the Headman's household in the village, and falls in love with the nubile young daughter of Silindu, called Punchi Menika. Silindu is a man apart, he belongs to a lower caste, and his daughters, Punchi Menika and Hinnihami, are called 'veddas' in the village – that is to say wild girls, strange girls, partly external to the normal life of the village. That the Headman's relative chooses to ally himself with one of these girls is considered a disaster, both by the Headman's family, and later on by Silindu's. As Leonard is at pains to point out, the caste system is kept in place by both high castes and low castes, and both endorse the system as it is.

Leonard carefully explains the conventions: 'In towns and large villages there are, especially among people of the higher castes, many rigid customs and formalities regarding marriages always observed.' But he goes on to say that in small villages, for economic reasons, these customs often go by default. There is, however, even in small villages, a distinction between a wife and a concubine. Moreover, the mixing of castes is regarded with equal disfavour by both upper and lower caste.

Babun knew well enough his brother-in-law's dislike of Silindu, and the contempt with which the 'veddas' were regarded by other villagers. He knew that his sister and Babehami would be very angry with him if he chose a wife from such a family.

(p. 52)

The Headman's wife, hearing of the proposed alliance across the castes, breaks out in outrage:

'Ohé! So we are to take veddas into the house, and I am to call a pariah sister! A fine and a rich wife! A pariah woman, a vedda, a daughter of a dog, vesige duwa! Ohé! the headman's brother is to marry a sweeper of jakes! Do you hear this? Will you allow these Tamils[1] in your house? Yes, 'twill be a fine thing in the village to hear that the headman has given his wife and daughters to Rodiyas,[2] leopards, jackals!'

[1] A favourite form of abuse among the Sinhalese is to call someone a Tamil.
[2] Rodiyas are the lowest Sinhalese caste.

(p. 54)

The structure of castes is here reinforced by the structure of races. Leonard is punctilious in his use of race distinction, which he had obviously studied closely. He includes at one point a footnote which seems to belong more to an anthropological treatise than to a work of fiction:

There are two distinct races in Ceylon, Tamils and Sinhalese. Their language, customs, and religions are different. The Tamils are Dravidians, probably the original inhabitants of India; they are Hindus in religion. The Sinhalese are Aryans, and their religion is Buddhism. The Tamils inhabit the north and east of the island, the Sinhalese the remainder. (footnote p. 106)

But this technical appreciation of the differences between Sinhalese and Tamil is central to the meaning and action of the novel.

Leonard tells us in *Growing* that Tamil was the first eastern language that he learnt, and also that he came to like the Tamils in a mild way, though he makes it clear that he much prefers the Sinhalese, and this on religious grounds. The Sinhalese are Buddhists, and there is something in their religion which fits well with Leonard's temperament. 'I am essentially and fundamentally irreligious, as I have explained in *Sowing*, but, if one must have a religion, Buddhism seems to me superior to all other religions' (*Growing* p. 159).

Thus, Leonard brings considerable erudition and sympathy to bear on the way Sinhalese and Tamils regard each other. There seems to be little doubt that Leonard is setting up in this earlier novel a series of social and racial distinctions which correspond to the social and racial distinctions he was to make in *The Wise Virgins*. Just as in the first novel the Sinhalese are Buddhists and high caste, the Tamils Hindu and low caste, so in the second novel, the gentiles are represented as Christian and high class, while the Jewish family, the Davises, to which the Leonard-*persona* Harry belongs, is represented as of Hebrew religion and of lower-middle to lower class. In both novels, the plot hinges on an attempt made by a pair of lovers to cross, to dare, to brave, the doubly reinforced taboos of caste and race; and in both novels the attempt fails.

Leonard reinforces the hopelessness of the attempt of Babun

Appu and Punchi Menika to succeed against the prejudices of their society, by twice 'doubling' the situation in the later phases of the novel. The second 'vedda' daughter of Silindu, Hinnihami, is lusted after by the one-eyed 'vederala' or medicine man. It is made clear that the 'vederala' is possessed of supernatural powers and is therefore not clearly assimilable to any caste. In his attempt to force the caste system, and take Hinnihami to himself, he uses sorcery on Silindu, and this is only resolved through trance, exorcism, rape, and finally a strange ritual execution, in which Hinnihami and her pet deer are stoned to death by the villagers, whose patience has come to an end. Thus Leonard seems to want to emphasise that deviance from caste-approved marriage or concubinage will end badly, whether that deviance is chosen (as in Punchi Menika's case) or forced upon her by bad luck (as in Hinnihami's case).

The second reinforcement of the major theme is the third main episode of the novel, in which Punchi Menika again becomes the object of desire, this time of a disreputable speculator, Fernando, who moves into the village. His low character is explicitly given through his race:

He was not a Sinhalese, and spoke Sinhalese very badly. Some people said he was a Tamil: his black skin and curly black hair pointed to the fact that he had Kaffir blood in his veins.

(p. 144)

'Some people said he was a Tamil.' This is an explicit judgment, not only upon race, but upon moral worthiness. And indeed, Fernando turns out to be a villain. He lusts after the very girl, Punchi Menika, whose alliance with the high-born Babun Appu brought about all the original trouble. In an elegant double structure, we see disaster again descend from the abuse of the caste system. Just as Hinnihami had been forced by the 'vederala' or medicine man, so Punchi Menika, on her second time round, is forced by the 'mudalali', the crook Fernando. His plot fails, but he spreads confusion, suffering and finally death by his intervention into a system he does not belong to or understand. Punchi Menika returns finally to her village, the jungle encroaches, and as she lies dying a giant boar snuffles its way into the hut. The jungle has reclaimed the village, down to its very last occupant.

The problems are immense, and it is obviously in some hope of trying to find solutions to them that Leonard undertakes his fictionalised algebra (for that is what his novels are). The first problem is the problem of class, and the enormous social and cultural gap which exists between classes. A higher class feels itself as irrevocably and unquestionably superior to a lower class, and this makes emotional commerce between members of different classes doubly difficult. Only a 'maverick' member of a higher class will be sufficiently detached from the group to entertain serious feelings for a member of a lower class. Hence the importance laid, in Leonard's novels, on the non-conforming member of a family, the only hope for commerce between a man and a woman from different classes.

Second, there is the problem of race. This seems at times to be Leonard's major preoccupation. His sense of being Jewish, and to that extent his sense of being cut off from equal and acknowledged commerce with the gentiles, is insisted upon for page after page. The sceptical reader is invited to read *The Wise Virgins* for himself. The theme is more or less obsessional.

Third, Leonard introduces into his second novel a new problem, the problem of feeling: how to feel, what to feel, how to express what one feels. So great has been the effect of a century's moralising pietism and hypocrisy that the return to the normal feelings of the heart and the body is almost insuperably difficult.

In *The Wise Virgins*, then, Leonard takes it upon himself to analyse, in a lightly fictionalised form, these three problems. Class and race are equally important. The problem of feeling, common to both strata of characters portrayed, occupies a slightly subordinate position, but is still important in the total economy of the novel.

There are three families involved, two socially equal and divided only by race, one socially superior and separated from both by class, and from one also by race.

Two of the families live in 'Richstead', a London suburb which is obviously a composite form of Richmond and Hampstead, the suburbs which adjoin, and which lie in each case to the west of, Putney and Highgate, with which Leonard had personal associations.

The two families who live in Richstead are given as equal in class terms. The Garland family consists of Mrs Garland and her four unmarried daughters. The Davis family, which is Jewish, consists of Mr and Mrs Davis, their son Harry, the gifted and 'advanced' artist-figure (Leonard's *persona* in the novel), and his rather colourless sister Hetty. The Davises are obviously modelled on memories of Woolf family life at a time which preceded the death of Leonard's father. Leonard's father is given very precise delineation in the third chapter.

The third family is given as socially superior, and as inhabiting a distant part of London. This family is distanced from the two Richstead families by race, class and geography. The well-to-do Mr Acton Lawrence, obviously a composite form of Leslie Stephen and a host of others, has two unmarried daughters, the wise virgins, presumably, of the novel's title. Camilla corresponds to Virginia Stephen, Katharine to Vanessa Stephen, and the modelling is not only accurate and precise, it also goes into considerable detail.

The Lawrences are portrayed as rich, bourgeois, idle, aesthetic, advanced, cosmopolitan and yet limited by their Kensington milieu. For instance Acton Lawrence cannot think, once he has consumed two plates of strawberries, how to get through the empty hours to dinner. He reads all day. His tolerance is only a form of inertia or spiritual sloth. Harry sees all this when he visits Camilla, and is torn in a conflict between admiration for the solidity and security of this well-to-do family, and contempt for its spiritual vacuity.

However, Harry begins to court Camilla, the daughter who corresponds to Virginia. The delineation of Leonard's bride before her marriage, and in her family surroundings, is not only brilliant, it is in many ways accurate to the point of being cruel. Leonard did not spare Virginia's feelings when writing about her, any more than she spared his when writing about him.

Harry's motives in courting Camilla are not clearly presented or analysed, but there is a definite sense that the Lawrence milieu represents a way out of a situation (in Richstead) which was for Harry both lifeless and without any form of future. Another reason why the motives of courtship are not analysed is that this precisely is one of the major problems in the novel: how to feel, and how to analyse feelings. Harry is not at all sure that he is really 'in love with' Camilla and spends a great deal of time analysing his state verbally and conceptually.

The first major theme of *The Wise Virgins*, then, concerns class difference. The difference between the lower-middle-class, more or less crudely vulgar and materialistic inhabitants of 'Richstead', and the elegant inhabitants of Mayfair, Kensington, Bayswater, or even Bloomsbury in its new modern guise, is insisted upon throughout the book. Not a page but reinforces this point: that the sensitive young Jewish man from the urban stretches of 'Richstead' is embarrassed by, and ashamed of, the vulgarity and poverty of spirit from which he comes.[1] Harry spends much of his time lecturing Gwen, one of the four Garland girls, on how she must wake up to life, read Ibsen and Dostoevsky and so on, but he knows the whole attempt is hopeless. The vulgarity, the limitation is irredeemably ingrained. He himself, Harry the artist and freethinker, has somehow escaped it, but cannot rise above it without help from elsewhere. He therefore goes to art school, consorts with advanced artists, one of whom is recognisably Roger Fry (there is mention of 'significant form', at which Harry is meant to be adept) and engages Miss Camilla Lawrence as his model.

But this attempt to penetrate into the upper reaches of society is matched by a parallel development between the two 'Richstead' families. Mrs Garland, who has four unmarried daughters to dispose of, and Mrs Davis, who has an attractive son as well as a daughter to dispose of, see mutual advantage in getting to know each other better. But from the first, the racial problem is there:

'I only saw Mrs Davis and the daughter. They both seemed very nice – rather foreign, I think.'

'I expect they're Jews,' said May.

'Do you know', Mrs Garland said in her low, serious voice, 'I be-

---

[1] In *Beginning Again* (pp. 74–5) Leonard explicitly states that his relationship to bourgeois, gentile society was extremely ambiguous: 'I was an outsider to this class, because, although I and my father before me belonged to the professional middle class, we had only recently struggled up into it from the stratum of Jewish shopkeepers. We had no roots in it.' He adds: 'I am ambivalent to aristocratic societies, disliking and despising them and at the same time envying them their insolent urbanity.' This is 'Harry' to the letter.

lieve, May, you're right; I think they may be. They don't seem to go to church.'

There was a silence. A feeling of disappointment came over Gwen. 'But what are they *like*, mother?' she said.

(p. 20)

After the first tea party has been engineered, and the four Garland girls have been exposed to the charms of Harry, there is the following immediate reprise:

'They're Jews,' said May, when the front door was shut and they had wandered back into the drawing-room.

'And what if they are?' said Gwen rather sharply.

'I hate Jews.'

'*I* don't like Jews,' said Janet, as if she was rather astonished to find that she did not like them.

'What Jews do you know? We don't know any.'

'There was May Isaacs at school, horrid little beast; I suppose you'll say she wasn't a Jew? Besides, I know the Davises now.'

'I don't see anything to hate in the Davises, May,' said Mrs Garland gently.

'I don't see anything much to like in them, at any rate,' said May.

'Then why did you ask her to come on the river with us? I heard you,' said Gwen.

'One must say something.'   (p. 48)

It is not as if Leonard is letting this theme of the constant, buried antipathy of gentile towards Jew happen merely adventitiously in his novel. The feeling is central to the whole of Harry's experience. In a conversation with one of the intimates of the Lawrence circle, Harry suddenly expresses the sense of anxiety and mistrust which the gentile comfortableness of the Lawrence milieu always produces in him:

Harry turned on him. 'You're a Christian,' he said contemptuously, brutally.

'I hope not,' Trevor smiled.

'I'm a Jew.'

'Yes, I know. Well?'

'You can glide out of a room and I can't: I envy you that! But I despise you. I like that big baby sitting all day long in his arm-chair, but I despise him. I admire your women, your pale women with their white skins and fair hair, but I despise them.'

'Do most Jews feel like that?'

'All of them – all of them. There's no life in you, no blood in you, no understanding. Your women are cold and leave one cold – no dark hair,

no blood in them. Pale hair, pale souls, you know. You talk and you talk
and you talk – no blood in you! You never *do* anything.'
　'Why do you think it's so important to do things?'
　'Why? Because I'm a Jew, I tell you – I'm a Jew!'

(pp. 76–7)

It is an ambiguity of feeling. There is an immense envy for all that
security, all that ease, all that sense of belonging. And there is
also a contempt, very profound, for the whole superficial and
unreal unnaturalness of the Lawrences and their social set.

When talking to his social equal Gwen Garland, back in Richstead, Harry can afford to be a little more relaxed, and shows too
that he can assimilate his sense of Jewishness at a social level
where he does not already feel threatened:

She wanted to move about. She got up and they walked on slowly
between the trees.
　'I believe,' she began haltingly, 'I have felt that. I've been discon-
tented. It seems all so meaningless sometimes. But there's no one to talk
to. You must think me an awful fool.'
　'My good child, of course I don't. You're about two years old – that's all
the matter with you.'
　She laughed. 'And you?'
　'I'm about seventy-two. I've never been two. I wish the devil I had, but
Jews are born old, you know; they know good and evil from their birth,
they take it in with their mother's milk, their original mother having
eaten those apples – and they usually choose to follow the evil from the
start. But I'll make a very good father confessor, philosopher, instructor,
and guide to you. You must know things, if you want to live – unless you
care to remain two years old all your life.'
　'I don't think I do. But how *can* one know things in Richstead?'
　'You can read, that's always a beginning. Read Dostoievsky.'

(pp. 106–7)

Harry is so much in command intellectually, that he can afford
these gibes at his own expense about his Jewish inheritance.
Gwen does not of course realise how significant the matter is.

But when Harry is finally invited to spend the weekend with
the Lawrences at their country cottage, this whole matter comes
to a serious and deliberate climax. The Lawrence family and its
gentile friends are all lying in deckchairs near the house.

After a while they saw Harry walk across the garden in front of the
house, go through the gate in the fence, and lie down in the field.

'I didn't know they had taken up that fellow,' said Wilton.
'Which fellow?' said Arthur irritably.
'That Jew fellow. Who picked him up? Camilla, I suppose.'

(pp. 139–40)

The matter is thus explicitly put in terms of what gentiles say about Jews behind their backs. The tone is not only condescending, it is actually hostile and contemptuous. Harry, in going to lie down in the field, and not joining the gentiles at rest by the house, is deliberately setting up a kind of racial space distinction. And he is immediately conscious of the price:

He felt the eyes of those above him in the garden; two, four, six, eight little loopholes of critical hostility. There they were behind his back, watching him . . .

(pp. 141–2)

Harry lies there in the sun, aware of their condescension, their unspoken sense of their difference from him. He thinks with affection of his father, who took an interest in life and in politics, and fought each day as a separate challenge. And, in view of what Leonard says again and again in his autobiography, a half century later, it is significant that this sense of the unspoken, latent, but very real hostility of the gentile toward the Jew should issue out into a semi-conscious reverie of the perennial lot of the Jew: to be scorned, despised, attacked, humiliated. As if presciently aware of a certain photograph that was to impress him so terribly later in life, Leonard allows Harry to predict what will happen when gentile hatred of the Jew is unleashed:

Well, he would be in bed by twelve to-night. Thirteen hours before that! And he would dream there, dream deliberately before he settled to sleep, dream of what he wanted to have and what he wanted to be. Why shouldn't he do that now and slip away into another world from these hard and bitter things? He tried. He thought of himself standing up on some raised platform above a crowd, a hostile crowd threatening him. Stones were thrown, there was blood on his face, but he stood there shielding – someone, from the stones. His arm fell limply to his side, but he stood up straight still.
  He flung himself over on his back. It wouldn't do, in the full sunlight and with the gentle breeze on his face.

(pp. 142–3)

Suddenly Katharine (Vanessa) comes down to him, crossing racial space as it were, and deliberately linking up the spaces of gentile and Jew. She is sufficiently independent of the prejudices of her race and class to carry off this kind of gesture. Yet, and nevertheless, her very first remark to Harry, as he lies there in the grass, makes explicit both the levels of implication of the previous pages. The only difference is that she is young enough, and charming enough, to speak it without offence:

'Well, Harry, I see you're following Arthur's advice, and adopting the first principle of Christianity and Sunday.'

He looked up. Katharine stood beside him under a large white umbrella.

'What's that? It isn't Sunday either, you know.'

'To make yourself uncomfortable. For me the first day out of London is always Sunday.' She sat down by his side.

(p. 143)

Harry absorbs this barb, well meant as it is, as he absorbs all the implied gentile comments about difference of race, and the talk turns to Camilla, about whom Katharine has ostensibly come to talk to him.

At this point, another theme of extreme importance is built into the novel. It is clear that while Harry is physically attracted by the charms of Katharine (Vanessa) he is far from sure what his relationship is with Camilla.

'I don't think Camilla does.'

Camilla's name came with a curious shock to Harry. For the first time he realised how much he had thought about her in the last weeks. It seemed to him that he *had* been in love with her. Was he now in love with Katharine? Through the physical attraction which he was at the moment feeling for Katharine Camilla's name had come with the shock of a blow. By an act of will he stiffened his body and his mind.

'What does Camilla do?'

(p. 146)

Harry is subject to two very strong forms of attraction in the wise virgins. He is also torn between them, torn between the attraction for the fleshly, embodied sensual Katharine (Vanessa) and the ethereal, virtually unembodied Camilla (Virginia). Katharine, richly attractive as she is, sits and warns Harry about her sister's inability to distinguish fiction from reality:

Katharine noticed the change of voice and tone, consciously steadied by Harry.

'I sometimes think there is no dividing line in Milla, between her dreams, I mean, and her realities. She doesn't pretend. When we were children, you know, she never said: "Let's pretend." We had a game, I remember, called explorers: we turned the nursery table upside down, tied a cloth across the legs, and sailed in it across the nursery floor to New Spain and wonderful western islands which father read to us about of an evening out of Hakluyt. I used to say: "Let's pretend we're explorers," but Milla never did. I'm almost ashamed to think how old we were when we last played explorers, but the floor was still really the Atlantic to Camilla and the table a galleon. And she's just the same now, I'm sure; she never says to herself: "Let's pretend." She never thinks of the brilliant things she might have said, but of the brilliant things she did say.'

'And did she?' Harry laughed. 'You seem to hint that she didn't.'

'God knows. Sometimes of course she did, and sometimes she didn't. It's of no importance to her; that's her danger.'

Harry looked across the meadow to the garden and Camilla under the trees. She seemed immeasurably far from him, herself like a dream. For the moment the idea of being in love with her was absurd. So white and delicate and fair, she was not a woman, but a fine lady in a dream or a play infinitely remote from him. And Katharine was very near; here was flesh and blood, moving him now as it flushed the fair skin red and the full lips. He could imagine kissing and being kissed; he could imagine marriage and a calm life of marriage, and that face across the breakfast-table and a copper urn. But he couldn't imagine kissing Camilla: fine ladies and Dresden china don't kiss one or pour out one's morning tea behind a copper urn.

(pp. 147–8)

Since Katharine belongs to physical reality so strongly, Harry is very willing to take her view of her sister at face value. When Katharine speaks of the 'danger' involved in waking Camilla up, she has the whole force of the 'fair skin and full lips' behind her. So, in predicting that Camilla will be a 'dangerous' bride, she has already physically half-convinced her listener by her mere presence.

One sister can distinguish reality from fantasy, and is full of the joy of life and very fleshly. The other sister cannot distinguish reality from fantasy, is ethereal and tries not to inhabit her body at all. But the clever thing about Leonard's fictional account is that we see how this distinction, delivered by the fleshly sister from a close, even intimate distance, takes on all the more power and conviction from the fact that the other sister is far away, remote and untouchable. The geographical space between the Lawrence family with Camilla, and the Jewish guest down in the field with Katharine, is used to reinforce the sense that Katharine must be right about her sister. Under these circumstances her view seems intensely reasonable and likely. All the more so when the attractive sister launches out on a very plausible, but very damning, theory about Camilla:

Then he came back again to her last remark, which had lain latent in his thoughts: 'That's her danger.'
'Her danger?' he asked. 'How is it dangerous to her?'
'Perhaps it's not so dangerous to her as it is to other people.'
She smiled both at the boldness of her remark and at her own thoughts. She did not feel or see what he was feeling for her. The intervals between his and her remarks she put down to his caution and reserve. Here was a young man in love who would never give himself away – never, until he had arrived at the determination to do so. She liked confidences, especially from men. She would have liked some sign, even though he was in love with her sister, of his being moved by her presence. She felt their intimacy, so close together on the grass under the eyes of those in the garden; but so little from his side seemed to be coming from their closeness. At any rate he had her sympathy. She thought she saw suffering in his eyes, and she determined that he should recognise her sympathy.
'You meant dangerous to her, you know,' he began again. 'In what way?'
She smiled to think that he was avoiding what was dangerous to him. 'Well,' she said, 'I do think it's dangerous not to face facts. Not that Milla doesn't face them, exactly. She isn't a coward or sentimental, but she simply doesn't know the difference between facts and – and, well, I suppose, her own dreams. I sometimes think she's never completely awake – and somnambulism is notoriously dangerous. Suppose somebody woke her up one day much too suddenly.'
He understood now what people meant when they talked of Katharine Lawrence's depth. She was enfolding him in her large and tolerant sagacity, soothing him with her unastonished wisdom. And Camilla herself became to him still more unreal, still more of a dream.
'Perhaps it's impossible to wake her up,' he said.
'Perhaps. But the person who does or tries to – the danger to him!'
'And hasn't anyone?'
'Oh, well, people have fallen in love with Camilla; but you can't take that very seriously – because she doesn't, you know. You've heard of poor Arthur; he's fallen in love with her several times. There has never

been any danger there, because even in her wildest moments she has never dreamed of being in love with him.'

He looked at her in silence, right into her eyes, quite steadily in a way in which one does not look directly at a person once in ten years. She met his eyes steadily too and smiling.

'You are kind', he said. 'And amazingly beautiful.'

Her eyes dropped at once, and she even blushed a little. It came as a surprise to her for the moment – and she was not easily surprised. It was a little ridiculous, and a little unpleasant to her, and yet she was pleased too, excited, flattered. Just at first she thought that possibly she might have been mistaken, that he was not in the least in love with Camilla; and then she came down again to a calm, sensible view of it. One had to expect these things from men, to women unintelligible and unexpected. And the unexpectedness was just the charm to her as a woman.

(pp. 148–50)

It may be for merely dramatic purposes that Leonard has his hero Harry waver between the physical attractiveness of the one sister, and the ethereal sexless quality of the other, but the point is made, nevertheless, that whoever attempts to 'wake' Camilla from her sexless sleep will be in great 'danger'. Retrospectively, this view must have held for Leonard a great deal of explanatory power, and I think that he came more and more to accept Vanessa's view that Virginia was from birth unable to distinguish dream from reality. The idea expressed here by Katharine–Vanessa to the effect that, when as children they had played explorers with the nursery table turned upside down, 'the floor was still really the Atlantic to Camilla and the table a galleon' – this idea was to take on in Leonard's mind, with time, the force of a certainty.

Even as a child, it would appear, Virginia had always been taken in by her own fantasies, and she believed what she was doing in fantasy to be taking place in real life. Placed in Leonard's mind by Vanessa, this theory, fully accepted, would motivate many of his actions on his return from his honeymoon.

After this conversation, and sealing it off at the latter end as it were, as its corresponding passage had introduced it, the impossible barrier of race is violently re-introduced:

As she did not speak he thought she was offended. He burst out almost angrily:

'I suppose I ought not to have said that. Good God! I was just thinking before you came out here how beastly people are to one another. I tell you I hated you all, because – because I thought you hated me. Well, not hated perhaps – despised, disregarded: don't you know what that feeling is? No I suppose you don't; women don't – not if they are beautiful. One can't talk to people, can't say what one wants – feels. It's just as if they were mere blocks of stone set up around one, like so many tombstones. And then it all seemed simply silly what I had been thinking, when you came and talked as you did. I thought I knew what you meant: I thought you understood, were kind. And now I've spoilt it all, I suppose.'

(pp. 150–1)

When he is not with her, Harry cannot imagine that Camilla is an actual woman of flesh and blood. Partly due to his attraction for the other sister, and partly due to the innate difficulty of expressing any feeling in a strong or committed way, Harry spends his time split between transcendence and desire, spirit and body. But when she is with him, some inkling of her fleshly presence gets through to him regardless.

'Let's go up on to the hills,' he said.

He had felt a sudden desire to talk to her alone, but now that he was walking by her side he did not know how to begin, or indeed exactly what he wanted to say. Before his conversation with Katharine, the idea that he might be or become in love with Camilla had been continually with him and had given him pleasure. Somehow or other that conversation had suddenly brought him to a full stop and shown him where he was going. As he had looked at Katharine, and realised the beauty of her face and body, the stability of her character, he had almost cried out within himself absurdly: 'If I am to be in love, why the devil am I not in love with her?' The reality of his whole feelings began to seem doubtful to him, and the reality of Camilla. What could she possibly have to do with him? There persisted in his mind that image of her as a fine lady, infinitely remote, something not to be touched, in silk and satin and lace and fine linen, and with lady's-maids around her.

Now that she was actually walking by his side the pleasure in her mere presence returned to him.

(p. 154)

In the light of all that happened, that note of longing for 'the stability of her character', with reference to Katharine–Vanessa, is very ominous.

The hidden question, the problem of the racial difference, does not take long to re-appear. As they walk across the hills, Harry goes into the question of what it means to be Jewish at considerable length, while pacing along beside the object of his devotion (though he is not sure she *is* the object of his love). This passage is so full of information about the way that Leonard must have regarded his marriage with Virginia, and certain racial disparities and irregularities in it, that it must be quoted at length:

'Worth? Worth while? Yes, perhaps that's it – that's what makes you different from them.'

'That's because I'm a Jew. Oh yes, you see what I mean, of course. We wait hunched up, always ready and alert, for the moment to spring on what is worth while, then we let ourselves go. You don't like it? I see you don't; it makes you shrink from me – us, I mean. It isn't pleasant; it's hard, unbeautiful. There isn't sensibility, they call it, in us. We want to *get*, to feel our hands upon, what's worth while. Is it worth while? Is it worth *getting*? That's the first and only question to buzz in our brains.'

Camilla was silent. She believed what Harry was saying. It made her sad. She distinctly did not want him to be like that. And then she ought to be making up her mind. She did not want to have to think of such things, to have to make up her mind about anything. She wanted to enjoy the gayness of sun and wind and the song of larks. She sat down, resting her elbows on her knees and her face on her hands. . .

'We're born that way; I suppose we were born that way twenty thousand years ago in Asia. Personally I'm proud of it. I like it. (The only thing that a Jew is sentimental about is Judaism, you know.) I don't like softness. I'm different from Arthur and Wilton, and – good Lord! – I'm different from you, and always will be. One can't be born again; once and for all one has one's father and mother in one, in every cell of one's body, so they say. I am a good Jew; I obey the fifth commandment, and honour my father and my mother – at any rate in myself. We aren't as pleasant or as beautiful as you are. We're hard and grasping, we're out after definite things, different things, which we think worth while. We don't drift, we watch and wait, wait and watch. Down here I've enjoyed myself, enjoyed myself immensely, but even here not like you others. I feel it. It's pure and fresh here, somehow, this air and sky, the trees and grass and the long, lazy days. The country – it's like the highest art, it purges the passions. One is more like what one was as a boy. But there it ends with me. I just feel it aesthetically. I can never give way to it, and settle back in my chair to chatter with a pure heart and childlike mind, like Arthur. I'm still looking out to get hold of things which – which are worth while.'

'And what is worth while?' said Camilla very slowly and wearily.

Harry hesitated. He had been speaking almost angrily, with a desire to hurt her, to expose himself and to justify himself. What was worth while? There was one thing which at the back of his mind he had all through half believed that he meant as worth while. But he only half believed it, and he shrank from, did not dare the putting of it into words.

'Money,' he said, 'money, of course. That's the first article of our creed – money, and out of money, power. That's elementary. Then knowledge, intelligence, taste. . .'

Harry stopped and looked at Camilla, waiting for her to say something. All the time that he had been speaking, Katharine's words were in her mind: 'You'll have to make up your mind.' Still she did not want to have to make up her mind; everything was too difficult. She felt that she had met here something that was strange to her. It was as if she were being jarred and jolted out of a pleasant, peaceful country of smooth roads and country lanes and dreamy fields into a desert of jagged rocks and stones. She wanted to say something to bring herself back into the old pleasant dreamy lanes and fields, but she could not. She watched the great stretch of land and the winding river and the smoke hanging over the sleepy village at her feet.

She was surprised to hear Harry laugh. 'Well, I've enjoyed myself immensely,' he said, 'but I'm going away.'

'Why? What do you mean? Surely you are coming up with us this afternoon?'

'No, I think I'll go by the next train. I'm going to run away for good.'

'From us?'

'Yes, from you.'

'Why?'

'Why? Damnation! one never knows quite why one runs away – because one's afraid, I suppose. If you make me put it in words you'll make me give the wrong impression, or say more than I mean. I'm in a reasonable panic, that's all.'

'I don't understand what you mean. What has happened? It's something to have made a new friend. We thought we had in you; we were congratulating ourselves on it.'

Harry thought for some time before he answered. Camilla felt strangely impersonal, and yet interested, even excited, as to what was coming next.

'I expect that's it,' he said in a voice in which there was now no trace of heat or anger. 'You want me to change my groove. You would hate to change yours; you want to go on as you've always gone on. I mean all of you. Well, so do I. It doesn't do, it is not worth it – not when you see what's going to happen, and that you'll never get what you want, if you want it. You don't like me.'

It came as a shock to Camilla. She was not sure exactly what he meant. She felt so impersonal herself that she could not believe that he meant it very personally. Katharine would say that now was the very moment for her to make up her mind. But it seemed all too far off for her to consider it in that light; also, she had that queer desire which comes to people in crises to remain passive, to watch what will happen, to take no part oneself in the altering of things.

'You know that isn't true,' she said. 'This is simply silly, Harry. We all like you.'

'Not as I am. You may like me as you are, and of course I could become so – but I won't, I never will, you know.'

'That's absurd. We like you as you are.'

Her voice was affectionate, almost pleading now. Harry sat down by her side. His anger left him suddenly; he looked back nervously over what he had said to see whether he had not been making a fool of himself, and he was inclined to think that he had. Camilla suddenly touched him gently on the arm and laughed.

(pp. 156–61)

The strands here are expertly woven. What is surprising is that Leonard can afford, in print, to be so explicit and so painfully precise. He tries to define his Jewishness in terms of a reality antithetical to the gentile reality, but finding the case to be so difficult to define, falls back into angry and frustrated cliché. Harry's outburst can be read as a defiance of gentile superiority, or an envy of it, it can be read as a feeling of threat from it, or a desire to repudiate it, or perhaps all of these. But since Camilla is central to Harry's inner debate, everything hangs on whether or not these rebellious feelings of his strike any kind of answering chord in her. And as the text clearly shows, she again and again tries to avoid the implications of what he is saying, again and again tries to take refuge in the familiar and the beautiful, the unproblematic. Harry's fear of a judgment, pronounced by the gentiles against him, is so deep-seated, that his final assertions that he 'will' not become like the Lawrences ('but I won't, I never will, you know') read more like a statement of intention than a statement of fact. But the very passion with which he utters them shows that he feels the difference to be insuperable. So what is to become of his love for Camilla, and will she be able to reciprocate it?

The novel turns aside to follow the progress of the friendship of Harry and Gwen Garland of Richstead. Walking with her, Harry, feeling no sense of social threat, is again able to make remarks at his own expense and suddenly even refers to himself as that powerfully Romantic figure, the Wandering Jew. This prompts Gwen to suggest that they should run away together:

'Hurrah! We're off now – we will never come back to lunch. But we'll go together, Harry. You're showing me the way – you're not that – that – oh, I don't like your calling yourself that.'

'Jew? Why not? I am one, and proud of it too. And the everlasting one. And the point of him is, you know, that there never is any kingdom for him to find.'

'Do you – do you mind being a Jew, Harry?'

'No, I like it – I'm proud of it. *You* don't like them, of course.'

'I? Oh no, Harry, don't think that – it isn't true. I don't know any except you.'

'But you'd rather I wasn't one,' Harry laughed.

Gwen blushed. 'No – no, that isn't true; not now – now that I know you. I remember – '

She stopped, remembering that afternoon in the garden at Richstead and the swifts screaming round the house and the little cold douche of disappointment at hearing that the Davises were Jews. A faint shadow from the past seemed to fall upon her. It was as if for one sudden moment she realised that she was at a dangerous point in life; she was vaguely conscious of being the same Gwen as that one who sat in the garden with May and Ethel, but broken loose, drifting to what? How far?

'You remember?' Harry broke in on her thoughts. 'What? Out with it, Gwen.'

'I didn't like it when I heard you were Jews.'

(pp. 267–9)

How on earth is Harry Davis, the promising young Jewish intellectual, to deal with this stupid, infantile feeling, which is so deeply embedded in Richstead that Gwen is not even conscious of offering a bitter observation? He *has* to escape to the society of Camilla and the painters of Bloomsbury. There is nowhere else for him to go. And yet, do not they, too, the gentiles of Bloomsbury, also feel this unspoken prejudice, this feeling that they are 'different' from him? There seems to be no way out at all. And it is in realising that this *is* the conclusion that the novel drives towards, that we can see perhaps some of the hidden motivations for Leonard's refusal to treat his wife's breakdown in 1913 as something entirely explicable, even as something which he had every reason to expect.

There is another reason why Leonard might well have
expected the collapse of 1913 when it came. This has to do with
the third of the three problems treated in this novel, as in the
earlier one: the appalling difficulties of being able to feel something, emotionally and sexually, for another person.

The final interview between Harry as suitor and Camilla is
disastrous. It clearly transpires that Camilla has *no feelings* for
Harry. It is a more terrible form of refusal than any kind of
protestation could be:

He opened the studio door: Camilla was standing by the fireplace.

'Hullo, Harry,' she said. He shut the door and walked over to her
without saying anything. He saw her face flush red and her lips tremble.
She sat down in a chair and looked up at him. His mouth was dry and he
had to gulp before he said:

'I suppose you know I'm in love with you. I have been for weeks.'

She did not say anything. He noticed a curious movement in her
throat.

'I can't stand this any longer,' he said. 'The suspense – doubt – I can't
stand it any longer. You must end it, one way or the other.'

He stood over her, looking down at her. To her there seemed to be in
him something threatening almost, and alien. His whole body trembled
slightly. As he stood there in that attitude of desire and waiting and
excitement, beaten down under his short, sharp words, she realised to
the full that he left her completely cold.

'But I'm not in love with you, Harry. I'm not in love with you,' she said
suddenly.

(pp. 212–13)

This passage has resonances of so many other passages – in
diaries, letters, and in Virginia's own novels, that it must correspond to a situation both Leonard and Virginia saw themselves
living through many times. There are sections of his autobiography where Leonard admits that Virginia's first relation to him
was of this kind. In the perception (of Camilla) that 'there was
something threatening almost, and alien', there is the echo of
many of Virginia's letters of the engagement period, and in his
notation 'His whole body trembled slightly' we seem to be watching that very man whom Thoby Stephen described to his sister
only a few years earlier:

another astonishing fellow – a man who trembled perpetually all over.
He was as eccentric, as remarkable in his way as Bell and Strachey in

theirs. He was a Jew . . . I was of course inspired with the deepest
interest in that violent trembling misanthropic Jew who had already
shaken his fist at civilisation and was about to disappear into the tropics
so that we should none of us ever see him again.

(*Old Bloomsbury*, in Schulkind p. 166)

This must have been, again and again, the predicament of
these two people. In this scene, we can see the fervour, the
indecision and the anxiety of the man; the coolness, withdrawal,
dispassionate refusal, of the loved woman. The situation is of
course underlined, as the novel has patiently shown, by the dual
difference in class and in race. These three things now come
together, in one moment of crisis, to make the setting up of a
mutual feeling, of a mutual physical attraction, an impossibility.
As so many times in life, doubtless, so here in the novel, the
attempt to build up a relationship which should be in any way
mutual and reciprocal, ends for both in pain, failure and chagrin.

And the status of physical desire, of emotion even, as such, is
constantly at issue in this novel. The agony of unsatisfied physical desire is described in a little vignette where another suitor for
Camilla's hand, Arthur, confides his inmost thoughts to Harry
one evening:

'Oh, I don't know, I don't know. That's what makes it so unbearable –
the suspense. I sometimes think I'll go off, break with it all completely. I
have too; I've gone off into the country for weeks, to ride hard, walk
hard, forget, but it's no use. I come cringing back, whistled to heel again
like some damned little puppy-dog. I wonder if any woman understands
what it is to a man. They don't realise that we've got bodies. That's what
makes it so intolerable: unless they are loose and vile they have no
passions. What's noble in us is vile in them.'

(pp. 136–7)

The gaps are very wide. The tortured personage called Arthur
seems to speak very largely on behalf of Harry when he asserts
that women do not know what desire is, being more desirous of
being desired than of giving any kind of physical satisfaction to
their suitors. The sense of alienation from the body is tremendous. Camilla, having seen the beaten and despairing Harry go
out of the room after his proposal to her, meditates as follows:

Camilla did not move when Harry shut the door softly behind him. A momentary storm had passed through and stirred the room and her life. It is so rare to see anyone moved by violent feelings, that at the sight our own begin to surge up and toss and tumble in a sympathy which for want of a better name we vaguely call excitement. And she had been the centre and cause of this storm. The room had grown very quiet, full of the heavy hush of Sunday. She closed her eyes. She was not depressed, only physically rather tired. After all, had she anything to regret, anything to reproach herself with? This was life, surely, the romance and fire of it, these strange meetings and partings of human beings, one caught and entangled immediately with another only to be torn apart and washed away in the turmoil of incompatible, unsatisfied desires.

Desires! How strange they were! Harry – she pitied Harry – had a desire for her, but she had no desire for him. There it was in a sentence. It was pleasant to be with him, to talk to him, to know that he was in love with her – that was exciting too; it had pained her to see his pain; but all this was not love; there was no desire. Perhaps she was incapable of love, perhaps she did not wish this odd convulsion, passion, to overthrow her life.

(pp. 221–2)

'There was no desire.' In her letter to Harry which she writes later in the novel, Camilla writes:

It's the romantic part of life that I want; it's the voyage out[1] that seems to me to matter, the new and wonderful things. I can't, I won't look beyond that. I want them all. I want love, too, and I want freedom. I want children even. But I can't give myself; passion leaves me cold. You'll think I am asking for everything to be given and to give nothing. Perhaps that's true.

And then there's so much in marriage from which I recoil. It seems to shut women up and out. I won't be tied by the pettinesses and the conventionalities of life. There must be some way out. One must live one's own life, as the novels say.

(p. 315)

It is but a short way from this letter, to the letter Virginia sent to Leonard on 1 May 1912:

Then, of course, I feel angry sometimes at the strength of your desire. Possibly, your being a Jew comes in also at this point. You seem so foreign . . . I'm half afraid of myself. I sometimes feel that no one ever has or ever can share something – It's the thing that makes you call me like a hill, or a rock. Again, I want everything – love, children, adventure, intimacy, work . . .

[1] The reference to the novel Virginia was 'ceaselessly re-writing' during 1912–13 cannot be accidental. *The Voyage Out* is Virginia's account of the problem Leonard treats in *The Wise Virgins*.

One wonders whether it was quite by chance that Leonard, the Latin scholar, hit upon Camilla, 'attendant at a sacrifice', as a name for his fictional Virginia. 'But I can't give myself; passion leaves me cold', writes Camilla. 'As I told you brutally the other day, I feel no physical attraction in you. There are moments – when you kissed me the other day was one – when I feel no more than a rock', writes Virginia to Leonard on 1 May 1912. It is noticeable that Virginia succumbed to two so-called 'mental illnesses' in January and February 1912. Leonard had proposed marriage to her on 11 January, and repeated his offer twice by letter. Was this totally unconnected with the stress which Virginia obviously found too much on that occasion? The approach of male desire terrifies Camilla: it obviously did Virginia too. This is a problem which, in a marriage, cannot but augur badly.

It would not be at all surprising, then, if, returning from a honeymoon with Leonard in 1912, a honeymoon during which Virginia had found true what she had always suspected of herself ('But I can't give myself; passion leaves me cold'), she succumbed to an access of total depression.

When Virginia writes in her letter 'There are moments – when you kissed me the other day was one – when I feel no more than a rock', one thinks back to the inner reflection of young Harry as he watches Katharine–Vanessa very close to him:

And Katharine was very near; here was flesh and blood, moving him now as it flushed the fair skin red and the full lips. He could imagine kissing and being kissed; he could imagine marriage and a calm life of marriage, and that face across the breakfast-table and a copper urn. But he couldn't imagine kissing Camilla: fine ladies and Dresden china don't kiss one or pour out one's morning tea behind a copper urn.

(p. 148)

It is of importance, obviously, that kissing was associated in Virginia's mind with the nocturnal embraces of George Duckworth 'cuddling and kissing and otherwise embracing me in order, as he told Dr Savage later, to comfort me for the fatal illness of my father – who was dying three or four storeys lower down of cancer' (*Old Bloomsbury*, in Schulkind p. 160). Consequently, when Virginia writes in her letter to Leonard that, when kissed, she feels 'no more than a rock', we are obviously presented, not with an inability to respond to male desire, but a refusal to do so. To become like a rock is to some extent the result of a deliberate pulling-back from the implications of a kiss; it has to do with refusal of sexuality, not ignorance of it, but mistrust of it, bad memories of it.

In this context, the two brief exchanges between Harry and Katharine in the field, much earlier in the novel, take on a certain malign significance:

Then he came back again to her last remark, which had lain latent in his thoughts: 'That's her danger.'
  'Her danger?' he asked. 'How is it dangerous to her?'
  'Perhaps it's not so dangerous to her as it is to other people.'
(p. 148)

'Perhaps it's impossible to wake her up,' he said.
  'Perhaps. But the person who does or tries to – the danger to him!'
  'And hasn't anyone?'
  'Oh, well, people have fallen in love with Camilla; but you can't take that very seriously – because she doesn't, you know.'
(p. 149)

The concept of Virginia not *wanting* to 'wake' is here explicitly linked with the idea that Virginia's passion, once awoken (or discovered), would be more or less fatal to the man who marries her. If indeed Leonard took seriously Vanessa's view of Virginia ('Katharine's Opinion of her Sister'), as I think all the evidence showed that he did, then he would deliberately have blinded himself to the meaning of the collapse after the honeymoon of 1912. After all, Vanessa had been right. It might well have appeared that way; and this might explain what otherwise appears a complete mystery – why a young man, recently returned from his honeymoon, should go and consult her sister about his wife's mental health (*Beginning Again* pp. 151–2). It happened that Roger Fry was there too, and, since Vanessa had always believed that this would happen when Virginia married, and since Leonard valued her opinion so highly, the talk of 'madness' and 'insanity ' and 'illness' begins to have an origin in Vanessa's view that 'the Goat' had 'always been mad' and that now marriage had pushed her over the edge.

The family myth that Virginia, 'the Goat', was unpredictable, awkward, gauche and a figure of ridicule seems to have its origin as far back as the Stephen nursery. Professor Bell writes:

There was some technique for making her turn 'purple with rage'. What it was we do not know; but Thoby and Vanessa knew and there were terrible occasions when she did turn a colour which her sister described as 'the most lovely flaming red'. It would be interesting to know how this was done, still more interesting to know whether, as Vanessa surmised, these paroxysms were not wholly painful to Virginia herself.

(I, 24)

The secret of how to turn a childhood companion to 'the most lovely flaming red' is not hard to penetrate for anyone who reflects a moment on his own early days. The secret is to aggravate and exacerbate a known weakness till the child under attack loses control of himself. Obviously Vanessa and Thoby were experts at doing this to Virginia, rendering her mad with anguished fury. It is an easy trick for any sibling to master.

This tendency to flaming rage is, anyway, connected with the appellation 'the Goat' as Quentin Bell then explains. Recounting a situation which must have been intensely embarrassing for Virginia as a child, he concludes:

It was this and similar misadventures which earned her, in the nursery, the title of 'The Goat' or more simply 'Goat', a name which stuck to her for many years.

(I, 24)

The situation in question belongs to the realm of acute bodily embarrassment. It would seem then as if the taunt about 'the Goat' usually followed an incident in which, embarrassed and maddened, Virginia turned 'the most lovely flaming red'. Another clear origin for Virginia's later terror of her own body and shame about its functions.

It is certainly arguable, from a close reading of the chapter called 'Katharine's Opinion of her Sister', as well as from the passages where Camilla and Katharine are shown talking to each other, that Leonard's view of Virginia came to be essentially Vanessa's. If that is the case, some of his behaviour of 1913 would begin to make sense. If we do not argue that way, and if we do not make some such assumption, the actions of Leonard in the early and middle months of 1913 are, to me at least, incomprehensible.

But given the powerful mass of evidence in *The Wise Virgins*, I think the conclusion is more or less forced upon us that the sexual side of the marriage collapsed so early because Leonard half-expected that Vanessa's predictions would come true, and half-recognised that his marriage across class and race had inevitably failed to produce physical passion in his bride.

What Leonard did not do was to show his novel to the specialists. Had he done so, much might have appeared quite explicable in the behaviour of his bride. But Leonard wrote his book in private, and Virginia suffered in hospitals in private, and (presumably) they never discussed what they might have had in common in their distress. But Leonard had, under his hand, a perfect explanation of how what had come to pass would have come to pass, and the inevitability of its having come to pass. The reasons why he wrote the novel, and the reasons why it is only once mentioned in the most glancing way in the autobiography, may have to do with the fact that Leonard realised that he had tried to make a situation, which he had already shown to be theoretically impossible, work: as if an architect were to write a book explaining that there could never be a single-arch bridge built over the Channel, and then tried to build one, and been amazed when it collapsed.

It is indeed striking how little Leonard says about *The Wise Virgins* in his autobiographical account of the years 1911–18. So far as I can see he mentions the novel only once in *Beginning Again*, and that is to dismiss it in two sentences, one of which refers to: 'My second novel *The Wise Virgins* was published in 1914 simultaneously with the outbreak of war. The war killed it dead and my total earnings from it were £20' (p. 91). The novel is not mentioned in the index.

This reticence might give one reason to pause. Why, having worked out his own dilemma so clearly, even harshly and acidly, on paper, should Leonard not, in considering the years of the war and of Virginia's so-called 'madnesses', reflect at all on that novel and its place in their early married life? The novel is clearly Leonard's account of some of the difficulties inherent in his marriage with Virginia, seen from his point of view. He gives no evidence in his autobiography about how he came to conceive the novel, plan it, write it and publish it, nor does he reflect on its place in the literary reciprocity set up between himself and Virginia after 1912.

Obviously, some of the reasons why Leonard wrote the novel were so urgent and pressing in 1913–14 that he could not reflect on them, even in his riper years, without acute discomfort. He therefore decided not to consider the matter fully in his autobiography.

Yet the problem is still unresolved. Leonard does not tell us when he wrote the novel, but we are permitted to assume that he wrote it some time shortly before, or some time shortly after, the marriage in 1912. If he wrote the novel before the marriage, it might have served him as some form of preliminary analysis of what was likely to go wrong in the marriage. If he wrote it after the marriage, it may have served him as some kind of analytic engagement with what was going wrong in the marriage. For the three major structures of difficulty which he sets out so ably in the novel were common to both himself and to Virginia.

Nevertheless, he chose not to connect his analysis in fiction, and his analysis in life, on one level of reflection. This may go a long way towards explaining why Virginia felt herself so isolated in London in 1913, and why, after the disastrous interview with Wright and Head of 9 September, she took veronal (see chapter 9). For who, if not Leonard, could have understood how difficult the marriage was proving for her? And he had taken sides against her (so it would have seemed to her), by siding with Head in his analysis that she was 'very ill'.

In real life (and we have Leonard's own repeated word for this) it seemed to Virginia as if Leonard were part of a conspiracy against her, a conspiracy of doctors and nurses. And if, in real life in 1913, Leonard asserted during psychiatric interviews that he found his wife's behaviour 'insane' and 'ill', then might not this be a ground for terrific outbursts of abuse which, Leonard tells us, his wife hurled at him in 1915? 'In the second stage of violent excitement, she was violently hostile to me, would not talk to me or allow me to come into her room' (*Beginning Again* p. 161). Bell writes of the 1915 attack: 'Virginia was violent and screaming, and her madness culminated in virulent animosity towards

Leonard himself' (II, 26). On the same page, Bell quotes Vanessa who writes: 'She won't see Leonard at all & has taken against all men. She says the most malicious & cutting things she can think of to everyone and they are so clever that they always hurt.' Neither Leonard nor Bell is explicit about what it was that Virginia shouted in her so-called madness; but we have it from Vanessa that, whatever it was she said, her accuracy was formidable. Perhaps her remarks were so hurtful because they contained a very large amount of truth?

Virginia read *The Wise Virgins*, in a single day, on 31 January 1915, and writes out her view of the book in her diary for that day. This reading follows the attacks of 1913–14 by a long way, so it was in two senses retrospective. First, it was about a period which had preceded their marriage. Second, it was about a period within their marriage which was now over. Virginia does not openly resent the novel, she shows a clever tolerance of it, rather preferring it to Leonard's Blue-book interests:

. . . I started reading The Wise Virgins, & I read it straight on till bedtime when I finished it. My opinion is that its a remarkable book; very bad in parts; first rate in others. A writer's book, I think, because only a writer perhaps can see why the good parts are so very good, & why the very bad parts aren't very bad. It seems to me to have the stuff of 20 Duke Jones' in it, although there are howlers which wd. make Miss Sidgwick turn grey. I was made very happy by reading this: I like the poetic side of L. & it gets a little smothered in Blue-books, and organisations.

(*Diary* I, 32)

But the amount of repression here is massive, and might account for much of the violence of the outbursts of 1915. Who would be able to guess, from this level account of *The Wise Virgins*, that Leonard's novel exposes her to the world in a most unflattering way, exposes her inmost weaknesses with almost scientific precision? Who would have guessed from this that Virginia had been reading an account, either of why her marriage to Leonard was bound to fail, or why her marriage to Leonard had already failed?

The outbursts of 'violent hostility' towards Leonard in 1915 could have been partly due to the sense of betrayal which Virginia might have felt, and repressed, in January of that year when she read *The Wise Virgins*. Partly due, of course. But we should notice a subtle inflection in Vanessa's account of 1915, a generalisation of what may have been up to then a private and personal issue: 'She won't see Leonard at all & has taken against all men.'

~~~~~~

CHAPTER 7

The ordeal of 1912

I shrink from the years 1897–1904 – the seven unhappy years. So many lives were free from our burden. Why should our lives have been so tortured and fretted? by two unnecessary blunders – the lash of a random unheeding flail that pointlessly and brutally killed the two people who should, normally and naturally, have made those years, not perhaps happy but normal and natural. Mother's death: Stella's death. I am not thinking of them. I am thinking of the stupid damage that their deaths inflicted.

(*A Sketch of the Past*, in Schulkind p. 117)

The assumption that the double collapse that Virginia suffered in 1913 was a return of 'the' old 'madness', the recurrence of a definite 'insanity' that had struck Virginia down at least twice before, needs some investigation. There is much evidence in the newly published autobiographical materials edited by Jeanne Schulkind to show that Virginia's breakdowns in 1895 and in 1904 had a localised cause and an entirely explicable origin. If that is so, then it is at least possible that the so-called 'madness' of 1913 also sprang from a localised cause and an entirely explicable origin.

What was Virginia's mental and emotional state in 1912? A brief backward glance at the 'seven unhappy years' and the years which followed these, will allow an insight into an extremely tense and anxious state of mind, which only needed one further crisis in order to become intolerable.

First, as Virginia insists again and again in *A Sketch of the Past*, the death of Julia Stephen meant not only the end of certainty, reassurance and a sense of order, but also the end of an epoch and a way of life. The death of her mother was absolutely shattering to

Virginia. Her pain comes through this late text again and again as a sense of bitterness against a fate that had struck so hard and so pointlessly. The two deaths of 1895 and 1897 were perceived as actual attacks on Virginia's own sense of security:

But at fifteen to have that protection removed, to be tumbled out of the family shelter, to see cracks and gashes in that fabric, to be cut by them, to see beyond them – was that good?

(Schulkind p. 118)

It is quite easy to see, now that we have the materials in the Schulkind collection, that the mental collapse of 1895 was directly due to the death of Julia Stephen and the sense of unreality it engendered:

What a jumble of things I can remember, if I let my mind run, about my mother; but they are all of her in company; of her surrounded; of her generalised; dispersed, omnipresent, of her as the creator of that crowded merry world which spun so gaily in the centre of my childhood . . . there it always was, the common life of the family, very merry, very stirring, crowded with people; and she was the centre; it was herself. This was proved on May 5th 1895. For after that day there was nothing left of it. I leant out of the nursery window the morning she died. It was about six, I suppose. I saw Dr Seton walk away up the street with his head bent and his hands clasped behind his back. I saw the pigeons floating and settling. I got a feeling of calm, sadness, and finality. It was a beautiful blue spring morning, and very still. That brings back the feeling that everything had come to an end.

(*A Sketch of the Past*, in Schulkind p. 84)

Julia Stephen's centrality in the family, a centrality we knew of from our reading of *To the Lighthouse*, but which is now given explicit confirmation in the autobiographical writings, turned out to act as a malign influence when it was suddenly knocked away. Virginia perceives the death of her mother, not only as a personal loss, but as a deprivation of meaning. The world was suddenly perceived quite differently: instead of gyrating round one loved person, it suddenly could not gyrate at all. It banged and bumped around in every direction, wildly, pointlessly, unreally. None of the old coherences was there to rely on. This kind of experience, surely, to a girl of thirteen, must have been sufficient cause for a temporary loss of mental control? The psychological reality is recalled quite clearly and explicitly in *A Sketch of the Past*. Julia's death led to a sense of unreality, of falsity, in the rest of the family. They could not deal with their own emotions. Everyone broke down in one way or another. Sir Leslie Stephen himself broke down:

Father used to sit sunk in gloom. If he could be got to talk – and that was part of our duty – it was about the past. It was about 'the old days'. And when he talked, he ended with a groan. He was getting deaf, and his groans were louder than he knew. Indoors he would walk up and down the room, gesticulating, crying that he had never told mother how he loved her.

(p. 94)

Again and again the explicit connection between Julia's death and a new sense of unreality, is struck. All the children felt it, each in his or her own way. 'I see us now, all dressed in unbroken black, George and Gerald in black trousers, Stella with real crape deep on her dress, Nessa and myself with slightly modified crape, my father black from head to foot' (pp. 93–4). These strange clothes made it all unreal:

With mother's death the merry, various family life which she had held in being shut for ever. In its place a dark cloud settled over us; we seemed to sit all together cooped up, sad, solemn, unreal, under a haze of heavy emotion. It seemed impossible to break through. It was not merely dull; it was unreal. A finger seemed laid on one's lips.

(p. 93)

The tragedy of her death was not that it made one, now and then and very intensely, unhappy. It was that it made her unreal; and us solemn, and self-conscious. We were made to act parts that we did not feel; to fumble for words that we did not know. It obscured, it dulled. It made one hypocritical and immeshed in the conventions of sorrow.

(p. 95)

There was this aspect:

There were no more parties; no more young men and women laughing. No more flashing visions of white summer dresses and hansoms dashing off to private views and dinner parties, none of that natural life and gaiety which my mother had created. The grown-up world into which I would dash for a moment and pick off some joke or little scene and dash back again upstairs to the nursery was ended.

(p. 94)

But there was a further aspect. It was immediately after her mother's death that Talland House in St Ives was sold. The truncating of the whole world of summer and holiday at the same moment as the truncating of the whole social world of London, must have meant a doubled sense of unreality for Virginia – and indeed for the other children too. The magical world of summer reality, the world of beach, town, quay and lighthouse which Virginia recalls with such nostalgia in *A Sketch of the Past*, had gone:

Next summer an hotel had risen in the middle of our view. My mother complained, the view was spoilt. A great square building, the colour of oatcake, stood there. And so, one October, a house agent's board appeared on our lawn. For some reason it required painting. I was allowed to fill in some of the letters from a pot of paint. No tenants came. The danger was averted. And then mother died. And perhaps a month later, Gerald went down to St Ives: some people called Millie Dow wanted to take the house. Our lease was sold to them; and St Ives vanished for ever.

(pp. 116–17)

Talland House, the very symbol of meaningful continuity, was no more. A world of summers had been lost in unreality.

On top of the death of her mother, came the death of Stella Duckworth, in the most dramatic and unreal circumstances: ecstatic love, between Stella and Jack Hills, a long-drawn-out engagement, a romantic wedding, then after three months' marriage, Stella's meaningless death. The death of Stella reinforced Virginia's conviction that the world was a meaningless, hostile, arbitrary and cruel place. But, for those very reasons, Virginia's sense of reality was powerfully reinforced too:

I would see (after Thoby's death) two great grindstones (as I walked round Goode Tye) and myself between them. I would typify a contest between myself and 'them' – some invisible giant. I would reason, or fancy, that if life were thus made to rear and kick, it was at any rate, the real thing. Nobody could say I had been fobbed off with an unmeaning slip of the precious matter. So I came to think of life as something of extreme reality.

(*A Sketch of the Past*, in Schulkind p. 118)

That is surely the harvest of these deaths – that, after an invasion of a sense of unreality in 1895, and an ensuing bout of extreme depression, the sense of life as being 'something of extreme reality' was given to the world in the novels. In a sense, the novels are about just this: what is 'reality'? And the origin of the sense of 'extreme reality' is in the abrupt and violent deaths of 1895–1906, those which temporarily shook her balance.

We should not forget either, in examining the forces at work in Virginia's mind in 1912, the effect of that fourth death, Thoby's, in 1906. The whole of *The Waves* is dedicated to the memory of Thoby. Thoby's death is the death of an ideal.

We must also remember that the deaths of her mother and of Stella took place in Virginia's early teens. She herself documents at length how embarrassed and ashamed she was of her own body, from as far back as she can remember. The emergence into adolescence and young womanhood under these circumstances of continual death and unreality cannot have been easy. When she was thirteen, her mother died. When she was fifteen Stella died.

During the years from 1895 to her father's death, Virginia was coping with a further sense of unreality brought about by the sexual attentions of George Duckworth. These continued un-abated, she tells us, until her father died in 1904 – she was then twenty-two. And in 1906 Thoby died. Thoby may be considered as Virginia's ideal of a complete man; as her mother had been her ideal of a complete woman. Thoby is celebrated for his complete-ness in *Jacob's Room*, and for his ideality in *The Waves*. For Virginia, from thenceforth, all men were to be a poor substitute for Thoby.

The collapse of 1904 seems as explicable, and as predictable, as the first collapse of 1895 had been. In 1897, after Stella's death, there does not seem to have been any sort of overt nervous collapse. Nevertheless, one can legitimately wonder by what sort of narrow margin it was averted.

There was a further reason why the collapse of 1904 took place, again to do with George. For the significance of this, we have again to reflect a moment on Virginia's sense of her own embod-iment.

We know, from earlier sections of *A Sketch of the Past*, how profoundly Virginia had been offended by Gerald's explorations of her 'private parts' at Talland House when she was 'very small'.

We have also had reason to note the continuing interference which took place from George around the time of Julia Stephen's death. This would have been enough in itself to have given Virginia a sense of unease in her own body, a deep mistrust of her own reactions and a deep suspicion of her own feelings.

But on top of this, we have to add the fact that George, during the years Virginia was a teenager and emerging into her early twenties, had yet a further relationship with her. George Duckworth was not only the 'lover' of the Stephen girls, he was also a *pater familias* well before the death of Sir Leslie, and took upon himself the double task of being the promoter of the social careers of Vanessa and Virginia, while at the same time being their sternest critic. This is documented in *A Sketch of the Past* (pp. 130–7) and *22 Hyde Park Gate* (passim).

George had decided to 'launch' the Stephen girls socially. First he tried with Vanessa, but gave up after a while, in the face of her severe discouragement. Then he turned his attentions to Virginia. Virginia's will-power, or sense of self-preservation, was obviously not as developed as Vanessa's and she was doubly under George's dominion.

The extreme of embarrassment was achieved because George simultaneously held Virginia in two conflicting positions. His avowed aim was to 'launch' Virginia on a giddy social climb, and therefore he procured invitations for her to all the best parties in London. But in order to arrive at these soirées, Virginia had to dress up and appear under George's scrutiny for approval. And it appears that this approval was rarely given, or, if it was given, was given grudgingly and in such a way as to undermine any confidence Virginia might have in her own body, her clothes, or her bearing. Scrutinised by George, her nocturnal companion, in the bright light of common day for her dress-sense and her social acceptability, Virginia was in a doubly ambiguous relation to him. It would have been enough to give anyone a sense that the body was suspect, ambiguous, shameful, or ridiculous. And these are the main attitudes Virginia came to hold about the body in general, and about her own in particular.

At 7.30 we went upstairs to dress. However cold or foggy it might be, we slipped off our day clothes and stood shivering in front of washing basins. . . I would stand in front of George's Chippendale glass trying to make myself not only tidy but presentable. . . Down I came: in my green evening dress; all the lights were up in the drawing room; and there was George, in his black tie and evening jacket, in the chair by the fire. He fixed on me that extraordinary observant . . . gaze with which he always inspected clothes. He looked me up and down as if [I] were a horse turned into the ring. (*A Sketch of the Past*, in Schulkind p. 130)

This last image fitly expresses what Virginia thought of herself under this scrutiny. So far, bad enough. But then something much worse happens. Virginia's whole bearing and presence is undermined and disconfirmed by George:

Then the sullen look came over him; a look in which one traced not merely aesthetic disapproval; but something that went deeper; morally, socially, he scented some kind of insurrection; of defiance of social standards. I was condemned from many more points of view than I can analyse as I stood there, conscious of those criticisms; and conscious too of fear, of shame and of despair – 'Go and tear it up', he said at last, in that curiously rasping and peevish voice which expressed his serious displeasure at this infringement of a code that meant more to him than he would admit.

(p. 130)

The origin of Virginia's view of her own body as ridiculous – looked at, penetrated, examined, undressed, criticised, disconfirmed – lies surely here. 'He looked me up and down as if [I] were a horse turned into the ring . . . I was condemned from many more points of view than I can analyse as I stood there . . .' 'Go and tear it up.' And this is the treatment meted out to a woman whom he was, in 1904, 'cuddling and kissing and otherwise embracing' while Sir Leslie was 'dying three or four storeys lower down of cancer'.

Any adolescent may be embarrassed when turning up for family inspection before a big dance. But to be scrutinised in that particular way, by that particular person, and for those particular reasons, must have presented for Virginia a self-contradictory series of experiences which ended in horror and confusion. Her body was spurned and ridiculous, her clothes were ghastly, her manners were unacceptable, her bearing was socially subversive. 'Go and tear it up.'

While they were actually doing the social rounds, George was in the ambiguous double rôle of presenter and censor. He was anxious to show the best side of his protégée, and yet extremely critical of the slightest breach of protocol on her part. One such evening, a dance at Lady Sligo's, is recounted in some detail in *22 Hyde Park Gate* (pp. 151ff.). This double scrutiny, after the initial one which had sent her upstairs to change her dress in shame, must have been unendurable. That it was so is evidenced by the story Virginia recounts in *22 Hyde Park Gate* – a story which has as its aim to show that on occasion even the worm can turn. It is highly significant that the whole story should depend upon the use of Greek. Reference is deliberately made to Plato, in some kind of revenge perhaps for George's constant meddling with her at her Greek lessons. Virginia uses Greek to discountenance George:

George had always complained of Vanessa's silence. I would prove that I could talk. So off I started. Heaven knows what devil prompted me. . . The ancients, I said, discussed everything in common. Had Lady Carnarvon ever read the dialogues of Plato? . . . I felt that I was earning George's gratitude for ever. Suddenly a twitch, a shiver, a convulsion of amazing expressiveness, shook the Countess by my side; her diamonds, of which she wore a chaste selection, flashed in my eyes; and stopping, I saw George Duckworth blushing crimson on the other side of the table. I realised that I had committed some unspeakable impropriety.

(Schulkind p. 152)

Yes, and probably quite deliberately. The dialectic of submission and resentment felt by Vanessa and Virginia for George is quite subtly presented in Virginia's account. George was always associated with Greek in Virginia's mind.

George meanwhile had secured a cab. He was much confused, and yet very angry. I could see that my remarks at dinner upon the dialogues of Plato rankled bitterly in his mind.

(p. 153)

And, after the dance:

I went up to my room, took off my beautiful white satin dress, and unfastened the three pink carnations which had been pinned to my breast by the Jews' harp. Was it really possible that tomorrow I should open my Greek dictionary and go on spelling out the dialogues of Plato with Miss Case? I felt I knew much more about the dialogues of Pato than Miss Case could ever do. . .

Sleep had almost come to me. The room was dark. The house silent. Then, creaking stealthily, the door opened; treading gingerly, someone entered. 'Who?' I cried. 'Don't be frightened', George whispered. 'And don't turn on the light, oh beloved. Beloved – 'and he flung himself on my bed, and took me in his arms.

Yes, the old ladies of Kensington and Belgravia never knew that George Duckworth was not only father and mother, brother and sister to those poor Stephen girls; he was their lover also.

(p. 155)

George Duckworth's hypocrisy is emphasised again and again by Virginia, and this overlay of hypocrisy in public must have been, given what Virginia knew of George's real relation to her, an invitation to divide reality very strongly into inner reality and mere social appearance. George's doubled attentions spring from repression, but they are also perfect instruments for setting up repression in Virginia. From outside, she is stared at, but inside she is agonised. Outside, she attempts to keep calm and to behave decorously. Inside she is in terror. Outside, she appears virginal and innocent. Inside, she knows that she is complicit in a strange game of mingled lust and disgust. Her body is not really hers: it is public property, and everything that George did to push her forward in brilliant company only made her own body more problematic to her. The dance at Lady Sligo's is a perfect example.

After two hours of standing about in Lady Sligo's ball-room . . . of being left without a partner, of being told by George that I looked lovely but must hold myself upright, I retired to an ante-room and hoped that a curtain concealed me. For some time it did. At length old Lady Sligo discovered me. . . On that occasion George was lenient. We left about two o'clock, and on the way home he praised me warmly, and assured me that I only needed practice to be a great social success.

(p. 151)

George is both there as promoter ('I looked lovely but must hold myself upright') and also as critic, as judge ('On that occasion George was lenient'). Virginia is constantly looked up and and down by George as if she were 'a horse turned into the ring'. He is determined that it is his view of her which shall count. And all the time he is secretly in a totally different private relationship with this girl. 'As we drove across the Park he stroked my hand,

and told me how he hoped that I should make friends with Elsie. . .' (p. 151). Always the doubled relationship, personal intimacy coupled with social distance. This whole long process must have contributed to a dissociation in Virginia's sense of her own body, of whom it belonged to, and what were proper uses of it. The letter to Leonard of 1 May 1912 makes perfect sense in this context. George's work had been done only too well: Virginia feels 'no more than a rock' when Leonard kisses her. It is a question whether she could have been expected to feel otherwise. And all this, and much more besides, was going on in the years which led up to, and culminated in, her father's death. The collapse of 1904 makes complete sense in this context, as do the birds singing in Greek.[1]

In her paper *Old Bloomsbury*, Virginia sharply differentiates two phases of Bloomsbury's history. There is the period which ran from 1904 to 1907, when Vanessa married. This is the period of abstraction ('It depends what you mean by beauty'), of endless verbal discussion and logical debate. This is also the period of the 'buggers' and the lack of physical attraction between the men and the women in the group (Schulkind pp. 167–70). Then, as from 1907, there is a new, 'liberated' period, when sex becomes a major topic and the affairs of the 'buggers' are endlessly discussed (pp. 170–4).

Through the experience of 'Bloomsbury', Virginia writes, a certain degree of freedom in sexual matters was achieved. But it is clear from what she says there that the embargoes of the earlier, sterile and abstract period of 'Bloomsbury' were completely successful in holding at bay certain kinds of freedom. It is doubtless true that, through the experience of new freedom, new friends and different kinds of discussion, Virginia threw off some of the fears of childhood and adolescence. But it seems that one ought not to confuse verbal freedom with freedom from inner fear. Virginia was still technically, perhaps, a virgin when she married

[1] A great deal of the 'hidden relationship' between George and Virginia can be seen in the photograph reproduced on p. 15 of George Spater's and Ian Parsons's *A Marriage of True Minds* (Jonathan Cape and Hogarth Press 1977). George's stance – arrogant, possessive, intimate – is in stark contrast to Virginia's, which is 'cancelled out', negated, frozen. This photograph is most revealing of the adolescent embodiment of Virginia.

Leonard, but the intervening years of discussion and freedom had obviously done nothing to make certain deeply implanted fears less strong. The question of marriage was resolutely put aside. But one afternoon Vanessa said, ' "Of course, I can see that we shall all marry. It's bound to happen" – and as she said it I could feel a horrible necessity impending over us; a fate would descend and snatch us apart just as we had achieved freedom and happiness' (*Old Bloomsbury*, in Schulkind p. 170). Marriage would be a new form of servitude. The new free, non-dependent life of Bloomsbury was going to be all too brief. Marriage did not appeal to Virginia, and for years I think she struggled against the necessity of recognising that it would one day happen. It was seen rather as an impending danger which could be put off for a long while.

And then suddenly it was 1912, and Virginia realised she was thirty.

The pattern of stress and upset which was to culminate in the double collapse of mid-1913, has its local origin, I am fairly sure, at the beginning of 1912, when Leonard first proposed to Virginia. This pattern is traceable in the letters. Leonard proposed marriage on 11 January 1912, and repeated his proposal in two further letters. Virginia's reply (13 January 1912, *Letters* I, no. 600) stalls. 'There isn't anything really for me to say, except that I should like to go on as before; and that you should leave me free, and that I should be honest'. This non-committal attitude corresponds to the period studied in *The Wise Virgins*, before the final interview between Harry and Camilla.

Then there is a gap of several weeks in the letters, and the next letter, dated 7 February, to Katherine Cox, refers to a period of illness already over: 'I've been ill, but I'm practically all right again now. It was a touch of my usual disease, in the head you know' (no. 602). A letter to Violet Dickinson of mid-February 1912, refers to a further period of enforced relaxation: 'I'm so sorry, but Savage is making me spend a fortnight in bed, as I cant sleep. It is very ridiculous' (no. 604). The editor's note reads: 'On 16 February Virginia returned to Jean Thomas's nursing home at Twickenham.'

It seems that there must be some connection between the two

proposals of marriage (Sydney Waterlow's had preceded
Leonard's) and the renewed stress, inability to sleep, and restlessness. The nearness that marriage had suddenly assumed
must have struck her with sudden force. Her sleep is punctuated
by 'miraculous dreams' or 'wild dreams' (nos. 602, 603). Virginia
emerges from the nursing home armed again with her usual
swashbuckling humour which she always uses to defend herself
precisely against the taunt of 'madness'. In a letter to Leonard
she writes: 'I shall tell you wonderful stories of the lunatics. By
the bye, they've elected me King. There can be no doubt about
it. I summoned a conclave, and made a proclamation about
Christianity' (5 March 1912, no. 606).

This theme of Christianity is closely connected with Miss Jean
Thomas, who was an ardent and convinced Christian. On
Christmas Day 1910, Virginia wrote to Vanessa telling her that
she had received Tolstoy's 'What I believe' from Jean Thomas.
'She sent a long serious letter with it, exhorting me to Christian-
ity, which will save me from insanity. How we are persecuted!
The self conceit of Christians is really unendurable' (no. 546).
Writing to Violet Dickinson on New Year's Day 1911, Jean
Thomas's Christianity is again made the butt of ironic ridicule:

Miss Thomas came down for a night, in an interval between discharging
a woman who wished to commit murder, and taking one, who wants to
kill herself. Can you imagine living like that? – always watching the
knives, and expecting to find bedroom doors locked, or a corpse in the
bath? I said I thought it was too great a strain – but, upheld by Christianity, I believe she will do it.

                                                        (no. 549)

I think there can be little doubt that Jean Thomas's ardent
Christianity, and her desire to propagate it, is behind much of the
ironic contempt expended on the figure of Miss Kilman in *Mrs
Dalloway*. The association of Christianity and the nursing home
run by Miss Jean Thomas was being set up, definitely, as an
element of persecution in that novel yet to be written.

But, quite obviously, Leonard was not yet conceived of as a
lover or a husband. Her tone about him in her letter to Molly
MacCarthy of March 1912 is extremely cold and distant: 'I don't
really worry about W[oolf]: though I think I made out that I did.

He is going to stay longer anyhow, and pérhaps he will stay in England anyhow, so the responsibility is lifted off me' (no. 608). The editors note: 'Determined to resign from the Ceylon Colonial Service if Virginia would agree to marry him, Leonard had asked the Colonial Office on 14 February to extend his leave by four months, for personal reasons.'

In March 1912, Virginia regards the matter of making up her mind about Leonard as a 'responsibility' she would gladly be rid of. If he is going to be in England anyway, so much the better, for then things can take longer, but, in any case, a sudden decision by herself was not required. This thought gives Virginia obvious relief. And this letter lies only a little over four months away from the marriage to Leonard on 10 August 1912.

In the middle of March, Virginia is again under some form of sedation, for she writes to Sydney Waterlow, her other suitor, 'I've been a shameful time in writing, but one day after another has been knocked on the head by sleeping draughts. They are a good deal worse than sleeplessness. . . At this moment I'm kept from visitors, but in a week or two I shall be alright' (21 March, 1912, no. 609).

This must be the third period of enforced relaxation since January. Something is obviously worrying Virginia intensely. At this point it is worth looking again briefly at Leonard's activities during this time. Virginia had read some of *The Voyage Out* to Leonard in March 1912:

I thought it extraordinarily good, but noticed even then what a strain it was upon her. Then came the emotional strain of our engagement and she got a severe headache and insomnia and had to go for a time to a nursing home in Twickenham and rest there. Her doctor was Sir George Savage, a mental specialist at the head of his profession. He was also a friend of her family and had known her ever since her birth. I went to see him quite early on in 1912 and he discussed Virginia's health with me as a doctor and as an old friend. He was very friendly to me, but impressed me much more as a man of the world than as a doctor.

(*Beginning Again* pp. 81–2)

What is so striking about this account is that Leonard refers to the novel as if *it* were a strain upon her (as opposed to what the novel was obviously about, the difficulties of engagement). He refers to 'the emotional strain of our engagement' as if that phrase explains itself, almost as if it was quite normal that an engagement should put such a strain upon a woman that she had to be hospitalised. And then there is the question of Leonard going himself to have chats with Sir George Savage about the mental health of a woman to whom he was not yet even engaged, a woman to whom he was not going to be engaged for a few more months yet, and whose response to his proposal had been so distant as to constitute almost an outright refusal. Yet, 'quite early on in 1912', Leonard was discussing her case with her physician. In view of some of Virginia's later claims about 'conspiracy' (claims in which Leonard always professes to see no justice), this early collaboration between a man who knew nothing about her and a man to whom she was not engaged may well have a significance.

Then comes the major letter of 1 May 1912, in which Virginia goes a long way to accepting Leonard as fiancé, but without actually saying that she accepts him. Indeed, the letter is scattered with pointers of danger, indications of warning, notes and hints which should have alerted the suitor to very troubled water ahead, especially in what would concern the sexual side of their marriage. Nevertheless, ignoring all these pointers, indications and hints, Leonard decided. The editorial note runs: 'This letter decided Leonard. He resigned from the Colonial Service, and his resignation was accepted on 7 May.'

The wording and phrasing of this letter (no. 615) is so complex, so problematic, and so shot through with difficulties, that it might have seemed equally reasonable, if not more so, to have returned to Ceylon. Anyone accepting a bride on such clearly spelt-out conditions as Virginia gave Leonard to understand on 1 May, would surely be entering his marriage with his eyes wide open.

1 May 1912. Three months and nine days before the pair marry. The woman, who has been in and out of hospital and often under sedation since Leonard first proposed to her in January, accepts (on terms which amount effectively to a refusal) a suitor who himself may well have felt that his return to Ceylon this time would have meant the beginning of a dreary and prolonged end.

Leonard was thirty-one. His return to Ceylon would have meant that he would have been perhaps nearer forty than thirty when he next came home on leave.

What we see in May 1912, then, is a woman more or less frantic with distress about a marriage which she cannot manage, and yet can no longer see any way of putting off, and a man who, having observed the effect upon her of his proposal, and having talked with her physician, decides to throw up a career in the Colonial Service in order to marry her.

The letters which Virginia writes to her various female friends, to inform them of the forthcoming marriage with Leonard, all stress one major fear: that contact might be cut off. Virginia goes out of her way to boost Leonard's image in her account of him, to give honest forewarning that Leonard is a Jew, and then to beg for no sudden or abrupt termination of a long friendship. This pattern runs through letters 620–9.

To Violet Dickinson she writes:

I've got a confession to make. I'm going to marry Leonard Wolf [sic] . He's a penniless Jew. I'm more happy than anyone ever said was possible – but I *insist* upon your liking him too. May we both come on Tuesday?

(no. 620)

To Madge Vaughan:

I want to tell you I'm going to marry Leonard Wolf [sic]. He was one of Thoby's greatest friends. I'm very happy–and I know you'll be glad.

May we come and see you some day? I want you to know him, and I don't mean there to be any lapse in our friendship, which has always been a joy since – oh what years ago!

(no. 621)

To Janet Case:

I want to tell you that I'm going to marry Leonard Wolf [sic] – he is a penniless Jew. He was a friend of Thoby's, – and I'm so happy . . . May we come and see you? You've always been angelic to me – no, much nicer than angelic, and I want you to like him. It has been worth waiting for.

(no. 622)

To Ottoline Morrell:

This is to tell you that I'm going to marry Leonard Woolf. I'm very happy – and find him more necessary every day. Do you like him? I hope so, because I want to be a friend of yours all my life.

(no. 624)

To Violet Dickinson:

My Violet,
Friday is no good – would Saturday do? If not, it must be one day next week. Please settle, (except Tuesday and Wednesday) It was idiotic to put you off – I've been rather headachy, and had a bad night, and Leonard made me into a comatose invalid.

We want very much to come. He is a most charming man, and I get steadily happier. By the way, my novel is getting on, in spite of interruptions, and L. wants me to say that if I cease to write when married, I shall be divorced.

Please have us.

Yr. VS

(no. 625)

The appeal is absolutely direct: 'Please settle . . . We want very much to come . . . Please have us.' But running through this is the constant fear of the marriage, evidenced by the fact that Virginia is again sleeping badly and having to have sedatives of some kind. What is new is the information that now Leonard is in charge of the sedation. Already in June, six weeks before the marriage, Leonard is in control of the medications: 'Leonard made me into a comatose invalid'. The pattern which is to be established officially immediately after the marriage, whereby Leonard is the nurse of a sick woman, is already visible well before the marriage.

The importance of the novel, *The Voyage Out*, is always emphasized. It is a structure in Virginia's thinking. The book is her work, that is her *raison d'être*, she is going to be a writer. At the time, before *The Voyage Out* was anything more than a series of drafts, it must have been little enough to hold on to. All the more so in that its subject, the difficulties of engagement and marriage, were being lived out even as the book was being written. The book is a refuge, and Leonard's insistence that she should continue to write when married is another of her flourishes by which the real question at issue is turned back to front, like the 'you will

probably wonder why on earth he should marry me' to Lady
Robert Cecil. The determination to hang on to writing at all costs
is clearly visible: it is the only strand holding her sense of identity
together. Marriage is like that puddle of water in *The Waves*, when
Rhoda stands immobile in horror before it: 'Identity failed me.' At
this point of her life, *The Voyage Out* is Virginia's identity.

The fear that announcing her engagement to Leonard might
mean the termination of a very old friendship runs through all
these letters. To Lady Robert Cecil she writes:

I am very very happy, and I hope when I'm married that you will come
and see me – or ask me to see you – oftener than in the past. Now please
bear this in mind.

(no. 629)

And in an effort to make Leonard's image more acceptable,
Virginia occasionally strains verisimilitude:

Meanwhile, how am I to begin about Leonard? First he is a Jew: second
he is 31; third, he spent 7 years in Ceylon, governing natives, inventing
ploughs, shooting tigers, and did so well that they offered him a very
high place the other day, which he refused, wishing to marry me, and
gave up his entire career there on the chance that I would agree.

(To Madge Vaughan, no. 628)

Or, even more extravagantly, in a letter to Lady Robert Cecil,
labours to give Leonard a kind of terrible *machismo*:

I think you will like him – though you will probably wonder why on earth
he should marry me – considering that he has ruled India, hung black
men, and shot tigers.

(no. 629)

These letters of information which Virginia wrote to her old
friends and lovers in June 1912 cost her a great deal of effort. Her
decision may well have been so shocking, so unexplainable, even
to herself, that she found announcing the matter almost beyond
her literary powers. What remains clear, however, is this: that, in
every case, Virginia felt that this announcement of her engagement to Leonard might have cost her the friendship of one of her
lifelong allies and friends.

The approaching nearness of the marriage worries Virginia
continually. Writing to thank Lady Robert Cecil for an early

wedding present (two months before the event), Virginia repeats
her request that she and Leonard should be received for tea.
Perhaps the arrival of the wedding present well before the marriage, and before Lady Robert had met Leonard, struck her as a
prelude to the breaking off of relations. In any case, Virginia is
sugar sweet in her note:

My dear Nelly,
  When I got home yesterday I found my first wedding present – yours.
If they're all going to be as nice, I shall be in luck. I love your old glasses,
which will adorn my table, directly I have one. You are extremely clever,
as well as nice.
  This is the prelude to asking whether we may come to tea with you –
and would Tuesday next week suit? That seems the first afternoon.
Heaven knows what happens to them – they melt away, and I shall soon
find myself confronted by a wedding day. Is it an awful experience? Will
you tell us truthfully about it, when we come – that is if we may come?
  Thank you again – I wish there was some new way of saying that
which came out absolutely truthfully.
                                        Your aff. VS

                                                    (no. 630)

  'Is it an awful experience?' The naïve question is menacing in
this context because of the brave distance held and maintained
between inner fear and outer nonchalance.
  Virginia is obviously under tremendous strain through June
1912, and it was at this time, or thereabouts, that Leonard took it
upon himself to add considerably to the strain, by introducing the
question of whether or not Virginia should have children. One
can only assume that he found Virginia's sedation and hospital-
isation during 1912 extremely worrying. His conversations with
Sir George Savage must have touched upon the matter of
whether or not Virginia should have children, and Leonard
decided to over-rule Savage's advice that she should, by collecting evidence from other medical authorities to the effect that she
shouldn't. The ambiguities present in the situation emerge from
Leonard's own account of his actions that year:

I went to see him quite early on in 1912 and he discussed Virginia's health
with me as a doctor and as an old friend. He was very friendly to me, but
impressed me much more as a man of the world than as a doctor. In the
next few months, I became more and more uneasy about one thing. We

both wanted to have children, but the more I saw the dangerous effect of any strain or stress upon her, the more I began to doubt whether she would be able to stand the strain and stress of childbearing. I went and consulted Sir George Savage; he brushed my doubts aside. But now my doubts about Sir George Savage were added to my doubts about Virginia's health. There seemed to be more of the man of the world ('Do her a world of good, my dear fellow; do her a world of good!') in his opinion than of the mental specialist. So I went off and consulted two other well known doctors, Maurice Craig and T.B. Hyslop, and also the lady who ran the mental nursing home where Virginia had several times stayed. They confirmed my fears and were strongly against her having children. We followed their advice.

(Beginning Again p. 82)

Leonard lost confidence in Sir George Savage when Savage insisted that having children would do Virginia 'a world of good'. 'So I went off and consulted two other well known doctors . . . '. The 'so' has a logical force here. '*Since* Savage said that having children would do Virginia good, *so* I went to get opinions contrary to his.'

The clear implications are either that Leonard did not believe it was safe for Virginia to have children (his official motive) or that he himself did not want her to have children. This seems at least as likely as the first hypothesis. One thing may well have been very present to his mind: the current and popular belief, among certain circles of eugenics theorists, that people with histories (or family histories) of mental disease should not be allowed to have children. This theory was closely allied with theories of race, and almost always advanced in the context of the evident necessity of keeping the Empire's rulers strong. One of the most outstanding of these theorists was T.B. Hyslop. And it was to him, precisely, that Leonard went to get a medical opinion on the advisability of Virginia's having children.

In October of that very year, in an article in the *Journal of Mental Science*,[1] Hyslop published a long and detailed list of proposed

[1] *The Mental Deficiency Bill 1912*, by Theo B. Hyslop, M.D., F.R.S.E. A discussion on the legislative proposals for the Care and Control of the Mentally Defective, opened by Dr Theo Hyslop at the Annual Meeting of the Medico-Psychological Association held at Gloucester on July 12th, 1912, *Journal of Mental Science*, LVIII (October 1912). I am grateful to Mr Stephen Trombley (who is at present working on a study of Virginia Woolf and her doctors) for bringing the publications of Doctors Hyslop and Craig to my attention.

improvements to the Mental Deficiency Bill. The general thrust of his article was that the Mental Deficiency Bill was not nearly strong enough in discriminating against, and taking responsibility from, those persons whose marriage and offspring might weaken the national fibre and increase the number of genetically inferior people in Britain and her Empire. Hyslop entertained a naïve, almost crazy theory, that the vital energies of the Empire were being sapped, and that strong measures had to be taken against further decline. He writes in October 1912, for instance:

in spite of overwhelming evidence of the existence of much evil inheritance that tends to destroy the vital energies of the nation, there are many who will raise their voices in indignant protestation. One point for our consideration is whether this matter of preventing procreation by the mentally defective is of equal urgency to the other matters referred to in the Bill. I, for my part, believe that it is one of the most important and farthest reaching of the benefits proposed, and that this sub-clause alone raises the principle of the Bill to a higher plane than does any other item in it.

The importance of this question is so great that a great deal of discussion will inevitably centre round it. We, who have to concern ourselves with the problems of degeneration, know quite well that much of the defective-mindedness prevalent nowadays might in the future be obviated. We also know that, unfortunately for the welfare of the race, our advice and protests are only too frequently entirely ignored by those who seem incapable of thinking of anything beyond the gratification of their own individual desires.

Such was Hyslop, the guardian of the purity of blood in the race. In a paper of 1905, Hyslop had written:

The public mind is at present much agitated by the alleged prevalence of physical deterioration, by the diminished birth-rate, and by the increase in infantile mortality. In the House of Lords, not long ago, the Bishop of Ripon gave it as his opinion that the facts revealed in the report of the Inter-departmental Commission on Physical Deterioration were pregnant with danger to the empire. He contended that, unless some steps were taken, the British race would no longer be able to maintain its position as a colonizing and as a ruling power.

(*British Medical Journal* (14 October 1905), II, 941)

Hyslop goes on in that paper to endorse the Bishop of Ripon's opinion up to the hilt, adding that the new breed of intellectual women was sapping ancient energies, and that the women who wanted to do 'mental work', like writing and so on, would damage the general health of their offspring. An example of his views should be quoted:

Woman's mission in this world is, according to Napoleon, that of breeding as many children as possible. Moralists are more generous, however, and assign her a double rôle of wife and mother. We may go further still and recognize that her mission is not only familial but social also, with a duty to perform toward her fellow-creatures and to help the destiny for which she was created. We grant her the right of being a great civilizing agent as well as an ornament, but, intending woman to be mother, Nature fashioned her destiny for her. The departure of woman from her natural state to an artificial one involves a brain struggle which is deleterious to the virility of the race. Nowadays the average female child – at the period of greatest susceptibility to mental, moral, and physical influences – is subjected to the pressure of modern methods of education ill calculated to prepare her for anything but a mental or nervous rôle in life. The physiological processes of puberty make greater demands on girls than on boys, and girls are handicapped by considerations which ought to make them realize the futility of forcing education and undertaking work which only too frequently renders them neurotic and sexually incompetent. When we look the facts in the face and note the divergence of our women from the life-rôle entrusted to them by Nature, are we inspired with confidence as to the results for future generations?

(p. 942)

This seems to me a classic of its kind. Hyslop's eugenics, mixed with his concern for the Empire and a kind of Gilbert and Sullivan grasp of Darwinism, is beyond serious comment. His obituary in the *British Medical Journal* for 25 February 1933 (i, 347), represents him as a great sportsman, musician, composer, painter and writer, a man of irrepressible good spirits and boundless energy. But the obituary ends on a darker note: 'His latter days were saddened by something in the nature of a neurosis. He developed an anxiety state in consequence of air raids during the war. Later this became manifest as a sort of tic of the shoulders and face, and ultimately the malady bore a strong resemblance to paralysis agitans.' A curious latter-day revenge taken by the spirit.

What of Maurice Craig, the other specialist Leonard went to consult in 1912? In 1906, he had been appointed Physician in Psychological Medicine at Guy's Hospital, in succession to Sir George Savage. He represents a far more modern type of mind than Savage's, and a far less superstitious one than Hyslop's. Considered as a prototype of Sir William Bradshaw, the eminent Harley Street practitioner in *Mrs Dalloway*, it is interesting that during the First World War Craig had done a great deal of work in connection with shell shock. Another interesting connection between Craig and the fictional Sir William Bradshaw is that on 2 November 1922, that is to say during the very period when Virginia was writing *Mrs Dalloway*, Sir Maurice Craig as he then was (he was knighted in 1921) gave the Bradshaw Lecture to the Royal College of Physicians.[1] In his preamble, Craig recalls the historical figure, Dr William Wood Bradshaw, who was born in 1801, and whose wife had endowed the lecture in memory of her husband in her will. Craig, struggling obviously to find some medical point of connection with Bradshaw, comments wryly of Bradshaw: 'At the age of 43 he matriculated at Newton Hall, Oxford, and was granted a degree without any examination. He never did much practice, but it is on record that he was generous and charitable in his treatment of the poor.' It is possible that some published report of this Bradshaw lecture gave Virginia the name of her fictional neurologist.

What sort of views did Craig hold? For his time, relatively enlightened ones. Craig takes a great deal of trouble to point out that neurological upsets can have psychological concomitants. In his lecture, for instance, he makes a statement which is sobering in its implications:

The close relationship of mind and body has long been recognised, but in practice this inter-relationship has been largely lost sight of and the tendency has been to investigate them apart to the detriment of our knowledge of each. It shows how dominated we are by tradition when we realise that it is customary for a student to pass through his medical instruction in the wards of a hospital with little or no thought given to the mental aspect of the patients he has been observing.

If that was still true in 1922, it would surely have been all the more an unquestioned assumption before the war.

This observation in the Bradshaw Lecture, in the context of the treatment of Virginia after 1913, has its significance:

[1] Published in *The Lancet* (4 November 1922), II.

Emotion arising from whatever cause quickly affects the appetite and digestion, and if it persists there is a steady deterioration in the body weight and in the general health of the patient, and yet it is common to see these conditions being treated as if the error in the digestion were the primary cause and indeed, the physician too often remains in entire ignorance of the fact that some disturbance of emotion is the real cause of the mischief. Therefore it is clearly important for every physician to have some insight into the mental make-up of his patient.

Whether or not Craig was in such calm possession of these views when he talked to Leonard in 1912, it is impossible to say. But the fact that Craig has to make these points at all shows how the mental patient was generally regarded at that time. Craig inherited what must be regarded as the dominant assumptions of British neurology, to the effect that all mental disease was, at base, a matter of 'nerves' gone wrong, and that the physiological approach in neurology was the one most likely to be right. But he was also critical of these assumptions. Hence the very cautious suggestion, in 1922, that 'the mental make-up of his patient' may itself be at least as important as the physiological symptoms, such as loss of appetite.

Whether or not, in 1912, Craig pronounced against Virginia's having children, I do not know, but the clear import of Leonard's account is that he concurred with Hyslop. And as for Jean Thomas, what would she have said, what could she have said, she whose entire experience of Virginia had been that of tending a nervous 'case' who had several times run out of control and had several times been an inmate of her establishment?

Leonard had, then, taken elaborate measures and carried out extensive research into his wife's mental state before they were married. Indeed, he had done more than just make enquiries: he had arrived at a point where, on the question of having children, he could place three medical opinions against one.

Some of the assumptions in Leonard's mind, when this decision was taken for himself and Virginia, must have had to do with the nature of the recurrent 'madness' that Virginia was traditionally claimed to have. It looks therefore as if Leonard, when he went ahead with the marriage in August 1912, did so with his eyes more or less open. But it is extraordinary how many subjective factors, even in 1912, Leonard had managed to leave out of account. There is a sense in which the woman he married in August 1912 was totally unknown to him. She was in another sense a woman about whom Leonard chose not to know a great many things.

It is obvious that, during the course of 1912, Virginia's own floating fear and vague apprehension had caused her many sleepless nights, headaches and restlessness, which had been treated on several occasions by rest, sequestration and sedation. Behind Virginia lay the breakdowns which followed the death of her mother and her father. Leonard was already, by June, her acknowledged medical supervisor. The move from engagement to marriage was extremely rapid – just over two months. Virginia feared that the engagement would cost her most of her friends. She was holding on to her novel, *The Voyage Out*, as the only truly stable element in her life. Leonard was busy consulting medical authorities on her ability to have children, and had secured a majority view against. Then came the honeymoon. And within three months of their wedding, on their return to London Leonard was consulting Vanessa, Roger Fry and other medical authorities on her mental state. By July 1913 she had her first collapse, and after the interview with Wright and Head on 9 September, and the veronal attempt, she was sent to Dalingridge Place to recuperate.

A return of a traditional 'madness'? Quite obviously not. What happened in 1912 and 1913 was due in very large measure to the events, the strains, and what were already seen by Virginia as the 'conspiracies', of 1912 and 1913.

vvuvvvuvvi

'Butter, cream, and eggs and bacon'

Whatever the kind, nature and origin of Virginia's previous history of nervous distress, what happened in 1913 must be considered, I think, as belonging to a different kind and nature and springing at least partly from a different origin.

Within a year of their marriage and honeymoon in 1912, Virginia was, it would appear from Leonard's account, in a state of suicidal depression so grave that psychiatric help was needed. And within the same year, Leonard and Virginia took up new substitute rôles within their marriage. Leonard is no longer the husband so much as the nurse. Virginia is no longer the wife so much as the patient. He is sane. She is 'insane'. He consults doctors and visits 'mental specialists'. She behaves with the utmost irrationality and violence towards the nurses. The first years of their marriage, as Leonard describes them in *Beginning Again*, were of unrelieved horror.

What Leonard does not emphasise, and what indeed he does not enquire into, is the striking fact that all this takes place almost immediately after the marriage and the honeymoon. This deserves a moment's reflection, if only to put the question, which Leonard does not put, as to whether this 'madness' of 1913–15 were not due to new pressures, as distinct from old pressures, on Virginia's psychic balance.

I was already troubled and apprehensive when we returned from our honeymoon in the autumn of 1912. All through the first seven months of 1913 I became more and more concerned, for the danger symptoms or signals became more and more serious. In January and February she was finishing *The Voyage Out*, writing every day with a kind of tortured intensity.

(Beginning Again p. 148)

I am at a disadvantage, as everyone is, in not having access to private papers, memos, journals, letters, medical reports and so on, which have never been published, or which may have been destroyed if indeed they ever had a written form. Yet the account that Leonard gives is deliberately free from detail, and deprived of evidence. We get his view of something going gravely wrong with his new wife, but we are never given her view; and her behaviour is seen, as it were from the outside, by a kind but puzzled spectator, as intensely irrational and furiously obscure.

But Virginia did give her own account – of a sort – years later, in *Mrs Dalloway*. In that novel, she is able, after a decade's reflection, to return to the dreadful experience of 1913–15, and give her description of it. But it is useful, if only to establish the sheer distance between Leonard's kind of mind and Virginia's, to study their two accounts of the events separately. Leonard's indeed, deserves detailed attention on its own.

One thing at least is clear. It was Leonard who took the initiative in going to consult psychiatrists about his wife's health, and we have his own word for it that he did this without telling her, and as early as 1912, before their marriage. That she was behaving in a way which showed intense stress I do not doubt, but there must have been some cause for this in Virginia's inner or subjective life. There is a high probability, I would have thought, that, especially in the first years of a marriage, a close and intimate series of discussions with one's new spouse would have helped enormously. It would have been of vital importance for Virginia and Leonard to have talked together of the causes, rather than the 'symptoms', of Virginia's mental distress. To go to an outside source, a 'mental specialist' completely unknown to either of them except in the vaguest possible social way, was, it seems to me, a strangely premature thing to do. He, however talented, could hardly have got to the problems more quickly or more accurately than Leonard, if only because Leonard had known Virginia and her friends for years, and had the precious asset of being married to her and therefore (presumably) enjoying a greater intimacy with her than any 'mental specialist' could ever achieve.

But no. It was Leonard, alarmed, who went to consult 'mental specialists' and went to see them independently. Virginia constantly hurled the taunt of 'conspiracy' at Leonard during 1913–15 and from her point of view there was quite a lot that must have looked like conspiracy in the way Leonard was always in secret league with the psychiatrists.

For instance, Leonard kept a secret medical journal on Virginia from as early as January 1913.

Very occasionally in times of crisis, when I want to make the record unintelligible to anyone but myself, I make my entries in cypher mainly composed of a mixture of Sinhalese and Tamil letters. My diary of the year 1913 shows very clearly the rapid progress of Virginia's illness and of my apprehension. From January to August I noted almost daily the state of her health, whether she could work, how she slept, whether she had sensations of headache; and in August I began to keep the diary in cypher.

(*Beginning Again* p. 149)

On 22 August Leonard paid a personal visit to Sir George Savage, unaccompanied by Virginia, and 'explained the situation'. When Leonard returned to Gordon Square, 'I discussed the whole situation with Vanessa and with Roger, who happened to be there . . . Roger suggested that he should take me at once to Dr. Henry Head, a brilliant physician whom he knew well, and see what he would say' (*Beginning Again* pp. 151–2). All this seems extraordinarily external, somehow. There is some quality about it which does not 'ring true' in a man married for only one year. He seems prepared to take advice from family, friends and psychiatrists, but not to treat Virginia herself as being a possible clue to the solution of the mystery.

Leonard seems very prepared to fall in with the family view (the traditional Stephen family view) that 'of course the Goat is mad'. He does not oppose this judgement, or in any way strenuously examine it. On the contrary, as we can see from the chapter 'Katharine's Opinion of her Sister' in *The Wise Virgins*, he had more or less swallowed Vanessa's view of Virginia's instability hook, line and sinker. He treats his wife, from the beginning, as someone with 'symptoms'. To treat one's newly married bride as some kind of alien and foreign person, possessed of 'symptoms', as someone who is 'insane', and to consult all and sundry in secret about her, without asking her advice or putting her in the picture afterwards, has all the appearances of a refusal on Leonard's part to enquire into why his wife was showing such signs of stress.

The symptoms of headache increased, she could not sleep, she would hardly eat anything. She could not work and became terribly depressed, and what was most alarming, she refused to admit that she was ill and blamed herself for her condition.

(*Beginning Again* p. 150)

These, then, are the 'symptoms'. 'Symptoms', though, of what? In themselves, they tell us nothing except that Virginia was desperately concerned about something which she was repressing. These 'symptoms' surely point to a condition of inner distress: they are not themselves co-extensive with Virginia's illness. These 'symptoms' point to something; they are not there merely to be pointed at, as further examples of a traditional 'madness'.

In other words, from the first days of their marriage, Leonard and Virginia had taken up their positions, dug their trenches, for what was to be a war which lasted a lifetime. She would take refuge in nervous stress, and he would be there to protect and to nurse. And this, extreme as it may sound, would be only natural in a marriage which rested on no secure physical base.

One cannot tell from Leonard's account of their marriage, and certainly I do not know of any other source which could tell us, whether any real attempt was made by the two to discuss what was worrying Virginia so intensely. It would seem not. And that would be incredible in itself, except for the equally strange nature of what it was that was worrying Virginia so intensely: the fact, precisely, that this was going to be a quite exceptional marriage, in which certain things were not going to be discussed, nor certain emotional issues treated seriously. Virginia was probably unwilling to speak about the Duckworths, and unable to make the transition from such a description to some kind of positive suggestion. She was being entombed, so to speak, in a relationship in which her partner would not listen to, or could not understand, what she had to say, even had she been able to say some part of it directly – which she was probably not; a relationship whose very form was to be one in which she was to be the insane sufferer, and he to be the sane nurse, with a 'sense of proportion'.

If indeed it had been decided at some earlier point that she and Leonard were not going to have children; if the emotional problems of 'making contact' were as perilously difficult as *The Voyage Out* had made it clear they were; if there was to be no physical basis to the marriage – then the stress on Virginia would have understandably increased in the year after her marriage.

That would explain why the traditional 'Goat' madness sets in, in 1913. But – and this is the very point – it is *not* the traditional 'Goat' madness that is in question (if indeed that ever existed). That reputation was founded I suspect, by Vanessa. Her account of how the children used to drive Virginia deliberately into purple rages of frustration in the nursery must suggest that *that* form of 'madness' was probably no more than a passionate response to extreme provocation. This stress in Virginia's mind seems to me to be of a new kind, one which, because of the peculiar elements which led to it, Leonard was the last person to be able to understand or to help, since he was himself a major element in the problem.

Faced, probably, with a marriage that was as strange and as unacceptable to himself as it seemed to her, he made, however, a better job of adapting to it. And it was certainly not possible for him, given his narrow rationalist presuppositions, to take a view of his wife's illness which threw his own status in the marriage into doubt. He shut, as it were, the heavy swing door on empathetic understanding of what was wrong with Virginia. That he could not afford. The easier way out was to treat her as her family traditionally treated her: as insane. And this he does from two months after the honeymoon.

It was clear to him that she was 'ill'; but Virginia refused to agree with him: 'what was most alarming, she refused to admit that she was ill and blamed herself for her condition'. But Leonard has decided as early as January 1913 that she was 'ill'.

They went to a Fabian Conference in Keswick in July, and
Virginia took to her bed. When they got back to London, Leonard
decided to take her to see a 'mental specialist' Sir George Savage .
It was now eleven months since the marriage. Sir George Savage
prescribed a rest cure in a nursing home in Twickenham.

It was at this interview that Sir George Savage made Virginia
'a promise which led to catastrophe':

> he said that if she would agree to go to the nursing home for a week or
> two and rest absolutely in bed under Jean's directions, she could go away
> for a holiday in Somerset with me in August.
>
> (*Beginning Again* pp. 150–1)

Virginia and Leonard went down to Holford, at the foot of the
Quantock Hills on 23 August 1913. It was here that one of the
fundamental issues in Virginia's mental distress blew up. The
question of food arose.

Leonard represents the stay at Holford as a nightmare. He has
also been at considerable pains to recount how distressed Virginia was before they went there (*Beginning Again*, pp. 150–2).
She was indeed in such distress that Leonard hesitated to take
her at all. But Head concurred with Savage for once in believing
that it would be more dangerous to cancel the journey than to go.
So they went. And Leonard plunges into the matter of how excellent the food was at the Inn. Virginia refused to eat.

This may be more explicable in the light of one vital fact which
Leonard neglects to put into his autobiographical account of
the honeymoon of August 1912: it was to the Plough Inn, Holford, that he and Virginia went during the first week of their
marriage.

True, Leonard does say in his account of August 1913 that 'We
had more than once stayed at an inn in the little village of Holford
in the Quantocks' (p. 151), but he does not give any indication of
when that was. It surely makes a great deal of difference that it
was on their honeymoon.

In Leonard's account of the honeymoon itself, the three or four
days spent at Holford are simply elided. He writes as if their
honeymoon took them straight to Europe:

We were married, as I said some pages back, on Saturday, August 10,

1912. Then we went off for a long meandering honeymoon. In those days
I had the *wanderlust* almost perpetually upon me.

(Beginning Again p. 82)

But Quentin Bell is more precise:

Although she had been agitated earlier in the morning, Virginia enjoyed
both the ceremony and the party. When this was over she and Leonard
left for Asham in high spirits. They spent the night there and then went
to stay for a few days in the Quantocks before going abroad.

(II, 4)

And in his Chronology in Appendix B, Bell is even more precise
than that:

10 August. Marriage of Virginia Stephen and Leonard Woolf at St Pan-
cras Registry Office. They go to Asham for two days, return to London,
and then stay at the Plough Inn, Holford, Somerset.

(II, 227)

This is highly significant. If indeed on the 1913 visit Virginia
reacted with such hostility to the masses of good food which
Leonard describes at the Plough, it may well have something to
do with the fact that, for Virginia, this visit to the inn was a return
to the scene of very great previous strain. The return to the inn
may well have triggered off in her forces which she could no
longer control. The distress Leonard describes cannot be entirely
due to a mere disinclination to eat. There was something else
involved which precipitated the crisis.

It seems likely, then, that the Plough may have been the scene
of that 'failure' which Virginia recalls throughout *Mrs Dalloway*,
the 'failure' to be a proper wife to Richard Dalloway, and the
origin of the 'faults' for which Virginia ceaselessly berates herself
in the years following her marriage to Leonard. The Plough Inn at
Holford may well have been, for Virginia, the scene of one of her
greatest failures, when she 'failed' Leonard as a sexual partner, or
when she became conscious that she did not wish to become a
sexual partner at all.

If this is so, then Leonard's account of the return to the Plough
in 1913 makes sense: 'she was convinced that she was not ill, that
her condition was due to her own faults, and that eating and
resting made her worse' *(Beginning Again* pp. 154–5). That would

all fit. And the sudden desire not to eat would be a perfect cover for an anxiety that Virginia could no longer hide by any other means. The constant refusal of food would have been, that is to say, a deliberate distraction. What was really at issue was an intense unhappiness in her married life that Leonard was not prepared, or not able, to recognise. Hence he interprets her 'food' code straightforwardly as having reference only to food. By now he may have given up any hope of any close discussion on the question of sexual relations, and have tensed himself to play out the game on the level which Virginia chose. So Leonard determines to accept the rejection of food as good coin.

We have already seen how Virginia associated food with gluttony, gluttony with obesity, obesity with stupidity, and stupidity with being laughed at. Yet the rest cure, both at the nursing home in Twickenham, and also at Holford, was to consist very largely of eating.

It seems perverse in Leonard, but he determines to ignore this element in his wife's distress. He does not, at the very least, connect this hatred and fear of food with her 'illness' except to note constantly that it was irritating and irrational in her to keep on insisting that food was repellent to her. Leonard refuses to see that food was a distinct menace to Virginia. His own description of the food at the Plough Inn is almost deliberately Falstaffian:

Nothing could be better than the bread, butter, cream, and eggs and bacon of the Somersetshire breakfast with which you began your morning. The beef, mutton, and lamb were always magnificent and perfectly cooked; enormous hams, cured by themselves and hanging from the rafters in the kitchen, were so perfect that for years we used to have them sent to us from time to time and find them as good as or better than the peach-fed Virginian hams which one used to buy for vast sums from Fortnum and Mason. As for the drink . . . they gave you beer and cider which only a narrow minded, finicky drinker would fail to find delicious.
(*Beginning Again* pp. 153–4)

It is Leonard himself who asserts that there was a connection in his wife's mind between eating and guilt. Yet, after this description of the good bill of fare at the inn at Holford, he writes:

it was with the greatest difficulty that she could be persuaded to eat; she certainly suffered from various delusions, for instance that people laughed at her.

It is Leonard again who insists at very great length later in his autobiography that people did, empirically and as a matter of fact, laugh at his wife, and yet he asserts that her belief that people were laughing at her was a 'delusion'. The proximity of the sentence, 'it was with the greatest difficulty that she could be persuaded to eat', to his own Gargantuan description of the bill of fare at the Plough Inn is striking. Nor does he flinch at writing, at the end of that same paragraph:

Things grew steadily worse and it became impossible to get Virginia to eat or to try to rest – the only two things which might have done her good. After a few days both Ka and I agreed that it was not safe to go on at Holford and that I must, somehow or other, induce Virginia to come up to London and see a doctor.

(p. 154)

It seems fairly clear that on this occasion it was the issue of food which caused Virginia's distress to be increased rather than decreased. The issue was couched in terms of food because neither Leonard nor Virginia had the power to express the fact that what was really at issue, in that inn, was their failed honeymoon and their bodiless love. Food is thus a signifier in the unconscious discourse of both of them – she insisting she does not want it, he insisting she does – a double and symmetric inversion of the real issues. The sheer disproportion between the amount of food Virginia thought she needed, and the amount of food Leonard and Sir George Savage thought was good for her, was enough to increase the violence of the nervous condition, and in a sense, she was driven back into the hands of Savage by the very 'cure' he had prescribed.

Quentin Bell, who is obviously referring to some private evidence, comments on the stay at Holford:

But the pressures on Virginia did not relax: she thought people were laughing at her; she was the cause of everyone's troubles; she felt overwhelmed with a sense of guilt for which she should be punished. She became convinced that her body was in some way monstrous, the sordid mouth and sordid belly demanding food – repulsive matter which

must then be excreted in a disgusting fashion; the only course was to
refuse to eat.

(Bell II p. 15)

These interpretations may be based upon diaries or other private
material to which the public has no access. But there must have
been a fight about food at Holford. Bell gives a Swiftian reason for
her refusal: the sordidness of the mouth, the repulsiveness of the
matter and the disgustingness of the excretion. These layers of
symbolism were doubtless also present to her vision of things –
like Swift, she too may have despaired of a rational animal who
was so rudely incarnate. But whatever the most basic level of her
fear of eating, it seems obvious that a rest cure which depended
for its efficacy upon ever greater amounts of food was running
directly contrary to the psychic determinants of the problem.

CHAPTER 9

Virginia's own view
negated and disconfirmed

I went to Virginia and said that I thought we should not go on any longer in Holford; that I thought she was ill and so did her doctor and we were convinced that if she ate well and tried to rest she would soon recover as she had several times before; that she was convinced that she was not ill, that her condition was due to her own faults, and that eating and resting made her worse. I suggested that we should return to London at once, go to another doctor – any doctor whom she should choose; she should put her case to him and I would put mine; if he said that she was not ill, I would accept his verdict and would not worry her again about eating or resting or going to a nursing home; but if he said she was ill, then she would accept his verdict and undergo what treatment he might pre-scribe.

(Beginning Again pp. 154–5)

With these conditions agreed, they returned to London by train.

Next day we went to see Head in the afternoon. I gave my account of what had happened and Virginia gave hers. He told her that she was completely mistaken about her own condition; she was ill, ill like a person who had a cold or typhoid fever; but if she took his advice and did what he prescribed, her symptoms would go and she would be quite well again, able to think and write and read; she must go to a nursing home and stay in bed for a few weeks, resting and eating.

(p. 156)

Leonard puts his view of what is wrong first. Then Virginia puts hers. Arbitrating like a judge who is forced to decide which of the two appellants is to have favourable judgement, Head dis-confirms Virginia in one sweeping analogy so crude that it shocks even today. In view of the sheer crudity of his view, the fact that he dared to make it is perhaps less surprising. But in one stroke he knocked away Virginia's precarious hold on the situation. For (she must have felt, very strongly) if *she* did not know what was wrong with her, who did? And here is Head telling her that she does *not* know what is wrong with her.

The word and concept 'ill' is being used by Leonard also in just the same naïve sense in which Head himself uses it – 'she was ill, ill like a person who had a cold or typhoid fever'. There is no awareness in Leonard that no one word like 'ill' will even remotely do justice to the complexity of the situation.

Even more menacing than this naïveté, and a direct result of it, is the question of the outcome of the dispute between Leonard and Virginia as to whether or not she is 'ill'. She avers she is *not* 'ill'. It is Leonard's firm conviction that she *is* 'ill'. There is, so to say, a struggle of *wills* as to which of them is 'right'. To be disconfirmed in her own verdict in her own mind will mean for Virginia that she has to 'undergo' the treatment the new 'mental specialist' will prescribe. Note the overtones of 'undergo' – Leonard is not unaware of the horrors of these 'rest' treatments, but he does not allow them to modify his decision. Why on earth Leonard should have wanted to prevail against his wife on this matter is beyond comprehension – surely a subtler way would have been to fall in with his wife's hypothesis that she was not 'ill' and to have tried to work it out together? But no, Leonard believes that mental illness is like having a broken leg, and that a specialist can say in one word whether or not it is broken.

So, as they come to London to see Head, they are locked in a battle of wills. Virginia is determined that, when she puts her side of the story to Head, she will affirm that she is not 'ill', only that 'her condition was due to her own faults and that eating and resting made her worse'. But Leonard was determined that Head should decide that his wife was 'ill'. And so Head's agreement with Leonard about Virginia's own view of her own inner state falls like a double judgement on her, utterly destroying her own sense of rightness, her own sense of identity.

I think it is inevitable that we should read those passages in *Mrs Dalloway*, between the 'ill' Septimus Smith and the successful Harley Street practitioner Sir William Bradshaw, as a direct reconstruction of certain passages of the conversation which took place on the afternoon of the 9 September 1913. Without denying that *Mrs Dalloway* is a work of fiction written eight to ten years after that interview, it is possible, and I think reasonable, to deduce from that fictional account, an impression of what transpired that afternoon. The word 'ill' is what makes this virtually a certainty:

'We have had our little talk,' said Sir William.

'He says you are very, very ill,' Rezia cried.

'We have been arranging that you should go into a home,' said Sir William.

'One of Holmes's homes?' sneered Septimus . . .

'One of *my* homes, Mr. Warren Smith,' he said, 'where we will teach you to rest.'

And there was just one thing more.

He was quite certain that when Mr. Warren Smith was well he was the last man in the world to frighten his wife. But he had talked of killing himself.

'We all have our moments of depression,' said Sir William.

Once you fall, Septimus repeated to himself, human nature is on you. Holmes and Bradshaw are on you. They scour the desert. They fly screaming into the wilderness. The rack and the thumbscrew are applied. Human nature is remorseless.

(p. 108)

If we assume, which seems reasonable, that some such train of thought as that contained in the last paragraph was running through Virginia's own mind through that interview with Head and Leonard, when they were insisting that she was 'ill' and must go into a home, and when she was having her own view 'remorselessly' disconfirmed, then it is not surprising that, immediately upon returning home from that interview with Head, Virginia swallowed 'a very large dose' of veronal tablets.

It was only by immediate emergency action that her life was saved. Septimus 'had talked of killing himself'. We know from Leonard's account that Virginia had spoken of killing herself at Holford, and that the journey by train back to London was a constant suspense in case Virginia should throw herself out of the train door, in spite of Leonard's and Ka's presence. Thus this threat of 'killing herself' must have been made much of in the interview of 9 September. The legal implications of this were that a person was considered thereafter unfit to run his own life and was deprived of his freedom. The novel makes overt reference to this when Sir William proposes 'rest' in a 'home'. Within the context of the novel, we know why Septimus had talked of killing himself: the memories of war are too terrifying, and he is haunted by what he had seen. It is given in the novel as perfectly reasonable that anyone who had seen what Septimus had seen should find a return to 'normal' conditions intensely difficult. No doubt, had he not 'talked of killing himself', he would have been offered a choice of whether he wanted to go and 'rest' in a 'home' or not. But having talked in this extravagant way, no such choice was offered to him.

Virginia, through the figure of Septimus Smith in *Mrs Dalloway*, was using an 'objective correlative' to her own situation. Just as she could not externalise the horror of her incarceration in her marriage, Smith cannot externalise the horror of being unable to feel. What is in common between Virginia's desperation and the fictional character Septimus Smith's desperation is precisely this inability to feel, which had haunted *The Voyage Out* and *Night and Day*. That is what is in question, that is what cannot be verbalised or externalised, and that is why Virginia hits on the idea of particularly violent war experience leading to numbness of feeling as an 'objective correlative' to her own mute state. Not only could Virginia not feel, but she could not say that she could not feel. Add to that a threat of suicide, and both medicine and the law were against her. So, both in the case of Virginia Woolf, and of her fictional *persona* Septimus Smith, the real drama takes place as someone in a state of trauma desperately tries to right himself, coping valiantly but alone with a reality for which there are no words, and which civilised society on the whole wishes officially to ignore.

Virginia's mental condition was not so much 'ill' as anguished. This is what psychiatry could not afford to recognise. Her condition was one of metaphysical or existential despair, since the kind of anguish she was going through had silence for its form. Her condition was very like that of the 'Shadowgraphs' whom Kierkegaard describes in *Either/Or*, whose outer silence is in exact proportion to their inner suffering. She needed subtle treatment, she needed existential, even theological, aid. What she did not need was rest, or food, or sequestration from the world.

The immediate result of not being listened to was a desperate attempt upon her own life. Leonard recounts the events as follows:

I was with Savage at 6.30 when I got a telephone message from Ka to say that Virginia had fallen into a deep sleep. I hurried back to Brunswick Square and found that Virginia was lying on her bed breathing heavily and unconscious. She had taken the veronal tablets from my box and swallowed a very large dose. I telephoned to Head and he came, bringing a nurse . . . Head, Geoffrey, and the nurse were hard at work until nearly 1 o'clock in the morning. Head returned at 9 next morning (Wednesday) and said that Virginia was practically out of danger. She did not recover consciousness until the Thursday morning.

(*Beginning Again* pp. 156–7)

Now the gloves are off. Obviously Virginia *is* 'ill'. Why? Because she tried (apparently without motive, or at least for no reason that anyone was prepared to see) to kill herself. Once she had made that attempt she had made the enforced 'rest' and sequestration a legal necessity, an inevitability. She has also confirmed Leonard in his own worst fears. His wife is indeed very 'ill'. He can see no reason why this particular day should have produced a suicide attempt.

We have to note why Leonard was out of the house when it happened. He was embarrassed that they had consulted a new psychiatrist (Head) without telling the old one (Savage) so he went off to explain matters. He felt that it was more important to carry out this belated act of courtesy than to sit with his wife after an interview which (we clearly see from the result) must have driven her to despair:

We returned to Brunswick Square and then a catastrophe happened. Vanessa came and talked to Virginia, who seemed to become more cheerful. Savage had not known that we were seeing Head and a rather awkward situation had arisen about that. Head asked me to see Savage and to explain how it had come about that I had brought Virginia to see him; he wanted me to arrange for him to have a consultation with Savage next day. I went off to Savage, leaving Ka with Virginia.'

(*Beginning Again* p. 156)

It must have seemed to Virginia that Leonard was part of that professional league which had ganged up against her, and which was determined to insist that she was 'ill' until she actually became so. It is difficult to understand a situation in which a husband can be so genuinely unaware of what a medical opinion has cost a wife, that he could actually leave her alone (having 'won his case', so to speak, against his wife, in alliance with Head), and go straight out of the front door again to confer with another 'mental specialist'.

It must have seemed to Virginia that Leonard was hand in glove with all the people she most feared and detested, the people who wanted to affirm that she was 'ill'. There is no obscurity about why she took the veronal. She had been disconfirmed in her assessment of her own mental condition, Leonard had 'won' against her, the forfeit was going to be that 'she would accept his verdict and undergo what treatment he might prescribe'. Terrified, deserted, with everyone against her, she felt it was too much. As she was later to express it through Septimus Smith: 'Once you fall . . . human nature is remorseless.'

The matter is described ten years later in *Mrs Dalloway*. Virginia has set forth an exact analogy to her own case in presenting the dilemma of Septimus Smith. Just as Virginia had asserted that she was not 'ill' and yet had had her judgment disconfirmed by the 'mental specialist', so Septimus Smith (although he is quite aware that he is far from well and acknowledges that he needs help of some kind) has his own view of the matter disconfirmed by the breezy Dr Holmes, who insists that 'there was nothing whatever the matter with him' and that he is *not* therefore 'ill'. When Sir William Bradshaw, however, insists that Septimus *is* 'ill', Septimus revolts (silently, for he is not allowed to express his view) against the judgment, perceiving that Sir William has understood nothing of what was really troubling him. Whichever way you choose to argue it (the fictional case spells out the implications of the real life interview), the experts are there primarily to disconfirm your own view of what is wrong with you:

Wouldn't it be better to do something instead of lying in bed? For he had had forty years' experience behind him; and Septimus could take Dr. Holmes's word for it – there was nothing whatever the matter with him.

And next time Dr. Holmes came, he hoped to find Smith out of bed and not making that charming little lady his wife anxious about him.

Human nature, in short, was on him – the repulsive brute, with the blood-red nostrils. Holmes was on him. Dr. Holmes came quite regularly every day. Once you stumble, Septimus wrote on the back of a postcard, human nature is in you. Holmes is on you. Their only chance was to escape, without letting Holmes know; to Italy – anywhere, anywhere, away from Dr. Holmes.

(Mrs Dalloway p. 102)

In the novel, the equivalences are completely consistent, only the sexes of the married pairs being inverted for obvious reasons:

Virginia (who denies she is 'ill')	= Septimus Warren Smith (who 'could not feel' and knows that he is not well but certainly does not concur either with Holmes's view that 'there is nothing whatever the matter with him' nor with Bradshaw's view that he is 'very ill')
Leonard (who asserts his wife is 'ill')	= Rezia Warren Smith (who is terrified by the behaviour of her husband: 'Her husband, she said, was mad' (*Mrs Dalloway* p. 104))
Sir Henry Head (who asserts Virginia is 'ill')	= Sir William Bradshaw (who asserts Septimus Smith is 'very ill')
Diagnosis ('nursing home, resting and eating')	= Diagnosis ('one of *my* homes . . . where we will teach you to rest')

The only difference is that whereas in real life it was Virginia herself who protested she was not 'ill' against the doctors, in the novel it is the bluff Holmes who asserts this of Septimus: only to have his judgment contemptuously dismissed by the Harley Street specialist. But common both to the 'real life' and the fictional cases was this: the *patient's own view* of what was wrong was disconfirmed by 'experts' and *did not count*. Terror sets in, thoughts of suicide began to occur. In the novel Septimus begins to plan suicide *as a direct result* of Holmes's visit (p. 103). And on that historic afternoon of 9 September 1913, Virginia seized the bottle of veronal and swallowed what she doubtless expected to be a fatal dose.

Not only was Virginia's view of herself disconfirmed, and the description 'ill' fixed round her neck for ever, but there was an even more serious problem. She had attempted suicide.

In those days, if anyone was in Virginia's mental state, dangerously suicidal, it was customary to certify them. The procedure took place before a magistrate who, on a doctor's certificate, made an order for the reception and detention of the person either in an asylum or in a nursing home authorised to take certified patients. Doctors were naturally unwilling to take the risk of leaving a suicidal patient uncertified in a private house.

(Beginning Again p. 158)

In 1913, to have offered to commit suicide, or to threaten it, was regarded as virtually a criminal act, after which the patient's own view of his own destiny could no longer be consulted. He or she became the moral equivalent of a prisoner. Decisions would now be taken on behalf of such people by 'competent authorities'. The thought of Virginia being certified and sent by a magistrate to an asylum for the insane was too much for Leonard to bear. He went to look at some asylums and was horrified. He therefore had to bargain with the psychiatric establishment:

I told the doctors that I was prepared to do anything required by them if they would agree to her not being certified. They agreed not to certify her, provided I could arrange for her to go into the country accompanied by me and two (at one time four) nurses.

(Beginning Again p. 158)

The situation, of sudden physical imprisonment by the machinery of the law, was obviously terrifying not only to Leonard but also to Virginia. They both suddenly realised that they were running the risk of being separated for good. The moment is caught with all its anxiety in *Mrs Dalloway*, when Septimus Smith's wife, Rezia, pleads (in vain) for her husband's reprieve:

Her husband was very seriously ill, Sir William said. Did he threaten to kill himself?

Oh, he did, she cried. But he did not mean it, she said. Of course not. It was merely a question of rest, said Sir William; of rest, rest, rest; a long rest in bed. There was a delightful home down in the country where her husband would be perfectly looked after. Away from her? she asked. Unfortunately, yes; the people we care for most are not good for us when we are ill.

(p. 107)

At this critical moment, the solution appeared in the form of a *deus ex machina*: 'George Duckworth came to our rescue and offered to lend me his country house, Dalingridge Place. George was Virginia's half-brother . . . '

Given that part of the collapse of 1913 must have been caused by sexual molestation by George Duckworth, this decision to send Virginia to 'rest' under his roof at this lowest moment of her resistance can only reinforce the virtual certainty that Leonard was ignorant of George Duckworth's rôle in his wife's past. Leonard writes a page or two about his good nature and his distinguished social status, and adds (with horrifying effect for those who know the reality) that 'He was an extremely kind man and, I think, very fond of Vanessa and Virginia':

He was a man of the world or at any rate what I think a man of the world in excelsis should be. As a young man he was, it was said, an Adonis worshipped by all the great and non-great ladies. He was still terribly good looking at the age of 45. A very good cricketer, Eton and Trinity College, Cambridge; he knew everyone who mattered . . .

(*Beginning Again* p. 159)

When Leonard wrote these words, decades after the events of 1913, he must still have been totally unaware of the furies which tormented his wife at the thought of George Duckworth.She, obviously, could not summon the courage to tell him about the matter. So she submitted to being taken to Dalingridge Place, rather than to a lunatic asylum.

It is interesting too, if we are concerned to measure the distance between the way that Leonard perceives the events and characters of 1913 and the way that Virginia was perceiving them, to observe the major difference between her own and Leonard's assessment of the physical appearance of George Duckworth. From the autobiographical accounts in *Moments of Being*, we know that Virginia did not at all concur with Leonard's view of him as a paragon of male beauty.

Thus it was that, immediately after the disconfirming inter-

view with Dr Head, and after her stomach had been pumped
following the veronal attempt, she was taken down to George
Duckworth's country house to recover. No wonder the birds
began to sing in Greek again!

The point is that her insanity was in her premises, in her beliefs. She
believed, for instance, that she was not ill, that her symptoms were due
to her own 'faults'; she believed that she was hearing voices when the
voices were her own imaginings; she heard the birds outside her window talking Greek; she believed that the doctors and nurses were in
conspiracy against her. These beliefs were insane because they were in
fact contradicted by reality.

(*Beginning Again* p. 164)

Given what we now know, from the autobiographical writings in
Moments of Being about George's connection with Greek, this
passage has a terrible irony about it. The 'reality' being questioned here is no longer Virginia's, but Leonard's. The connections between the birds singing in Greek and Dalingridge Place
are now easy for us to make. But Leonard obviously did not know
what awful memories of sexual molestation he was reviving. At
Dalingridge Place, disconfirmed, branded as 'ill' by Head and
'insane' against her own protestations, deprived of her freedom
to decide her own destiny, saved from the humiliation and the
lunatic asylum only by a kindness on the part of the doctors,
Virginia is forced to lie and rest in George Duckworth's bed, in
George Duckworth's house. She is forced to eat great quantities
of food, against her will. There are four nurses, two by day and
two by night. And, to cap it all, she is unable to tell Leonard why
this particular bed is insufferable for her: she dare not. Her
non-communication with him is complete on this matter. He
does not even suspect what he is putting his wife through, and
insists on the full 'cure' of food, administered by nurses. 'These
beliefs were insane because they were in fact contradicted by
reality.' The 'reality' for Virginia was to be lying in George Duckworth's bed and in his house, and unable to speak a word about
it, even to Leonard.

But he remembered. Bradshaw said, 'The people we are most fond of
are not good for us when we are ill.' Bradshaw said he must be taught to
rest. Bradshaw said they must be separated.

'Must', 'must', why 'must'? What power had Bradshaw over him? 'What right has Bradshaw to say "must" to me?' he demanded.

'It is because you talked of killing yourself,' said Rezia. (Mercifully, she could now say anything to Septimus.)

So he was in their power! Holmes and Bradshaw were on him! The brute with the red nostrils was snuffing into every secret place! 'Must' it could say! . . .

Even if they took him, she said, she would go with him. They could not separate them against their wills, she said . . .

Septimus could hear her talking to Holmes on the staircase.

'My dear lady, I have come as a friend, ' Holmes was saying.

'No. I will not allow you to see my husband,' she said.

He could see her, like a little hen, with her wings spread barring his passage. But Holmes persevered.

'My dear lady, allow me . . . ' Holmes said, putting her aside (Holmes was a powerfully built man).

Holmes was coming upstairs. Holmes would burst open the door. Homes would say, 'In a funk, eh?' . . .

(Mrs Dalloway pp. 162–4)

How many times must not Virginia herself have been treated like that? A slight woman can easily be 'put aside' by 'a powerfully built man'. Subjective opposition is of no avail. The medical machine will move on regardless. Wives will be barred, put aside, left behind. The ambulance will take the man, struggling, straitjacketed, against his will, to a home, where he will be submitted to enforced rest, enforced feeding, without anyone near and dear. If anything is needed to knock an unstable mental balance into actual confusion, this is the sort of treatment to achieve it. Violence, action carried out against the express will of the patient, and in total isolation from all that he knows and loves – what can one expect but 'violence' during some phases of the 'treatment'? But Virginia was 'insane', 'ill'. It was useless for her to protest that she was not. No appeal is allowed. Holmes is a powerfully built man.

CHAPTER 10

'Taboo against eating — guilt'

And so Virginia was sent down to George Duckworth's country residence, Dalingridge Place, for a rest cure which should be accompanied by a large and nourishing amount of food.

From Leonard's account of this period three things stand out clearly. Virginia deeply resented being there. Virginia resented and fought against the enforced diet. Virginia spoke in veiled terms about guilt which she connected with eating. From Leonard's own point of view we learn that the entire episode was most distressing, that Virginia was violent on occasion, and that she could argue most persuasively about why she should not be at Dalingridge and why the treatment was wrong because her present unhappiness was due to her own faults. Leonard professes to see no sense in any of these claims, and spends a good deal of his time in a quasi-philosophical exposition about how infuriatingly sane and consequent are the arguments of the insane.

Let us take the question of food first. Leonard's account is as follows:

In the first weeks at Dalingridge the most difficult and distressing problem was to get Virginia to eat. If left to herself, she would have eaten nothing at all and would have gradually starved to death. Here again her psychology and behaviour were only a violent exaggeration of what they were when she was well and sane. When she was well, she was essentially a happy and gay person; she enjoyed the ordinary things of everyday life, and among them food and drink. Yet there was always something strange, something slightly irrational in her attitude towards food. It was extraordinarily difficult ever to get her to eat enough to keep her strong and well. Superficially I suppose it might have been said that she had a (quite unnecessary) fear of becoming fat; but there was something deeper than that, at the back of her mind or in the pit of her stomach a taboo against eating. Pervading her insanity generally there was always a sense of some guilt, the origin and exact nature of which I could never discover; but it was attached in some peculiar way particularly to food and eating. In the early acute, suicidal stage of the depression, she would sit for hours overwhelmed with hopeless melancholia, silent, making no response to anything said to her. When the time for a meal came, she would pay no attention whatsoever to the plate of food put before her and, if the nurses tried to get her to eat something, she became enraged. I could usually induce her to eat a certain amount, but it was a terrible process. Every meal took an hour or two; I had to sit by her side, put a spoon or fork in her hand, and every now and again ask her very quietly to eat and at the same time touch her arm or hand. Every five minutes or so she might automatically eat a spoonful.

(*Beginning Again* pp. 162–3)

Leonard consistently and insistently professes himself unable to guess or understand why his wife should have associated eating with 'a sense of some guilt'. Yet we have the testimony of Leonard's own biography, and in the very same volume, to the effect that Virginia was perceived in public space, in the street, in Lewes High Street, as odd, peculiar, remarkable and, in particular, laughable.

During our life together there was one fantastic recurring example of this fact which again and again I noted with astonishment. If you walk in the streets of London or any other large European city, you will see every now and then persons, particularly women, who in the eye of God must appear indescribably ridiculous. There will be fat or lean, middle aged or elderly, women dressed up in some exaggeration of the exaggerated contemporary fashion which could in fact only – and that doubtfully – be carried off by some rare and lovely young thing. They are ludicrous and laughable caricatures of female charm. Virginia, on the other hand, by any standard of taste was a very beautiful woman and many people would have applied to her the rather dubious description 'distinguished looking'; she had, too, I think, a flair for beautiful, if individual, dresses. Yet to the crowd in the street there was something in her appearance which struck them as strange and laughable. I am one of those people who merge in a crowd anywhere. Even in a foreign town, though I am not dressed exactly like the native inhabitants, no one notices and I pass – in appearance – for a Spaniard in Barcelona or a Swede in Stockhom. But in Barcelona and in Stockholm nine out of ten people would stare or stop and stare at Virginia.

(*Beginning Again* pp. 28–9)

This is the first piece of evidence which Leonard gives us about the *degree* to which Virginia attracted attention. To claim that 'nine out of ten' people would 'stare or stop and stare' at his wife, is obviously meant seriously. How seriously are we to take it?

And not only in foreign towns; they would stop and stare and nudge one another – 'look at her' – even in England, in Piccadilly or Lewes High Street, where almost anyone is allowed to pass unnoticed.

(p. 29)

The degree to which she attracted attention then, in an open public space, whether English or foreign, was so marked that people actually nudged each other and drew each other's attention to her as she passed. If one accepts Leonard's evidence as literally true, then, and it is obviously literally that he intends it, we have to assume that walking in public must for her have been a kind of nightmare of continual exposure, a sense of continually being looked at. 'They did not merely stop and stare and nudge one another; there was something in Virginia which they found ridiculous' (p. 29). Leonard obviously is not trying to be facetious, or ironic.

'Some monstrous female caricature, who was accepted as ordinary by the crowd, would go into fits of laughter at the sight of Virginia.' Does he mean this literally? That people would burst into 'fits of laughter' at the mere sight of his wife? It is an amazing thing to state categorically, as he does here.

I always found it difficult to understand exactly what the cause of this laughter was. It was only partly that her dress was never quite the same as other people's. It was partly, I think, because there was something strange and disquieting, and therefore to many people ridiculous, in her appearance, in the way she walked – she seemed so often to be 'thinking of something else', to be moving with a slightly shuffling movement along the streets in the shadow of a dream. The hags and harridans and bright young things could not restrain their laughter or their giggles.

(p. 29)

This is extraordinary testimony from a man who complied with psychiatric advice to feed his wife so that a person 'who went in weighing seven stone six comes out weighing twelve'. Leonard must surely have been aware that his wife had an almost unbearably vivid impression of the effect she had on other people, out there in public space. Why did he not develop his reflection to the point of asking himself how his wife regarded her actual weight and figure? 'The cynosure of neighbouring eyes' she certainly was. She knew that; he knew it; and he knew that she knew it. Did he never ask himself why she attached feelings of 'guilt' and 'fault' to food? What her own feelings about this incipient laughter were we shall gather in a moment.

This laughter of the street distressed her; she had an almost morbid horror of being looked at and still more of being photographed – which is the reason why there are very few photographs of her in which she looks her natural self, the real everyday self which one saw in her face in ordinary life from hour to hour. A curious example of this nervous misery which she suffered from being looked at occurred when Stephen Tomlin (Tommy, as he was always called) sculpted the bust of her now in the National Portrait Gallery.

(p. 30)

It is part of the continual mystery of Leonard's account of his wife, that he should never connect her fear of scrutiny, her consciousness of ridicule, with her mistrust of food. Virginia's novels are scattered with references to how painful she found actual scrutiny.

With the greatest reluctance she was eventually induced by him to sit for him. The object of each sitting was naturally to look at her, which Tommy did with prolonged intensity. It was a kind of Chinese torture to her.

Leonard goes on to relate the 'aura' of Virginia to her genius:

I was saying that in her day to day, everyday life she thought and talked and acted, to a great extent, as other people do, though there was always this element or aura in her which was strange and disquieting to ordinary people so that in self-defence, in order to reassure themselves, they giggled or roared with laughter. I think this element was closely connected with the streak in her which I call genius.

(p. 30)

It seems to me in every way significant of the tragedy of this embodied misalliance, that Leonard should insist to the end on being baffled by his own evidence, and come to the conclusion that Dryden was right when he wrote:

Great wits are sure to madness near allied,
And thin partitions do their bounds divide.

The judgement, in its curiously deliberate (self-imposed) insensitivity, does form a part of the larger picture which Leonard entertained of his wife – the one he wrote out in *The Wise Virgins*. In his autobiography he writes several times, and obviously believed, that his wife was 'insane'. If he genuinely believed that she was from time to time actually 'insane', then his acknowledgment of the 'missing half' in Dryden's couplet, 'genius', fits naturally into the picture. Part 'insane', part 'genius', such was undoubtedly Leonard's view of his wife.

Now it seems perverse in Leonard to be able to write all this about his wife's physical appearance at pages 28–30 of *Beginning Again*, and then to insist that he can attribute no meaning whatsoever to the taboo against eating in Virginia's mind. 'Pervading her insanity generally there was always a sense of some guilt, the origin and exact nature of which I could never discover; but it was attached in some peculiar way particularly to food and eating.' In view of Leonard's own account of his wife in the street, this seems deliberate self-deception. Leonard did not fail to understand the connection; but he decided that he would not see the connection.

This was doubtless because he had a simple belief in the régime handed out by Henry Head. If Head said Virginia should eat, and Head was 'a man at the top of his profession', then Virginia had to eat. Her constant refusal of food became a mere irritant.

Leonard tells us that at Dalingridge there were four nurses, 'two on duty in the day, and two at night. For some time Virginia was extremely violent with the nurses, but after about a month she became slightly better and it was possible to have only two nurses' (*Beginning Again* p. 164).

Was there absolutely no reason for Virginia's violence to the nurses? Was absolutely no violence offered to Virginia? There is in Leonard's account a distinct suggestion that the most difficult part of the rest cure was in getting Virginia to eat, as well as a suggestion to the effect that a recalcitrant patient will have to be made to eat. I am very much afraid that Leonard, in a misled belief that Virginia needed a great deal of food, however great her own repulsion for it, allowed a considerable degree of coercion to be brought to bear upon her. Virginia may not actually have been

force fed, but the two nurses' attempts to get Virginia to eat may
have been fairly powerful ones, even if, as appears also from
Leonard's account, these attempts were mostly unsuccessful in
the end. But the situation in which two nurses take it upon themselves to get a patient to eat is itself potentially violent if the
patient violently resents their intrusion. And two nurses is a lot at
any one time – Virginia was not strong, she was slightly built.
Leonard writes that 'she became enraged'. When? 'When the time
for a meal came, she would pay no attention whatsoever to the
plate of food put before her and, if the nurses tried to get her to eat
something, she became enraged.' It all depends, I suppose, on
how hard the nurses tried. If they really put their backs into it,
there may well have been violence, but it would be quite difficult
to say from which side the violence was coming. However that
may be, the nurses must usually have failed in their object, for it
clearly transpires in Leonard's account that the only person who
could successfully get her to eat was himself, and this took very
long periods of time as well as the creation of an almost total
abstraction in the patient:

I could usually induce her to eat a certain amount, but it was a terrible
process. Every meal took an hour or two; I had to sit by her side, put a
spoon or fork in her hand, and every now and again ask her very quietly
to eat and at the same time touch her arm or hand. Every five minutes or
so she might automatically eat a spoonful.
　　This excruciating business of food, among other things, taught me a
lesson about insanity which I found very difficult to learn – it is useless to
argue with an insane person. What tends to break one down, to reduce
one to gibbering despair when one is dealing with mental illness, is the
terrible sanity of the insane.

　　　　　　　　　　　　　　　　　　(*Beginning Again* pp. 163–4)

What Leonard is obviously referring to here is the logical consistency of the insane: he goes on to list some of the factors of
delusion in her mind which she irritatingly and doggedly goes on
repeating, even though 'These beliefs were insane because they
were in fact contradicted by reality.' One of these factors of
'insanity' in his wife, one which must have reduced Leonard to
'gibbering despair', is the belief that food was the one thing she
did not need. Her 'terrible sanity' consisted in always arguing
from her own premises and not Leonard's and Head's.

But Virginia has given, in *Mrs Dalloway*, a literal description of the reason why she hated food so much. She could not have been more explicit:

To his patients he gave three-quarters of an hour; and if in this exacting science which has to do with what, after all, we know nothing about – the nervous system, the human brain – a doctor loses his sense of proportion, as a doctor he fails. Health we must have; and health is proportion; so that when a man comes into your room and says he is Christ (a common delusion), and has a message, as they mostly have, and threatens, as they often do, to kill himself, you invoke proportion; order rest in bed; rest in solitude; silence and rest; rest without books, without messages; six months' rest; until a man who went in weighing seven stone six comes out weighing twelve.

(pp. 109–10)

Surely it is impossible to deny that this is a direct comment upon the 'cure' meted out to her by Dr Head in 1913? It gives us the direct clue as to why Virginia hated and feared food so much, and milk: the rest cure added half her normal weight again.

The 'man' who is submitted to rest and feeding treatment goes in weighing seven stone six. What is grotesque is that 'he' can come out after treatment weighing twelve stone. But this is the very weight Virginia herself reached after her 'cure' of 1913–15. In October 1915 she wrote to Lytton Strachey: 'I am really all right again, and weigh 12 stone! – three more than I've ever had, and the consequence is I can hardly toil uphill' (Bell ii, 29).

Let us assume that Virginia's weight in 1913 lay somewhere between the fictional seven stone six in *Mrs Dalloway* and the implied previous maximum of nine stone in the letter to Strachey. Let us assume that it was just under nine stone. Then the figure of 'twelve stone', which would represent for Virginia a quite unprecedented maximum weight, must have had a certain malign significance for her personally. It is an all-time record, a quite unnatural burden: she can 'hardly toil uphill'.

The figures thrown out in *Mrs Dalloway* as if at random ('until a man who went in weighing seven stone six comes out weighing twelve') have a certain deliberateness, a certain specific, chosen quality, which gives to them a resonance of authenticity. It was no surprise to find, in a recent account of the marriage of the Woolfs, that the figures which are given in the novel are very close to the weight of Virginia before, and very close indeed after, her enforced convalescence at Dalingridge.

In George Spater's and Ian Parsons's book *A Marriage of True Minds*, there is a photograph of Leonard's diary record of Virginia's weight over the period 1914–15. Opposite it is a note of the authors which reads as follows:

On September 30, 1913, three weeks after her suicide attempt, Virginia weighed 8 stone 7 pounds. Leonard's tabulation shows that she had gained more than a stone by January 13, 1914, and put on another three stone by the end of 1915 – a gain of roughly 60 pounds in a little more than two years.

(p. 73)

Opposite the page from Leonard's journal, there is a photograph of Virginia at her new weight after the cure. It is obviously related to 'toiling uphill' since Virginia is in walking clothes, with hat, stick, overcoat and scarf, standing by a country wall. The note to it reads:

Virginia, still weighing over 12 stone, went to Cornwall in 1916 with Leonard and Margaret Llewelyn Davies. Years later she wrote, 'unless I weigh 9½ stones I hear voices and see visions and can neither write nor sleep'.

(p. 73)

A little earlier in their account, Spater and Parsons write:

Leonard carefully watched what Virginia ate and weighed her regularly, entering the results in his diary. Between October 1, 1913 and October 14, 1915 her weight increased from 8 stone 7 pounds to 12 stone 7 pounds – a gain of nearly 50 per cent! Photographs taken of Virginia about the time she reached this peak show her as surprisingly plump. After her recovery in 1915 her weight was allowed to fall to the more normal level of something over 9 stone.

(p. 69)

If indeed Virginia's traditionally recognised and acknowledged 'more normal level' was indeed 'something over 9 stone', one wonders why it was conceived necessary to push her up to a weight she had never had before, twelve stone seven pounds, which would have been in her case a positively grotesque exaggeration of anything she could carry. For the feeding which began at Dalingridge was of course continued after she left George's country house on 18 November 1913. Spater and Parsons tell us that Virginia weighed eight stone seven pounds on 30 September, and we know from Leonard's diary page reproduced in their book that on 13 January 1914 she weighed nine stone nine pounds. That is to say that Virginia put on sixteen pounds in those three months. That is a considerable increase in so short a time, and testifies to great assiduity in the feeding programme. It could hardly have been achieved with the odd five-minutely spoonful that Leonard represents himself as getting her sporadically to swallow, so the 'four nurses, two on duty in the day, and two at night' must have had some success after all.

But after leaving Dalingridge the régime must have been kept up, for we can see from Leonard's diary that Virginia maintained a weight of roughly nine and a half stone throughout 1914. Indeed, the régime must have been increased, because in April 1915 she passed the ten stone mark and kept spiralling upwards for another eight months. By October 1915 she is twelve stone seven pounds.

Even if her weight had been increased at Dalingridge and after to something between nine and a half and ten stone, quite enough would have been achieved. Virginia herself must have been aware of this, and been distracted when nobody would listen to her. Virginia could well see that there was no point in engaging on a feeding programme which was eventually to lead her to '12 stone 7 pounds – a gain of nearly 50 per cent!' as Spater and Parsons put it. And yet she had to acquiesce, since it was part of the convention of 'insanity' that the 'ill' person did not know what was in his or her best interests. The patient's own point of view was not of interest to anyone, a state of affairs which is very little changed in psychiatric practice even today.

Consequently, there would have been from Virginia's point of view, every reason to oppose the régime of food, since she herself did not believe in the cure, and knew full well in her own mind that food was not the answer to her problems. There was a case, at Dalingridge, for trying to raise her weight a little – say by a stone. But that would have been at best only a very small contribution to a cure. The Spater and Parsons book throws another shaft of light on Virginia's health during the summer of 1913:

For ten years following the suicide attempt, Leonard kept records of Virginia's menstrual periods, presumably because of the possibility that her mental disorders coincided with the occurrence of an unusually long interval between periods.*

*In 1913 there was a 98 day interval between periods (from August 6 to November 12) when Virginia's weight fell to its lowest recorded level. Virginia was then extremely ill, and under the care of four nurses. There is no indication that she was pregnant.

(p. 69)

Of course there is not.

The interesting aspect of that information is precisely that this ninety-eight day period began in August 1913 and only ended in November 1913, during which time Virginia succumbed, at the Plough Inn, Holford, to the worst attack of depression that she had had in her marriage. August has been described by Leonard, earlier in this book, mainly in terms of the wonderful and plentiful food that the Plough provided. Leonard told us that Virginia would not eat. But now we know that, not only was Virginia's weight somewhere in the region of eight and a half stone – much too low, dangerously low for her – but also that the stress and strain on her was so great that her menstrual period, which should have begun in the first week of September, did not in fact begin until November. And 9 September was the date of the fateful interview and the veronal attempt.

All the evidence seems to point to the conclusion that the stress and strain Virginia was suffering arose, not from grossly empirical causes like underweight, nor from mythical entities like 'madness' or 'insanity', but from precisely those psychological tensions engendered by the marriage. For this reason, Virginia could clearly see that no grossly empirical 'cure', like feeding and rest, would ever have any point of intersection with what was really troubling her. Her greatest anxiety must have been engendered by realising that no-one was going to listen to her point of view at any point, that she was the one person in this saga whose view did not count. No wonder she 'grew violent' with the nurses.

Leonard's insistence that he can make neither rhyme nor

reason out of Virginia's refusal of food at Dalingridge now clearly appears as a refusal, not a failure, of comprehension. The connection between food and fear, weight and ridicule, is only too glaringly obvious.

CHAPTER 11

'Conspiracy'

It must have seemed for all the world as if Leonard were indeed in a conspiracy against her. 'The point is', writes Leonard 'that her insanity was in her premises, in her beliefs'. Leonard then lists five cases in which Virginia's premises were mistaken. The fifth is as follows: 'she believed that the doctors and nurses were in conspiracy against her':

This excruciating business of food, among other things, taught me a lesson about insanity which I found very difficult to learn – it is useless to argue with an insane person. What tends to break one down, to reduce one to gibbering despair when one is dealing with mental illness, is the terrible sanity of the insane. In ordinary life, as her writings, and particularly her essays show, Virginia had an extraordinarily clear and logical mind; one of the most remarkable things about her was the rare combination of this strong intellect with a soaring imagination. There were moments or periods during her illness, particularly in the second excited stage, when she was what could be called 'raving mad' and her thoughts and speech became completely unco-ordinated, and she had no contact with reality. Except for these periods, she remained all through her illness, even when most insane, terribly sane in three-quarters of her mind. The point is that her insanity was in her premises, in her beliefs. She believed, for instance, that she was not ill, that her symptoms were due to her own 'faults'; she believed that she was hearing voices when the voices were her own imaginings; she heard the birds outside her window talking Greek; she believed that the doctors and nurses were in conspiracy against her. These beliefs were insane because they were in fact contradicted by reality. But given these beliefs as premises for conclusions and actions, all Virginia's actions and conclusions were logical and rational; and her power of arguing conclusively from false premises was terrific. It was therefore useless to attempt to argue with her: you could no more convince her that her premises were wrong than you can convince a man who believes he is Christ that he is mistaken. It was still more useless to argue with her about what you wanted her to do, e.g. eat her breakfast, because if her premises were true, she could prove and did prove conclusively to you that she ought not to eat her breakfast.

(*Beginning Again* pp. 163–4)

The extent of the sheer intellectual incompatibility evident in these lines between Leonard's way of looking at things and Virginia's, is frightening, even at this date, and must account for her feeling so hopelessly cut off, so conspired against. 'These beliefs were insane because they were in fact contradicted by reality' shows a complete refusal of the truths of the perspectival world, the world of which Virginia was to become the foremost literary exponent.

For Leonard never transfers himself imaginatively into his wife's own position in space. He refuses to allow even a possibility that Virginia's 'premises', as he calls them, might have their own kind of validity, a validity created by the position in space which Virginia occupied. He could not entertain even the remote suspicion that, seen from where Virginia found herself, the idea of 'conspiracy' was a very natural one, and one that had a lot to recommend it. Indeed, Leonard seems genuinely unaware that some of his acts must have looked conspiratorial to his wife. At Holford, when he asked Virginia which doctor she would agree to see, her offer to see Dr Head staggered him. 'It was to Head that I wanted her to go, but I had always anticipated insuperable difficulties to getting her agreement to consult him. She could not possibly have known that *I* had consulted him . . . ' (*Beginning Again* p. 155).

So Leonard refuses to allow even the possibility that conspiracy exists because it does not appear to him to exist. He takes no account of what might have appeared to his wife. Indeed, if one looks carefully down the list of 'premises' which were 'insane' in Leonard's eyes, it becomes clear that the only evidence Leonard can offer for his wife's 'insanity' is a list of points on which Virginia disagreed with *him*.

Leonard's list of 'insane' 'premises' is fascinating. It is so self-evident to Leonard the rationalist that his premises were correct and sane, and that Virginia's premises were incorrect and insane, that he systematically interprets disagreement with him as evidence of insanity as such.

It seems clear to me that with 'four nurses, two on duty in the day and two at night' it could very well have appeared to Virginia that there *was* a conspiracy against her, especially as she disagreed inwardly with the diagnosis of the 'mental specialist' that she was 'ill'. She did not believe that they were right to call her 'ill', 'insane' and so on. Nor could she have believed that the best way to get her well again was by enforced rest and overfeeding. She hated being made artificially inactive. She was cut off from her friends and the London life which she loved more than anything else in life, as the whole of *Mrs Dalloway* so repeatedly testifies. And yet Leonard asserts that Virginia's belief that she was the victim to a 'conspiracy' was 'insane' because it was 'in fact contradicted by reality'. But whose reality?[1]

It must have seemed to Virginia, in short, that she was the victim of an act of arbitrary force. The passion with which she recalls the powerlessness of the patient in front of the great 'mental specialist' is still only just in control when she comes to write this, ten years later:

There in the grey room, with the pictures on the wall, and the valuable furniture, under the ground-glass skylight, they learnt the extent of their transgressions; huddled up in arm-chairs, they watched him go through, for their benefit, a curious excercise with the arms, which he shot out, brought sharply back to his hip, to prove (if the patient was obstinate) that Sir William was master of his own actions, which the patient was not. There some weakly broke down; sobbed, submitted; others, inspired by Heaven knows what intemperate madness, called Sir William to his face a damnable humbug; questioned, even more impiously, life itself. Why live? they demanded. Sir William replied that life was good. Certainly Lady Bradshaw in ostrich feathers hung over the mantel-piece, and as for his income it was quite twelve thousand a year. But to us, they protested, life has given no such bounty. He acquiesced.

[1] The question is a philosophical one. Edmund Husserl gives it powerful statement in *The Crisis of European Sciences*, paras 47, 48 and 49. Restating the problem proposed by Protagoras, and never fully answered by Plato, Husserl proposes that our intentional construction of a world is a direct result of the horizon of the world we have, and that a shift in horizon-consciousness will give a distinct shift in what is taken to be true or false. The relation of horizon validities is one Husserl takes to be unsolved. But the debate between Leonard and Virginia is a stark illustration of the problems which arise when horizonal validities are ignored or forgotten.

They lacked a sense of proportion. And perhaps, after all, there is no
God? He shrugged his shoulders. In short, this living or not living is an
affair of our own? But there they were mistaken. Sir William had a friend
in Surrey where they taught, what Sir William frankly admitted was a
difficult art – a sense of proportion. There were, moreover, family affection; honour; courage; and a brilliant career. All of these had in Sir
William a resolute champion. If they failed, he had to support him police
and the good of society, which, he remarked very quietly, would take
care, down in Surrey, that these unsocial impulses, bred more than anything by the lack of good blood, were held in control. And then stole out
from her hiding-place and mounted her throne that Goddess whose lust
is to override opposition, to stamp indelibly in the sanctuaries of others
the image of herself. Naked, defenceless, the exhausted, the friendless
received the impress of Sir William's will. He swooped; he devoured.
He shut people up. It was this combination of decision and humanity
that endeared Sir William so greatly to the relations of his victims.

But Rezia Warren Smith cried, walking down Harley Street, that she
did not like that man.

(Mrs Dalloway pp. 112–13)

The tone here is only just under control. It testifies to the difficulty Virginia has in writing about a violence which she herself
had been submitted to, and which she still cannot quite come to
terms with or master. The violent use of words here recalls
violence done.

These beliefs were insane because they were in fact contradicted by
reality. But given these beliefs as premises for conclusions and actions,
all Virginia's actions and conclusions were logical and rational; and her
power of arguing conclusively from false premises was terrific. It was
therefore useless to attempt to argue with her: you could no more
convince her that her premises were wrong than you can convince a
man who believes he is Christ that he is mistaken.

(Beginning Again p. 164)

This particular argument of Leonard's, which he must have
regarded as a *reductio ad absurdum* which would shatter false
premises, obviously recurred during the conversations at Dalingridge, and Virginia includes it acidly in her own text of ten years
later. It must have struck her as being particularly unjust, for the
tone in which she writes is still imbued with bitter irony:

Worshipping proportion, Sir William not only prospered himself but
made England prosper, secluded her lunatics, forbade childbirth, penalised despair, made it impossible for the unfit to propagate their views

until they, too, shared his sense of proportion – his, if they were men, Lady Bradshaw's if they were women . . . so that not only did his colleagues respect him, his subordinates fear him, but the friends and relations of his patients felt for him the keenest gratitude for insisting that these prophetic Christs and Christesses, who prophesied the end of the world, or the advent of God, should drink milk in bed, as Sir William ordered; Sir William with his thirty years' experience of these kinds of cases, and his infallible instinct, this is madness, this sense; his sense of proportion.

(*Mrs Dalloway* p. 110)

A 'sense of proportion', 'these prophetic Christs and Christesses': these phrases toll back and forth between Leonard's account of Dalingridge and Virginia's in *Mrs Dalloway*. The arguments, verbalisations, appeals and refusals, must have turned very much on the matter of what was a sane premise, what an insane one. And naturally enough, in his enumeration of Virginia's insane premises, Leonard has to vent his irritation about the matter of food:

It was still more useless to argue with her about what you wanted her to do, e.g. eat her breakfast, because if her premises were true, she could prove and did prove conclusively to you that she ought not to eat her breakfast.

(*Beginning Again* p. 164)

It simply does not occur to Leonard that, to Virginia, her premises *were* true. There were, from her point of view, excellent reasons why she should not eat her breakfast. But it is always a battle of *wills*: 'It was still more useless to argue with her about what *you* wanted her to do.'

These fights over the matter of food must have involved enormous amounts of stubbornness and resistance on both sides. In *A Marriage of True Minds* emphasis is placed on Leonard's stubbornness, and he is quoted as saying, 'from my very early years I have had in me, I think, a streak of considerable obstinacy' (p. 2). The authors continue:

At a *New Statesman* board meeting when he was in his eighties Leonard made an extremely serious charge against one of the *New Statesman* employees. The employee was immediately able to refute the charge by written documents, and demanded an apology. All the other directors agreed that an apology was in order. Leonard simply sat still, shaking, saying nothing, then slowly explained that ever since he was a boy he had never apologised regardless of circumstances, and that he could not do so now. He was asked, alternatively, to withdraw the charge he had made. After a long wait he said he would withdraw it – 'reluctantly'.

(p. 2)

With will-power like that, and an utter conviction that Virginia's premises were all wrong, the pressure brought to bear on Virginia at Dalingridge must have been colossal.

At the base of the whole failure of communication at Dalingridge, is the problem that Virginia had already treated in *The Voyage Out*, and Leonard was to treat in *The Wise Virgins*: the difficulty of self-expression. In a highly verbalised milieu, in which failure to make yourself precisely clear in logical verbal bits was a failure at once intellectual, social and moral, the things which needed careful, tactful, indirect expression were at a discount, or failed to survive altogether.

Virginia could not express what she felt was wrong with her. There were no words. To be battered with Leonard's constant artillery fire about sane and insane 'premises' must have made things much worse. If Virginia could have explained what was distracting her, she doubtless would have done so. But she could not. Not in so many words.

That is why her indictment of Sir William Bradshaw comes to rest on his failure to take account of what the patient either could not say, or could only say in an indirect manner. Sir William Bradshaw fails to take account of the *presence* of the patient, his unspoken communication, his indirect manner of expressing his meaning through inarticulate gropings after words, or perhaps through silence itself:

Sir William himself was no longer young. He had worked very hard; he had won his position by sheer ability (being the son of a shop-keeper); loved his profession; made a fine figurehead at ceremonies and spoke well – all of which had by the time he was knighted given him a heavy look, a weary look (the stream of patients being so incessant, the responsibilities and privileges of his profession so onerous), which weariness, together with his grey hairs, increased the extraordinary distinction of his presence and gave him the reputation (of the utmost importance in dealing with nerve cases) not merely of lightning skill and almost infallible accuracy in diagnosis, but of sympathy; tact; understanding of the human soul. He could see the first moment they came into the room (the Warren Smiths they were called); he was certain directly he saw the man; it was a case of extreme gravity. It was a case of complete breakdown – complete physical and nervous breakdown, with every symptom in an advanced stage, he ascertained in two or three minutes (writing answers to questions, murmured discreetly, on a pink card).

(*Mrs Dalloway* pp. 105–6)

This is the central indictment of Sir William: he knows *at a glance*, immediately, before Septimus Smith has opened his mouth, what is wrong with him. For Sir William shares with Leonard the belief that mental matters are questions of concrete realities, yes/no, ill/not ill, normal/abnormal. There are no shades of grey (perhaps the irony of Sir William's car upholstery lies there). Everything is black or white. And God help you if it is black. For Sir William never listens to what you say: he has made up his mind in advance, has fitted the patient into a slot long before he opens his mouth, and everything the patient says only confirms the original diagnosis. As Smith enters the room, Sir William makes out his case history, instantaneously, his diagnosis, his treatment. By the time Septimus has sat down, his fate is sealed.

Must not Virginia herself have felt rather like Septimus Smith at that interview with Head on 9 September 1913? Did she not hear the stream of assertion and evidence flowing against her, first from Leonard's mouth and then from Head's? What chance had she of explaining that she wanted to be understood subjectively, as a person with emotional, sexual, psychological, philosophical, yes even theological, difficulties? She would have been unable even to express the fact that she wanted to be considered in this way. She may well have been so conceptually helpless that all she could feel was, like Rezia Smith, that 'she did not like that man', the ultimate conceptual helplessness before organised practical expertise. 'Ill', said Head. 'Ill', said Leonard.

Leonard took her back home and left her, to go and confer with George Savage. She was left alone. 'Holmes' would be coming soon, and the treatments, and the feeding, and the nurses and the isolation, and the total lack of talk, of exchange, or discussion, with Leonard, with anyone.

At Dalingridge would it not have seemed that the 'mental specialist' instead of being for his patient, was in fact against her? Would it not have seemed as if there was indeed a 'conspiracy'? In a few seconds the great man had seen what was wrong with her, and had made up his mind instantly. The questions he murmured discreetly, noting down the answers on a pink card, were only put in order to confirm his initial instantaneous diagnosis. He had delivered his opinion, and ushered them to the door.

She clung to his arm. They had been deserted.
But what more did she want?
To his patients he gave three-quarters of an hour. . .

vvv

'Forbade childbirth, penalised despair'

It is at least possible that Leonard's will imposed itself upon Virginia to an even greater extent than in his insistence that she was insane when she was trying to hang on to the belief that she was not. For it would appear that Leonard together with the psychiatrists decided that Virginia was not to have any children. This is lightly touched on in *Mrs Dalloway* in the scathing indictment of Sir William Bradshaw:

Worshipping proportion, Sir William not only prospered himself but made England prosper, secluded her lunatics, forbade childbirth, penalised despair, made it impossible for the unfit to propagate their views until they, too, shared his sense of proportion . . .

(p. 110)

It is possible that the pen of Virginia, as it wrote that, hurriedly added 'their views' to what was, as 'unfit to propagate', really a repetition of 'forbade childbirth'. Leonard after all would read this novel, as he read all the others. He would refuse to see the indictment of himself and the psychiatrists, but he might pick up a nearly factual accusation: that Leonard and the psychiatrists had agreed that she, Virginia, should not have any children.

We know from many sources that Virginia always entertained a secret envy for Vanessa's children, which she hid under a sophisticated barrage of independent talk, pretending children were not 'human' and so on. But since Leonard in 1912 kept on insisting that it would be dangerous to have children, the high likelihood is that, at some point before their marriage, Virginia eventually acquiesced.

The evidence is given in two phases in Leonard's autobiogra-

phy. The important passage in which Leonard describes his 1912
visits to Sir George Savage has been quoted at pp. 120–1. From
this passage, we can see a development in Leonard's own will.
First, it was Leonard, not Virginia, who began to have doubts as
to whether Virginia would be able to stand the strain of having
children. So, without his fiancée, he goes off alone to consult
Sir George Savage, who for once, says something half-way perceptive. It would doubtless have given Virginia an immense stability to have been able to reinforce the sense of her own identity by
actually having children of her own.

But one feels that behind this description of Leonard's is the
very firm wish that the psychiatrists should confirm him in his
view that she should *not* have children. When Savage fails to
come up to scratch, his opinion is dismissed as having in it 'more
of the man of the world . . . than of the mental specialist' (a
glaringly naïve opposition of terms in itself). So Leonard, determined to have his view confirmed that Virginia should not be put
to the strain of childbearing, goes off on his own again, always
alone, always without his fiancée's knowledge, to find some
respectable mental specialists who will confirm his view.

The 'conspiracy' theory, which he professes to be unable to
understand later on, begins to have its documentation here – in
Leonard's own account. But he was doubtless totally unaware
that his actions, taken together, might have looked like 'conspiracy' to his fiancée.

So he goes to two other 'well known doctors' and also 'the lady
who ran the mental nursing home where Virginia had several
times stayed'. There was probably no-one more likely than that
lady to confirm Leonard in his desire that Virginia should not
have children. As for T. B. Hyslop, he was famous for his view, as
we have seen, that the mentally unstable should not be allowed to
propagate. Leonard collects his materials carefully, and does not
stop collecting evidence until he has three voices against George
Savage's one. Then, he imposes his decision on Virginia: 'We
followed their advice.' We do not know anything about what
Virginia thought about this, for Leonard tells us nothing. The
'we' means: 'Virginia, at my request, followed my advice and the
advice of my advisers.' There is no note of free consent in that

'we'. It simply points to another step on Virginia's path into loneliness where her own wishes and desires were either not consulted, or actually over-ruled.

Later on, in 1913, Leonard eventually gets even George Savage to confirm him in his previous decision:

> she was continually suffering from bouts of intense worry and insomnia, and every now and again from the headache which was the danger signal of something worse. From time to time Sir George Savage was consulted, and some time in the spring it was at last definitely decided that it would not be safe for her to have a child.
>
> (*Beginning Again* p. 149)

'Forbade childbirth, penalised despair.' There are two passages in *Mrs Dalloway* which reflect on the outcome of these decisions between Leonard and the 'mental specialists'. The relation between Clarissa Dalloway and her husband Richard is in all points identical to the relation between Virginia and Leonard: one passage sums it all up, her husband's 'divine simplicity', the doctor's eternal régime:

> And there is a dignity in people; a solitude; even between husband and wife a gulf; and that one must respect, thought Clarissa, watching him open the door; for one would not part with it oneself, or take it, against his will, from one's husband, without losing one's independence, one's self-respect – something, after all, priceless.
>
> He returned with a pillow and a quilt.
>
> 'An hour's complete rest after luncheon,' he said. And he went.
>
> How like him! He would go on saying 'An hour's complete rest after luncheon' to the end of time, because a doctor had ordered it once. It was like him to take what doctors said literally; part of his adorable divine simplicity, which no one had to the same extent . . .
>
> (*Mrs Dalloway* p. 132)

It seems to me clear that this is how Virginia regarded Leonard – a good, naïve, trusting soul, literal, loving and essentially 'other': someone she hardly knew, and who hardly knew her. He is full of goodness and kindness, and it is part of his goodness 'to take what doctors said literally'. He is off (the rest of the page tells us) to help 'his Armenians, his Albanians' – a direct reference to Leonard surely, for he recounts at length in his autobiography how the massacre of the Armenians in 1894 had definitively moulded his sense of the world (*The Journey not the Arrival Matters* pp. 21–3), forcing him to recognise the presence of evil and to hate cruelty. Mrs Dalloway is left to rest for an hour after lunch. That leaves her, alone, with the tormenting problem of how to get through the long afternoon.

But the invalid longs for something she has not got, something they do not share, something they will never have. Her sense of deprivation amounts almost to a physical pain. It was renunciation: but how much it cost!

It was all over for her. The sheet was stretched and the bed narrow. She had gone up into the tower alone and left them blackberrying in the sun. The door had shut, and there among the dust of fallen plaster and the litter of birds' nests how distant the view had looked, and the sounds came thin and chill (once on Leith Hill, she remembered), and Richard, Richard! she cried, as a sleeper in the night starts and stretches a hand in the dark for help. Lunching with Lady Bruton, it came back to her. He has left me; I am alone for ever, she thought, folding her hands upon her knee.

(pp. 52–3)

It does seem as if Virginia, in tying together the idea of forbidding childbirth and penalising despair, has wished to link the concept of the imposition of will with the existential issue of the meaning and continuance of life. For Sir William does impose his will: 'Naked, defenceless, the exhausted, the friendless received the impress of Sir William's will. He swooped; he devoured. He shut people up.' And there must be some connection here with Virginia's own feeling that, in the psychiatric interviews of 1913, her view had not really been consulted. Perhaps there is some reference to this in the extremely subtle delineation of Lady Bradshaw, whose will to oppose Sir William's will had, at some moment in the past, been quietly demolished:

For example, Lady Bradshaw. Fifteen years ago she had gone under. It was nothing you could put your finger on; there had been no scene, no snap; only the slow sinking, water-logged, of her will into his.

(p. 111)

And Virginia does directly link the question of Sir William's all-conquering will with philosophical and even theological issues:

There some weakly broke down; sobbed, submitted; others, inspired by Heaven knows what intemperate madness, called Sir William to his face a damnable humbug; questioned, even more impiously, life itself. Why live? they demanded. Sir William replied that life was good . . . as for his income it was quite twelve thousand a year. But to us, they protested, life has given no such bounty. He acquiesced. They lacked a sense of proportion. And perhaps, after all, there is no God? He shrugged his shoulders.

(p. 112)

This remorseless imposition of Sir William's will has only one more stage to go before it is totally autocratic, and that step is taken in the next line:

In short, this living or not living is an affair of our own? But there they were mistaken. Sir William had a friend in Surrey where they taught, what Sir William frankly admitted was a difficult art – a sense of proportion.

(pp. 112–13)

All of these issues must have been discussed, in just these terms, in 1913. Three questions: Why live? Perhaps there is no God? This living or not living is an affair of our own? In all three cases, Sir William imposes his will, imposes a practical solution, like a kind of *pax psychiatrica*, over problems of existential theology.

For the real-life equivalent of this mood of Mrs Dalloway's one has only to read through volume II of Virginia's letters, which covers the period of her return from Dalingridge to Asham in late 1913 and early 1914. The tone is absolutely anguished. The sense of physical deprivation is unbearable. One senses that Virginia feels that her body has been estranged from her, confiscated, and that it will not be given back. One can see that physical relations between her and Leonard had been broken off completely. These endings are typical:

Old Mandril does want her master so badly and last night his empty bed was so dismal, and she went and kissed the pillow.

(8 March 1914)

How are you, my pet beast? Your old Mandril cries so pathetically when it crawls into its straw, and sees your basket empty.

(10 March 1914)

My pet, you would never doubt my caring for you if you saw me wanting to kiss you, and nuzzle you in my arms. After all, we shall have a happy life together now, wont we?

(14 March 1914)

The invention of this deprived language of Mongoose and Mandril allows of a kind of communication, but it is an impoverished one, resting on no physical foundation. The obvious aim of this animal code is to obviate the necessity of having to write in a way which assumes a continuing physical relationship. Obviously, Leonard did not intend physical relations to be renewed for a long while, and he was away a great deal, leaving Virginia to rest alone. She must have felt that her body had been taken away from her almost as a punishment. Conceiving children was a luxury which others would have to consider the merits of in their own good time. It was in fact no longer open to her to think in terms of conceiving children, and this only eighteen months into her marriage. The deprivations were terrific, impacted one into the other.

Mrs Dalloway, in the novel, is not childless, yet the novel aches with a sense of childlessness, aches with a sense of sensory and physical deprivation. Despair has indeed been penalised through the forbidding of childbirth. But childbearing, the continuance of life, is refused because according to certain eugenics propagandists of that time, of whom T. B. Hyslop was one of the most prominent, those who despair are unfit to propagate.

The novel is essentially a description of a man and a woman living together in a marriage which has long since resigned itself to having no physical base. Although Mrs Dalloway does have a daughter, this event is so long in the past that it is almost a mythical remembrance. Her daughter is grown up, and leading her own life, partly under the malign tutelage of Miss Kilman. Apart from a certain pride in her daughter, Mrs Dalloway seems to have no relation to her. She lives a nun-like, chaste existence, sleeping alone in her bedroom, and resting during the afternoons while her husband is away on committee work. There is no suggestion that there has been any physical contact for decades. The sense of childlessness is engendered partly by the awareness in the reader of this fact, and partly by the extreme distance which exists between Mrs Dalloway and her daughter. And it does not seem to me that, for all her final acquiescence in the combined wills of Maurice Craig, T. B. Hyslop, Jean Thomas and Leonard Woolf, Virginia ever forgave in her heart of hearts this violation of her own basic right to dispose of herself as she thought fit.

CHAPTER 13

'The birds talking Greek'

Listing the 'premises' he considers 'insane' during Virginia's collapse of 1913–14, Leonard writes:

> She believed, for instance, that she was not ill, that her symptoms were due to her own 'faults'; she believed that she was hearing voices when the voices were her own imaginings; she heard the birds outside her window talking Greek; she believed that the doctors and nurses were in conspiracy against her.
>
> *(Beginning Again* p. 164)

At an earlier point in the same volume, Leonard had recounted the matter of the birds singing in Greek with reference to one of Virginia's previous 'breakdowns'. It is not perfectly clear which breakdown Leonard is referring to, since he omits to count the one of 1904, but on Quentin Bell's evidence it seems likely that he is in fact referring to the one of 1904. Leonard writes:

> In the manic stage she was extremely excited; the mind raced; she talked volubly and, at the height of the attack, incoherently; she had delusions and heard voices, for instance she told me that in her second attack she heard the birds in the garden outside her window talking Greek; she was violent with the nurses.
>
> *(Beginning Again* pp. 76–7)

Quentin Bell has, as we have seen previously, traced the upsetting effect George Duckworth had on Virginia's adolescence. It is perhaps worth recalling this passage:

> At what point this comfortably fraternal embrace developed into something which to George no doubt seemed even more comfortable although not nearly so fraternal, it would be hard to say. Vanessa came to believe that George himself was more than half unaware of the fact

that what had started with pure sympathy ended by becoming a nasty erotic skirmish. There were fondlings and fumblings in public when Virginia was at her lessons and these were carried to greater lengths – indeed I know not to what lengths – when, with the easy assurance of a fond and privileged brother, George carried his affections from the schoolroom into the night nursery.

(I, 42–3)

What sort of lessons were these during which Virginia was sexually molested by George Duckworth? They were Greek lessons, amongst others. For this we have her own testimony, which Quentin Bell quotes at the foot of the same page as a footnote to the foregoing:

'. . . this led us to the revelation of all George's malefactions. To my surprise, she [Janet Case] has always had an intense dislike of him; & used to say "Whew – you nasty creature," when he came in & began fondling me over my Greek. When I got to the bedroom scenes, she dropped her lace, & gasped like a benevolent gudgeon . . .' V.W. to Vanessa Bell, [25th July] 1911.

(I, 43)

Later on, in describing the breakdown of 1904, Quentin Bell again refers explicitly to Greek:

She heard voices urging her to acts of folly; she believed that they came from overeating and that she must starve herself. In this emergency the main burden fell upon Vanessa; but Vanessa was enormously helped by Violet Dickinson. She took Virginia to her house at Burnham Wood and it was there that she made her first attempt to commit suicide. She threw herself from a window, which, however, was not high enough from the ground to cause her serious harm. It was here too that she lay in bed, listening to the birds singing in Greek and imagining that King Edward VII lurked in the azaleas using the foulest possible language.

All that summer she was mad.

(I, 89–90)

Thus we have two sets of testimony, Leonard's and Bell's (which doubtless leans on Leonard's) to the effect that, both in 1904 and in 1913–14, Virginia asserted that the birds outside her window were singing in Greek. It is obvious that one of the primary 'Greek' associations in Virginia's mind was George Duckworth, and, by extension, probably Gerald Duckworth. But there must have been many others.

References to Greek are scattered profusely through Virginia's writing – in novels, in essays, in letters and diaries. There are an immense number of them, and it is only gradually that their significance becomes clear.

For Virginia, Greek was a symbol for everything that she personally would never be able to attain to. Greek was an ideal, a touchstone, an abstraction of pure intellection. It represented a value like the logic of her friend Russell, the learning of her friends at Cambridge, the ethics of Moore. It was a symbol for her own failure, her own impracticality, her own shifting nature, her irrepressible unlearnedness.

She gives all this clear expression in one place, her essay 'On Not Knowing Greek', which appeared in the first volume of *The Common Reader* in 1925. The essay is rich in pointers to the unconscious reality of Virginia's mind. Her opening ploy is that Greek is so foreign to us that 'we do not know how the words sounded, or where precisely we ought to laugh, or how the actors acted, and between this foreign people and ourselves there is not only a difference of race and tongue but a tremendous breach of tradition'. So much by the way of modest disclaimer. Then the essential qualities of Greek art are slowly listed. Greek is 'the impersonal literature'. 'There is a cruelty in Greek tragedy which is quite unlike our English brutality.' It represents heroism, and fidelity. 'The stable, the permanent, the original human being is to be found there.' The Greek philosophers teach us that truth is not to be sought by mere intellection alone, but by the whole being, and the embodied being who lives a full life. 'Truth, it seems, is various; Truth is to be pursued with all our faculties' – a section which concludes a meditation on the discussions of Socrates' friends which is almost identical to the discussions described in Virginia's own account of *Old Bloomsbury*, with G.E.Moore and Saxon Sydney-Turner leading the talk.

But behind the descriptions of impersonal tragedy and philosophy, there lurks another set of images, running concurrently in Virginia's mind: 'Here we listen to the nightingale whose song echoes through English literature singing in her own Greek tongue.' Electra is adduced, for Electra 'speaks of that very nightingale: "that bird distraught with grief, the messenger of Zeus.

Ah, queen of sorrow, Niobe, thee I deem divine – thee; who evermore weepest in thy rocky tomb." ' The choruses in Greek tragedy are 'the undifferentiated voices who sing like birds in the pauses of the wind'. Sophocles 'selects what he wishes to emphasize and sings of white Colonus and its nightingale'. 'The nightingale has only to be named by Sophocles and she sings; the grove has only to be called ἄβατον, "untrodden", and we imagine the twisted branches and the purple violets.'

With such a rich orchestration of Greek motifs and birds singing of tragic and irredeemable situations, some of the normal associations in Virginia's mind when 'she lay in bed listening to the birds singing in Greek' appear to bear directly on Virginia's view of herself.

With reference specifically to the birds singing in Greek to Septimus Smith, the following passage is of interest:

Accustomed to look directly and largely rather than minutely and aslant, it was safe for them to step into the thick of emotions which blind and bewilder an age like our own. In the vast catastrophe of the European war our emotions had to be broken up for us, and put at an angle from us, before we could allow ourselves to feel them in poetry or fiction. The only poets who spoke to the purpose spoke in the sidelong, satiric manner of Wilfrid Owen and Siegfried Sassoon.

(Collected Essays i, 10)

This makes clear one of the technical reasons why the sparrow which chirps to Septimus Smith chirps in Greek. The sparrow sings 'freshly and piercingly in Greek words how there is no crime and, joined by another sparrow, they sang in voices prolonged and piercing in Greek words, from trees in the meadow of life beyond a river where the dead walk, how there is no death' *(Mrs Dalloway* p. 28). The emotion has to be 'put at an angle from us'.

The presence of 'Greek' in Virginia's unconscious always points to a necessary indirection, the presence of something which is too costly to entertain except in the mode of absence. The Greek tragedy, the nightingales singing of hopeless grief, all are there. But there is a further, even more precise, admixture.

Leonard himself was an excellent and distinguished Greek scholar. He recounts the anguish and the glory of a classical education in the first volume of his autobiography, *Sowing*. At St Paul's School, from 1894 to 1899, Leonard was forced through the most exacting classical training in order to fit him for the Oxford or Cambridge scholarship examinations (pp. 74–8).

At Trinity College, Cambridge, Leonard was a classical scholar, and did excellently in both parts of the Classical Tripos, even though he modestly affirms himself to have done much less well than either he or his mentors had hoped (p. 193). His first great friend was Saxon Sydney-Turner, who was a classicist of legendary ability. ('In one of the university scholarship examinations they set us for Greek translation a piece from a rather obscure writer which had a riddle in it. Saxon won one of the scholarships and it was said that he was the only person to get the riddle bit right. It was characteristic of him' (p. 103).) In the last three years of Leonard's stay at Trinity he shared rooms with Saxon Sydney-Turner in Great Court. Virginia herself, in *Old Bloomsbury*, recalls Sydney-Turner as 'an absolute prodigy of learning. He had the whole of Greek literature by heart' (Schulkind pp. 166–7).

Nor was it only Leonard and Saxon who were associated with Greek in Virginia's mind. The conversations which Virginia describes as being characteristic of the 'first phase' of Bloomsbury society, roughly from 1904 to 1907, were extremely reminiscent of the Socratic and the Platonic. In a Socratic manner everything was analysed and reduced abstractly to its primal verbal elements. But there was also the high aesthetic tone of Plato. The conversations were doubly redolent of fifth-century Athens, not only because the manner of them was Socratic and the matter of them largely Platonic, but also because they were largely conducted among homosexual classicists. Describing her unease in early 'abstract' Bloomsbury, Virginia writes:

I knew that there were buggers in Plato's Greece; I suspected – it was not a question one could just ask Thoby – that there were buggers in Dr Butler's Trinity [College], Cambridge; but it never occurred to me that there were buggers even now in the Stephens' sitting room at Gordon Square.

(Schulkind p. 172)

Eventually it did occur to her.

There is a possible inter-relation between Virginia's first stream of associations of Greek in the unconscious (abstraction, an ideal impossible of achievement, personal incapacity) and her second (Greek as expertise, Greek as knowledge, Greek as verbal brilliance). It is worth while reflecting on the possible ways in which these two streams of association might inter-relate. Some of the reasons why the birds continued to sing in Greek in 1913 have obviously to do with Leonard and Virginia together as mutually incapable. She could not help feeling that she had 'failed', that her 'faults' had found her out, that she would never come up to any of the standards expected of her. She also perhaps felt that the failure, the inability was not entirely her own: Leonard too had failed, had not come up to the impossible standards represented by 'Greek'. He had not been able to reach through her verbal world to help her in her distress. She had not been able to tell him, any more than the nightingale could, what was wrong. If Greek was high proficiency, an ideal of attainment and mastery, then both she and he had miserably failed.

It is also conceivable that, by the time Virginia came to write *Mrs Dalloway*, she had, overlying her original associations of George Duckworth with Greek lessons, a new verbal association, the music of T.S. Eliot's *The Waste Land*, which she had published with Leonard at the Hogarth Press in 1923. I think the influence of 'Tom' Eliot on Virginia in the years after the war is greater than has been realised. Not only many of the associations, but many of the images, which occur in *Mrs Dalloway* and *To the Lighthouse* particularly, seem to have their origin in Eliot's poetry, above all those which have to do with water, sexuality, repression and sterility. It is striking how close the symbolic meaning of parts of *The Waste Land* is to certain symbols in *Mrs Dalloway*. For instance:

> Above the antique mantel was displayed
> As though a window gave upon the sylvan scene
> The change of Philomel, by the barbarous king
> So rudely forced; yet there the nightingale
> Filled all the desert with inviolable voice
> And still she cried, and still the world pursues,
> 'Jug Jug' to dirty ears.

Eliot's immediate source is the poem by the Elizabethan poet Lyly:

What bird so sings, yet so does wail?
Oh, 'tis the ravished nightingale.
Jug, jug, jug, jeg, tereu, she cries,
And still her woes at midnight rise.

Eliot dryly gives the antique source, Ovid's *Metamorphoses*, in his
'Notes' to *The Waste Land*, but Virginia would not have needed
that hint to find in the sugestion of the ravished nightingale some
reference to her own mishandling by Gerald and George Duckworth. Philomela was kidnapped, raped, imprisoned and muti-
lated by her sister's husband Tersus – it is an easy leap to associate
half-brother with brother-in-law. And in *The Waves*, Jinny, lost in
reverie, refers to Eliot's nightingale singing 'Jug, jug, jug' in the
context of actual sexual penetration.

As a result of her terrible revenge, Philomela is changed into a
nightingale. She sings, therefore, in notes which have been
deprived of verbal meaning, but which are instinct with the
memory of suffering and violence.

It seems likely that the voices of the birds which sing to
Septimus Smith tell him of a state beyond death where atrocity
can be forgotten, and forgiveness achieved. It is significant that,
restored to freedom again and writing a novel ten years after the
events of 1913, Virginia should have made the birds in her novel
sing in Greek, as if to make the point, in some kind of revenge,
that in certain states of heightened consciousness, certain stimuli
can indeed be *directly* perceived as symbolically significant:

A sparrow perched on the railing opposite chirped Septimus, Septimus,
four or five times over and went on, drawing its notes out, to sing freshly
and piercingly in Greek words how there is no crime and, joined by
another sparrow, they sang in voices prolonged and piercing in Greek
words, from trees in the meadow of life beyond a river where the dead
walk, how there is no death.   (*Mrs Dalloway* p. 28)

The knowledge that Septimus Smith has gained from the
war is repeated to him by the birds that sing to him that the
dead are in Thessaly. However, it is also part of the knowledge that Virginia wants to express about the meaning of life
as such. The burden of guilt is transferred in the birdsong. For
one minute during the psychiatric interview with Sir William
Bradshaw, Septimus thinks he sees a way out. He might 'confess':

But if he confessed? If he communicated? Would they let him off then, Holmes, Bradshaw?

'I – I –' he stammered.

But what was his crime? He could not remember it.

'Yes?' Sir William encouraged him. (But it was growing late.)

Love, trees, there is no crime – what was his message?

He could not remember it.

'I – I –' Septimus stammered.

'Try to think as little about yourself as possible' said Sir William kindly. Really, he was not fit to be about.

(*Mrs Dalloway* p. 109)

> The change of Philomel, by the barbarous king
> So rudely forced . . .

No, Virginia cannot utter it. But it had to do with the nature of things. The song of the birds is theological, metaphysical.

The birds had been singing in Greek when Virginia lay in bed in 1904, they sang in Greek again in 1913 (*Beginning Again* p. 164), and they were singing in Greek to Septimus Smith after the Armistice and while Virginia was writing *Mrs Dalloway*,which was published in 1925. I think that the associations are cumulative, even though Gerald or George is always at the bottom of them. By the time Eliot had added his notation they had become the perfect symbol for a state of mind which, though apparently 'insane' and definitely incomprehensible to the outsider who had no intuition of the rôle of the Duckworths, is itself meaningful, indeed charged with meaning to the highest possible degree.

The meaning for Virginia herself was quite simply: she could not feel. She had been anaesthetised. Barbarously and rudely forced, she was a damaged thing, a spoilt, wingless bird. This may help to explain a constant theme, otherwise inexplicable or at least not explained, in Mrs Dalloway's mind. She constantly refers to herself as having 'failed', as having been deprived. The creeping feelings of guilt, with reference to her husband Richard, always have to do with herself as emotionally and physically damaged, maimed, unable, incapable.

Reference to Mrs Dalloway's sexual bereavement, to her sexual frustration, are scattered through the novel:

The hall of the house was cool as a vault. Mrs. Dalloway raised her hand to her eyes, and, as the maid shut the door to, and she heard the swish of

Lucy's skirts, she felt like a nun who has left the world and feels fold round her the familiar veils and the response to old devotions.

(p. 33)

Like a nun withdrawing, or a child exploring a tower, she went, up-stairs, paused at the window, came to the bathroom. There was the green linoleum and a tap dripping. There was an emptiness about the heart of life; an attic room. Women must put off their rich apparel. At mid-day they must disrobe.

(p. 35)

So the room was an attic; the bed narrow; and lying there reading, for she slept badly, she could not dispel a virginity preserved through childbirth which clung to her like a sheet. Lovely in girlhood, suddenly there came a moment – for example on the river beneath the woods at Clieveden – when, through some contraction of this cold spirit, she had failed him. And then at Constantinople, and again and again. She could see what she lacked. It was not beauty; it was not mind. It was something central which permeated; something warm which broke up surfaces and rippled the cold contact of man and woman, or of women together. For *that* she could dimly perceive.

(pp. 35–6)

For the sake of the narrative, a very slight modification to Virginia's own life is made (Mrs Dalloway, the fictional character, has had a child, and therefore her 'virginity' has been 'pre-served through childbirth'), but the description of an inviolate virginity, of a nun-like chastity is strongly proffered, in these descriptions of Mrs Dalloway's consciousness as she muses, as being literally true of Virginia Woolf herself. She refers so often and so pointedly to the nun-like state of her body, the narrow bed, reaching out for a hand in the dark and finding none, to her 'virginity' which she could not 'dispel' and which 'clung to her like a sheet'.

This raises the question of Virginia's gradual conversion of feeling towards the world of female desire, the quitting of the world of marriage for a softer experience. Male desire has become incomprehensible to her as for Mrs Dalloway:

yet she could not resist sometimes yielding to the charm of a woman, not a girl, of a woman confessing, as to her they often did, some scrape, some folly. And . . . she did undoubtedly then feel what men felt. Only for a moment; but it was enough. It was a sudden revelation . . . Then, for that moment, she had seen an illumination; a match burning in a crocus; an inner meaning almost expressed. But the close withdrew; the hard softened. It was over – the moment.

(p. 36)

She is left lying in her narrow bed, with her virginity wrapped round her like a sheet, awake in the darkness, waiting for Leonard–Richard to come back from one of his committee meetings.

Against such moments (with women too) there contrasted (as she laid her hat down) the bed and Baron Marbot and the candle half-burnt. Lying awake, the floor creaked; the lit house was suddenly darkened, and if she raised her head she could just hear the click of the handle released as gently as possible by Richard, who slipped upstairs in his socks and then, as often as not, dropped his hot-water bottle and swore! How she laughed!

(pp. 36–7)

Up creeps Richard Dalloway in his kind, solicitous way, in his socks, in an attempt to be silent, to let his wife 'rest'. It is a sardonic joke that he manages to drop his own hot-water bottle. But it is a humour which comes from extreme deprivation. 'How she laughed' is a grim notation.

The ironies at Leonard's expense are tender and delicate, yet they are there, as are the ironies at her own expense. But Leonard could hardly have afforded to see their married life from Virginia's point of view, through her eyes, given his oft-repeated view that she had been 'insane' and that she probably would be again. It is strange that Virginia herself could have expressed herself so clearly in fiction, and still not have managed to show Leonard in real life what she most longed for. Yet we know from *The Wise Virgins* ('Katharine's Opinion of her Sister') that Leonard had his counter-explanation for everything that had happened, and the coherence of his view depended for its continued existence upon the assumption that Virginia's mind was incapable of telling fantasy from reality. But perhaps Virginia knew that Leonard could never see what it was she wanted of him, and considered that, loving as he was, it was all her own fault, as she should never have married him. (Another cigarette. Let's get on with the next review – essay – novel – draft. Time must be filled in somehow, and writing is the best way to fill it. Those interminable reading lists: the Greeks, the Elizabethans, the eighteenth century, the modern novel, history, psychology, biography. For her, reading was morphia.)

What the birds sing to Septimus Smith in Greek has to do with an ideal world, a world that would be deathless, beyond death but still not deprived of consciousness like the nightingale in Yeats's *Byzantium*, a world that would be serene and unscarred by war. Or they may have been singing of the afterworld, beyond the Styx, where people are no longer plagued by bodies. But the birds that chattered in Greek outside Virginia's own window were probably reminding her of her own 'failures', first with her half-brother, then with her husband: 'Lovely in girlhood, suddenly there came a moment – for example on the river beneath the woods at Clieveden – when, through some contraction of this cold spirit, she had failed him. And then at Constantinople, and again and again.' Those birds singing in Greek must have been merciless critics.

Leonard in his account of Virginia's 'insanity', keeps on letting slip that, according to her, the upsets in her mental life were due to her own 'faults'. He never seems to have wanted to enquire into what, for her, these might have consisted in.

Why doesn't he enquire into them? Insofar as they were connected with George Duckworth, he obviously had no inkling of their significance. But insofar as he suspected they might also refer to his and her married life together, he might have known that for his wife her faults were the 'failures' she refers to in *Mrs Dalloway*, the 'failures' to allow or to respond to normal sexual feeling between man and wife. This would be to assume that she had instigated the break-up of their sexual relationship. But all the evidence seems to point the other way. If one reads the letters to Leonard which follow Virginia's return home in early 1914, it looks very much as if Leonard had ended all sexual activity with his wife, in the belief that she was too 'ill' for it. But, since their married life was based upon an agreement, it may well be that he would have refused to acknowledge that these 'failures' ('at Constantinople': change that to Provence, Spain, Valencia, Marseilles, Venice or any of the places mentioned by Leonard as being on their honeymoon itinerary) were 'failures' at all. They were, after all, as much his 'failures' as hers. Anyway it was he who decided that it would not be wise for her to have children. Leonard obviously adapted much more easily to the non-physical marriage than Virginia did, or at least it seems to have cost him less than it did her. So when Virginia speaks of 'faults', he may have felt obliged to expunge their possible referents in his mind. They thus became yet further evidence of her delusions.

Or it could well be that in freely associating 'Greek' with her own 'faults' Virginia was regretting her long sexual passivity with George Duckworth. In a sense, she had committed a grave 'fault' in that relationship, by allowing it to achieve such a degree of intimacy. But she could not explain this to Leonard: it would be too grossly embarrassing, too appallingly intimate. It would shatter too much between them. She may have realised that by allowing George's intimacies over a period of time she had effectively damaged her own responses beyond repair, and that here too she was gravely 'at fault' with regard to Leonard. All this Leonard could have known, but she made no effort to inform him.

But he should surely have suspected that the hints – 'birds singing Greek', 'faults', 'conspiracy' – amounted to *some* form of sense, even if he could not be sure what the 'conspiracy', as she saw it, consisted in. The answer to this must surely be that Leonard just did not want to admit the validity of his wife's view of their marriage. It would have been too expensive for him. We know a good deal about Leonard's state of mind, while his wife lay in George Duckworth's house in 1913, because we possess *The Wise Virgins*.

CHAPTER 14

Was Septimus Smith 'insane'?

Sir William Bradshaw assures Mrs Warren Smith that her husband is 'very, very ill', even though Dr Holmes equally unperceptively, has assured her many times that there is nothing at all the matter with her husband. Both were wrong, of course, and for the usual reasons: if you approach something with preconceived notions you will have little difficulty in satisfying yourself that you are correct.

For he is not, in Sir William's sense of the word, 'very ill'. Nor is there, in Dr Holmes's sense of the phrase, nothing the matter with him. The reality of Septimus's mental condition falls between these two judgements, one falsely clinical, the other clinically false. When, a decade after the events of 1912–13 Virginia decided to write a novel which would include an account of what it feels like to be in a state of nervous collapse, and to be treated by so-called experts who understand nothing whatsoever about the root causes of the 'symptoms' they take themselves to be treating, she had to think long and hard about how to achieve her aim. In introducing the figures of Septimus and Rezia Warren Smith into her novel, she took a calculated risk. What she had to decide was whether she could 'deal with' the events of 1912–13 and 1915 or not. Just as she decided, a few years later, to 'exorcise' her parents and the problems of her childhood by writing *To the Lighthouse*, so she seriously set herself to 'exorcise', in *Mrs Dalloway*, the horror and the terror of the months which followed her marriage to Leonard.

What Virginia has done, in inventing the character of Septimus Warren Smith, is to find an extremely subtle and cogent symbol for what really was wrong with her in 1912–13. For Septimus Smith's root problem is that 'he could not feel'.

Now we know from *The Voyage Out* and *Night and Day*, as well as from Leonard's novels of 1913 and 1914, that the major problem both Virginia and Leonard experienced was how to feel: how to feel emotions, how to control them, how to direct them, how to integrate them into the feelings of someone else. And as the novels show, the problem occasionally appeared so grave as to be insoluble.

Septimus Smith is presented as a young man who goes to the war, makes friends with his officer, Evans, sees Evans killed, and prides himself on being able to take this in his stride without faltering. His career is given in a very few words:

Septimus was one of the first to volunteer. He went to France to save an England which consisted almost entirely of Shakespeare's plays and Miss Isabel Pole in a green dress walking in a square. There in the trenches the change which Mr. Brewer desired when he advised football was produced instantly; he developed manliness; he was promoted; he drew the attention, indeed the affection of his officer, Evans by name . . . when Evans was killed, just before the Armistice, in Italy, Septimus, far from showing any emotion or recognising that here was the end of a friendship, congratulated himself upon feeling very little and very reasonably. The War had taught him. It was sublime.

(pp. 95–6)

Virginia has chosen in Septimus a perfect 'objective correlative' for her own state of mind in 1912–13. Smith sees Evans killed. He congratulates himself on his resilience. And then the horror sets in, he cannot feel.

In this way, and in giving Septimus Smith just precisely *this* problem, Virginia has created a symbol which exactly corresponds to the unspoken and incommunicable elements of her own problem in 1912–13. Then, shocked and isolated, she could not feel, and she could not express her feelings. She was treated in an entirely external and 'behavioural' way, which took no account of her inner dilemma. In Septimus Smith, and the 'treatment' he receives, Virginia has the symbol she needs.

She has been extremely careful to give Septimus Smith's emotional anaesthesia a particular origin, a definite cause, and a precise moment in time. There is an exact originating moment for the shock which leads to the anaesthesia. And then there is a long drawn-out, indeed endless, period when the price he has to pay comes home to him:

The War had taught him. It was sublime . . . he became engaged one evening when the panic was on him – that he could not feel.

  For now that it was all over, truce signed, and dead buried, he had, especially in the evening, these sudden thunder-claps of fear. He could not feel . . . but something failed him; he could not feel . . . beauty was behind a plane of glass. Even taste . . . had no relish to him . . . But he could not taste, he could not feel . . . his brain was perfect; it must be the fault of the world then – that he could not feel.

(pp. 96–8)

Having established, in symbolic form, that extreme shock can anaesthetise the feelings (her own problem in marriage after her dealings with the Duckworths subtly symbolised), Virginia goes on to show that such a shock can lead *directly* to the conviction that the world itself is entirely without meaning. She makes this point once only, but with absolute mastery:

It might be possible, Septimus thought, looking at England from the train window, as they left Newhaven; it might be possible that the world itself is without meaning.

(p. 98)

These are, philosophically and humanly, the central lines in the book. And they are given to us immediately after the eight-fold repetition of 'he could not feel', and only two pages after the death of Evans. The death of Evans leads to the inability to feel. This in its turn leads to a philosophical conclusion: the world might well be without meaning. And this leads inevitably and at once, to the theme of childbearing. Virginia, in the course of four pages of *Mrs Dalloway*, ties these themes inextricably together. Septimus begins to read. All the great texts of the world now have a different meaning, and it is exactly at this point of ultimate disgust and refusal, that the question of having children is thrust upon Septimus:

Here he opened Shakespeare once more. That boy's business of the intoxication of language – *Antony and Cleopatra* – had shrivelled utterly. How Shakespeare loathed humanity – the putting on of clothes, the getting of children, the sordidity of the mouth and the belly! This was now revealed to Septimus; the message hidden in the beauty of words. The secret signal which one generation passes, under disguise, to the next is loathing, hatred, despair. Dante the same. Aeschylus (translated) the same . . .

Love between man and woman was repulsive to Shakespeare. The business of copulation was filth to him before the end. But, Rezia said, she must have children. They had been married five years . . .

She must have a son like Septimus she said . . .

One cannot bring children into a world like this. One cannot perpetuate suffering, or increase the breed of these lustful animals, who have no lasting emotions, but only whims and vanities, eddying them now this way, now that.

(pp. 98–9)

In the closed circuit represented by this diagram:

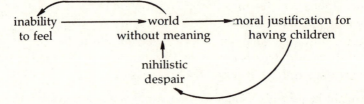

Virginia Woolf has, in her symbolic character Septimus Smith, reconstituted *exactly* the structure of problems she herself had when she was examined by two neurologists on 9 September 1913 and sent to Dalingridge Place. The inability to feel was her greatest problem. This led inevitably to a developed *Weltschmerz* in which her own actions, and those of others, seemed ridiculous and meaningless. The question of whether or not to have children compounded these problems: in her own case, Leonard's refusal to have children supported by selected medical advice; in Septimus's case the refusal to countenance children because of a moral decision that there is no justification for them.

This three-fold problem leads to a state of nihilistic despair, and this leads back into, and reinforces, the second stage of the problem, the conviction that the world is really meaningless and hostile.

And it is in this state, and unable to utter a word *about* this state, that Virginia is seen by Henry Head on 9 September 1913, and

Septimus Smith is seen by Sir William Bradshaw in the novel of ten years later.

The inadequacies of an approach which would attempt to intervene in a state of mind which is more theological or philosophical than neurological or physiological, are made the butt of Virginia's scorn in the novel.

'You served with great distinction in the War?'
  The patient repeated the word 'war' interrogatively.
  He was attaching meanings to words of a symbolical kind. A serious symptom to be noted on the card.

(p. 106)

If a psychiatrist wants to understand what is wrong with his patient, surely the first thing he should be attentive to is the meanings the patient attaches to words. The fact that they are 'symbolical' is not so much a 'serious symptom' as a ray of hope: from the unravelling of the symbolic meanings the patient is attaching to words there may come an insight into how he can be helped. But we know already that Sir William Bradshaw is closed to the subjective dimension of Smith's problem:

'The War?'the patient asked. The European War – that little shindy of schoolboys with gunpowder? Had he served with distinction? He really forgot. In the War itself he had failed . . .
  He had committed an appalling crime and been condemned to death by human nature.

(p. 106)

Virginia's subtle use of the psychic cause of Septimus's mental collapse ('the War') allows her to reinforce her symbol twice over. Just as Septimus Smith's problem is his inability to feel, so the reason for this is what he has become aware of as reality during his war experience. In terms of Virginia's own life, just as her problem is her inability to feel, so the reason for this is what she has become aware of as reality during the years since her mother's death. This cannot be expressed in speech in 1913, but by 1925 Virginia has found her sufficient symbol: the horror of war, the mercilessness of man to man.

There must have been many thousands of young men returning from that war who had recently seen reality as Septimus Smith saw it. It cannot have been at all exceptional for young men

whose nerves had been shattered by the war to return home
mentally and morally wrecked. These are the young men Wilfred
Owen writes of in his poem 'Mental Cases':

> – These are the men whose minds the Dead have ravished.
> Memory fingers in their hair of murders,
> Multitudinous murders they once witnessed.
> Wading sloughs of flesh these helpless wander,
> Treading blood from lungs that had loved laughter.
> Always they must see these things and hear them,
> Batter of guns and shatter of flying muscles,
> Carnage incomparable, and human squander
> Rucked too thick for these men's extrication.
>
> Therefore still their eyeballs shrink tormented
> Back into their brains, because on their sense
> Sunlight seems a blood-smear; night comes blood-black;
> Dawn breaks open like a wound that bleeds afresh.
> – Thus their heads wear this hilarious, hideous,
> Awful falseness of set-smiling corpses.
> – Thus their hands are plucking at each other;
> Picking at the rope-knouts of their scourging;
> Snatching after us who smote them, brother,
> Pawing us who dealt them war and madness.

The mode of presence which the war has, both to Owen and to
the men whose condition he describes, cannot be dismissed by
Sir William Bradshaw, though he may write on pink cards and
murmur discreetly until kingdom come. There is another order of
experience present here. The peculiarly grave kind of failure
which Virginia is indicting is the failure to give attention to the
order and kind of experience from which Septimus Smith is
suffering.

Septimus Smith, sitting in the sun, sees the past all the time,
exactly in the manner of Owen's poem:

The dead were in Thessaly, Evans sang, among the orchids. There they
waited till the War was over, and now the dead, now Evans himself –

'For God's sake don't come!' Septimus cried out. For he could not look
upon the dead.

But the branches parted. A man in grey was actually walking towards
them. It was Evans! But no mud was on him; no wounds; he was not
changed. I must tell the whole world, Septimus cried, raising his hand
(as the dead man in the grey suit came nearer) . . .

And that is being young, Peter Walsh thought as he passed them. To be having an awful scene – the poor girl looked absolutely desperate – in the middle of the morning.

(Mrs Dalloway pp. 78–9)

The man in the grey suit whom Septimus Smith sees as Evans is of course Peter Walsh crossing the Park on his way from Clarissa Dalloway. But just as, in Owen's poem, it is made clear that all that there is of the present for these 'Mental Cases' is the past, so Septimus Smith cannot help but perceive Peter Walsh as Evans. But this imposed necessity, by which all presents take place in an actual past, creates a kind of *reality* with which the psychiatrist must come to terms.

Despite Rezia's interventions to the effect that Septimus 'served with the greatest distinction', in the war, and was promoted, Septimus's own irony about 'that little shindy of schoolboys with gunpower' would be lost on Bradshaw. And it must surely be part of the point that to be unaware of the irony implicit in the discourse of the patient is to fail utterly to understand why the patient is 'attaching meanings to words of a symbolic kind'. As Sir William notes this 'serious symptom' on his pink card, Septimus is obviously deciding that the man is a fool (although potentially a dangerous fool) and therefore there is no further point in trying to make his meaning understood.

It is certainly part of Virginia's intention in her depiction of the psychiatric scene to throw into relief the fact that the psychiatrist is deliberately blinding himself to three sorts of evidence. First, Bradshaw makes no attempt to investigate, or understand, how the world in fact appears to his patient. Second, he ignores the embodiment of his patient, which would doubtless be highly significant: extreme nervousness, absence of attention, a sense of his being bodily absent, being bodily 'somewhere else'. And third, he ignores the most important kind of evidence of all – the verbal associations and puns that Smith makes, his inversion of values, his tone of muddled contempt. The psychiatrist who *refuses* to pay attention to these three bands of signifying activity is not only failing in his job, he is actually falsifying and damaging it.

Virginia is particularly careful to emphasise the significance of

Smith's embodiment, that is to say, the way he 'lives' his body and the way the world appears to him 'through' his body. Septimus has been given to the reader, right from the beginning, as being in a state of peculiar attentiveness, in which objects in the world 'out there' suddenly seem to coalesce and to gleam with intense and personal meaning.

The case of the mysterious car in Bond Street is a perfect example:

And there the motor car stood with drawn blinds, and upon them a curious pattern like a tree, Septimus thought, and this gradual drawing together of everything to one centre before his eyes, as if some horror had come almost to the surface and was about to burst into flames, terrified him. The world wavered and quivered and threatened to burst into flames.

(p. 18)

In the park, his surroundings speak directly to him:

he saw Regent's Park before him. Long streamers of sunlight fawned at his feet. The trees waved, brandished. We welcome, the world seemed to say; we accept; we create. Beauty, the world seemed to say.

(p. 77)

Virginia describes Septimus Smith's state of bodily awareness as being one of quite intolerable sensitivity:

Scientifically speaking, the flesh was melted off the world. His body was macerated until only the nerve fibres were left. It was spread like a veil upon a rock.

He lay back in his chair, exhausted but upheld. He lay resting, waiting, before he again interpreted, with agony, to mankind. He lay very high, on the back of the world. The earth thrilled beneath him. Red flowers grew through his flesh; their stiff leaves rustled by his head . . .

But he himself remained high on his rock, like a drowned sailor on a rock. I leant over the edge of the boat and fell down, he thought. I went under the sea. I have been dead, and yet am now alive, but let me rest still, he begged (he was talking to himself again – it was awful, awful!) . . .

(pp. 76–7)

Smith experiences the world as a perpetual bombardment of intolerably loud noises, sharp feelings, bright light, clear insights – in other words, his body has ceased to act as a buffer between him and the world. He has grown beyond and out of the normal protective barriers which the body affords. Indeed he is unaware of his body. Everything has become present mentally in an intolerable way. But Sir William Bradshaw chooses to ignore all this semantically rich evidence of the body and reduces it to mere delayed shell-shock. Smith's way of sitting in the chair at the interview, his way of speaking, of holding himself, should have been instinct with a thousand pointers to the lived reality he is trying, through his body, to bring to the others' attention (his only hope of reprieve). But his whole mode of embodiment is discounted.

The mode of symbolic discourse used by Septimus is similarly disallowed. The distinction he makes between 'The European War' and 'the War itself' is full of implications which lead down into the unconscious struggle with the failure to find meaning in what he has been through. It is not as though Smith speaks stupidly, or dully, or incoherently. Everything he says has its point only too clearly made. Yet in the psychiatric situation, where his symbolic reference-system is refused and discounted, everything he says argues against his sanity, argues for his internment.

It seems very clear that this refusal of recognition of the patient's embodied state in the fictional psychiatric interview is a direct comment upon what took place in 1913. What problems of embodiment Virginia was engaging with in 1912–13 we know from *The Voyage Out*. But it is highly unlikely that these problems were in any way taken account of in Henry Head's diagnosis. He was, after all, a neurologist, and the belief that all 'nervous' diseases were in some way reducible to a physiological upset was common to all the specialists Virginia was taken to. Yet herein lies the difference between taking account of a body as a mere object, and the body as 'lived'. A physiological analysis may be appropriate in the first case, but the second will require a phenomenological awareness of the lived intentionality which the body is attempting to express. Sir William says the ultimately silly thing:

'Try to think as little about yourself as possible,' said Sir William kindly. Really, he was not fit to be about.

(p. 109)

Who, one wonders, is not really fit to be about? For his own self is the one thing Septimus cannot stop thinking about – that and his complicity in human nature, and the horror and cruelty of men.

I imagine that that identical sentence was said to Virginia Woolf by Head when she was sent down to the country. Or it may have been similar to the one Leonard recounts, from the lips of 'the great Dr Saintsbury, as he shook Virginia's hand' outside his Harley Street rooms: 'Equanimity – equanimity – practise equanimity, Mrs Woolf' (*Downhill All the Way* p. 51). Anyway, Sir William's dismissal is the sort of remark that a human being endowed with a normal sense of justice retains for a lifetime. Both Septimus and Virginia Woolf were judged to be 'very, very ill'.

Virginia had proposed, mutely and without being able to express the internal inter-relationships of its structure, a certain view of the world which, while intensely unacceptable to the objectivity of that time, still made perfect sense to herself and held together absolutely coherently as a set of beliefs. She attempted, in the person of Septimus Smith, to propose that this world view be examined on its merits, and answered as it deserved to be answered. But both in her own case, and in Septimus's, the answer was the same: evidence inadmissible. Verdict: 'insane'.

But:

He could not feel . . . beauty was behind a pane of glass. Even taste had no relish to him . . . But he could not taste, he could not feel . . . his brain was perfect; it must be the fault of the world then – that he could not feel.

(pp. 97–8)

And:

It might be possible, Septimus thought, looking at England from the train window, as they left Newhaven; it might be possible that the world itself is without meaning.

(p. 98)

Meaning has drained out of the world.

The state Septimus is suffering from is not any which can be reached by, or intersected by, psychiatric expertise. It was the same with Virginia in 1913. Septimus is in despair. And he suffers, as Virginia obviously did, from what one might call the vision of ontological emptying. Suddenly, as if someone has extracted the plug from the bottom of the world, the colour begins to drain out. Objects are deprived of reality, of distinctness, of colour. The most remarkable description of this actual process is in the long soliloquy by Bernard at the end of *The Waves*. The ten paragraphs which show it happening run from 'For one day as I leant over a gate' at page 201 to the paragraph which ends 'Look, this is the truth' on page 204. This is the world 'seen without a self', and it is terrifying. The landscape is one of utter desolation.

The scene beneath me withered. It was like the eclipse when the sun went out and left the earth, flourishing in full summer foliage, withered, brittle, false . . . The woods had vanished; the earth was a waste of shadow. No sound broke the silence of the wintry landscape. No cock crowed; no smoke rose; no train moved. A man without a self, I said. A heavy body leaning on a gate. A dead man. With dispassionate despair, with entire disillusionment, I surveyed the dust dance.

(p. 202)

With the seventh paragraph, the light begins to return to things, and in the eighth, a kind of double self walks like a ghost, invisible, through the landscape.

So the landscape returned to me; so I saw fields rolling in waves of colour beneath me, but now with this difference; I saw but was not seen. I walked unshadowed; I came unheralded.

(p. 203)

In the latter paragraphs describing this transformation, the world is filled again with colour and meaning, but, having lived through the experience of absolute, total, deprivation, the 'self' which sees it sees also through it and knows it to be a mere cover for the ontological greyness and deprivation which lies always underneath. The passage from appearance to reality has been achieved, and the return to appearance also made. Thus the self 'saw but was not seen'. That is because this self has penetrated 'to the other side of appearances'.

The description is terrifying, however, and one can feel exactly how the world appeared to Virginia when she was called 'mad'. It is suddenly destitute, grey, motionless, sapless, fleshless, without hope, without green, without water, without life, without

desire, without comfort, without illusion. There is also that
accompanying image, 'No fin breaks the waste of this immeasur-
able sea'. And it is fascinating that the way this ontological
draining of the world is experienced, is given in terms of absorption of colour, as if objects, like the images on a television set, can
be 'drained' of their colour at the turning of the knob, and then
have their colour returned to them by a turn of the fingers the
other way:

Then off twists a white wraith. The woods throb blue and green, and
gradually the fields drink in red, gold, brown. Suddenly a river snatches
a blue light. The earth absorbs colour like a sponge slowly drinking
water. It puts on weight; rounds itself; hangs pendent; settles and
swings beneath our feet.

(p. 203)

In 1913, the idea of a colour television set where the colour
could be drained out of the objects on the screen at the flick of a
wrist, and restored to them gradually or rapidly, would not of
course have been available. But at several points in her writing
Virginia has explained what this gradual ebbing of colour and
reality from the world looked like, and we can use this modern
technological simile to make the imaginative leap easy for ourselves.

If the world can thus be drained, emptied, as the ebb of colour
happens, then the state we have to describe may well have some
kind of physiological explanation, but it also needs a name which
can be used with respect and modesty by those who are not
similarly afflicted. Psychiatric labelling is not what is required
here: on the contrary, an act of almost religious respect should be
put in place of assertive technical talk. Here is a phenomenon in
the spiritual life of man which has as yet no name, and which yet
Virginia Woolf has described. Some few others have described
the *state* as well: Beckett no doubt, Kafka, Kierkegaard, Pascal,
Shakespeare. But I know of no other description of *the actual
transformation* than Virginia's. In those ten paragraphs at the end
of *The Waves*, she describes the way into this deprived, drained
landscape, and the way back again into the world of colour.
The world bleeds to death in front of her eyes, and gradually
the colours and reality of the world are restored. This is not

madness. The problem is ours, for we have to reckon with a reality for which we have as yet no name, and of which Virginia has given the very first description in the literature of the world.

CHAPTER 15

Virginia's embodiment

The question of the way in which Septimus sees the physical world, and the way that kind of vision is ignored or disallowed by Sir William Bradshaw, brings in its train the question of embodiment generally in Virginia's novels.

By 'embodiment' I mean, borrowing a concept from Merleau-Ponty, the way the 'lived body' perceives the world. Embodiment in this sense is an activity, not a passive process. It is everything that Locke ignored in his theory of the passivity of experiential atoms breaking into an empty mental space, and everything that the great Romantic poets wished to re-introduce when they spoke of the world we 'half perceive and half create'. In that Romantic conception, whether Kant's, Hegel's, Blake's or Wordsworth's, of a world which is created by perception, brought into active being by perception, the phenomenological conception of the activity of consciousness in the 'lived body' may well have its hidden historical origin. Be that as it may, the view which Merleau-Ponty has of our perceptual process, a view which emphasises the manner in which the 'lived body' takes an active part in conferring the meanings we wish to confer upon the world through our 'intentionality', is a view which seems to be an exact parallel, in the realm of philosophy, to what Virginia Woolf attempted in her novels. In Virginia Woolf, indeed, phenomenology found its novelist. The ways the body is 'lived', is active in creating, and participating in, a world of meanings, is her theme throughout her fictional career. The various ways in which the body is active in perceiving and creating a world is given clearly in the case of Septimus Smith. How the world appears to him is given, in all its flickering oscillation between control and panic, in a dozen places where perception becomes active in bringing a world of meaning into being, a world of meaning which is, however, inter-subjectively disconfirmed, to borrow a concept from Husserl, by Smith's counter-subjects in the world. That he is disconfirmed, that his 'intentionality' projected over the world seems odd and strange even to his wife, is part of the genius of the novel. We see, at one and the same moment, how a world could appear like that to someone in Smith's embodied state, and also how the world is not in fact, for his embodied counter-subjects, like that. We get the brilliance, the inspiration, the wonder, and at the same moment (or a split second after) we see that this is a world view that will get itself disconfirmed. In giving Septimus Smith such a carefully graduated series of embodiments through *Mrs Dalloway*, Virginia opens up the whole question of how the world is perceived through and by means of the fact that we inhabit bodies which are themselves creators of meaning in the world of created meanings.

But now let us look at the testimony of *The Waves*. It could be that by a free variation of perspectives, Leonard's and Virginia's own, we shall see the other side of what was utterly obscure to Leonard:

'I shall edge behind them,' said Rhoda, 'as if I saw someone I know. But I know no one . . . The door opens; the tiger leaps. The door opens; terror rushes in; terror upon terror, pursuing me . . . Throwing faint smiles to mask their cruelty, their indifference, they seize me . . . I must take his hand; I must answer. But what answer shall I give? I am thrust back to stand burning in this clumsy, this ill-fitting body, to receive the shafts of his indifference and his scorn, I who long for marble columns and pools on the other side of the world where the swallow dips her wings . . . A million arrows pierce me. Scorn and ridicule pierce me. I, who could beat my breast against the storm and let the hail choke me joyfully, am pinned down here; am exposed. The tiger leaps. Tongues with their whips are upon me. Mobile, incessant, they flicker over me. I must prevaricate and fence them off with lies. What amulet is there against this disaster? What face can I summon to lay cool upon this heat? . . . Hide me, I cry, protect me, for I am the youngest, the most naked of you all.'

(*The Waves* pp. 75–6)

Exposedness is the key note. The body is experienced as open, exposed, threatened, surrounded, scrutinised, menaced. Rhoda is the character in *The Waves* in whom this experience, which was Virginia's, is particularly emphasised.

'Hide me, I cry, protect me, for I am the youngest, the most naked of you all.' The experience on Lewes High Street here has its fictional counterpart. This is the voice which was hidden within the silent and apparently self-sufficient woman whom Leonard so wonderingly shepherded. Here is the agony that she internalised, during those walks in public space. An acute sense of exposedness is testified to here. It is not only the feeling we all know, of being awkward, of being looked at, of feeling ill at ease.It is a positive obsession by the idea that all eyes are on her. And from Leonard's own testimony, we know that she was correct. All eyes *were* on her, and 'nine out of ten' people stopped to stare, to nudge each other, to laugh or to giggle.

. . . I am broken into separate pieces; I am no longer one . . . But I am not composed enough, standing on tiptoe on the verge of fire, still scorched by the hot breath, afraid of the door opening and the leap of the tiger, to make even one sentence. What I say is perpetually contradicted. Each time the door opens I am interrupted. I am not yet twenty one. I am to be broken. I am to be derided all my life. I am to be cast up and down among these men and women, with their twitching faces, with their lying tongues, like a cork on a rough sea. Like a ribbon of weed I am flung far every time the door opens. I am the foam that sweeps and fills the uttermost rims of the rocks with whiteness; I am also a girl, here in this room.

(pp. 76–7)

'What I say is perpetually contradicted.' 'I am to be broken. I am to be derided all my life.' It seems that in creating the character of Rhoda, Virginia wished to 'exorcise' a certain view of herself, as she had 'exorcised' her own mental state in *Mrs Dalloway*, and 'exorcised' her parents in *To the Lighthouse*. Rhoda's embodiment, the pain and embarrassment it brought with it, is exorcised in these passages of despair, of intense inwardness, of intense conviction. It seems as if Rhoda feels that she has been created only to be the butt of other people's scorn, or the object of other people's laughter. 'What I say is perpetually contradicted . . . I am to be derided all my life.' Others are 'lords and owners of their faces' (Shakespeare, Sonnet 94), she is not ever to be so.

One form of embodiment in *The Waves*, then, Rhoda's, is presented as the experience of continuous physical exposure. If we assume that Rhoda is one, very prominent, aspect of Virginia's experience of her own embodiment, then we can deduce that she went through a martyrdom of embarrassment and anxiety. It was for her as if she were constantly in a room of people, looked at by them all the time, ridiculed by them, and stark naked. Every glance goes home, every laugh comes to rest on exposed flesh. She is undressed, open, simply exposed (both in the sense of being shown up, and also in the sense of being exhibited) to every eye in the room. 'Hide me, I cry, protect me, for I am the youngest, the most naked of you all.'

This kind of embodiment also involves two related fears: the fear of time, and the fear of purposelessness. Like Septimus, Rhoda cannot really believe that time is real or that any of her purposes in life have any intrinsic worth or validity:

'If I could believe,' said Rhoda, 'that I should grow old in pursuit and change, I should be rid of my fear: nothing persists. One moment does not lead to another. The door opens and the tiger leaps. You did not see me come. I circled round the chairs to avoid the horror of the spring. I am afraid of you all. I am afraid of the shock of sensation that leaps upon me, because I cannot deal with it as you do – I cannot make one moment merge in the next. To me they are all violent, all separate; and if I fall under the shock of the leap of the moment you will be on me, tearing me to pieces. I have no end in view. I do not know how to run minute to minute and hour to hour, solving them by some natural force until they make the whole and indivisible mass that you call life . . . But there is no single scent, no single body for me to follow. And I have no face.'

(p. 93)

The image relates directly back to the obsessional inner discourse of Septimus Smith ('They scour the desert' etc.). And through this linkage, we can clearly see that in some respects, Rhoda's embodiment is not unlike Septimus Smith's. For both, the world is experienced as a place of incipient violence, unleashed ferocity, and personal insecurity.

The common affectivity of Rhoda and Septimus Smith points to a common fear, which must have been Virginia's, the fear of suddenness and the fear of ordinary experience, which she knows she cannot deal with. The 'shock of sensation' leaps upon her, like the tiger, because she cannot make sense of experience in the normal way.

I am afraid of the shock of sensation that leaps upon me, because I cannot deal with it as you do – I cannot make one moment merge in the next. To me they are all violent, all separate; and if I fall under the shock of the leap of the moment you will be on me, tearing me to pieces.

(p. 93)

Bernard is suddenly used as a 'focus', seeing Rhoda from the outside:

Rhoda loves to be alone. She fears us because we shatter the sense of being which is so extreme in solitude – see how she grasps her fork – her weapon against us.

(p. 95)

Even though Rhoda is seen from the outside, the significance of the object she grasps in her hand is correctly assimilated. Rhoda herself has told of an earlier moment of 'humiliation' at a garden party when she was young:

Also, in the middle, cadaverous, awful, lay the grey puddle in the courtyard, when, holding an envelope in my hand, I carried a message. I came to the puddle. I could not cross it. Identity failed me. We are nothing, I said, and fell. I was blown like a feather, I was wafted down tunnels. Then very gingerly, I pushed my foot across. I laid my hand against a brick wall. I returned very painfully, drawing myself back into my body over the grey, cadaverous space of the puddle. This is life then to which I am committed.

(p. 46)

A miniature Odyssey. 'Indentity failed me.' But bravely she perseveres, drawing herself back into her body in the face of the threat offered by the 'cadaverous space of the puddle'.

We now have access to the source, in the Schulkind collection, for this experience, which Virginia retained as a painful initiatory moment of existential insecurity all her life:

What then has remained interesting? Again those moments of being. Two I always remember. There was the moment of the puddle in the path; when for no reason I could discover, everything suddenly became unreal; I was suspended; I could not step across the puddle; I tried to touch something . . . the whole world became unreal.

(*A Sketch of the Past*, in Schulkind p. 78)

It is yet further confirmation of the thesis that Rhoda's embodiment is primarily modelled on Virginia's when this threat of suspension is met by a reaching out to touch something. This is Rhoda's constant ploy when faced with a situation which deprives her of all indentity.

'Identity failed me.' This must be, we begin to realise, one of the central structures of the body-consciousness of Virginia. The tiger leaps, the terror springs. Fitted awkwardly into a body at which everybody laughs, she suffers inwardly all kinds of daily mortification and humiliation. She withers when hostile glances penetrate her, glances which reduce her to shivering jelly, without identity.

In order to reinforce the validity of Rhoda's own kind of embodiment, Virginia builds into her novel her physical exact opposite, Jinny. Jinny, because she is at home in her body, is not afraid of glances, and accepts the male regard not as a terror, but as a pleasure. There are other characters in *The Waves* too who are free of the pain of being looked at. Thinking enviously of them, Rhoda says:

They are immune . . . from picking fingers and searching eyes. How easily they turn and glance; what poses they take of energy and pride!

(p. 102)

This sense of being 'picked at', 'plucked at' by eyes, by glances, as if the body were being pinched or assaulted indecently, occurs consistently and constantly in the meditations of Rhoda:

I must start when you pluck at me with your children, your poems, your chilblains or whatever it is that you do and suffer. But I am not deluded. After all these callings hither and thither, these pluckings and searchings, I shall fall alone through this thin sheet into gulfs of fire. And you will not help me. More cruel than the old torturers, you will let me fall, and will tear me to pieces when I am fallen.

(pp. 158–9)

Her sense of identity must have been precariously balanced. Again and again she insists she has 'no face'. This is a strange statement for a woman whose face was, by all accounts, the most striking thing about her. Everyone remarked upon the luminous beauty of her face. Perhaps Vanessa Bell, in her famous portrait of Virginia faceless, was making the point through empathy with her sister's deepest feeling about herself. For Virginia, as she knew herself from the inside, had no face:

But here I am nobody. I have no face. This great company, all dressed in brown serge, has robbed me of my identity. We are all callous, unfriended. I will seek out a face, a composed, a monumental face, and will endow it with omniscience, and wear it under my dress like a talisman . . . I promise myself this. So I will not cry.

(p. 24)

The lack of a face is unhesitatingly connected with the theme of callousness, the theme of the pack scouring the desert. The others, they have faces:

'That is my face,' said Rhoda, 'in the looking-glass behind Susan's shoulder – that face is my face. But I will duck behind her to hide it, for I am not here. I have no face. Other people have faces; Susan and Jinny have faces; they are here. Their world is the real world. The things they lift are heavy. They say Yes, they say No; whereas I shift and change and am seen through in a second. If they meet a housemaid she looks at them without laughing. But she laughs at me. They know what to say if spoken to. They laugh really; they get angry really; while I have to look first and do what other people do when they have done it.

(pp. 30–1)

The sense of a world of reality which other people have, those others who are 'lords and owners of their faces', is immediately connected in the code of embodiment-consciousness with a threat to identity and a reliance upon other people's gestures and words in an emergency. It would seem as if emergencies (verbal or social emergencies) actually threw into jeopardy Virginia's trust in continued existence as such. From dislocated moment to dislocated moment, she lives perpetually in the fear of exposure.

Therefore I hate looking-glasses which show me my real face. Alone, I often fall down into nothingness. I must push my foot stealthily lest I should fall off the edge of the world into nothingness. I have to bang my hand against some hard door to call myself back to the body.

(p. 31)

This fear of looking at herself in the mirror we now know, since the publication of *Moments of Being*, is associated directly with the experience of shame and guilt at Talland House. 'When I was six or seven perhaps, I got into the habit of looking at my face in the glass. But I only did this if I was sure that I was alone. I was ashamed of it. A strong feeling of guilt seemed naturally attached to it . . . I thus detect another element in the shame which I had in being caught looking at myself in the glass in the hall. I must have been ashamed or afraid of my own body.' There follows the story of the sexual molestation by Gerald Duckworth (Schulkind pp. 67–8).

At the famous dinner party at the centre of the novel, Rhoda's concerns run consistently and predictably:

'The swing door goes on opening,' said Rhoda. 'Strangers keep on coming, people we shall never see again, people who brush us disagreeably with their familiarity, their indifference, and the sense of a world continuing without us. We cannot sink down, we cannot forget our faces. Even I who have no face, who make no difference when I come in (Susan and Jinny change bodies and faces), flutter unattached, without anchorage anywhere, unconsolidated, incapable of composing any blankness or continuity or wall against which these bodies move.'

(p. 87)

It is the sense, then, of a body (in which one happens to be situate) moving unattached, unconsolidated, in a sense not yet even created, amorphous, faceless, that haunts her. She feels unstable, threatened at her very centre. Everything, whether animate or inanimate, is a potential threat to her. Anything whatever, from whatever order of creation it may happen to come, is an abyss of nothingness into which she, faceless and unhelped, may sink at any moment, for ever. There is a sense in which she recognises that no-one could help her at that moment of utter annihilation, the problem dwelling so intimately in herself.

One central symbolic connection that develops in richness as the novel progresses is the assertion 'I have no face' associated with images of foam, spray, sea-water: pointing to the future, as we uneasily begin to apprehend.

But there is no single scent, no single body for me to follow. And I have no face. I am like the foam that races over the beach . . . I am whirled down caverns, and flap like paper against endless corridors, and must press my hand against the wall to draw myself back.

(p. 93)

That pressing of the 'hand against the wall to draw myself back' has an analogous structure to the early encounter with the 'cadaverous' puddle at school, when Rhoda recalls 'I laid my hand against a brick wall'. Since Rhoda's embodiment is so closely modelled on Virginia's it is no surprise to find, in the autobiographical account of the puddle (Schulkind p. 78), the exactly similar reaction: 'There was the moment of the puddle in the path . . . I was suspended . . . I tried to touch something.' Standing in a group of people, and unobserved by them, how many times must Virginia herself not have reached out to touch some solid object to steady her sense of identity? A fork or a glass, a handbag or a chair-back, a wall or a door-jamb, pressing her hand against something in order to draw herself back, this structure of Virginia's own embodiment is surely inferrable from the consistency of Rhoda's reactions when threatened by nonidentity.

I walked straight up to you instead of circling round to avoid the shock of sensation as I used. But it is only that I have taught my body to do a certain trick. Inwardly I am not taught; I fear, I hate, I love, I envy and despise you, but I never join you happily. Coming up from the station, refusing to accept the shadow of the trees and the pillar-boxes, I perceived, from your coats and umbrellas, even at a distance, how you stand embedded in a substance made of repeated moments run together; are committed, have an attitude, with children, authority, fame, love, society; where I have nothing. I have no face.

(pp. 157–8)

That theme of childlessness again, as if the absence of a child 'out there' in public space, a child who owed its existence to her, deprived her of a central hold over her own identity. But even time does not cohere for her: she envies others who can stand 'embedded in a substance made of repeated moments run together'. She cannot put the world together as the others do, and get it right every time, naturally, without even trying. She only has to walk down a corridor, and some housemaid will laugh at her. The whole of existence is against her: everything laughs at her, contradicts her, deprives her of a face and an identity and a moment to stand entimed in.

This sense of being perpetually contradicted is strangely strong for a woman whom we have been taught to regard as the most brilliant literary lion of Bloomsbury society. 'They say Yes, they say No; whereas I shift and change and am seen through in a second.' She repeats this several times in the novel: 'They say, Yes; they say, No; they bring their fists down with a bang on the table. But I doubt; I tremble; I see the wild thorn tree shake its shadow in the desert.' She could not be more explicit: 'What I say is perpetually contradicted. Each time the door opens I am interrupted. I am not yet twenty one. I am to be broken. I am to be derided all my life' (p. 77). And then, ominously, always there, almost unnoticed, the sea image, the water image:

I am to be cast up and down among these men and women, with their twitching faces, with their lying tongues, like a cork on a rough sea. Like a ribbon of weed I am flung far every time the door opens. I am the foam that sweeps and fills the uttermost rims of the rocks with whiteness; I am also a girl, here in this room.

(p. 77)

'Oh, life, how I have dreaded you,' said Rhoda, 'oh, human beings, how I have hated you!'

(p. 145)

This passionate outburst is the prelude to the swan-song of Rhoda in the novel (pages 145–7), and contains the whole recalled reality of her life, her flight from life; and the water imagery is dangerously dominant. The outburst which opens this passionate meditation of a whole woman refers us briefly back to a previous moment, the moment of the dinner at the centre of the novel:

Rhoda comes now, from nowhere, having slipped in while we were not looking. She must have made a tortuous course, taking cover now behind a waiter, now behind some ornamental pillar, so as to put off as long as possible the shock of recognition, so as to be secure for one more moment to rock her petals in her basin. We wake her. We torture her. She dreads us, she despises us, yet comes cringing to our sides because for all our cruelty there is always some name, some face, which sheds a radiance, which lights up her pavements and makes it possible for her to replenish her dreams.

(p. 86)

Louis (seeing Rhoda from the outside) has yet hit on the central structure of her dependence–fear relationship unerringly. And, thinking how much she must have suffered, it is perhaps not surprising that the imagery which flows through Rhoda's meditations becomes more and more world-weary, becomes more and more drugged with desire for escape, for transcendence. As so often in the work of Virginia, water represents the resolution of warring and jarring contraries that cannot be reconciled. It represents the end of the hurtful dominance of the male mind, and a feminine passing into peace.

I threw my bunch into the spreading wave. I said, 'Consume me, carry me to the furthest limit.' The wave has broken; the bunch is withered. I seldom think of Percival now.

Now I climb this Spanish hill; and I will suppose that this mule-back is my bed and that I lie dying. There is only a thin sheet between me now and the infinite depths . . . Now the bed gives under me. The sheets spotted with yellow holes let me fall through . . . We launch out now over the precipice. Beneath us lie the lights of the herring fleet. The cliffs vanish. Rippling small, rippling grey, innumerable waves spread beneath us. I touch nothing. I see nothing. We may sink and settle on the waves. The sea will drum in my ears. The white petals will be darkened with sea water. They will float for a moment and then sink. Rolling me over the waves will shoulder me under. Everything falls in a tremendous shower, dissolving me.

(pp. 146–7)

The text gives us clearly to understand, though it is not directly stated, that Rhoda, at the end of her sufferings, will commit suicide by water.

There is an earlier moment in the novel when this resolution through water was clearly touched upon. Significantly enough, it is at the dinner held to celebrate the departure of Percival to India, and to his death:

It makes no sign, it does not beckon, it does not see us. Behind it roars the sea. It is beyond our reach. Yet there I venture. There I go to replenish my emptiness, to stretch my nights and fill them fuller and fuller with dreams. And for a second even now, even here, I reach my object and say, 'Wander no more. All else is trial and make-believe. Here is the end'.

(pp. 99–100)

These passages fulfil a premonition, present in the text almost from the very beginning, a premonition that the tortured journey through an embodiment impossible to sustain will end in a death by water:

Oh, to awake from dreaming! Look, there is the chest of drawers. Let me pull myself out of these waters. But they heap themselves on me; they sweep me between their great shoulders; I am turned; I am tumbled; I am stretched, among these long lights, these long waves, these endless paths, with people pursuing, pursuing.

(p. 20)

This then, Rhoda's, is one aspect of the experience of embodiment in *The Waves*. But all of the other characters are there to 'fill out' other possibilities which are related to, or the inverse of, the embodiment of Rhoda. Rhoda is the central point in a measure of possibilities which stretches from the extreme, nervous, childless sensuality of Jinny, across to the enrooted, earthy naturalness of Susan.

Jinny is fully embodied in a way which Virginia envied: she is pretty, sexy, attractive, a friend to men. Her whole life is one unbroken and unashamed sexual escapade. Such an embodiment was denied to Rhoda and must represent one of the aspects of embodiment about which Virginia felt most ambiguously. At the other extreme, Susan is sunk in the loam of the farming life, with her feet planted squarely on the face of the revolving globe. She inhabits, without any sense of strain, the seasons, the weathers, the lands that surround her. She has children. She has animals, crops, fruits, tasks, recognised limits and recognised identity, which is continually being confirmed by others, just as Jinny's is. If Jinny is embodied sexually, Susan is embodied naturally. Both embodiments, however, take their force from being defined in terms of what Rhoda's embodiment most significantly lacks: either sexual experience, or children, or both.

Common to both Jinny and to Susan is this reinforcement of identity through repetition. Whereas Rhoda finds each time a new time, and each meeting a new threat, for the other two women, each time is a further success, and each meeting a further achievement. Successful repetition reinforces their sense of being 'real', of existing, of having faces, names, careers, bodies.

The male characters in *The Waves* have the function of 'doubling' what is given explicitly in the case of Rhoda. It is no accident, for instance, that all three male characters, Bernard, Neville and Louis, suffer predominantly from a sense of insecurity.

All three suffer from the same basic lack of confidence in their presence in the world as Rhoda does. Louis, for instance, eating a lunch in a café, looks 'at the little men at the next table to be sure that I do what they do' (p. 67). He too is constantly aware of the swinging door, letting in new and potentially hostile people: 'the door perpetually shuts and opens. I am conscious of flux, of disorder; of annihilation and despair' (p. 67). He is not like the others around him: that is his problem, just as it is Rhoda's. 'Where then is the break in this continuity? What the fissure through which one sees disaster?'(p. 68). The others accept their food from the waitress and there is no sense of strain in this action. But he cannot. 'I am not included.' He sees 'eternity. It is a stigma burnt on my quivering flesh by a cowled man with a red-hot iron' (p. 69). All this is going on while Louis is simply having lunch in a café. He is existentially not at home in his own skin. And of course, the central embodiment-structure which is Rhoda's seems inevitable when the time comes to pay the waitress and leave the café:

I am always the youngest, the most innocent, the most trustful. You are all protected. I am naked. When the waitress with the plaited wreaths of hair swings past, she deals you your apricots and custard unhesitatingly, like a sister. You are her brothers. But when I get up, brushing the crumbs from my waistcoat, I slip too large a tip, a shilling, under the edge of my plate, so that she may not find it till I am gone, and her scorn, as she picks it up with laughter, may not strike on me till I am past the swing-doors.

(pp. 69–70)

There again is the characteristic that Leonard has told us about, the readiness of the others in the street, in the café, to turn and stare, to laugh, here in 'scorn'. Why should Louis be so afraid of 'scorn'? He whips out of the door before the waitress can find her tip, anxious to escape her laughter and derision. We recognise in Louis's dilemma the same anxiety Rhoda has constantly suffered. And he half projects her solution, too: 'I, who would wish to feel close over me the protective waves of the ordinary' (p. 68). Louis, too, lives in fear of ridicule, of laughter, of disconfirmation.

The passage quoted above, although it issues from a male consciousness, is there to reinforce the central structure of embodiment in the novel, which is undoubtedly Rhoda's. When the men suffer from anxiety, suspense or terror, they see the world in exactly the same way as Rhoda does.

Nowhere is this better illustrated than in that long sequence which precedes the dinner which is to celebrate Percival's departure for India. Here, through the eyes of Neville (again a Rhoda-substitute), we see those dreadful doors opening and shutting, the hostile guests coming in; and a kind of intentionality is set up through which, and because of which, the whole room, the whole scene, is de-realised until Percival arrives. The room exists in a kind of suspended chaos, full of potential hostility, and nothing is real until Percival arrives and confirms Neville in his own identity:

'It is now five minutes to eight,' said Neville. 'I have come early. I have taken my place at the table ten minutes before the time in order to taste every moment of anticipation; to see the door open and to say, "Is it Percival? No; it is not Percival." There is a morbid pleasure in saying: "No, it is not Percival." I have seen the door open and shut twenty times already; each time the suspense sharpens. This is the place to which he is coming. This is the table at which he will sit. Here, incredible as it seems, will be his actual body. This table, these chairs, this metal vase with its three red flowers are about to undergo an extraordinary transformation. Already the room, with its swing doors, its tables heaped with fruit, with cold joints, wears the wavering, unreal appearance of a place where one waits expecting something to happen. Things quiver as if not yet in being.'

(pp. 84–5)

Although it is Neville who purports to be observing, the feelings of suspense and anxiety overlap so exactly what we know to be the central obsessions of Rhoda that we are led back again and again to the undoubted, lived experience of Virginia herself, present in both male and female characters. Neville's consciousness exactly coincides with the consciousness of a female, a female moreover who feels herself particularly vulnerable in the public space where she sits, observed from all sides, and companionless, unsupported, isolated, unconfirmed. She could be anybody. Her 'identity has failed' her. The whole room is unreal. She sits and waits until a certain person should come, that person who will restore to her the very experience of being, the experience of actual real existence. There is something horrible, menacing, even phantasmagoric in the scene. We begin to know, from experience, as it were, what the embodiment of Virginia must have been like:

Things quiver as if not yet in being. The blankness of the white table-cloth glares. The hostility, the indifference of other people dining here is oppressive. We look at each other; see that we do not know each other, stare, and go off. Such looks are lashes. I feel the whole cruelty and indifference of the world in them.

(p. 85)

And one cannot miss the connection between the looks which are lashes, and the 'cruelty and indifference of the world' which are made manifest in these looks. It is Septimus Smith's vision again, endlessly repeated. And the vision consists, in the characters in *The Waves* as in Septimus Smith, in the experience of a chain of embodied perceptions which, endlessly repeated, lead always to the same result: nihilism, despair. It starts from an awareness of the body. The body is exposed; the looks are lashes; I am naked; the others are clothed; their looks pin me down, expose me, ridicule me; therefore the world is cruel, indifferent, hateful.

If one thinks back to the humiliations of 1913, these linked feelings do add up to a perfectly rational conclusion, given the bodily determinants. Given these determinants, Virginia had grounds for finding the world hostile, indifferent, menacing, finally evil and meaningless.

In moments of severe emotional stress, Virginia reached out for a solid object upon which she could momentarily lean, in order, through its solidity, to recompose the atoms of her jarred self. I think there may be a temporal correlative to this. In a situation of waiting, her being was unreal until something or someone solid came to her rescue. Here is an example, once again seen through the eyes of Neville:

Such looks are lashes. I feel the whole cruelty and indifference of the world in them. If he should not come I could not bear it. I should go. Yet somebody must be seeing him now. He must be in some cab; he must be passing some shop. And every moment he seems to pump into this room this prickly light, this intensity of being, so that things have lost their normal uses – this knife-blade is only a flash of light, not a thing to cut with. The normal is abolished.

(p. 85)

Virginia's relationship to the Impressionist school of painters can be discerned in that last image. One sees the flashes of light of Monet; for a moment, indeed, one sees the whole restaurant as a series of shifting planes of light and impression, no reality at all. But the unreality here is not set up by mere art, it is a mirror of a state of being which is utterly deprived of identity, of security, of self-assurance. There is indeed something morbid, something overdone, in the idea of a man waiting for another man with this intensity (Neville waiting for his admired Percival, in the novel). But I think the morbidity disappears once one recognises that Neville merely 'doubles' Rhoda.

Neville passes the moment of waiting in an agony of fear and apprehension. He observes Louis come in, and Louis observes Susan come in, and then Rhoda is seen (again presumably by Louis) creeping round behind things 'so as to put off as long as possible the shock of recognition'. We become aware of Neville's suspension again only after a while:

'The door opens, the door goes on opening,' said Neville, 'yet he does not come.'

(p. 86)

The whole restaurant is held in this spaceless, timeless, de-realised limbo of expectation and dependence. It is given as Neville's, of course, but it is Virginia's too. Susan observes Jinny come in.

'He has not come,' said Neville. 'The door opens and he does not come. That is Bernard . . . But without Percival there is no solidity. We are silhouettes, hollow phantoms moving mistily without a background.'

(p. 87)

And, of course Rhoda eventually takes over from Neville:

'The swing door goes on opening,' said Rhoda. 'Strangers keep on coming, people we shall never see again, people who brush us disagreeably with their familiarity, their indifference, and the sense of a world continuing without us. We cannot sink down, we cannot forget our faces. Even I who have no face, who make no difference when I come in (Susan and Jinny change bodies and faces), flutter unattached, without anchorage anywhere, unconsolidated, incapable of composing any blankness or continuity or wall against which these bodies move. It is because of Neville and his misery. The sharp breath of his misery scatters my being. Nothing can settle; nothing can subside. Every time the door opens he looks fixedly at the table – he dare not raise his eyes – then looks for one second and says, "He has not come." But here he is.'

'Now,' said Neville, 'my tree flowers. My heart rises. All oppression is relieved. All impediment is removed. The reign of chaos is over. He has imposed order. Knives cut again.'

(pp. 87–8)

The subtlety with which Rhoda becomes aware of her misery as emanating from Neville's equally profound misery scarcely covers over the very simple, but ingenious, technical device by means of which the misery and the de-realised suspension of Rhoda and Neville are one and the same. There is no felt 'break' between their two flows of consciousness, nor is there (in my view) a felt break between either of these consciousnesses and Virginia's own as she sat and waited in a public space. The de-realisation of space, the de-functionalisation of objects, the de-personalisation and de-humanisation of visual contact, all emerge as lived realities from the text. And when Percival finally appears, the whole of reality is suddenly reimposed, as if by magic, such that we feel in the triumphant 'He has imposed order. Knives cut again' the actual suppression of unreality through the presence of another. This person is needed, if the world is to take on and have a meaning, if ordinary objects like knives are to have a function. His presence is actually necessary to Rhoda–Neville–Virginia because, without him, none of them can survive as a secure identity, functioning continuously. This person is the loved person, the one who confirms one in one's identity. In the novel, this is Percival, a semi-mythical hero who never speaks, and dies a semi-mythical death in a semi-mythical land across the sea. He is not one of the six consciousnesses we study in such detail in the novel. His is a merely virtual presence. But the inter-relationships of the consciousness of Rhoda with her two female outer points of reference, and the consciousness of Neville, Louis and Bernard doubling Rhoda's, build up a kind of continuous mosaic of lived bodily experience which is recognisable and personal. This complex mosaic of possible and actual embodiments, this pattern of dependencies and fears, of suspensions and cancellations of identity, of terror and apprehension, is Virginia's.

CHAPTER 16

Führer, Duce, Tyrant

There is no more reason to call Virginia 'insane' or 'mad' when she stepped into the Ouse in 1941, than there had been on the other occasions of alleged insanity. As the 1930s ended, she saw what was coming. She had the sense that history was about to come to an end, that there was no future. The entries in *A Writer's Diary* show us how profoundly she felt that the society she had known was going to disappear. As she waited for war in 1939 she felt that the world she had known and lived in had but a few weeks to run, that her literary work, even as she prepared it, would have no readers and no meaning. She and Leonard made a suicide pact: if the Germans landed they were to commit suicide together by inhaling the fumes of the car engine in the closed garage. It is perhaps worth recalling this, in view of the fact that Virginia's suicide is often evidenced as the final proof of her 'madness'. Leonard had arranged his own suicide with Virginia in May 1940. Quentin Bell writes:

On 13 May, when the battle was at its height, they had discussed the question of suicide. They decided to poison themselves with the fumes of their car and Leonard kept enough petrol for this purpose in his garage; later they managed to get sufficient morphia from Adrian for a lethal dose. Throughout May and June Virginia refers frequently to the question of how and when they should make an end of themselves. Believing the war to be lost, she hardly doubts the necessity will arise, and looking into the future she sees nothing: 'I can't conceive,' she wrote, 'that there will be a 27th June 1941.'

(II, 216–17)

It is clear from this that the mere fact that Virginia committed suicide is no evidence at all for her alleged 'insanity'. Even Leonard, the rational, the sane, the balanced, expected to do this, and had taken his own precautions. One could even reason that their mutual suicide pact was a rational and defensible decision. Given that Virginia saw no future for herself, her work, her society, her country, her friends, was it not reasonable and dignified to consider suicide? Quentin Bell writes:

Even if one were optimistic enough to believe that there might be a grain of pity or magnanimity in the heart of such an enemy, it was quite certain that there would be none for a Jewish socialist and his wife; for them the gas-chamber would be an unlooked-for mercy.

(II, 216)

There is evidently nothing 'mad' in Virginia's feeling, in the middle of 1941, that the proper and dignified way for her was to put an end to things. Her last letter to Leonard, left on the table, makes this motivation quite explicit.

But one has to go further into this matter of the historical moment – Virginia proposed, in *Three Guineas* and *Between the Acts*, a certain probable shape of things to come. Although it has long been fashionable to deride *Three Guineas*, it does quite cogently develop a theme which was most germane to the rise and consolidation of the Third Reich – the relation of magnificent military uniform to sheer pugnacity. She pointed explicitly to the Führer and the Duce as examples of what she meant.

another picture has imposed itself upon the foreground. It is the figure of a man; some say, others deny, that he is Man himself, the quintessence of virility, the perfect type of which all the others are imperfect adumbrations. He is a man certainly. His eyes are glazed; his eyes glare. His body, which is braced in an unnatural position, is tightly cased in a uniform. Upon the breast of that uniform are sewn several medals and other mystic symbols. His hand is upon a sword. He is called in German and Italian Führer or Duce; in our own language Tyrant or Dictator. And behind him lie ruined houses and dead bodies – men, women and children.

(*Three Guineas* pp. 257–8)

Earlier in this book she ridicules the trimmings of the army, the church and the university, and had put in well-chosen photographs to make her point.

Your clothes in the first place make us gape with astonishment. How many, how splendid, how extremely ornate they are – the clothes worn by the educated man in his public capacity! Now you dress in violet; a jewelled crucifix swings on your breast; now your shoulders are covered with lace; now furred with ermine; now slung with many linked chains set with precious stones.

(pp. 35–6)

This in general. But military attire attracts Virginia's special distrust:

every button, rosette and stripe seems to have some symbolical meaning. Some have the right to wear plain buttons only; others rosettes; some may wear a single stripe; others, three, four, five or six. And each curl or stripe is sewn on at precisely the right distance apart; it may be one inch for one man, one inch and a quarter for another.

(pp. 36–7)

The ceremonies too are exotic, amazing, until one sees that they cover a quite different kind of signification:

But your dress in its immense elaboration has obviously another function. It not only covers nakedness, gratifies vanity, and creates pleasure for the eye, but it serves to advertise the social, professional, or intellectual standing of the wearer.

(p. 38)

Virginia's lifelong distrust of the male mind – its thrusting, pushing, deadening, analytic quality, is reinforced at the end of the 1930s by a feeling that in the rise of the Third Reich, male arrogance has reached the limit of what is endurable.

What connection is there between the sartorial splendours of the educated man and the photograph of ruined houses and dead bodies?[1] Obviously the connection between dress and war is not far to seek; your finest clothes are those that you wear as soldiers.

(p. 39)

The sheer arrogance of full military or academic dress directly provokes violent emotions:

We can say that for educated men to emphasize their superiority over other people, either in birth or intellect, by dressing differently, or by

---

[1] The photographs in question were sent 'with patient pertinacity' by the Spanish government about twice a week. 'They are not pleasant photographs to look upon. They are photographs of dead bodies for the most part' (p. 20).

adding titles before, or letters after their names are acts that rouse competition and jealousy – emotions which, as we need scarcely draw upon biography to prove, nor ask psychology to show, have their share in encouraging a disposition towards war. If then we express the opinion that such distinctions make those who possess them ridiculous and learning contemptible we should do something, indirectly, to discourage the feelings that lead to war.

(p. 40)

Because she believed that full academic and military dress were ridiculous and incited people to envy and malevolence, Virginia herself turned down honorary doctorates from Manchester (1933) and Liverpool (1939), refused to give the Clark Lectures at Cambridge in 1932, and, later in life, turned down an Order of Merit.

One of the reasons why *Three Guineas* was so unpopular was because it suggested that the whole of Europe was complicit with Hitler in acquiescing in, even wanting, armed strife. And this view lies behind *Between the Acts* which Virginia was writing in the last years of her life. The importance of the theme of clothes, of dressing-up and playing rôles, in *Between the Acts*, can hardly be over-emphasised. In the final 'scenario' of *Between the Acts* the actors, armed with mirrors and other shiny objects in which to catch the reflections of the audience, cause consternation and dismay among their audience by forcing them to face themselves:

Look! Out they come, from the bushes – the riff-raff. Children? Imps – elves – demons. Holding what? Tin cans? Bedroom candlesticks? Old jars? My dear, that's the cheval glass from the Rectory! And the mirror – that I lent her. My mother's. Cracked. What's the notion? Anything that's bright enough to reflect, presumably, ourselves?
Ourselves! Ourselves!
Out they leapt, jerked, skipped. Flashing, dazzling, dancing, jumping. Now old Bart . . . he was caught. Now Manresa. Here a nose . . . There a skirt . . . Then trousers only . . . Now perhaps a face . . . Ourselves? But that's cruel. To snap us as we are, before we've had time to assume . . . And only, too, in parts . . . That's what's so distorting and upsetting and utterly unfair.

(BTA p. 214)

'But that's cruel. To snap us as we are, before we've had time to assume . . .' what? Our costumes, obviously, is what she has in mind, our state robes, our cloaks and insignia, our doctorates and generals' batons, in other words the 'outer' symbols and trappings which do not correspond to an inner superiority, but are easily detachable from it.

It was the cheval glass that proved too heavy. Young Bonthorp for all his muscle couldn't lug the damned thing about any longer. He stopped. So did they all – hand glasses, tin cans, scraps of scullery glass, harness room glass, and heavily embossed silver mirrors – all stopped. And the audience saw themselves, not whole by any means, but at any rate sitting still.

The hands of the clock had stopped at the present moment. It was now. Ourselves . . .

The mirror bearers squatted; malicious; observant; expectant; expository.

(*BTA* pp. 216–17)

The mirror bearers both expound and expect. Expository: here you are, this is you, this is yourselves, 'undressed' and in everyday clothes, what are you? And also expectant: what are you going to make of yourselves? How are you going to react?

Virginia does not really want to make any distinctions in terms of nationality . Men are men, whether they be German, Italian or English. They are consumed with pride, arrogance and self-esteem, they can devise no way to oppose force except by crushing it with even greater force, and it seems to be generally agreed that it is men who have to put the matter to the arbitrement of swords and men who must fight the matter out. This all seemed intellectual poverty of the most base kind, but picked out attractively for the show of oncoming war. It is the women's job to wait, to mourn and eventually to tend the injured and bury the dead.

Scarcely a human being in the course of history has fallen to a woman's rifle; the vast majority of birds and beasts have been killed by you, not by us; and it is difficult to judge what we do not share.

(*Three Guineas* pp. 13–14)

Virginia Woolf, like Wilfred Owen, felt that it was the poet's function and duty to warn. In the figure of Septimus Smith she had given us a view of the effect of violent armed conflict on a man who had fought in the trenches, and she had also made the point that if his mind gave way under the strain, he would be treated as 'mad' and there would be no mercy for him. Neither would there be, Virginia was sure, for the survivors of the next war with Hitler. But the contemporary view of *Three Guineas* was that it reflected that famous unbalanced mind, and that its arguments were shallow:

Three Guineas was published in June 1938. It is the product of a very odd mind and, I think, of a very odd state of mind . . . A great many women wrote to express their enthusiastic approval; but her close friends were silent, or if not silent, critical. Vita did not like it, and Maynard Keynes was both angry and contemptuous; it was, he declared, a silly argument and not very well written.[1] What really seemed wrong with the book – and I am speaking here of my own reactions at the time – was the attempt to involve a discussion of women's rights with the far more agonising and immediate question of what we were to do in order to meet the ever-growing menace of Fascism and war. The connection between the two questions seemed tenuous and the positive suggestions wholly inadequate.

(Bell II, 204–5)

If one thinks for a moment of the exaggerated pomp and ceremony, of the goose-stepping parades and the impeccable military turn-out, of the splendid and terrifying banners and accoutrements of Hitler's Third Reich, Virginia's point surely makes perfect sense? The connection which Quentin Bell thought 'tenuous' is glaringly obvious. But it was a connection which Virginia's contemporaries did not wish to see, and therefore a connection they refused to see.

It is to the few fragments of her last years in *A Writer's Diary* that we must turn if we wish to understand the world view which Virginia had in 1938, 1939, 1940 and 1941. Although Quentin Bell assures us that from August 1940 till March 1941, Virginia was 'euphoric' and 'imperturbable' one suspects that he must have missed something, must have missed perhaps, reading *Between the Acts*. Quentin Bell writes:

This exchange took place in August 1940; by that time the Battle of Britain was approaching its climax and Virginia was passing from a mood of apprehension to one of quiet imperturbability.

Her serenity was perhaps a necessary prelude to the storm – by which I

---

[1] Keynes's judgment is delivered here with approval, as if it cancels out the absurdity of Virginia's case, without any need of further discussion.

mean that the workings of Virginia's mind may have been such that she had to pass from the terror of June 1940 to the final agony of March 1941 by way of an euphoric interval, and that this may have been just as much a part of her mental illness as all the rest.

(II, 221)

If you are convinced *a priori* that someone is mad, then even her being 'imperturbable' and 'euphoric' will be new evidence to support your hypothesis.

Bombs went on falling, and on 29 September one fell very close to Monk's House. Virginia swore at Leonard for slamming the window so noisily and then, realising what it was, went out on the lawn to see the raider chased back over Newhaven; but such things no longer worried her.

(II, 222)

I suspect that such things did worry her, but that her anxiety had been turned inwards, to be concentrated on writing *Between the Acts*, which is a vision of human evil imminently about to destroy civilisation. Virginia's view of the world was, *pace* Quentin Bell, at the other extreme from euphoria. She was engaging with the reality of Nazism, which she felt to be the end of history – anyway as she had known it, and as it could ever affect her.

Giles nicked his chair into position with a jerk. Thus only could he show his irritation, his rage with old fogies who sat and looked at views over coffee and cream when the whole of Europe – over there – was bristling like . . . He had no command of metaphor. Only the ineffective word 'hedgehog' illustrated his vision of Europe, bristling with guns, poised with planes. At any moment guns would rake that land into furrows; planes splinter Bolney Minster into smithereens and blast the Folly.

(*BTA* pp. 66–7)

Compare the entry in *A Writer's Diary* for 17 August 1938:

So, at supper, we discussed our generation: and the prospects of war. Hitler has his million men now under arms. Is it only summer manoeuvres or – ?

See too the following entry, for 28 August 1938:

And at any moment the guns may go off and explode us. L. is very black. Hitler has his hounds only very lightly held. A single step – in Czechoslovakia – like the Austrian Archduke in 1914 – and again it's 1914.

As usual with Virginia, the war is given symbolic dimensions. Throughout the afternoon which *Between the Acts* spans, Giles's rage is given as significant of political impotence. It is not just that he does not get on with his wife, or that he is angry with his own failure and cowardice in life, though both are true. His anger is the anger of futile fury against people who will not see what they are looking at, who will not take in the meaning of what is going on around them, in the world as well as in Miss La Trobe's highly symbolic play.

'We remain seated' – 'We are the audience'. Words this afternoon ceased to lie flat in the sentence. They rose, became menacing and shook their fists at you. This afternoon he wasn't Giles Oliver come to see the villagers act their annual pageant; manacled to a rock he was, and forced passively to behold indescribable horror.

(*BTA* p. 74)

Nothing in Miss La Trobe's play, trenchant and relevant as it is, could be called 'indescribable horror'. Giles is seeing what the play is about, what it involves, rather than what it is. He sees through the outer shell to what the play indicates is about to happen. Hence his vision is adequate to the occasion, which cannot be said of most of the rest of the audience. This is surely part of Virginia's point in her parody of the audience at the play: they will not see what the play is about.

But Giles cannot help doing so, since his vision of how things are corresponds to Virginia's. And significantly enough, a horrible thing happens to him as he wanders alone 'between the acts':

There, couched in the grass, curled in an olive green ring, was a snake. Dead? No, choked with a toad in its mouth. The snake was unable to swallow; the toad was unable to die. A spasm made the ribs contract; blood oozed. It was birth the wrong way round – a monstrous inversion. So, raising his foot, he stamped on them. The mass crushed and slithered. The white canvas on his tennis shoes was bloodstained and sticky. But it was action. Action relieved him. He strode to the Barn, with blood on his shoes.

(p. 119)

This scene again, though extremely disgusting, is hardly 'indescribable horror', yet, seen through Giles's eyes, it leads to that

horror. It is symbolic of that horror, of that disgusting thing like
'birth the wrong way round – a monstrous inversion'. Giles sees
the 'indescribable horror' coming up. Part of the horror is waiting
passively for the horror. So he stamps. But it is futile. The audience at the play see nothing, they refuse to see, and all he gets
from his wife is a belittling look:

'No,' said Isa, as plainly as words could say it. 'I don't admire you,' and
looked, not at his face, but at his feet. 'Silly little boy, with blood on his
boots.'

(p. 133)

Isa, like everyone else in the audience except Lucy, Virginia's
Julia-figure, refuses to see what is coming, the 'indescribable
horror'. It is an act of will. Any minor lunge like Giles's is
regarded as mere petulance. And so, in the circumstances of
universal refusal of vision, it is. Only Miss La Trobe, hidden
behind the bushes, trying, as she directs the play, to make her
audience see what is coming, is honest enough to reckon
inwardly with what is approaching.

In the middle of the vicar's speech of thanks, the impending
war suddenly looms again:

Mr Streatfield paused. He listened. Did he hear some distant music?
    He continued: 'But there is still a deficit' (he consulted his paper) 'of
one hundred and seventy-five pounds odd. So that each of us who has
enjoyed this pageant has still an opp . . .' The word was cut in two. A
zoom severed it. Twelve aeroplanes in perfect formation like a flight of
wild duck came overhead. *That* was the music. The audience gaped; the
audience gazed. Then zoom became drone. The planes had passed.
    '. . . portunity,' Mr Streatfield continued, 'to make a contribution.' He
signalled. Instantly collecting boxes were in operation.

(pp. 225–6)

The impending war has that degree of physical givenness in the
context of the village pageant, yet the audience merely 'gapes'
and 'gazes'. They do not believe that war will really come, or, if it
does, they do not believe that it will be really bad.

But the whole novel is a testimony to how bad Virginia herself
thinks it will be. Miss La Trobe, the eccentric lady who writes,
produces and directs the whole pageant from a point of seclusion
behind the bushes, is obviously one of the Virginia *personae* in the

novel. Her function, with this pageant, is to make the audience see:

Now Miss La Trobe stepped from her hiding. Flowing, and streaming, on the grass, on the gravel, still for one moment she held them together – the dispersing company. Hadn't she, for twenty-five minutes, made them see? A vision imparted was relief from agony . . . for one moment . . . one moment.

(p. 117)

And the stage was empty. Miss La Trobe leant against the tree, paralyzed. Her power had left her. Beads of perspiration broke on her forehead. Illusion had failed. 'This is death,' she murmured, 'death'.

(p. 165)

Grating her fingers in the bark, she damned the audience. Panic seized her. Blood seemed to pour from her shoes. This is death, death, death, she noted in the margin of her mind; when illusion fails. Unable to lift her hand, she stood facing the audience.

(p. 210)

These notations are surely enough to throw doubt on Quentin Bell's assertion that Virginia was feeling 'euphoric' and 'imperturbable'. The association between death, and the failure of 'illusion' or (which is the same thing) the power to make people see, is made a great many times. 'Hadn't she, for twenty-five minutes, made them see?'

The audience receives the first, historical scenes, with tolerant and superior good humour. The Elizabethan scene, the Restoration scene, and even the Victorian scene – even though this does make one of the characters, Mrs Lynn Jones, begin to muse, in a trance, about her childhood, which has now become more 'real' to her than the proceedings on the stage:

There was an interval.
'Oh but it was beautiful,' Mrs. Lynn Jones protested. Home she meant; the lamplit room; the ruby curtains; and Papa reading aloud.
They were rolling up the lake and uprooting the bulrushes. Real swallows were skimming over real grass. But she still saw the home.
'It was . . .' she repeated, referring to the home.

(pp. 201–2)

This is magic, but it is Miss La Trobe's magic, she who, like

Virginia, has used illusion to make people see. Real swallows were skimming over real grass, but still Mrs Lynn Jones sees nothing now but home. The play has thus worked: Miss La Trobe's effort has succeeded: Mrs Lynn Jones now sees. This is what art is for. It is 'relief from agony . . . for one moment . . . one moment'.

But it is when Miss La Trobe comes to the present that the audience refuses to co-operate.

Miss La Trobe stood there with her eye on her script. 'After Vic.' she had written, 'try ten mins. of present time. Swallows, cows etc.' She wanted to expose them, as it were, to douche them, with present-time reality. But something was going wrong with the experiment. 'Reality too strong,' she muttered. 'Curse 'em!'

(p. 209)

She has tried to make the time of the representation coincide with the time of the performance. But 'reality is too strong'. She stands there, with blood seeming to pour from her shoes, in agony. For what she wants to make them see, she cannot achieve. 'This is death, death, death, she noted in the margin of her mind; when illusion fails.'

Only the intuitive, feminine, Julia-figure in the novel, Lucy Swithin, sees what Miss La Trobe is trying to do. (But then of course, she 'sees' all the time.) Virginia allows Lucy to stick her head through the bushes to congratulate Miss La Trobe, in the middle of the performance:

Then, ignoring the conventions, a head popped up between the trembling sprays: Mrs. Swithin's.

'Oh Miss La Trobe!' she exclaimed; and stopped. Then she began again; 'Oh Miss La Trobe, I do congratulate you!'

She hesitated. 'You've given me . . .' She skipped, then alighted – 'Ever since I was a child I've felt . . .' A film fell over her eyes, shutting off the present. She tried to recall her childhood; then gave it up; and, with a little wave of her hand, as if asking Miss La Trobe to help her out, continued: 'This daily round; this going up and down stairs; this saying "What am I going for? My specs? I have 'em on my nose." . . .'

She gazed at Miss La Trobe with a cloudless old-aged stare. Their eyes met in a common effort to bring a common meaning to birth. They failed; and Mrs. Swithin, laying hold desperately of a fraction of her meaning, said: 'What a small part I've had to play! But you've made me feel I could have played . . . Cleopatra!'

She nodded between the trembling bushes and ambled off.

The villagers winked. 'Batty' was the word for old Flimsy, breaking through the bushes.

'I might have been – Cleopatra,' Miss La Trobe repeated. 'You've stirred in me my unacted part,' she meant.

(pp. 178–9)

Miss La Trobe, with her village pageant, has provoked Mrs Swithin, old as she is, to push through the bushes not only of reality but also of temporality, and to confide in Miss La Trobe that she has seen what she might in other circumstances have been. Miss La Trobe accepts this. 'Their eyes met in a common effort to bring a common meaning to birth. They failed.' Even so, their communication has been what this book, and indeed Virginia's whole career was all about: the effort to make people see.

But the villagers wink after Mrs Swithin as she ambles off. ' "Batty" was the word for old Flimsy . . .'.

Virginia's ploy in *Between the Acts* is directly related to her contention in *Three Guineas*: put on the clothes, and all will acknowledge your rôle. The audience try to recognise which of the well-known local characters it may be who now appears clothed as England, Law or the Elizabethan Age.

Everyone was clapping and laughing. From behind the bushes issued Queen Elizabeth – Eliza Clark, licensed to sell tobacco. Could she be Mrs. Clark of the village shop? She was spendidly made up. Her head, pearl-hung, rose from a vast ruff. Shiny satins draped her.

(p. 101)

Reason held the centre of the stage alone. Her arms extended, her robes flowing, holding orb and sceptre, Mabel Hopkins stood sublimely looking over the heads of the audience. The audience gazed at her. She ignored the audience.

(pp. 148–9)

A pompous march tune brayed. 'Firm, elatant, bold and blatant,' etc. . . . And once more a huge symbolical figure emerged from the bushes. It was Budge the publican; but so disguised that even cronies who drank with him nightly failed to recognise him; and a little titter of enquiry as to his identity ran about among the villagers.

(p. 188)

Can clothes then, make such a vast difference to people that we fail to recognise Eliza Clark licensed to sell tobacco, Mabel Hopkins, or the local publican, under their impressive robes? Yes indeed. There is speculation among the audience as to who these notabilities might be, so effective is the visual distance between their normal humble station in the village and their new prestige in their full regalia.

Clothes make the man, suggests Miss La Trobe: or at least, clothes make what man wishes himself to be *taken as*. None of the people who rise up at the village pageant *is* Reason, the Elizabethan Age, or Law. But dressed to look the part, they can easily engender enough confusion in those who know them best to carry the impersonation off for a while.

There are two sorts of 'illusion' going on at the village pageant. One, the obvious one, is the one here described. But the other sort of 'illusion' is far more subtle, and it is the one that Miss La Trobe is attempting to create. This has to do with making the audience see through the play to the threadbare reality which lies behind it: 'ourselves'.

We, dressed in our slacks, open shirts and tennis shoes, sitting at ease in the village, without our costumes of medical, literary, military or ecclesiastical superiority upon us, we have to see through the pageant, to 'ourselves'. When we have seen that we have seen everything.

For we are the hollow men, the straw men, stuffed and propped against each other. That is Virginia's view of us in *Between the Acts*. Eunuchs, sexless men, petulant men, perverts, arrogant men, destructive men, half-men, toad-squashers, well-wishers, cheerers from the side-lines: geriatric, impotent, confined to our wheel chairs, undressed, naked, absurd, defenceless, self-deluded, helpless, beyond help.

Outwardly Virginia may have been calm, as Leonard reports in his autobiography, but inwardly she must have been grappling with hopelessness. Leonard says that he too felt that the end of civilisation was upon them:

There we sat in May 1940, Moore, Desmond, Virginia, and I in the house and under a hot sun and brilliant sky in the garden, in a cocoon of friendship and nostalgic memories. At the same time the whole weekend was dominated by a consciousness that our little private world was menaced by destruction, by oecumenical catastrophe now beginning across the Channel in France . . . even hope was a kind of self-indulgence and self-deception.

(The Journey not the Arrival Matters p. 49)

During the months of the phoney war, when everything seemed to be for the moment inexplicably suspended, there was this incessant feeling of unreality and impending disaster . . . There was a curious atmosphere of quiet fatalism, of waiting for the inevitable . . .

(The Journey p. 53)

If Leonard could feel it, G.E. Moore could feel it, Desmond Macarthy could feel it, why should Virginia not have felt it? All of them felt it, the impending disaster, the destruction of civilisation as they had known it. Outwardly Virginia may have appeared cheerful and relaxed – but inwardly, she felt it. Yet Leonard's notations are as puzzling as usual. Either she wrote *Between the Acts* as an ironic joke, or else she managed to conceal her real feelings with more than ordinary effectiveness. For Leonard writes:

Virginia's diary shows clearly that this life gave her tranquillity and happiness. On October 12 she wrote etc.

(The Journey p. 70)

Another entry in her diary (October 2), which I reprinted in *A Writer's Diary*, gives vividly her mood that autumn, a kind of quietism and open-eyed contemplation of death . . .

(The Journey p. 72)

It was only in the first days of 1941 that the deep disturbance in her mind began to show itself clearly.

(The Journey p. 77)

It may have been only in the first days of 1941 that the *outer* show of mental stress began to be apparent, because by then she had more or less completed *Between the Acts*. But that the stress had been going on inwardly is amply testified to by the novel itself.

Leonard must have been taken in by his wife's outer calm. He felt, he says, no fear:

The German planes just above my head, I was glad to find, left me perfectly calm and cold, the whole incident seeming to be completely unreal, and in fact in all the many 'incidents' of the kind which took place in subsequent years I never myself felt or saw anyone else feeling fear.

(The Journey p. 32)

No, his main feeling about war was one of boredom:

Having lived through the two world wars of 1914 and 1939, I can say that my chief recollection of war is its intolerable boredom . . . If I ever prayed, I would pray to be delivered, not so much from battle, murder, and sudden death, but rather from the boredom of war.

(The Journey pp. 64–5)

Leonard himself was calm:

It was a pause, only a pause, as we waited for the next catastrophe; but we waited in complete calm, without tension, with the threat of invasion above our heads and the bombs and the bombing all round us.

(The Journey p. 69)

Although he read *Between the Acts* in 1941, he can still, thirty years later in his autobiography, seriously put to himself the question why his wife took the extraordinary and unexpected decision to commit suicide after her (outwardly) calm and 'euphoric' 1940.

Looking back from Virginia's suicide in March 1941 to the last four months of 1940, I have naturally often asked myself why I had no forebodings of the catastrophe until the beginning of 1941.

(The Journey p. 69)

There was the petrol in the garage, the photograph of a Jew with his fly open mocked by the Gestapo, the mutual suicide pact, the sense of the end of an epoch, the evidence of *Between the Acts* and *Three Guineas*; but Leonard, as late as 1969, still professes himself puzzled.

What was the real state of her mind and her health in the autumn and early winter of 1940? I thought at the time and still think that her mind was calmer and more stable, her spirits happier and more serene, than was usual with her.

(The Journey p. 69)

Leonard seems in this case to have failed to make sufficiently intuitive connections between inner states and outer behaviour.

Death, I think, was always very near the surface of Virginia's mind, the contemplation of death. It was part of the deep imbalance of her mind.

She was 'half in love with easeful Death'. I can understand this, but only intellectually; emotionally it is completely alien to me.

(*The Journey* p. 73)

And yet he had read *Between the Acts*. That must indeed have been an incomprehensible text. And partly, indeed, it was incomprehensible because, for the last time, Virginia presented her double portrait of herself and Leonard in that novel, and he could not afford to recognise the justice of his own portrayal. In the tragic conflict between old Bartholomew Oliver and Lucy Swithin, his sister, is the very last variation on the theme that has run through every major novel since *The Voyage Out*. It is the theme of emotional, rational, intellectual and human incompatibility between two human beings, Leonard and Virginia Woolf.

CHAPTER 17

Incompatibility

Virginia enters emotionally and physically into all the characters of her novels, but there is always one central point of consciousness, one central kind of embodiment, which is that of the Virginia *persona* in each novel. This privileged Virginia *persona* is presented as being locked in conflict with another privileged *persona* whom, from the time of *The Voyage Out*, we can always recognise as being partly Leonard. In *Between the Acts*, there can be little doubt that the two opposed characters Bartholomew Oliver, known as Bart for short, and his sister, the bird-like, diaphanous, mystical, intuitive Lucy Swithin, represent respectively Leonard and Virginia.

Other characters represent aspects of the problem lying between Bart and Lucy, of course. Mrs Manresa, the 'child of nature' who manages to flirt with three men simultaneously and is embodied in that happy, unself-conscious way we remember in Jinny in *The Waves*, represents that free self-access which Lucy has never had and so much envies. Giles, the son of old Oliver, is out of love with his wife, consumed with the sense that he is a coward and a failure: and in him we recognise old prototypes like Mr Ramsay and Tansley in *To the Lighthouse* – largely modelled, so far as self-reproach and morbid self-pity go, on recollections of Sir Leslie Stephen, no doubt.

Isabella Oliver, married unhappily to Giles and aware of his willingness to let Mrs Manresa, the 'child of nature', trail her coat for him, and who reciprocates by taking Mrs Manresa's gigolo friend William Dodge in tow for a while, is locked in a battle of non-communication with her husband which we recognise from as far back as *The Voyage Out* and *Night and Day*. Isa, as she is known, and her husband Giles do not exchange so much as a word during the proceedings of the afternoon, locked in hostile and mutually resentful silence. Only in the last line of the novel do they begin to speak. And in the silence, in the locked-up, emotionally sterile relationship between Giles and Isa, we see one further variation on the theme of the engagement (or the marriage) without passion, without communication through the body, and with all feelings dammed up inside.

The relationship between old Bartholomew Oliver and his sister Lucy Swithin is central to the novel, because the disagreement between Bart and Lucy is not one which, like Mrs Manresa's with William Dodge, or Giles's with Isa, is capable of mutation, progress and resolution. It is incapable of any resolution whatsoever, since Bart and Lucy are locked together in a struggle about the nature of rationality until the end of their days.

In the struggle between Bart and Lucy, Virginia has painted her last, biggest, and most daring full-length portrait of herself and Leonard. By making Bart and Lucy brother and sister, she has done away, at a stroke, with the embarrassing and unnecessary dimension of sexuality. Their relationship can be studied 'pure', so to speak. What we have in the struggle between Bart and Lucy, last owners of the great house as the war encroaches and the end of an epoch draws near, is a struggle between two kinds of mind which are not only mutually opposed, but actually vowed to each other's destruction. Or rather, Bart is slowly (and obviously) destroying Lucy, though I do not think that Lucy's kind of mind represents a real or felt threat to Bart. Bart's attitude to his sister is one of pure rationalism. He destroys her illusions, he attacks her faith (she is depicted as a Christian, hanging on desperately to the crucifix around her neck as her last refuge), belittles her remarks, and behaves in a generally superior, blunt and condescending manner towards her. She never hits back, but with every blow from Bart, she subsides a little further into total pessimism.

Dryness, rationalism, reduction is the keynote to Bart's character.

'It's very unsettled. It'll rain, I'm afraid. We can only pray,' she added, and fingered her crucifix.

'And provide umbrellas,' said her brother.

Lucy flushed. He had struck her faith. When she said 'pray,' he added 'umbrellas.' She half covered the cross with her fingers. She shrank; she cowered . . .

(BTA p. 31)

And, as if anxious that the point be taken, Virginia adds, almost at once, another example of the same thing:

'Tell me, Bart,' said Mrs. Swithin turning to her brother, 'what's the origin of that? Touch wood . . . Antaeus, didn't he touch earth?'

She would have been, he thought, a very clever woman, had she fixed her gaze. But this led to that; that to the other. What went in at this ear, went out at that . . .

'Touch wood; touch earth; Antaeus,' he muttered, bringing the scattered bits together. Lemprière would settle it; or the Encyclopædia.

(BTA p. 32)

The timid, halting appeal to Bart's erudition is met by the dismissive contempt of his reaction, and, typically, he turns, this latter-day instantiation of Sir Leslie, to Lemprière or the Encyclopedia. They would 'settle it', for it is, is it not, a matter of 'fact'?

Bart, as he flips through the pages of his 'authority' is himself struck by a question:

But it was not in books the answer to his question – why, in Lucy's skull, shaped so much like his own, there existed a prayable being? She didn't, he supposed, invest it with hair, teeth or toenails. It was, he supposed, more of a force or a radiance . . .

(pp. 32–3)

The rationalist mind has certain definite limits. It cannot understand 'imbecility',[1] and it cannot conceive what a religious impulse would be like. Anyone who has any such impulse would be (we remember from Gerald Brenan) wilfully cultivating illusions.

Virginia has encoded her own dilemma in the symbol of the Christian faith, God, a 'prayable being'. Like other symbolic substitutions in earlier novels (mathematics, geometry and astronomy for retreat from male desire with Katharine Hilbery in Night and Day, for instance; and the death of Evans for Septimus's inability to feel in Mrs Dalloway), this substitution is simple but

[1] See The Journey not the Arrival Matters pp. 49–52.

subtle. Christianity, God, a 'prayable being' must surely correspond to a spiritual value which would transcend the world of
rationalist certainty. Behind the crucifix that Lucy so nervously
grips (and which acts as a shield against the verbal dryness of
Bart), there lies the conviction that the world is full of values and
meanings which are unavailable to the rationalist mind, full of
radiances and subtleties which the rationalist mind is not only
blind to but actively denies. The crucifix, God and the 'prayable
being' are Lucy's last resort in front of the battering ram of her
brother's rationalist reductivism. (One recalls the violence of Mr
Ramsay in *To the Lighthouse*: 'into this delicious fecundity, this
fountain and spray of life, the fatal sterility of the male plunged
itself, like a beak of brass, barren and bare.') The enquiry into the
origin of the saying 'Touch wood' is concluded by another defeat
for Lucy:

'What's the origin – the origin – of that?'
  'Superstition,' he said.
  She flushed, and the little breath too was audible that she drew in as
once more he struck a blow at her faith. But, brother and sister, flesh and
blood was not a barrier, but a mist. Nothing changed their affection; no
argument; no fact; no truth. What she saw he didn't; what he saw she
didn't – and so on, *ad infinitum*.
  'Cindy,' he growled. And the quarrel was over.

(pp. 33–4)

'What she saw he didn't; what he saw she didn't'; but, bound
together in lasting affection that is more like a 'mist' than a bond,
they are together for life. This must surely have reference to the
position which the marriage of Leonard and Virginia had
reached.

At the end of the long afternoon which is *Between the Acts* the
shadows lengthen. Two of the longest shadows which fall across
this novel are the shadows of books, books of the major precursor
in Virginia's development. John Stuart Mill's *Autobiography* tells
in a famous passage of how the firm, indeed oppressive, intellectual love of his father had to be broken through, before life could
be regained. The turning point in his life was reading Wordsworth, and realising that it was permitted to feel.

The other shadow is that of the two essays on Bentham (1838) and Coleridge (1840) in which Mill, drawing on his own past intellectual experience, presents his two thinkers as necessary antagonists in the evolution of the nineteenth century. In the light of that phrase in *Between the Acts*, 'What she saw he didn't; what he saw she didn't', Mill's own formulation is relevant: 'Each of them scarcely sees anything but what the other does not see.'[1] 'In every respect the two men are each other's "completing counterpart": the strong points of each correspond to the weak points of the other.'[2]

The major disjunction Mill wishes to establish is the one between parts and whole. He describes Bentham's method[3] as that of 'detail': breaking each question into as many parts as he considers necessary to solve it, while Coleridge fears to forsake the whole problem at any point for fear of leaving something vital out of consideration.

Considering the lateness of the afternoon in *Between the Acts* – not only in Virginia's own life but also in the life of that society with which she identified herself above all – Mill's personal struggle with James Mill and with Bentham, and his analysis of the cast of mind of Bentham and of Coleridge, are useful in reminding the reader of the novel that the problem at issue between Bart and Lucy had been a living one, if not a central one, since Descartes was opposed by Pascal. Bart and Lucy do not only struggle in their own private anguish, they are also part of the central intellectual tradition of Europe since the great rationalist laid down his *Cogito* as the rule of all reflection: the rigid exclusion of the thinker from the thought. Not Pascal, not Rousseau, not Wordsworth or Coleridge, can actually prevail against his *fiat*, but each nevertheless makes his attempt to have the whole reconsidered. 'Above, the air rushed; beneath was water. She stood between two fluidities, caressing her cross.'

'Ourselves,' she murmured. And retrieving some glint of faith from the grey waters, hopefully, without much help from reason, she followed the fish; the speckled, streaked and blotched; seeing in that vision beauty, power, and glory in ourselves.

(BTA pp. 239–40)

---

[1] *Mill on Bentham and Coleridge*, ed. F.R. Leavis (Chatto 1950), p. 101.
[2] *Ibid*. p. 102. [3] *Ibid*. p. 48.

This opposed view of the relation of parts to whole seems to be exactly what has finally got itself set up as the intellectual condition of the Woolfs. Unsupported by any history of physical understanding, their originally opposed kinds of mind have developed separately over the years along their own natural lines, and have now reached a position where they do indeed think very differently on most matters. It is not exaggerated to say that they now occupy *opposed* mental positions. In the opening pair of exchanges between Bart and his sister, one can see what is at issue between Leonard and Virginia. Leonard's mind divides and holds apart, Virginia's fuses and merges. Where he sees no connection, she sees a dozen.

Something which makes the analogy between the real-life Leonard and the fictional Bart very clear, almost a parable of concision, is the very early scene where Isa's little boy is 'looking into the heart of light, the silence', and Bart suddenly, for a joke, leaps at him from behind a tree, giving him an almighty scare and shattering the vision:

The little boy had lagged and was grouting in the grass. Then the baby, Caro, thrust her fist out over the coverlet and the furry bear was jerked overboard. Amy had to stoop. George grubbed. The flower blazed between the angles of the roots. Membrane after membrane was torn. It blazed a soft yellow, a lambent light under a film of velvet; it filled the caverns behind the eyes with light. All that inner darkness became a hall, leaf smelling, earth smelling of yellow light. And the tree was beyond the flower; the grass, the flower and the tree were entire. Down on his knees grubbing he held the flower complete. Then there was a roar and a hot breath and a stream of coarse grey hair rushed between him and the flower. Up he leapt, toppling in his fright, and saw coming towards him a terrible peaked eyeless monster moving on legs, brandishing arms.
    'Good morning, sir,' a hollow voice boomed at him from a beak of paper.
    The old man had sprung upon him from his hiding-place behind a tree.

(BTA pp. 16–17)

Such was the concentration of the little boy that he had lost any sense of distinction between the senses. He had been seeing the world as entire, and whole. Such was the degree of purity and concentration in his gaze, that the leaf and the earth smell of yellow light. But rationalism splits and divides. Suddenly the old man bursts in, for a joke. Unity is broken, the unity of the self, of nature, and of the senses. (What do little boys like? thinks the Benthamite. A joke. What kind of joke? Let's leap at him in a paper mask from behind a tree.) The result is that the dream is shattered and the little boy topples back in fright, the unity smashed and the mood broken.

That 'beak of paper' must surely have some reference, used as it is to smash unity by Mr Oliver, to the 'beak of brass' which Mr Ramsay, in *To the Lighthouse*, brings down again and again on his wife, demanding sympathy. 'Beak of paper', 'beak of brass', both obviously male symbols of aggression and attack, are used to scatter unity in the passion of rationalism.

That Leonard stands as model for old Mr Oliver is obvious if one compares the following two passages:

'Good morning, sir,' a hollow voice boomed at him from a beak of paper.

The old man had sprung upon him from his hiding-place behind a tree.

'Say good morning, George; say "Good morning, Grandpa,"' Mabel urged him, giving him a push towards the man. But George stood gaping. George stood gazing. Then Mr Oliver crumpled the paper which he had cocked into a snout and appeared in person. A very tall old man, with gleaming eyes, wrinkled cheeks, and a head with no hair on it. He turned.

'Heel!' he bawled, 'heel, you brute!' And George turned; and the nurses turned holding the furry bear; they all turned to look at Sohrab the Afghan hound bounding and bouncing among the flowers.

'Heel!' the old man bawled, as if he were commanding a regiment. It was impressive, to the nurses, the way an old boy of his age could still bawl and make a brute like that obey him. Back came the Afghan hound, sidling, apologetic. And as he cringed at the old man's feet, a string was slipped over his collar; the noose that old Oliver always carried with him.

'You wild beast . . . you bad beast,' he grumbled, stooping. George looked at the dog only. The hairy flanks were sucked in and out; there was a blob of foam on its nostrils. He burst out crying.

(*BTA* pp. 17–18)

The original of Flush was a golden cocker spaniel called Pinka which had been given to Virginia by Vita. It became, essentially, Leonard's dog . . . Leonard had a feeling for animals which was, on the surface at all events, extremely unsentimental. He was gruff, abrupt, a systematic disciplinarian, extremely good at seeing that his dogs were obedient, healthy, and happy. Whenever one met Leonard there would be a brief shouting match between him and whatever dog or dogs happened to be there, at the end of which the animals would subside into whining passivity and Leonard would be transformed from a brutal Sergeant-Major into the most civilised of human beings.

(Bell II, 175)

The whole function of the incident where Bart leaps out from behind a tree and shatters the vision of unity enjoyed by the little boy George is, precisely, to destroy the illusion, to substitute the parts for the whole, the empirical world for the world of reverie and insight. That is what Bart intends to do. He can see well enough, presumably, that the little lad is lost in contemplation, with his nose stuck deep into the flowers. Ordinary knowledge of human reactions to shock might have informed him in advance that the little boy would get a terrible fright if suddenly bawled at from close at hand. Nevertheless, to the Benthamite no state of inwardness is to be respected. Shatter it at once, in the interests of good sense!

George is too terrified to do anything except gaze at him, and at the dog, until eventually, coming out of his shock 'He burst out crying.' But Bart learns nothing about what has happened. He is totally closed to inwardness, therefore cannot respond when he sees it shattered, even in a child.

He burst out crying.
Old Oliver raised himself, his veins swollen, his cheeks flushed; he was angry. His little game with the paper hadn't worked. The boy was a cry-baby. He nodded and sauntered on, smoothing out the crumpled paper and muttering, as he tried to find his line in the column, 'A cry-baby – a cry-baby.'

(BTA p. 18)

'Can't take a joke. Only jumped out at him for fun. No sense of humour. Why stare into the flowers anyway – silly thing to do' – one can imagine the train of thought in Bart's mind as he 'saunters on'. And to make sure that he has made his point, he tells the boy's mother, Isa, later, with his usual brutal bluntness:

'Your little boy's a cry-baby,' he said scornfully.
'Oh,' she sighed, pegged down on a chair arm, like a captive balloon, by a myriad of hair-thin ties into domesticity. 'What's been happening?'

'I took the newspaper,' he explained, 'so . . .'

He took it and crumpled it into a beak over his nose. 'So,' he had sprung out from behind a tree on to the children.

'And he howled. He's a coward, your boy is.'

She frowned. He was not a coward, her boy wasn't. And she loathed the domestic, the possessive; the maternal. And he knew it and did it on purpose to tease her, the old brute, her father in law.

She looked away.

(pp. 25–26)

I do not suppose that this last reaction of dislike is Virginia's towards Leonard: it is here 'Isa's'. But old Oliver's train of thought is related to Leonard's, and so is the total inability to see why the little boy should have been scared and howled. All good clean fun. Why bring emotions into it?[1]

It is immediately after this that Lucy, Bart's sister, enters and Bart 'strikes her faith' twice.

The theme of the single vision and the multiple vision is continued throughout the novel. Indeed, that is really what, at base, it is about. Bart enjoys 'single vision and Newton's sleep'. Lucy's vision is Coleridgean, or Blakean. It happens again when, 'between the acts' of the play, Bart has wandered off by himself to meditate on why his son and his daughter-in-law should be so unsatisfied together.

The dog, who had followed him, flopped down on to the floor at his feet. Flanks sucked in and out, the long nose resting on his paws, a fleck of foam on the nostril, there he was, his familiar spirit, his Afghan hound.

The door trembled and stood half open. That was Lucy's way of coming in – as if she did not know what she would find. Really! It was her brother! And his dog! She seemed to see them for the first time. Was it that she had no body?[2] Up in the clouds, like an air-ball, her mind touched ground now and then with a shock of surprise. There was nothing in her to weight a man like Giles to the earth. . .

. . . He looked sardonically at Lucy, perched on her chair. How, he wondered, had she ever borne children? . . .

She was thinking, he supposed, God is peace, God is love. For she belonged to the unifiers; he to the separatists.

(pp. 138–40)

[1] The reader should look up the story of the 'imbecile' boy, compassion for whom Leonard could not understand, in *The Journey not the Arrival Matters* pp. 49–52.

[2] At this point, the 'her' seems to refer, ambiguously, both to his sister, Lucy, present before him, and also to his daughter-in-law, Isa, who cannot 'keep' his son Giles from Mrs Manresa. But the absence of 'body' is a key factor.

Here again the central, irreconcilable split between Bart and Lucy is given exact expression. 'She belonged to the unifiers; he to the separatists.' She is Coleridge, he is Bentham. 'What she saw he didn't; what he saw she didn't – and so on, *ad infinitum*.'

After the play put on by Miss La Trobe is over, and the gramophone has insisted 'Dispersed are we' for so long, it is up to Lucy to make some kind of sense of what has happened, to pull together the 'dispersed' threads of the afternoon and re-unite the various people in the great house. During the performance, she had made (following a line of thought explicitly presented in *Three Guineas*) this observation:

'The Victorians,' Mrs Swithin mused. 'I don't believe,' she said with her odd little smile, 'that there ever were such people. Only you and me and William dressed differently.'

(p. 203)

Immediately after comes this, the emphasis on insight, unifica-tion, the Coleridgean:

Mrs. Swithin caressed her cross. She gazed vaguely at the view. She was off, they guessed, on a circular tour of the imagination – one-making. Sheep, cows, grass, trees, ourselves – all are one.

(p. 204)

And it is indeed Mrs Swithin alone who sees what Miss La Trobe is up to with her pageant. As the machine in the bushes goes tick, tick, tick, as it does so many times, when it isn't going chuff, chuff, chuff (a notation of passing time which also indicates existential fear just below the surface), she suddenly comes out of her excursion of 'one-making'.

'D'you get her meaning?' said Mrs. Swithin, alighting suddenly. 'Miss La Trobe's?'
Isa, whose eyes had been wandering, shook her head.

(p. 204)

Mrs Swithin 'sees' of course what Miss La Trobe is about. And she thinks it right, since the gifted authoress of the village pageant has not made an appearance to be publicly thanked during the vicar's speech, that she and Bart, as owners of the great house, should go up and thank her personally after the guests have gone.

Then, coming up behind him, 'Oughtn't we to thank her?' Lucy asked him. She gave him a light pat on the arm.
How imperceptive her religion made her! The fumes of that incense obscured the human heart.

(p. 237)

This is one of those occasions when Virginia's irony turns into outright sarcasm. Bart ('He strolled alone past the trees. It was here, early that very morning, that he had destroyed the little boy's world. He had popped out with his newspaper; the child had cried') rebuffs his sister's suggestion that Miss La Trobe should be thanked (for a performance whose meaning, and hence whose quality, has totally escaped him) with rationalistic contempt. 'How imperceptive her religion made her!'

'She don't want our thanks, Lucy,' he said gruffly. What she wanted, like that carp (something moved in the water) was darkness in the mud; a whisky and soda at the pub; and coarse words descending like maggots through the waters.
'Thank the actors, not the author,' he said. 'Or ourselves, the audience.'

(pp. 237–8)

In the following two pages Virginia sharply contradistinguishes Lucy's capacity for unifying vision from the bluff rationalism of her brother. Lucy stares into the waters of the pool, watching the fish.

Then something moved in the water; her favourite fantail. The golden orfe followed. Then she had a glimpse of silver – the great carp himself, who came to the surface so very seldom. They slid on, in and out between the stalks, silver; pink; gold; splashed; streaked; pied.
'Ourselves,' she murmured. And retrieving some glint of faith from the grey waters, hopefully, without much help from reason, she followed the fish; the speckled, streaked, and blotched; seeing in that vision beauty, power, and glory in ourselves.
Fish had faith, she reasoned. They trust us because we've never caught 'em. But her brother would reply: 'That's greed.' 'Their beauty!' she protested. 'Sex,' he would say. 'Who makes sex susceptible to beauty?' she would argue. He shrugged who? Why? Silenced, she returned to her private vision; of beauty which is goodness; the sea on which we float. Mostly impervious, but surely every boat sometimes leaks?

He would carry the torch of reason till it went out in the darkness of
the cave. For herself, every morning, kneeling, she protected her vision.

(pp. 239–40)

In that sad slow dialectic is the whole essence of the tragedy of
Leonard and Virginia Woolf. Bart opposes Lucy's vision with
reductivism. She grabs on to anything, to keep faith, faith in
beauty, faith in goodness. 'He would carry the torch of reason till
it went out in the darkness of the cave.' There she has hit the
problem exactly. 'For herself, every morning, kneeling, she protected her vision.' And there she has given her own account of
what so puzzles Leonard in his autobiography when he asks
himself what Virginia's state of mind and health in 1939, 1940,
and 1941 may have been? She was trying to protect her vision,
firstly against the terrifying approach of total war, and secondly
in spite of a lifetime's belittlement, disappointment, fear and
effort.

Miss La Trobe goes off unthanked.

She crossed the terrace and stopped by the tree where the starlings had
gathered. It was here that she had suffered triumph, humiliation, ecstasy, despair – for nothing. Her heels had ground a hole in the grass.

(*BTA* p. 245)

And yet, even as this other Virginia moves off (she does indeed
direct her steps towards the pub, as Bart forecast), she is beginning to conceive her next play. As soon as one production is over,
vision begins again and art begins to work, the magic of art.
Virginia transforms the image of the fish pool (there was one at
Monks House and she must have stood looking into it for many
hours) for the third time. First Lucy Swithin studied its occupants
as denizens of a world of beauty and goodness which our daily
world destroys. Then, in a second use of the same images, Bart
reduced all beauty to procreation and biology, and asserted that
Miss La Trobe needs nothing so much as 'a whisky and soda at
the pub; and coarse words descending like maggots through the
waters'. Now Miss La Trobe begins to conceive her new play in
terms of germinations at the rich murky bottom of the pool.
Sitting in the pub she muses:

Words of one syllable sank down into the mud. She drowsed; she nodded. The mud became fertile. Words rose above the intolerably laden dumb oxen plodding through the mud. Words without meaning – wonderful words . . . She set down her glass. She heard the first words.

(pp. 247–8)

And there we lose sight of Miss La Trobe. The scene is again the impossibly strained *ménage à quatre* at the great house. Giles and Isa are waiting until the old people shall have gone off before they launch into a quarrel and mutual recriminations that they have been storing up all day. Bart reads the paper ('Like a fish rising to a crumb of biscuit, Bartholomew snapped at the paper' – a cruel final reduction of his own reduction within the 'code'). And night falls. Lucy is absorbed with the book about the prehistoric world, and the time scheme seems to be moving back at the speed of light, thousands of years a second, so that the final conflict between Giles and Isa can be sufficiently primal, prehistoric and 'original'.

But meanwhile, there is one final pen-portrait of Bart as he sits in his chair, which is so accurately a representation of how Leonard must have looked in the gloaming at Rodmell on so many occasions, that I cannot feel it is put in by accident, nor that we strain credulity by seeing in this portrait Leonard as Virginia, struggling to 'protect her vision', must so often have seen him:

The great square of the open window showed only sky now. It was drained of light, severe, stone cold. Shadows fell. Shadows crept over Bartholomew's high forehead; over his great nose. He looked leafless, spectral, and his chair monumental. As a dog shudders its skin, his skin shuddered. He rose, shook himself, glared at nothing, and stalked from the room. They heard the dog's paws padding on the carpet behind him.

(p. 255)

This is not only, surely, a picture of Leonard in profile at Rodmell, going off to bed followed by his dog, it is also the vision of life that Virginia was beginning to see was to be hers ever more hopelessly as the war approached. The sky was 'drained of light, severe, stone cold. Shadows fell.' It is a lunar effect she tries for here, emphasising that all life and hope is passing from the world.

The window was all sky without colour. The house had lost its shelter. It was night before roads were made, or houses. It was the night that

dwellers in caves had watched from some high place among rocks.
(p. 256)

It is a return to the very origin of things, of time; a landscape deprived of all hope. There is no-one to talk to there. The very sky is 'drained of light, severe, stone cold'. Neither Lucy, nor Miss La Trobe, could survive there very long. It is a return of the 'ontological draining' of the world that we examined in *The Waves*. The whole world is emptied of colour, being and meaning. It is without comfort, without illusion. It is the world 'seen without a self', seen from the other side of appearances.

This was the state of mind, then, that Virginia was in, in 1940. Far from going 'insane', she was reacting in a most beautiful, responsible, idealistic and creative manner to a world getting ready to hurl itself into barbarous conflict. Virginia, faced with a world like that, could see no hope. There were, she felt (*A Writer's Diary* reiterates this), no friends about, no 'circle'. All were, as the gramophone at the pageant insisted, 'dispersed', there was no circle in terms of which meaning could be created, or in terms of which hope could be generated. There was no help coming, or at least Virginia could not see where it might come from. The world was becoming primeval, bare, merciless, hopeless, stone cold.

It is a state of mind in which suicide, far from being 'insane', becomes a natural, and even an understandable, desire.

CHAPTER 18

Octavia Wilberforce: 'oak and triple brass were around her breast'

Between the Acts was finished on 23 November 1940.

'It was only in the first days of 1941 that the deep disturbance in her mind began to show itself clearly', writes Leonard in his autobiography. Apparently, *Between the Acts* had been conceived and written without any noticeable disturbance of mind, so far as Leonard could see. 'Round about January 25, I think, the first symptoms of serious mental disturbance began to show themselves. She fell into what she called a "trough of despair".' Normally, Leonard says, Virginia's attacks were preceded by the well-known signs of trouble – 'the headache, the sleeplessness, the inability to concentrate . . . But this time there were no warning symptoms of this kind. The depression struck her like a sudden blow.'

By mid-January 1941, Leonard had begun to have his suspicions. He went, typically enough, to discuss his wife privately with some third person. This time he chose Octavia Wilberforce, who 'practised as a doctor in Montpelier Crescent, Brighton, and lived there with Elizabeth Robins'. It would appear that their social acceptability was such that Octavia would make the ideal doctor for Virginia (*The Journey* p. 80).

It is not made at all clear by Leonard whether Octavia Wilberforce had any special psychiatric qualifications or abilities which would have fitted her to help the author of *Between the Acts*. She was consulted as a *doctor*:

She had, to all intents and purposes, become Virginia's doctor, and so the moment I became uneasy about Virginia's psychological health in the beginning of 1941 I told Octavia and consulted her professionally.

(The Journey p. 86)

This is precisely the démarche which had, in 1912–13, been the first action in a series which led finally to the veronal attempt. Leonard had certainly not drawn the conclusion, from the events of 9 September 1913, that consulting experts about his wife, without her presence, led her to feel more, not less, isolated, and increased her sense of having no-one to turn to.

There is slightly more information in *A Marriage of True Minds* by Spater and Parsons, but the general line of their interpretation is still squarely that of Leonard and of Quentin Bell. In 1940, they say, things were physically more difficult than they had been in 1913:

First, Leonard's regimen of calm, rest and good food could not be followed. Second, Virginia was tortured by the thought that since she had gone mad in the First World War it was likely that the same thing would happen during the Second.

(p. 182)

It is obvious from this sentence that Spater and Parsons do not intend to nuance their use of the word 'mad' any more than Professor Bell does. And the automatic equivalence set up in this sentence shows that the conceptual level they are working at is the same as Bell's.

Spater and Parsons include however (p. 182) a few more details about the visits of Octavia Wilberforce than we find either in Leonard or in Bell. Virginia was obviously deep into reflection on her family, her father, her mother, Stella, but Octavia clearly did not have much patience with this, any more than Leonard did. 'Poor Leonard is tired out by my interest in my family and all it brings back', Virginia is quoted as saying.

But there is one major clue, missed by Octavia, which we are able, in the light of what we now know of Virginia's embodiment, to interpret for its full significance:

[Virginia said] that her father had 'made too great emotional claims upon us and that I think has accounted for many of the wrong things of my life . . . I never remember any enjoyment of my body'. When Octavia asked what she meant, Virginia said, 'you adored the woods and games

– I never had that chance', on which Octavia commented: 'It was all for her I gather intellectual and emotional – no healthy hunting outdoor outlet.'

(p. 182)

That remark is truly worthy of Dr Holmes. But for us, who take some account of the way Virginia experienced her adolescence, her marriage and her life, that sudden twist of evasion is significant to the highest degree. It is quite pathetic. She says 'I never remember any enjoyment of my body.' That would have been the moment to enter into a subjective dialogue with Virginia, wheedling her little by little towards an assurance that these things could be understood. But 'asked what she meant' – 'What exactly do you *mean* by *that*?' in the true blue rationalist manner – she sees the danger, and rapidly twists out of the road: 'you adored the woods and games – I never had that chance', an absolutely visible evasion.

Spater and Parsons list the terrors of the winter of 1940–1, but do not derive from their observations, any more than Leonard did, that Virginia was living in a state of nervous terror (p. 181). Neither do they see, in the image of Virginia scrubbing floors because she could not write and felt so cut off from her friends, anything more than an odd quirk in someone obviously tending towards insanity. Indeed they endorse Leonard's oft-repeated position up to the hilt: 'Up to this point Virginia had been claiming (as she characteristically did when she was ill) that there was nothing wrong with her' – this is always taken as firm evidence of insanity by Leonard and others. But, Spater and Parsons continue:

. . . at tea on March 12 she finally confessed that she had been 'feeling desperate – depressed to the lowest depths, had just finished a story. Always felt like this – but specially useless just now.'

(p. 183)

She had 'just finished a story'. That story is *Between the Acts*, the document which contains all one could ever hope to know about Virginia's state of mind in 1940–1. But Octavia had not read it, it was still just 'a story' for her, as she came to tea bringing her milk and cream.

'Virginia had looked "almost scared" at the first tea on December 9, 1940', say Spater and Parsons. No wonder she looked so scared. She could easily see through Leonard's motive in asking Octavia so often to tea, though Leonard presumed she could not. Her own explanation for her suicide of 1941 is quite clear in what she says at this time:

There was another tea on March 21 at which Virginia told Octavia that her two biographies, *Orlando* and her book on Fry, were 'failures'; that she could no longer write: 'I've lost the art . . . I'm buried down here – I've not the stimulation of seeing people. I can't settle to it'; and that she 'had taken to scrubbing floors when she couldn't write – it took her mind off.'

(p. 183)

The three major points established here would be enough to explain the suicide of the author of *Between the Acts*. Indeed, her own firm conviction that, with that novel and her biography of Roger Fry, she had 'lost the art' of writing would be enough in itself to make sense of her decision. For, ever since *The Voyage Out*, she had defined herself in terms of her writing. Deprived of her writing, she was deprived of a *raison d'être*, deprived of her identity. The world had drained of colour, of meaning. She was seeing the world 'without a self'. It all fits.

The final interview of 27 March, as reported by Quentin Bell, is almost grotesquely menacing:

Octavia replied [to Virginia] that the mere fact that she had had this trouble before and that it had been cured should be a reason for confidence. If you have your appendix removed, she said, nothing will remain but the scar; a mental illness can be removed in the same way if you don't inflame the wound by dwelling upon it.

(II, 225)

The level of this kind of analysis is so primitive, that it is not surprising that Virginia's sense of having no-one to talk to was increased. She may well have felt that it was simply childish, and that no form of hope lay in such medical science.

Just as, in 1913, Dr Henry Head had 'told her that she was completely mistaken about her own condition; she was ill, ill like a person who had a cold or typhoid fever' (*Beginning Again* p. 156), so now Dr Octavia Wilberforce told Virginia in all seriousness that mental illness could be removed in the same way as an appendix 'if you don't inflame the wound by dwelling upon it'.

It seems otiose to suggest that the state of psychiatric expertise had not increased much, in 1941, from what it had been in 1913; it might to all intents and purposes be the psychiatric expertise of the middle ages. That this level of medical talk was conceptually primitive must have been quite evident to Virginia herself, and she obviously did not feel that it was worth arguing the issue. She saw the hopelessness of that. If people were seriously prepared to compare mental illness with a cold, typhoid fever or an appendix, it must have seemed to her that they were all, and Leonard with them, well out of the range of intelligent criticism, and that there was nothing she could do about it but submit.

Both Leonard and Quentin Bell insist, once more, that Virginia fought against being called 'mentally ill'. Indeed, her refusal to admit this plain fact is yet another confirmation for Quentin Bell's view that she was simply mad:

It was a symptom of Virginia's madness that she could not admit that she was mentally ill; to force this knowledge upon her was, in itself, dangerous. But by 26 March Leonard had become convinced that the risk must be taken and that she must be persuaded to see a doctor.

(II, 224)

Leonard is of course the origin of this passage. He writes:

Desperate depression had settled upon Virginia; her thoughts raced beyond her control; she was terrified of madness. One knew that at any moment she might kill herself. The only chance for her was to give in and admit that she was ill, but this she would not do.

(*The Journey* p. 91)

It is, once again a battle of wills just as it had been in 1913. She will not 'give in'. She refuses to admit that she is ill.

It was essential for her to resign herself to illness and the drastic regime which alone could stave off insanity. But she was on the brink of despair, insanity, and suicide.

(*The Journey* p. 91)

How Virginia struggled! She fought to the very last not to be called 'insane', 'mad', 'mentally ill'. But always there was Leonard, writing descriptions of her in his secret diary in Tamil characters and consulting medical experts in her absence, urging her to 'give in', 'to resign herself to illness', to resign herself to 'the drastic regime which alone could stave off insanity'. If ever there was a man working against his own interest, it was Leonard. If ever a woman struggled to remain alive, it was Virginia. She would not admit that she was insane. And this of course, quite rightly, because she was not.

And the most astonishing thing is this: that although Leonard *explicitly recalls* the action he took in 1913 when he took Virginia to see Dr Head, he had learnt nothing from this mistake in the intervening thirty years. He was determined to repeat his mistakes (both of them) of 1913 in identical form in 1941.

On Wednesday March 26th, I became convinced that Virginia's mental condition was more serious that it had ever been since those terrible days in August 1913 which led to her complete breakdown and attempt to kill herself. The terrifying decision which I had to take then once more faced me. It was essential for her to resign herself to illness and the drastic regime which alone could stave off insanity. But she was on the brink of despair, insanity, and suicide. I had to urge her to face the verge of disaster in order to get her to accept the misery of the only method of avoiding it, and I knew at the same time that a wrong word, a mere hint of pressure, even a statement of the truth might be enough to drive her over the verge into suicide. The memory of 1913 when the attempted suicide was the immediate result of the interview with Dr Head haunted me.

(The Journey pp. 91–2)

But in the intervening thirty years, it had not occurred to Leonard that the actual suicide attempt was not only a result of the interview with Head: it was at least as much a result of Leonard's having left Virginia after this interview, in order to apologise to Savage for having been to see Head *(Beginning Again* p. 156). For Virginia, there had been a double sense of desertion, and it was this that had led to the veronal attempt.

In 1941, Leonard repeated the formula exactly. Here is the account of Quentin Bell:

The interview was difficult. Virginia at once declared that there was nothing the matter with her. It was quite unnecessary that she should have a consultation; she certainly would not answer any questions.

'All you have to do,' said Octavia, 'is to reassure Leonard.'

(II, 225)

Two capital points recur immediately from the 1913 situation, then. Virginia asserts she is *not* ill, and is disconfirmed. And Virginia is distressing Leonard so much that the main thing to be achieved is to reassure him. In other words, it is his estimate of the situation that has to be confirmed, not hers. It does not matter much what she thinks is wrong with her (if anything). What matters is that Leonard's diagnosis (that she is mentally 'ill') should be confirmed.

It is at least partly a verbal matter, a matter of mere words. Leonard insists on the formula 'insane', and Virginia rejects the formula 'insane'. That there was something wrong with Virginia, I do not for a moment deny: no doubt she was desperate, no doubt she needed help: but no attempt seems to have been made to discover *what* was wrong with her, and how she saw her own situation. At least neither Leonard nor Bell tells us of any such attempt.

Virginia, threatened by Octavia about having to reassure Leonard, is brought to a stop for she is, of course, devoted to him:

Then she added that she knew what kind of symptoms Virginia felt, and asked to examine her. In a kind of sleep-walking way Virginia began to undress and then stopped.
  'Will you promise, if I do this, not to order me a rest cure?'
                                                              (II, 225)

It is almost too pitiful to watch. Frightened, afraid of the power of doctors to order rest cures, Virginia, half-undressed, tries to bargain with her judge. If Octavia Wilberforce knew in advance 'what kind of symptoms Virginia felt', it is curious that she should ask 'to examine her' and even more curious (this being a psychiatric interview) that the form of examination should require Virginia to 'undress'.

'Will you promise, if I do this, not to order me a rest cure?'
  'What I promise is that I won't order you to do anything that you won't think it reasonable to do. Is that fair?'
  Virginia agreed and the examination continued, but not without many protests. She was like a child being sent up to bed.
                                                              (II, 225)

I do not know what evidence Quentin Bell has for that last comment, but it fits well enough. Here is one of the subtlest and most perceptive minds of her time being treated just like a child, threatened with a hated rest cure, and 'being sent up to bed'.

Then something very interesting occurs, but it is difficult to gather from Bell's account just what form of words was used:

In the end she did confess some part of her fears, fears that the past would come back, that she would be unable to write again.

(II, 225)

I find the word 'confess' here significant. But it is difficult to reconstruct what was going on, since there is so little published evidence of any kind as to what was asked and what was said. It would appear that Virginia felt that she would probably be able to satisfy Octavia Wilberforce, and Leonard, if she 'did confess some part of her fears', although there is no evidence that the situation was such that she could have expressed any part of what was really worrying her. For was not the situation a replay of the one in 1913, the one which had been recorded in *Mrs Dalloway*, in which the specialist knows *in advance* what is wrong with the patient, and is so sure of his diagnosis that there is no need for the patient to say anything? The whole point of the 'psychiatric' section of *Mrs Dalloway* is that nobody is interested in what the patient's own view of his condition is. This was true in 1913; it was true in 1941; and the psychiatric situation today, insofar as it is still conceptually pre-Laingian, is all too often run according to the same assumptions.

Then there was a private consultation between Octavia and Leonard. What were they to do; should Virginia be under the surveillance of a trained nurse? It might easily be a disastrous measure . It seemed, both to Leonard and to Octavia, that the consultation had done some good.

(II, 225)

One recalls Octavia's opening remark to Virginia ' "All you have to do," ' said Octavia, ' "is to reassure Leonard." ' Leonard was now reassured. Virginia had done what was asked of her.

But who, in all this, had been concerned with reassuring *her*? Who had tried to contact her in the strange space in which she was adrift? What follows next in Bell's account gives us the time-scale we need to understand what the effect of the interview was:

The Woolfs went back to Rodmell and Octavia returned to bed. She wrote Virginia a note, as gentle and as reassuring as she could make it, and on the following evening rang up, but by that time it was too late.

(II, 225–6)

Just as, in 1913, the direct result of the interview with Dr Head was attempted suicide, so in 1941, the direct result of the interview with Octavia Wilberforce is attempted suicide – only this time it succeeds. Just as, in 1913, Virginia's desperate assertion that she was not 'ill' was disconfirmed by Dr Head and then disconfirmed by Leonard, so in 1941 her refusal to admit she was 'ill' was disconfirmed implicitly by Leonard and by Octavia Wilberforce, who disregarded Virginia's opening assertion that 'there was nothing the matter with her. It was quite unnecessary that she should have a consultation', and who said that 'she knew what kind of symptoms Virginia felt'.

The inevitable conclusion seems to me that the direct result of the disconfirmation in 1913 and of the disconfirmation by Octavia Wilberforce in 1941 was a suicide attempt, and that the reason behind both attempts was that Virginia felt no-one had asked her what *she* was really feeling nor enquired of her what her own view of her mental state might be.

Leonard obviously did not expect Octavia Wilberforce to talk to Virginia in the sense in which a Freudian analyst talks to his patient: long sessions of analysis, self-examination, discussion, free-association and so on. It was not in Leonard's mind, obviously, that Octavia could come at some deep-seated mental trouble in his wife, which he himself Leonard ('As for intelligence . . . I would back myself against all of them'), could not have got at. Nor was it, obviously, in Octavia Wilberforce's mind.

It was not, in other words, in the minds either of Leonard or of Octavia Wilberforce that Virginia should be analysed at the level of words, ideas, concepts, hopes and fears, at all. That does not seem even to have been considered by either of them. And if it was not considered, what hope could there have been of Virginia being helped? For her mental problems were existential ones.

And the image of 'madness' as something which 'enters into' his wife is constant throughout Leonard's autobiography. He sees the madness arrive, something external, attacking her from without. When Leonard saw the attack coming he speaks entirely in terms of physical reactions to the stimulus:

The desperate difficulty which always presented itself when Virginia began to be threatened with a breakdown – a difficulty which occurs, I think, again and again in mental illnesses – was to decide how far it was safe to go in urging her to take steps – drastic steps – to ward off the attack. Drastic steps meant going to bed, complete rest, plenty of food and milk. But part of the disease was to deny the disease and to refuse the cure.

(*The Journey* p. 86)

Leonard's view of the externality of her affliction was shared by Octavia Wilberforce. So 'confessing' a little here and there, in what is visibly a stratagem to bring the interview to an end, Virginia is defeated once again. There is nothing she can say, since no-one wants to hear it.

She must 'give in', said Leonard. 'All you have to do is to reassure Leonard', said Octavia Wilberforce. Virginia had done her best, obviously, in the interview, to say whatever it was that would reassure Leonard, for Bell says 'it seemed, both to Leonard and to Octavia, that the consultation had done some good'.

And yet, goes the orthodox view, she *must* have been 'insane' – does not her drowning herself prove that beyond any doubt? And (this is always the final appeal) what of the letter Virginia left on the table before she walked down to the river? The text of the letter, which Leonard reproduces on pages 93–4 of *The Journey*, runs as follows:

Dearest,
  I feel certain that I am going mad again. I feel we can't go through another of those terrible times. And I shan't recover this time. I begin to hear voices, and I can't concentrate. So I am doing what seems the best thing to do. You have given me the greatest possible happiness. You have been in every way all that anyone could be. I don't think two people could have been happier till this terrible disease came. I can't fight any longer. I know that I am spoiling your life, that without me you could work. And you will I know. You see I can't even write this properly. I can't read. What I want to say is I owe all the happiness of my life to you. You have been entirely patient with me and incredibly good. I want to say that – everybody knows it. If anybody could have saved me it would

have been you. Everything has gone from me but the certainty of your goodness. I can't go on spoiling your life any longer.

I don't think two people could have been happier than we have been.

V.

A preliminary draft of the letter, written on her writing block in her work room, is given as a footnote on page 93.

Does she not here admit that she was 'going mad'? Does she not refer to hearing 'voices'? Does she not assure Leonard that if anybody could have saved her it would have been him? That she owes all the happiness of her life to Leonard?

To any reader who had not previously known of Virginia's suicide letter it must have come as a shock, with its sudden stark acknowledgment of the madness she had spent so many years denying.

She is now saying she is going mad 'again', that she cannot go through 'another' of those terrible times, that she will not recover 'this time', phrases which necessarily imply that she knew she had been mad before.

Certainly that is what the words mean, but can they possibly be true? They cannot be, *unless* all her previous protestations had been untrue, unless she had been living a lie, unless so much of her novels had been based on that same deception.

Whatever criticisms may have been levelled against Virginia Woolf, dishonesty of mind has never been one of them. It is surely impossible to believe that everything she had ever said to Leonard (and to the world) about her alleged madness had been untrue: so it must be the suicide note which was untrue, written as it was for its specific purpose, as her last message to Leonard.

The explanation for the letter seems to be this – Virginia is explaining to Leonard, in terms which make sense to him, that she cannot endure any more. The difficulty is that she has to explain this matter in terms he can understand. It is useless (she has come to realise) to try and explain to him in her terms. The basic disparity between their two world views was so enormous that there was no possibility of justifying her decision to Leonard in her own terms. She had to reassure him in the terms he habitually used: 'mad', 'terrible disease', 'hear voices' and so on.

That Virginia was devoted to Leonard and deeply grateful to

him for all the care and concern, is clear. She had tried to 'reassure' him in the situation of the psychiatric interview, and had done her best, no doubt, after they had returned to Rodmell that afternoon, to contain her emotion. When it became apparent to her that suicide was her only way out, the very last thing she wanted to do was to hurt Leonard, or to imply that, in any degree, he was responsible for her dying. She wanted to give him an absolutely clean record, so far as her death was concerned. And that is why, with her mind no doubt already on the river and the walk to it, she takes such care to say and say again, that he could not have been more patient with her, that nobody could have done more for her, and so on. She even says that 'I don't think two people could have been happier than we have been.' Preparing to die, she writes the most generous letter of which she is capable. Her prime concern is to make sure that he will never reproach himself for her death.

All who knew Leonard speak of his untiring devotion to Virginia, and the single-minded purity with which he devoted himself to her salvation. Within his limits, within the narrow limits of his vision, he had done his best. He had tried to give her happiness, to protect her, to preserve her from hurt and to keep her career afloat. He had laboured with forces too great for him, and which he did not understand. So in her final letter she stresses that nobody could ever have done more for her than he had done.

And this is true. We watch here the most tragic end of this engagement of Leonard and Virginia: they part, profoundly devoted to each other, in complete misunderstanding. She cannot explain to him what she sees, and what really tortures her. He cannot get her to accept that all she is threatened by are baseless fears and unjustified remorse.

The misunderstanding is total and tragic. What he sees, she does not; what she sees, he does not. In her last letter, Virginia writes that she is beginning to hear voices. But those voices, 'Edward VII in the azaleas using the foulest possible language', the voices of the birds singing in Greek, as well as the voices of her mother and father, of George Duckworth, were voices whose meaning she had never explained to Leonard, voices whose meaning she was incapable of explaining to him.

Consequently, she cannot explain to Leonard why she is walking into the river. There is too much he does not know about her, too much that she dare not tell him, too much that she does not even dare to recall to her own memory. She has, however, to explain her action somehow. How to do it?

The only way out, is to fall into the language and idiom of Leonard himself. Of all the people who have cited this last letter it does not seem to me that there is one who realises that this is the only piece written by Virginia which is written in Leonard's language and which incorporates Leonard's world view. It is the only 'fraud' of her career. The language, the idiom, the conceptual limits, are Leonard's and not hers. Determined to give total exoneration to Leonard, attempting to explain why she is doing what she is doing, she can think of only one way of being convincing: she has to use Leonard's own style, and observe the contours of Leonard's own understanding. The last letter is the most generous fraud, and the most magnificent deception, in modern literature.

Leonard lived on to write his autobiography in the calm faith that he had done everything that could humanly have been done for his wife, until madness seized her and insanity prompted her to suicide. The letter worked. Virginia's last profound concern for Leonard's spiritual survival was totally effective in persuading Leonard that he was in no way responsible for her death.

Nothing changed their affection; no argument; no fact; no truth. What she saw he didn't; what he saw she didn't – and so on, *ad infinitum*.

There was nothing they could say to each other to cancel their tragic incompatibility either, though. There was nothing for it, but the walk down through the fields to the river.

ww

Death by shrapnel or
death by water

> Full fathom five thy father lies
> Of his bones are coral made
> Those are pearls that were his eyes . . .

Water is Virginia's central symbol. Water, the sea, the waves: in these symbols, the meanings, moods and varieties of her experience find their synthesis, their point of repose. At least three of her novels – *The Voyage Out*, *To the Lighthouse* and *The Waves* – have the sea in their very titles, and the sea is part of their structure too. But there is scarcely a page of her novels where the sea, or water, does not make a fleeting appearance, as if her imagination was rocked on the swell of an invisible current of water which ran ceaselessly through her thinking.

Counting the frequency of images in literary texts is usually one of the more fruitless aspects of scholarship, but there are occasions when the results can be startling. Marie-Paule Vigne has shown that:

across all the novels, water alone occupies almost *one half* of the cosmic vocabulary: 48% (about 4,500 words) against 52% (4,850) for all the other elements *together*. Water predominates in all the novels taken individually, and in five of the nine, occupies a more important place than all the other elements put together: 52% in *The Voyage Out*, 53% in *Jacob's Room*, 54% in *The Years*, and a proportion of ⅔ in *Orlando* and *To the Lighthouse*.[1]

It is irrelevant, in the case of Virginia Woolf, to point to Freud, to Jung, or to Bachelard. That water is an archetype or a symbol, the maternal element or the feminine liquid, the origin of Aphro-

---

[1] 'Reflexions on a Theme: Virginia Woolf and Water', in *Virginia Woolf: Colloque de Cerisy* (Editions 10/18, Paris 1977), p. 180.

dite or a mythical matrix, is equally irrelevant. We feel the pre-
dominance of water as we read, but it is convincing that when
the references are counted, they do empirically predominate over
all other images from the natural world taken together.

I think that water played such a permanent and powerful part
in Virginia's thinking and writing because it represented for her
two things, both of which had an entirely personal value and
meaning. First, it represented the kind of intellection which was
not abrupt, logical, male, hacking, dominant, fractious and
pseudo-logical; but smooth, flowing, integrating, harmonious.
Second, it represented the possibility of the resolution of intolerable conflicts in death.

Men divide. Women harmonise. This is the theme of much
of her writing. Hence, whatever the symbol of the male mind –
Lighthouse, brazen beak, scissors, pocket-knife, Gibbon, the
Encyclopedia or Lemprière – their polar opposite is the flowing,
the liquid, the merging, the cool. Male thought creates fissures
and cracks. Female presence fills the interstices of things, brings
calm and resolution, soothes male vanity and quiets male pride.
Men esteem 'facts', they are 'solid', or 'brilliant' or 'a failure', and
they have Fellowships at Cambridge (or soon will, or ought to).
The women esteem insight, vision, beauty, harmony, colour.
Often, as a male character in the novels goes on and on about
some matter of more importance to his ego than to knowledge
itself, a female character will be watching the foliage, noting the
change of colours on the sea, or meditating inwardly on some
breach that she can now heal. It happens incessantly in *The
Voyage Out*, where the Bloomsbury models are 'placed' ceaselessly by Helen, who watches the sunset or admires the beauty of
the flowers. But it happens throughout the novels. The characters of *To the Lighthouse* would not be able to complete one day in
peace (Virginia implies) if it were not for Mrs Ramsay and Lily
Briscoe taking pity, soothing, calming, reassuring, forgiving,
bringing water into the desert of male arrogance and intellectu-
ality.

This basic opposition of the male and female mind is, I believe, incapable of resolution. There is a very wise and a very
insightful book, which I much esteem, *Feminism and Art*, by

Herbert Marder,[1] which suggests at length that Virginia was searching through her life for something which she called on one occasion 'the adrogynous mind', the mind which should include both male and female qualities. And who would deny that this would be the ideal solution? But I do not think it is possible, if only because men and women are physically present in the world in such different ways (their embodiment is so radically different), and the way in which they see the world is therefore necessarily too opposed, for such a happy resolution as 'the androgynous mind' to be anything more than a conceptual possibility.

No doubt Virginia herself entertained the idea of 'the androgynous mind' and worked at it, especially during the period of witing *A Room of One's Own*.[2] But this does not mean that the androgynous mind is a real possibility. Men being embodied as they are, their minds will normally be of the Ramsay – Tansley kind: stuck at Q and desperately struggling to get to R in the conceptual world, as Virginia herself said of Mr Ramsay. The male mind, and Ramsay's is an excellent example of it, modelled on one of the finest rationalist intelligences of the nineteenth century, will remain as it is until it peters out. 'He would carry the torch of reason till it went out in the darkness of the cave', as Virginia writes of Bart in *Between the Acts*. The line, from the early intellectuals in *The Voyage Out* and *Night and Day*, modelled on Virginia's own early suitors like Lytton Strachey, through Ramsay and Tansley of *To the Lighthouse*, to Bart of *Between the Acts*, is unbroken. It is the line of the male mind at its rationalist best, the mind of Leslie Stephen, G. E. Moore, Bertrand Russell, Lytton Strachey, Maynard Keynes and so on. This male mind has been portrayed in the novels again and again as egocentric, rough, bruising, insensitive, hammering, dominant, 'fact'-obsessed, cynical, reductive, ironical, contemptuous.

And the female mind at its best has been given equally long, thorough and patient treatment in the 'magical' ladies from Helen in *The Voyage Out* and Mrs Hilbery in *Night and Day*, through Mrs Ramsay and Lily in *To the Lighthouse*, to Lucy Swithin in *Between the Acts*. These magical ladies do not so much 'think' as know,

[1] University of Chicago Press 1968.
[2] See Marder, *Feminism and Art* ch. 4 *passim*.

they do not so much ratiocinate as arrive at conclusions and perceptions, they do not so much 'carry thought out' at the expense of other people, as arrive at thought in order to make other people's lives easier.

Following Herbert Marder, though, there have been at least three major attempts to heal the intolerable splits in Virginia's novels by referring to the concept of the androgynous mind. James Naremore opposes 'the world of the self, the time-bound, landlocked everyday world of the masculine ego, of intellect and routine' to the 'world without a self – watery, emotional, erotic, generally associated with the female sensibility'.[1] Nancy Topping Bazin, adopting Leonard's account of his wife as manic-depressive (*Beginning Again* pp. 76–7) as self-evident, clear and definitive, associates 'an essentially feminine vision of life' with her alleged 'mania', and 'an essentially masculine vision of life' with her 'depression', and sees the dialectic set up between these as being the polarity set up between the mother and the father, expressed through Mrs and Mr Ramsay.[2] Alice Van Buren Kelley divides the fiction up into 'the factual world', which is the world of 'the intellect' and 'objective reason', and the 'world of vision' where objects 'transcend themselves to take on universal significance'.[3]

While all of these critics have isolated warring opposites and jarring contraries, I do not believe that any one of them has shown in his or her book that it was indeed through 'the androgynous mind' that the resolution was achieved. For me the warring opposites and jarring contraries are and remain a fact of experience in the novels. There is just no way to close the gap in a harmonious wave of Prospero's wand, the world of embodiment being so brutally and irrevocably what it is.

Indeed, it seems to me that all attempts to close the gap between experienced opposites by invoking the concept of the androgynous mind are a kind of wish fulfilment. It could well be that this wish fulfilment is originally and primarily Virginia's own, that it is through some such concept that she envisages, in a

[1] *The World Without a Self* (Yale University Press 1973) p. 245.
[2] *Virginia Woolf and the Androgynous Vision* (Rutgers University Press 1973) p. 6.
[3] *Virginia Woolf: Fact and Vision* (University of Chicago Press 1973) pp. 4–6.

better world than this, these warring contraries coming into harmony and peace. But I do not observe her achieving this harmony in any of the characters in the novels.

The gaps experienced in the novels are just too wide to cross or annihilate by the adept use of any single word or concept. Indeed, even though Virginia does see Shakespeare and others as endowed with what she calls an androgynous mind, she points to it even there (in *A Room of One's Own*) as an ideal entity, 'a consummation devoutly to be wished', which occurs only in certain towering peaks of human intellection. She does not observe it commonly around her in the society she knows, indeed what she indicts there (as in so many places in the novels) as 'self-conscious virility, men writing only with the male side of their brains', is what she finds to be the all-too-common problem. Androgyneity might be a superb solution, but she does not regard it as in any way an achieved state. It is an ideal state, towards which we tend.

Besides that, *Orlando*, in which the theorists of the androgynous mind come most happily home to rest, is a 'fantasy', and remains that. It is an escape from the felt split of male–female experience. Indeed, *Orlando*, if it proves anything, proves how fundamentally the male–female *fact* makes of androgynous experience a merely possible idea.

I think that the concept of the androgynous mind was for Virginia, like water, a symbol that stood for resolution without in fact being any sort of resolution. It was a conceptual referent, an ideality. Insofar as Virginia points to androgynous minds in literature (Shakespeare, Coleridge, Proust), she is surely pointing rather to an achievement of empathy (a leaning over and into the experience of the opposite sex) rather than some sort of cancelling out of the basic duality between the sexes.

We remain, then, in the presence of two totally opposed kinds of mind, the male-rationalist mind, and the female-intuitive mind, and it appears that Virginia herself believed (in the novels) that never the twain would meet. Indeed, she went a good deal further: she suggested that the male mind and the female mind are not only incompatible, but actually hostile to each other. Not only does the egoistic fact-obsessed, reductive male mind oppose the intuitive, fluid, nature-aware female mind, but it seeks to destroy that female mind if it can. Whereas it is inconceivable that Mrs Ramsay should ever make her interlocutor 'feel small', impossible that she should ever 'score a point' against him, it is virtually always the case that the male 'intellectual' characters will more or less consciously do immense damage to others around them. At any rate, if there is any consciousness of causing hurt, it is suppressed ('He was incapable of untruth; never tampered with a fact; never altered a disagreeable word to suit the pleasure or convenience of any mortal being, least of all of his own children' – *TTL* p. 13). It simply does not matter if, in the course of expressing itself, the male mind causes pain, embarrassment or damage to others. It is immaterial to the male mind in the full sweep of its abilities if, in the course of its manoeuvres, some small craft is rammed and sunk. The male mind is expressing 'facts', or opinions which (in the case of Cambridge intellectuals) are indistinguishable from 'facts'. The female mind, if it is present, is required to knuckle under and get this matter straight.

'But you'll never see it!' he exclaimed; 'because with all your virtues you don't, and you never will, care with every fibre of your being for the pursuit of truth! You've no respect for facts, Rachel; you're essentially feminine.'

She did not trouble to deny it . . .

'But I like him,' she said, and she thought to herself that she also pitied him, as one pities those unfortunate people who are outside the warm mysterious globe full of changes and miracles in which we ourselves move about: she thought that it must be very dull to be St. John Hirst.

(*TVO* p. 361)

So much for 'the androgynous mind'! When it comes to the point, male fact-obsessed arrogance ('the pursuit of truth') simply causes the emotion of pity in the female breast. It is the same old dialectic we noted in real life: Sir Leslie was admirable and brilliant, yet he was (at home, in private, with his womenfolk) pitiable. The dialectic in Virginia's mind swung between admiration for the intellectual ability, and pity for the miserable squashed perceptual apparatus which could ever confuse 'the pursuit of truth' with the logical galvanisms which these intellectuals took to be that pursuit. Truth itself being so much more complex, it was unlikely that the logically limited male mind would ever stumble across it.

The talk is incessant, and 'the pursuit of truth' is doubtless engaged in 'with every fibre' of the being of each of the intellectuals present; nevertheless, the result is that everyone has missed or ignored some sorts of truth even as they sat there and argued. The truth of perception, for instance, or the truth of beauty, or the truth of nature. To balance the male outburst of Terence above, one could counterpose this, from the female mind, Helen:

'You've all been sitting here,' she said, 'for almost an hour, and you haven't noticed my figs, or my flowers, or the way the light comes through, or anything, I haven't been listening, because I've been looking at you. You looked very beautiful; I wish you'd go on sitting for ever.'

(*TVO* p. 379)

That is the female mind in action: the intellectual discussion that has been going on has been bracketed. The perceptual world has been preserved. The beauty of nature has been noticed. The logical errors of one or other party to the debate have been forgiven in a wider understanding. And the essential ugliness of a group of male intellectuals engaged 'with every fibre of [their] being in the pursuit of truth' has been transformed into a canvas of great beauty. Such is the ability of the female mind.

The quality of the female mind is liquid. Water is the symbol which indicates, all through the pages of Virginia's novels, that she is thinking as a woman. She is, in fact, trying to think in a way which no woman ever succeeded in achieving before: a way which is peculiarly female. She is aware of this explicitly: much of *A Room of One's Own* is concerned with the stylistic innovation that she herself, as a woman, has been capable of, and which her female predecessors were never allowed to try. She has been trying, in her novels, to create a model of the female mind in action.

Her paper 'Professions for Women' insists on this achievement, using the image of the female imagination as a violent descent into the deepest part of the lake: 'The line raced through the girl's fingers. Her imagination had rushed away. It had sought the pools, the depths, the dark places where the largest fish slumber' (*Collected Essays* ii, 287). In this paper, Virginia is very clear that she regards the female imagination as different from, and largely opposed by, the male imagination. She links this with 'telling the truth about my own experiences as a body', a difficulty she acknowledges she has not been able to solve. 'I doubt that any woman has solved it yet.'

But this female thinking is connected, fatally connected in Virginia's own case, with another, deeper movement of consciousness. Water is the resolution of intellectual argument, water is the cancelling of petty differences in one supreme liquid flow, water is the merging of opposites and the annulling of conflicts, but water is also the deep pull of unconsciousness, easy death. Water is dissolution of the self in something greater than the self. Water is the great forgiver, the great receiver, the great lover, the great divine element which makes all argument unnecessary and all strife unimportant. Water was the call to death itself. And never was the call of water more powerfully felt than in the face of the assault of the rationalist male mind.

Suddenly he said, 'Now we will kill ourselves,' when they were standing by the river, and he looked at it with a look which she had seen in his eyes when a train went by, or an omnibus – a look as if something fascinated him . . .

(*Mrs Dalloway* p. 74)

This is from *Mrs Dalloway*, where the conflict between the male mind and the female mind has been given a savage potentiation by the fact that Septimus Smith, as Virginia's *persona* in the novel, has been given a male exterior. But his fear is the fear of the male mind, the mind of Sir William Bradshaw and of Holmes, 'a powerfully built man'. Septimus lies in bed, ill. This is an obsessional situation in Virginia's fiction, and water always occurs in the reverie as a haunting temptation:

Outside the trees dragged their leaves like nets through the depths of the air; the sound of water was in the room, and through the waves came the voices of birds singing . . . Fear no more, says the heart in the body; fear no more.

(*Mrs Dalloway* pp. 153–4)

It is tempting to compare this with the reverie of Rachel in *The Voyage Out*, as she lies dying:

The heat was suffocating. At last the faces went further away; she fell into a deep pool of sticky water, which eventually closed over her head. She saw nothing and heard nothing but a faint booming sound, which was the sound of the sea rolling over her head. While all her tormentors thought that she was dead, she was not dead, but curled up at the bottom of the sea. There she lay, sometimes seeing darkness, sometimes light, while every now and then someone turned her over at the bottom of the sea.

(TVO p. 416)

This is from the first novel that Virginia wrote, the one which she ceaselessly revised and which covered the period of her engagement and marriage. This ambiguity about the depths of the sea, containing both pleasure and resignation, runs through all her fiction. The patient sees her nurses as 'tormentors', and takes pleasure in deceiving them. But, at any rate, she is safe from them now, safe at the bottom of the sea.

Indeed, the chapter in which Rachel lies ill is introduced by a passionate poetic acceptance of death by water, which takes the form of repeated quotations from Milton:

> Sabrina fair,
>> Listen where thou art sitting
> Under the glassy, cool, translucent wave.

This line, 'Under the glassy, cool, translucent wave' forms the beginning of an inner meditation in Rachel's mind:

The glassy, cool, translucent wave was almost visible before her, curling up at the end of the bed, and as it was refreshingly cool she tried to keep her mind fixed upon it.

(TVO p. 402)

However, even though the glassy, cool, translucent wave is a temptation, water always has its nasty memory associated with it too:

She shut her eyes. When she opened them again several more hours had passed, but the night still lasted interminably. The woman was still playing cards, only she sat now in a tunnel under a river . . .

In order to get rid of this terrible stationary sight Rachel again shut her eyes, and found herself walking through a tunnel under the Thames, where there were little deformed women sitting in archways playing

cards, while the bricks of which the wall was made oozed with damp,
which collected into drops and slid down the wall.

(TVO pp. 404–5)

We recognise that terror. George Duckworth haunts that
underwater tunnel. His presence is nightmarish but intermittent.
Only in water will the terrible dreams ever go away, and the
burden of life be lifted.

On this day indeed Rachel was conscious of what went on round her.
She had come to the surface of the dark, sticky pool, and a wave seemed
to bear her up and down with it; she had ceased to have any will of her
own; she lay on the top of the wave conscious of some pain, but chiefly of
weakness.

(TVO p. 423)

This experience of being at the bottom of the water is partly
pleasurable, in that 'she had ceased to have any will of her own'.
The release from responsibility is indeed a great refreshment, a
great disburdening. We recognise the ever present temptation
quite clearly in many of the most passionate passages of *The Waves*:

That is my ship. It sails into icy caverns where the sea-bear barks and
stalactites swing green chains. The waves rise, their crests curl . . .

(p. 13)

Out of me now my mind can pour. I can think of my Armadas sailing on
the high waves. I am relieved of hard contacts and collisions. I sail on
alone under white cliffs. Oh, but I sink, I fall!

(p. 19)

It is, of course, Rhoda, who, even as a child, is having nightmares. 'I am relieved of hard contacts and collisions' – that alone
is such pleasure for the too sensitive, haunted child. And,
although she recognises her nursery, yet already she is trying to
escape from 'people pursuing, pursuing':

That is the corner of the cupboard; that is the nursery looking-glass. But
they stretch, they elongate. I sink down on the black plumes of sleep . . .
Oh, to awake from dreaming! Look, there is the chest of drawers. Let me
pull myself out of these waters. But they heap themselves on me; they
sweep me between their great shoulders; I am turned; I am tumbled;
I am stretched, among these long lights, these long waves, these endless
paths, with people pursuing, pursuing.

(p. 20)

'I am relieved of hard contacts and collisions . . . these long waves, these endless paths, with people pursuing, pursuing.' That is the dual, tormented nature of water: it offers peace, resolution, release from the intolerable collisions of the world and the pursuit of the critical eye and the destructive tongue. Yet, it also means death, and is clearly recognised as such. The price for such deliverance from pursuit and hard-edged things is death:

Behind it roars the sea. It is beyond our reach. Yet there I venture. There I go to replenish my emptiness, to stretch my nights and fill them fuller and fuller with dreams. And for a second even now, even here, I reach my object and say, 'Wander no more. All else is trial and make-believe. Here is the end.'

(pp. 99–100)

Even more clearly, at the end of Rhoda's presence in the novel:

'Oh, life, how I have dreaded you,' said Rhoda, 'oh, human beings, how I have hated you! . . . I left Louis; I feared embraces . . . I implored day to break into night. I have longed to see the cupboard dwindle, to feel the bed soften, to float suspended, to perceive lengthened trees, lengthened faces . . .

(p. 145)

I threw my bunch into the spreading wave. I said, 'Consume me, carry me to the furthest limit.' The wave has broken; the bunch is withered. I seldom think of Percival now . . .

(p. 146)

We launch out now over the precipice. Beneath us lie the lights of the herring fleet. The cliffs vanish. Rippling small, rippling grey, innumerable waves spread beneath us. I touch nothing. I see nothing. We may sink and settle on the waves. The sea will drum in my ears. The white petals will be darkened with sea water. They will float for a moment and then sink. Rolling me over the waves will shoulder me under. Everything falls in a tremendous shower, dissolving me.

(p. 147)

'Rolling me over the waves will shoulder me under.' There is little fear of death there. There is a feeling that the struggles to love and be loved are far behind now. She left Louis – she 'feared embraces' – and she seldom now thinks of Percival, the much beloved central figure of their group in younger days. No, the days darken, and Rhoda imagines death coming to her in exactly the same terms in which she imagined it as a child in the nursery: 'the waters sweep me between their great shoulders . . . Rolling me over the waves will shoulder me under.'

It is indeed a powerful pull from underneath – the pull to unconsciousness, to freedom from individuality and responsi- bility – and it represents in itself so much of what Virginia could not find for herself in life. Water was the end, for instance, of words, arguments, differences of opinion. It was the end of Cambridge rationalism, of someone springing out from behind a tree as Bart does to the intent little boy George and shouting 'What exactly do you *mean* by *that*?' It was an end of Stephen- surrogates, all absorbed in their own male egoism and intellectual sterility, contradicting each other and reckoning up how many 'essential' philosophers there are in the world. It was the end of being contradicted and disconfirmed by 'mental specialists' and doctors, and it was an end too of the hated 'cures' which Leonard had grown to represent, an end to the stuffing-in of unnecessary food and the swallowing of unnecessary gallons of milk. It is amusing to note that Leonard is parodied as early as *The Voyage Out* for his belief in the virtues of milk for dying heroines, and also that he 'unconsciously' takes the side of the quack doctor Rodriguez against Helen, 'who seemed to have taken an unreasonable prejudice against him'! Indeed, it is in terms of nurses and milk that Rachel conceives her 'tormentors' when she is lying in a coma under her Miltonic water. In 1941 milk was still Leonard's remedy:

Octavia had been coming to see us about once a week, bringing cream and milk. These visits were, so far as Virginia was concerned, just friendly visits, but I had told Octavia how serious I thought Virginia's condition was becoming and from our point of view, the visits were partly medical.

(*The Journey* p. 91)

'From our point of view', that is from Leonard's and Octavia's. No wonder Virginia kept on suspecting 'conspiracy', which Leonard never ceased to deny.

More even that freedom from responsibility and from conflict, water represents the freedom from the conscious self, that hated, all-too-particular self which Virginia so much distrusted and resented. In one of the most famous passages in her writing, Virginia gives a marvellous, almost mystical, description of the death of personality in water experience, using this time, the *persona* of her mother Julia, Mrs Ramsay. If this had not been so clearly Julia on the 'wedge-shaped core of darkness' it could easily have been Julian of Norwich on the ecstasies of assimilation into God.

it was a relief when they went to bed. For now she need not think about anybody. She could be herself, by herself. And that was what now she often felt the need of – to think; well not even to think. To be silent; to be alone. All the being and the doing, expansive, glittering, vocal, evaporated; and one shrunk, with a sense of solemnity, to being oneself, a wedge-shaped core of darkness, something invisible to others . . . Beneath it is all dark, it is all spreading, it is unfathomably deep; but now and again we rise to the surface and that is what you see us by . . . There was freedom, there was peace, there was, most welcome of all, a summoning together, a resting on a platform of stability . . . Losing personality, one lost the fret, the hurry, the stir; and there rose to her lips always some exclamation of triumph over life when things came together in this peace, this rest, this eternity; and pausing there she looked out to meet that stroke of the Lighthouse, the long steady stroke . . .

(*TTL* pp. 99–100)

Although the image of water here is at one remove, there is no doubt that it is in terms of submerged life and surface life that Mrs Ramsay is meditating ('it is unfathomably deep; but now and again we rise to the surface and that is what you see us by'). Our public lives are surface lives. But, alone, in the evening, delivered from the restrictiveness of the multiple roles of wife–comforter–nurse to Mr Ramsay, and mother–comforter–unifier to her children, and beautiful vision–inspiration to her friends and guests, she can sink, a 'wedge-shaped core of darkness' down into the depths of herself, where all particularity is lost in unity, and all strife is lost in peace.

And here is Cam, meditating as the voyage to the lighthouse is finally under way:

They don't feel a thing there, Cam thought, looking at the shore, which, rising and falling, became steadily more distant and more peaceful. Her hand cut a trail in the sea, as her mind made the green swirls and streaks into patterns and, numbed and shrouded, wandered in imagination in

that underworld of waters where the pearls stuck in clusters to white
sprays, where in the green light a change came over one's entire mind
and one's body shone half transparent enveloped in a green cloak.

(TTL p. 281)

She sees her own body at the bottom of the sea, where one
'doesn't feel a thing', and surely the idea of 'pearls stuck in
clusters' must recall to the literate mind the echo of Shakespeare's
lines from *The Tempest*

> *Ariel's Song*
>
> Full fathom five thy father lies
> Of his bones are coral made
> Those are pearls that were his eyes
> Nothing of him that doth fade
> But doth suffer a sea change
> Into something rich and strange;
> Sea nymphs hourly ring his knell
> > Ding Dong
> Hark now I hear them, ding dong bell.

> *Ferdinand*: The ditty does remember my drown'd father;
> This is no mortal business, nor no sound
> That the earth owes.

Virginia, trailing her hand in the water and thinking herself
down into its cool depths, envisages her own body lying there at
the bottom of the sea, without any trace of unease or repulsion.
On the contrary it is beautiful. Rocked on the currents, not
feeling, her body, shining 'half transparent enveloped in a green
cloak', has obviously suffered the Shakespearean 'sea change'.
But death down there is beautiful and peaceful.

And Virginia may well also have had half-present to her as she
wrote this passage the overtones and suggestions of the fourth
movement of her friend 'Tom' Eliot's *The Waste Land*, which she
had helped publish with Leonard at the Hogarth Press some
years earlier:

> IV *Death by Water*
>
> Phlebas the Phoenician, a fortnight dead,
> Forgot the cry of gulls, and the deep sea swell
> And the profit and loss.

A current under sea
Picked his bones in whispers. As he rose and fell
He passed the stages of his age and youth
Entering the whirlpool.
Gentile or Jew
O you who turn the wheel and look to windward,
Consider Phlebas, who was once handsome and tall as you.

The father, drowned ('But I beneath a rougher sea' intones Mr Ramsay); Gentile or Jew; death by water; the sea-change; *The Tempest*:

So they heard Mr. Ramsay asking some question about the great storm at Christmas. 'She comes driving round the point,' old Macalister said, describing the great storm last Christmas, when ten ships had been driven into the bay for shelter, and he had seen 'one there, one there, one there' (he pointed slowly round the bay. Mr. Ramsay followed him turning his head.) He had seen three men clinging to the mast. Then she was gone . . . eleven ships . . . had been driven into the bay in a storm. Three had sunk.

(*TTL* pp. 253–4)

The death of these sailors, then, is what is running through Cam's mind as she trails her hand in the water and thinks 'They don't feel a thing there.' The dead sailors, like Phlebas, are rocked forever in peace on the sea-floor. There, no 'compacts against tyranny' are necessary; there are no 'people pursuing, pursuing'.

Death by water obviously had no terrors for Virginia. In a sense she regarded it as a happy release, a going home. Down there was her element. Down there she would not have to struggle any longer against forces which always looked likely to overwhelm her.

And water itself simply fascinates her, anyway. The beautiful passage where Lucy Swithin, alone after the long afternoon in *Between the Acts*, stares abstractedly into the lily pool in the garden, is full of intimations of death. But also, she draws great strength from the mere sight of the water, its vegetation, its beautiful coloured inhabitants down there:

Lucy still gazed at the lily pool. 'All gone,' she murmured, 'under the leaves.' Scared by shadows passing, the fish had withdrawn. She gazed at the water. Perfunctorily she caressed her cross. But her eyes went water searching, looking for fish. The lilies were shutting; the red lily,

the white lily, each on its plate of leaf. Above, the air rushed; beneath
was water. She stood between two fluidities, caressing her cross.

(BTA pp. 238–9)

The sense of the difference between the world of the air, and the
world of the water is carrying her away into a reverie. 'Above, the
air rushed; beneath was water. She stood between two fluidities
. . .'. There is obviously present to her some kind of temptation.
Both air and water are fluid, both are her elements. But water is
by far the more peaceful:

Then something moved in the water; her favourite fantail. The golden
orfe followed. Then she had a glimpse of silver – the great carp himself,
who came to the surface so very seldom. They slid on, in and out
between the stalks, silver; pink; gold; splashed; streaked; pied.
  'Ourselves,' she murmured. And retrieving some glint of faith from
the grey waters, hopefully, without much help from reason, she followed the fish; the speckled, streaked, and blotched; seeing in that
vision beauty, power, and glory in ourselves.

(pp. 239–40)

Virginia must often have stood staring down into one of the
ponds at Monks House at Rodmell. So here Lucy knows the
name of each kind of fish, the fantail, the golden orfe, the carp.
She knows their habits. She watches them intensely for their life.
She even manages, after a while, to retrieve 'some glint of faith
from the grey waters'. Without much help from reason (Bart has
just left Lucy to go back into the house) she follows the fish,
'seeing in that vision beauty, power, and glory in ourselves.'

  Finally it is to *A Writer's Diary* we must turn, if we wish to
understand how powerful the pull of the water became in 1940–1.

Sunday August 28th [*1938*]
  How deliberately we are digging ourselves in! And at any moment the
  guns may go off and explode us. L. is very black. Hitler has his hounds
  only very lightly held . . .

Saturday, September 10th [*1938*]
  Meanwhile the aeroplanes are on the prowl, crossing the downs.
  Every preparation is made.

Thursday, August 24th [*1939*]
  Whiffs of despair. Difficult to work . . . Haze over the marsh.
  Aeroplanes. One touch on the switch and we shall be at war.

Friday, August 16th [1940]
They came very close. We lay down under the tree. The sound was like someone sawing in the air just above us. We lay flat on our faces, hand behind head. Don't close your teeth said L. They seemed to be sawing at something stationary. Bombs shook the windows of my lodge. Will it drop, I asked? If so, we shall be broken together . . .

Monday, August 19th [1940]
Yesterday, 18th, Sunday, there was a roar. Right on top of us they came . . . The closest shave so far.

Saturday, August 31st [1940]
Now we are in the war. England is being attacked. I got this feeling for the first time completely yesterday; the feeling of pressure, danger, horror. The feeling is that a battle is going on – a fierce battle. May last four weeks. Am I afraid? Intermittently . . . I daresay if I write fiction and Coleridge and not that infernal bomb article for U.S.A. I shall swim into quiet water.

Wednesday, September 11th [1940]
A plane shot down before our eyes just before tea: over the racecourse; a scuffle; a swerve; then a plunge; and a burst of thick black smoke.

Saturday, September 14th [1940]
A sense of invasion – that is lorries of soldiers and machines – like cranes – walloping along to Newhaven. An air raid is on. A little pop rattle which I take to be machine gun, just gone off. Planes roaring and roaring . . .

Wednesday, October 2nd [1940]
Should I think of death? Last night a great heavy plunge of bomb under the window. So near we both started. A plane had passed, dropping this fruit . . . I said to L.: I don't want to die yet. The chances are against it. But they're aiming at the railway and the power works. They get closer every time. Caburn was crowned with what looked like a settled moth, wings extended – a Messerschmitt it was, shot down on Sunday.

Then comes the passage which Leonard cites in his description of Virginia's 'tranquillity and happiness', her 'quietism and open-eyed contemplation of death' during the autumn of 1940:

Oh I try to imagine how one's killed by a bomb. I've got it fairly vivid – the sensation: but can't see anything but suffocating nonentity following after. I shall think – oh I wanted another 10 years – not this – and shan't, for once, be able to describe it. It – I mean death; no, the scrunching and scrambling, the crushing of my bone shade in on my very active eye and brain: the process of putting out the light – painful? Yes. Terrifying. I suppose so. Then a swoon; a drain; two or three gulps attempting consciousness – and then dot dot dot.

If this passage is ever to prove anything, it is to prove not so much that Virginia did not want to die as such (of course she did not) as that Virginia did not want to die that way. The sheer force of the explosion, the 'crushing of my bone shade in on my very active eye and brain', that is what terrifies her. 'Terrifying', she says. The sense of physical pain, of being blown to pieces violently, is what terrifies her. As to actually dying, her reaction is almost resigned, philosophical: 'I shall think – oh I wanted another 10 years – not this'. It is being killed 'by a bomb' that terrifies her.

I think, in other words, that both Leonard and later Quentin Bell have not followed the thought process that lies behind the punctuation here:

I shall think – oh I wanted another 10 years – not this – and shan't, for once be able to describe it. It – I mean death; no, the scrunching and scrambling, the crushing of my bone shade . . .

'It – I mean death; no,' indicates that it is not death as such that she feared, although she regrets not having been allowed another ten years to write. No, that she has anyway described, over and over: descriptions of death abound in her work. '. . . death; no, the scrunching and scrambling, the crushing of my bone shade in on my very active eye and brain . . . painful . . . terrifying'. That is the way the punctuation invites us to read the passage: two meanings are running concurrently, and the punctuation allows us (if we read carefully) to distinguish them.

Death by water would be a very different thing, would it not? *Between the Acts*, alone, contains enough indications of the pull of desire, for Virginia 'standing between two fluidities', the pull of desire towards the water, and death by water. And there are the other novels too, packed with the same information. 'They don't feel a thing there, Cam thought . . . where in the green light a change came over one's entire mind and one's body shone half transparent enveloped in a green cloak.'

The entries about bombings go on and on.

Sunday, October 6th [*1940*]
Will it ever seem strange that L. and I walking on the marsh first look at a bomb crater: then listen to the German drone above: then I take two paces nearer L., prudently deciding that two birds had better be killed with one stone? They got Lewes at last yesterday.

Thursday, October 17th [*1940*]
I must black out. I had so much to say. I am filling my mind slowly with Elizabethans: that is to say letting my mind feed like the Red Admiral – the siren, just as I had drawn the curtains. Now the unpleasant part begins. Who'll be killed tonight? Not us, I suppose. One doesn't think of that – save as a quickener.

When they go up to London the following day, Leonard and Virginia have to see both their London homes, 52 Tavistock Square, and 37 Mecklenburgh Square, wrecked by bombs.

And running side by side with the actual fear of bombs, of being hit by a bomb and being physically exploded, runs the sense that an entire world has disappeared, crumbled, disintegrated, a world of people, friends, values, common history and common meaning:

Wednesday, September 6th [*1939*]
Yes, it's an empty meaningless world now. Am I a coward? Physically I expect I am. Going to London tomorrow I expect frightens me.

Saturday, June 22nd [*1940*]
at the moment, with *PH* [1] only to fix on, I'm loosely anchored. Further, the war – our waiting while the knives sharpen for the operation – has taken away the outer wall of security. No echo comes back. I have no surroundings. I have so little sense of a public that I forget about *Roger* [2] coming or not coming out. Those familiar circumvolutions – those standards – which have for so many years given back an echo and so thickened my identity are all wide and wild as the desert now. I mean, there is no 'autumn', no winter. We pour to the edge of a precipice . . . and then? I can't conceive that there will be a 27th June 1941.

The crisis is existential. This is not in the slightest the thought-process of a mind unhinged. '. . . the outer wall of security' has been knocked away. 'No echo comes back.' The 'standards'

[1] *Pointz Hall*, the original title for *Between the Acts*.
[2] *Roger Fry*, the biography she had recently completed.

which have thickened Virginia's identity are 'all wide and wild as the desert now'. 'No echo comes back. I have no surroundings.' It is uncanny, eerie. Where has everyone gone? What has happened to the world of yesterday, the world of values, standards, friends, security, 'echo'? Speak now, and who is there to hear? Surely this must have been the mood of millions of people in June 1940?

Wednesday, July 24th [1940]
All the walls, the protecting and reflecting walls, wear so terribly thin in this war. There's no standard to write for: no public to echo back; even the 'tradition' has become transparent . . .

Friday, July 26th [1940]
A large hedgehog was found drowned in the lily pool; L. tried to resuscitate it. An amusing sight. 2/6 is offered by the government for live hedgehogs.

Sunday, January 26th [1941]
Yes, I was thinking: we live without a future. That's what's queer: with our noses pressed to a closed door.

Sunday, February 16th [1941]
In the wild grey water after last week's turmoil.

Sunday, March 8th [1941]
I will go down with my colours flying.

Even the tiny fragments of Virginia's journals which we have in *A Writer's Diary*, show us that the evolution of Virginia's fear was part and parcel of the psychological and mental history of an entire nation in 1939–41. There was nothing 'mad' about the state of mind which felt there were no surroundings left, there was no echo, and that it was scarcely possible to imagine a 27 June 1941. Indeed, the fear of being blown to bits by a bomb must have been pretty nearly universal. And as for the feeling that 'we live without a future. That's what's queer: with our noses pressed to a closed door', who did not feel that, if only intermittently, in 1940 and 1941?

But there was a special reason for Virginia's own existential despair: the sense that she now had no public left to write for, no audience 'out there', no body of people who knew that she existed, that she was a writer, and that she was alive. Even the very concept of 'tradition', she felt, had become transparent. Whether her next novel was an advance on *Between the Acts*, or not, there would be no one left to judge – if indeed anyone had time even to care. As a writer, she had been deprived of her *raison d'être*. Most people, in 1941, were deprived of one sort of identity. Virginia was deprived of two.

Virginia could hardly spare one identity, let alone two. Indeed, the second was very largely a replacement of the first, which was only intermittently present to her, as we know from the fiction. What could Rhoda be, if Rhoda had no audience? What could Miss La Trobe become if the public had 'dispersed'? Reduced to her original embodiment, Virginia was too little assured of her ability to hold out, in the face of an increasingly male violence which threatened to blow her apart in pain, blood and guts. The war was a male thing: she had no responsibility for it. She had explained, in *Three Guineas*, why male arrogance, and male dressing-up, led to belligerence, envy, hatred and violence. Everyone had scorned her explanation, or refused even to comment upon it. The entry for Friday, 3 June 1938 runs:

Anyhow that's the end of six years floundering, striving, much agony, some ecstasy: lumping the *Years* and *Three Guineas* together as one book – as indeed they are. And now I can be off again, as indeed I long to be. Oh to be private, alone, submerged.

In 1941, it was the embodiment of Virginia which forced her decision. She could not face being blown to bits. The water was her friend, and had been her friend ever since she was a child in Cornwall. The water could be trusted. The water was peace. The water would receive her with the dignity that she felt she needed, and indeed, deserved.

ഝഝഝഝഝഝഝഝഝഝഝഝഝഝഝഝഝഝഝഝഝഝഝഝഝഝഝഝ

Writing Melymbrosia

It has perhaps not been sufficiently remarked with what awe, with what veneration Virginia Woolf regarded her friend E. M. Forster—as writer, as artist, as arbiter, not only as friend. It was his judgment which counted absolutely when she brought out a new novel. In October 1919 *Night and Day* is published. She waits for first reactions with trepidation. 'Of course if Morgan and Lytton and the others should be enthusiastic, I should think the better of myself', she notes in her diary on 21 October. Two more days pass. She writes 'I think I feel most doubtful about Morgan; after getting his report I shall be quite at ease. Three or four people count, & the rest save as a senseless clapping of hands or hissing are nowhere'. (*Diary* Vol I, p. 307, 23 October 1919) But, when it comes, Morgan's view is only just favourable, and a crisis ensues.

> After Clive's letter came Nessa's—unstinted praise; on top of that Lytton's: enthusiastic praise; a grand triumph; a classic; & so on; Violet's sentence of eulogy followed; and then, yesterday morning, this line from Morgan 'I like it less than the V. O.' Though he spoke also of great admiration, & had read in haste & proposed re-reading, this rubbed out all the pleasure of the rest.
>
> (*Diary* Vol I, pp. 307–8, 30 October)

It is clear that Forster's is *the* view she has been waiting for, the *critical* view, the one which counts. The degree to which she was cast down by its uncompromising honesty is reflected in the troubled syntax with which the entry continues:

> . . . this rubbed out all the pleasure of the rest. Yes; but to continue. About 3 in the afternoon I felt happier and easier on account of his blame than on account of the others' praise—as if one were in the human atmosphere again, after a blissful roll among elastic clouds and cushiony downs. Yet I suppose I value Morgan's opinion as much as anybodies.
>
> (p. 308)

'About 3 in the afternoon.' If we suppose that Forster's letter arrived in the morning post, then she must have taken nearly six hours to rally her defences and muster her courage again. Lunchtime on 29 October 1919 must have been a rather silent and gloomy affair.

It is because of the respect she has for Forster *as writer* that she so anxiously scrutinizes his view. A week later she is still reflecting on the import of Forster's judgment of *Night and Day*.

Morgan has the artist's mind; he says the simple things that clever people don't say; I find him the best of critics for that reason. Suddenly out comes the obvious thing that one has overlooked.

(pp. 310–1, 6 November)

Forster delivered the critical judgment on *Night and Day*, the one that others—Leonard, Lytton, Nessa, Violet—would not deliver: the judgment, in fact which she knew unconsciously she *needed* if she were to progress out of the relatively traditional format of *The Voyage Out* and *Night and Day* towards the sorts of innovative texts that she felt she had it in her to write, the sorts of innovatory texts that Forster himself had already produced. He was not only her mentor, he was her precursor, and to some extent her struggle to get free had to be with *him*.

In this struggle between the master and the pupil at around the time of the publication of *Night and Day*, the distinction clearly appears between Forster as friend and Forster as technical master. He freed her, by his harsh view of *Night and Day*, for the writing of *Jacob's Room* and the other modernist masterpieces she was feeling towards. But he could not be both friend and mentor at once. He chose, bravely, to be the mentor, thus showing himself to be the better friend. She, hoping for the lucky let-off that a friend would offer, yet hoped against hope that he would rise above friendship and give her an honest, craftsman-like, professional view. He did. At first she didn't like it, but then she settled to the wisdom of his decision, and even welcomed the new 'reality' that he thus gave her access to.

Nevertheless there had to come the moment of personal meeting, the moment of relaxation over the dinner table. Forster showed himself the friend, this time by offering as his view of *Night and Day* what is clearly a most generous deceit. What he had the courage to put on paper he did not have courage to deliver when face to face with Virginia Woolf. So he invented an account of the deficiency of *Night and Day* which seems quite adventitious, even arbitrary, but which had the effect of pacifying the wounded vanity of his pupil.

The doubt about Morgan and N. & D. is removed; I understand why he likes it less than V. O. &, in understanding, see that it is not a criticism to discourage. Perhaps intelligent critism never is. All the same, I shirk writing it out, because I write so much criticism. What he said amounted to this: N. & D. is a strictly formal and classical work; that being so one requires, or he requires, a far greater

degree of lovability in the characters than in a book like V. O. which is vague
and universal. None of the characters in N. & D. is lovable. He did not care how
they sorted themselves out. Nor did he care for the characters in V. O. but there
he felt no need to care for them. Otherwise he admired practically everything;
his blame does not consist in saying that N. & D. is less remarkable than t'other.

(p. 310, 6 November 1919)

Lovability! Nevertheless, Virginia Woolf seems completely taken in
by it, and does not notice that the price she has to pay for this relief is
that *Night and Day* is 'a strictly formal and classical work'. No doubt she
would have begun to wonder about the implications of *that* in the
morning, but for the moment Forster, by evading the task of critic and
adopting the role of friend, had already achieved his critical point. The
way lies clear to *Jacob's Room*, the freedom to write which surely must
largely have been given to her by Morgan Forster.

But the point I am trying to make is not primarily about literary debt
and literary influence. More important, it has to do with 'elective
affinities'. It was precisely E. M. Forster who could help Virginia Woolf
in 1919, at that critical point of her writing career, because he himself
could see so clearly what it was that she was attempting to do. After all,
he himself had started on a similar *oeuvre* a decade earlier, and had
tackled themes so similar to Virginia Woolf's that in some ways they
might have appeared to him as identical. He alone would have known
how to advise her, because he alone had the entry to her particular
problem. And he could clearly see that, if she wanted to attempt the
themes that she had it in mind to attempt, she had to abandon the
sterile path which led to *Night and Day*.

What in fact Forster had begun in his early novels was a study of
what the phenomenology then being developed by Edmund Husserl
was to call 'embodiment'. 'Embodiment' is a complex problem—and
early phenomenological attempts to solve it were operating from various starting points—but it is basically an attempt to reconstitute a
description of the lived body *as it is experienced from the inside*, together
with all the 'intentionalities' directed towards the outside world that
that embodiment has been constrained to adopt as its own.

In *Ideas II*, an early sketch of what will be the fifth *Cartesian Meditation*, Husserl attempts to devise various means of penetrating the
meanings of the Other as he appears in inter-subjective space. Various
methods of 'pairing', analogy and empathy all variously fail to allow of
a clean transcription of the meanings of the other. (See Paul Ricoeur,
Husserl: An analysis of His Phenomenology, trans. E. G. Ballard and L. E.
Embree [Northwestern University Press 1967], Chapters 3 and 5.) What
is fundamental to the Husserlian analytic enterprise, however, is that
the world *will be*, for me, *as I perceive it*. In this sense, what I experience

is *necessarily* true, for it is the very warp and weft of experience itself. It carries with it a corollary for fiction which was being discovered in the first decade of this century by E. M. Forster, and would soon be developed by Ford Madox Ford, James Joyce and, of course, Virginia Woolf. The philosophical insight into the importance for perception of embodiment is matched by a shift in the theory of fictional representation at the same period. Forster's *Where Angels Fear to Tread* (1905), *The Longest Journey* (1907), *A Room With a View* (1908) and *Howards End* (1910) are the documents which mark the transition from the old fictional mimesis to the new: from a mistaken attempt at 'direct' impersonal or objective narrative to the new, more rich and nuanced attempt at 'indirect', 'embodied' or subjective narrative.

Forster's technically innovative point of departure is that a world depends for the meanings it gives, or appears to give, upon the subjectivity and the embodiment of the observer himself or herself. This was so extremely innovative that he did not himself try to spell it out in theoretical terms at the time, and even now, 80 years later, it has the smell of rank heresy about it. It seems almost too strange, even now, to assert that the meaning that something 'out there' in the world will take on is a direct result of the observing subjectivity and the embodiment which 'encases' that subjectivity and 'intends' a world out there in an attempt to locate its meaning. It seems to run in the face of all received ideas about the objectivity of a world 'out there'. Yet a world 'out there' is only knowable to me through the perceptual apparatus which my body *is*; and the meaning which a world 'out there' has is only the meaning which my body allows me to perceive.

It is with this radically subjectivized fictional premise that Forster began writing. *A Room with a View*, though published third, was in fact the earliest in conception, and it is full of radical ideas of this sort. It studies the embodiment of two maiden ladies in a foreign country, who are utterly exposed to a rain of indecent, physical, material and indeed heretical suggestions which descend on them from all sides and at all times, and in the face of which they find they have no defences. They are 'without a Baedeker'. Experience breaks over them in a stream of unmediated particularity, and every event is recorded by Forster with his new fictional equipment—equipment which consists in doing away with all false mediating lenses and membranes and letting the reader go through the shock of experience at the same time and in the same rough manner as his two heroines have to experience it. It is in every sense—social, economic, physical, cultural, religious—a Voyage Out.

Forster's choice of a Voyage Out for his theme is a rich one for the novelist, and instinct with possibilities. What will happen 'out there' in Italy, in a country which is not 'Sawston', not 'Windy Corner', not

Protestant and certainly not genteelly middle-class, is anybody's guess; but that something will happen is virtually sure. Thus the theme of the Voyage Out is attended by a penumbra of the adventurous, the daring, the threatening and very possibly the wicked.

Its direct first effect is to throw into uselessness or non-applicability all those rules and prohibitions which, learned at home and perfected over the years, have now grown into a defensive second nature. Pointers to this dilemma scatter the early pages of *A Room with a View*.

'Mother wouldn't mind, I'm sure', said Lucy, but again had the sense of larger and unsuspected issues.

(*A Room with a View*, p. 33)

Lucy was puzzled. She was again conscious of some new idea, and was not sure whither it would lead her.

(p. 42)

She was sure that she ought not to be with these men; but they cast a spell over her. They were so serious and so strange that she could not remember how to behave.

(p. 44)

'Oh, good gracious me!', said Lucy, suddenly collapsing and again seeing the whole of life in a new perspective. 'Where, where?'

(p. 48)

'The world', she thought, 'is certainly full of beautiful things, if only I could come across them.'

(p. 61)

This situation is also socially, culturally and economically determined, and remarkably similar accounts of this estrangement from the sources of instinctual life—for the full presence of which 'Italy' is but a metaphor—are to be found everywhere in the autobiographical texts of this period. The young woman who has to emerge from the grip of strait-laced Victorian morality, while at the same time learning to make tasteful and canny use of a new freedom which seems terrifying in its limitlessness, is a subject which represents for E. M. Forster, as for Virginia Woolf later, something of a *rite de passage*. To illustrate the technical difficulties involved, I shall limit myself here to a consideration of their respective treatments of what might seem to be the most easy and natural of human exchanges, the kiss.

The kiss which (fleetingly) takes place between Lucy Honeychurch and George Emerson is the fulcrum of *A Room with a View*. Everything leads up to it, and everything leads away from it. In a certain sense this kiss—the possibility, the reality, the liberation of this kiss—is the *raison d'être* of the novel. It is a kind of statement of faith on Forster's part.

We have to note, first of all, that Lucy Honeychurch is *led* (as the duplicitous result of her own artless questioning) by a beautiful young Italian boy called Phaethon (whose kissing exchange with 'Persephone' on the driving seat of the carriage caused such upset among the English as the party ascended to see the view), but not misled by him. He leads her where she wants to go, even if she doesn't know where she wants to go. The last words her Italian seducer addresses to her when he has led her to the 'little open terrace, covered with violets from end to end' are, 'Courage! . . . Courage and love'. Lucy is thus ushered into a scene of natural beauty which Forster has orchestrated in his richest manner.

George had turned at the sound of her arrival. For a moment he contemplated her, as one who had fallen out of heaven. He saw radiant joy in her face, he saw the flowers beat against her dress in blue waves. The bushes above them closed. He stepped quickly forward and kissed her.

Before she could speak, almost before she could feel, a voice called 'Lucy! Lucy! Lucy!' The silence of life had been broken by Miss Bartlett, who stood brown against the view.

The rhapsodic style and the singing strings of young romance are thus interrupted, both thematically and stylistically, by a violent stylistic break. Partly this has to do, no doubt, with the theme and the point of the story Forster wanted to tell. But I suspect, too, that so violent a break also testifies to a limitation in the technical abilities of the writer to continue to describe what he wants to describe. Forster is attempting the kiss scene because he is interested in trying to do so, but finds that the exercise is getting beyond his powers to control. The embodiment of the writer himself and the present situation of his young female protagonist are too close, and some form of rapid closure has to be devised.

The theme of the kiss is one that Virginia Woolf was to make central to her own explorations in *The Voyage Out* (completed 1913, published 1915). The kiss is, after all, the motion that makes impossible the continuation of talk, and it was on talk that the young people of this period chiefly relied to get them through erotic situations. The kiss is also the declaration of something simple: affection, commitment, love, trust or whatever combination of these it may be, whereas talk always holds in its recesses the possible re-establishment of distance, hostility or independence. So the kiss, for the hero and heroine of these early twentieth century novels, is an affirmation of commitment which is physical, strong, non-verbal and to some extent unretractable, a form of contract. This is why the kiss is seen as so dangerous a transaction.

The first two novels of Virginia Woolf are full of talk between lovers who cannot summon up the courage, or the decisiveness, to cross over the physical barrier and enter the world of physical contact, the kiss. This inability of lover and beloved to stop talking and start kissing is in fact the major theme of both *The Voyage Out* and *Night and Day*. A passage like this gives the measure of the problem.

> They would have liked, had they dared, to take each other by the hand, but the consciousness of eyes fixed on them from behind had not yet deserted them . . . . After one of these glances she murmured, 'Yes, I'm in love. There's no doubt; I'm in love with you'. Nevertheless they remained uncomfortably apart . . . . This body of his was unreal; the whole world was unreal.
> 'What's happened?', he began. 'Why did I ask you to marry me? How did it happen?'
> 'Did you ask me to marry you?', she wondered . . . .
> 'We sat upon the ground', he recollected.
> 'We sat upon the ground', she confirmed him . . . .
> 'This is happiness, I suppose'. And aloud to Terence she spoke, 'This is happiness.'
> On the heels of her words he answered, 'This is happiness', upon which they guessed that the feeling had sprung in both of them at the same time.
>
> (*The Voyage Out*, pp. 285–7)

I think, therefore, that Forster's use of a violent swerve or closure when dealing with physical transactions between the sexes may have been assimilated by Virginia Woolf as she read his novels. There are two major uses of the kiss as transition in *The Voyage Out*. The first is the unexpected assault that the young heroine, Rachel Vinrace, has to endure from the mature Richard Dalloway, and which traumatizes her. The second, more complex and textually ambiguous, is the kiss which appears to take place between Rachel and her lover Terence, but may take place rather between Terence and Rachel's aunt Helen, during the excursion into the jungle which occupies the same structural place as the excursion to Fiesole in *A Room with a View*.

Forster's novels involve a Voyage Out—twice to Italy and, in the case of *The Longest Journey*, into prehistoric time as expressed by the Figsbury Rings and the geology of Wiltshire. But the Voyage Out as a physical reality is of course only an elaborate literary figure. It is the Voyage Out into life itself, into experience, and in particular the experience of love and death which the trope includes. In the case of Forster and Woolf it is also the Voyage Out into embodiment and all that this implies.

Virginia Stephen took many physical voyages out during the years 1905–11. She found that her own experience could be put to the service of the same literary trope as Forster had already adopted. A first Voyage Out was her trip with her brother Adrian from Liverpool to Oporto in March 1905. They visited Lisbon, Seville and Granada, re-embarking at Lisbon and reaching England again on Easter Sunday, 23 April 1905.

The terrible trip to Greece which ended in Thoby's death took place in September 1906. Thoby returned ill to England, while Vanessa and Virginia went on to Constantinople, where Vanessa was again ill herself. They were back in London on 1 November, and on 20 November Thoby died—of typhoid fever. This is a second model for *The Voyage Out*, and Thoby's illness and death are an obvious source for the illness and death of Rachel Vinrace at the end of the novel.

But by the middle of 1907, Virginia Stephen is at work on her 'novel'—then called *Melymbrosia*. According to the account of Quentin Bell, 100 pages were completed by the end of August 1908. This was followed by a third Voyage Out, when in September Virginia Stephen went with the Bells to Italy. They stayed in Siena and Perugia, they visited Pavia and Assisi. Returning by Paris, they were home in London by 1 October.

By early February 1909, 'seven chapters of *Melymbrosia* were read and criticized by Clive Bell'—hardly a critic whose views would have increased Virginia's confidence. But she pursues. Some form of the novel has now been on the stocks for 17 months. (This is the moment, 17 February 1909, when Lytton Strachey suddenly proposed to Virginia.) There was a fourth Voyage Out when Virginia accompanied Clive and Vanessa Bell to Florence in April 1909, and a fifth when Virginia had to leave suddenly for Turkey in April 1911 to rescue her sister, who had fallen ill at Broussa. The *dénouement* of this fifth Voyage Out must have vied, in the novelist's mind, with the tragic ending of the second (Thoby's death), and returning with Vanessa on the Orient Express to London on 29 April 1911 must have contained all the terror and uncertainty that foreign travel had traditionally come to imply.

Terror, uncertainty and—guilt. It was Forster who built into the idea of the Voyage Out the idea of the Fall. He encodes this very subtly in *A Room with a View*.

Then something did happen.

Two Italians by the Loggia had been bickering about a debt. 'Cinque lire', they had cried, 'cinque lire!' They sparred at each other and one of them was hit lightly upon the chest. He frowned; he bent towards Lucy with a look of interest, as if he had an important message for her. He opened his lips to deliver it, and a steam of red came out between them and trickled down his unshaven chin.

That was all. A crowd rose out of the dusk. It hid this extraordinary man from her, and bore him away to the fountain. Mr George Emerson happened to be a few paces away, looking at her across the spot where the man had been. How very odd! Across something. Even as she caught sight of him he grew dim; the palace itself grew dim, swayed above her, fell on to her softly, slowly, noiselessly, and the sky fell with it.

She thought 'Oh, what have I done?'.

'Oh, what have I done?', she murmured, and opened her eyes.

(p. 62)

This is, on the surface, merely a description of a young woman fainting in a public place. But it substitutes a series of impressionistic notations for events which the reader surmises must be taking place at the same time, but which the author neglects to describe. It is very tantalizing. The swoon is nothing less than the Fall itself—the Fall from innocence, the Fall into guilt, complicity, knowledge and sensuality. Forster equates the swoon in front of experience with the swoon into guilt, and in fact the moment Lucy Honeychurch recovers she discovers that she is involved, via the bloodstained photographs, with the young George Emerson.

The oscillation between knowledge and acceptance, which is the very structure of the Fall itself, that dizzying swoon towards submission which is experienced as pleasure and as dread equally, has been described by Kierkegaard in *The Concept of Anxiety*. The dizziness, the fumbling forward into areas unknown and also deeply distrusted, because felt as dangerous, is given again and again in the early drafts of *The Voyage Out*, which Louise DeSalvo has published as *Melymbrosia*.

'Yes' he said, 'I live there alone. But don't think that I'm to be pitied. I sometimes think life's been too easy for me. I've had too much happiness. If I'm ever gloomy it's my own fault. It comes of wanting too much—of wanting something so tremendously that the whole of my life will be worthless without it.' He stopped; the moments seemed to Rachel as messengers approaching.

'You know that I love you' he whispered. The messenger had arrived.

'Is it possible?' she exclaimed.

'And you?'

[E19/10] For answer she opened her arms.

More as people who grope, who push away a veil between them than as man and woman in midday they sought each other's arms. They embraced passionately.

'And now,' Rachel murmured, releasing herself and looking with dazed eyes into the distance, 'what have we done?'

'The most wonderful thing in the world' Hewet replied. He was trembling all over.

'Something terrible' she answered.[1]

[1] *Melymbrosia by Virginia Woolf: An Early Version of The Voyage Out*, edited with an introduction by Louise DeSalvo (The New York Public Library 1982), p. 197.

Immediately, as in the Forster passage, there are 'others' there to break up and break off the passion. But in this early draft the two lovers disregard the onlookers, only to plunge once again into the experience of terror:

Sounds stood out from the background making as it were a bridge across their silence; there was the swish of the trees and far off the rush of the water.

'Tell me you are happy' Hewet begged her.

'Happy?' she said. 'I am nothing.'

He sat by her side not touching her.

'It will mean' she said after a time, 'living with you all my life.'

She paused and then looked at him for the first time with life in her eyes. 'What happiness!' she cried.

'Oh that you should say that!' he burst out, as if released from agony.

'We must not move' she said after a time. 'We must let it all begin round us—life—this wonderful life.' Again they heard the cries and the water.

'O Terence,' she cried suddenly. 'The dead! My mother is dead!'[2]

The sudden discovery of love—the fact that they love each other—is still only partly verbalisable. The past hovers over them, and it is only a matter of seconds before that dark outrider of present happiness—sin—is named, and integrated:

[*289*: E19/11] He comforted her. 'In everything we shall be together, Rachel. With you to help me . . . . . . Ever since I met you,' he continued, 'life's been different. It's over now, the waiting, playing about, observing. All that's been so unsatisfactory, all the things I've had to pretend, all I've had to put up with in default of better—I shan't waste time on them again. Half my life I've wasted-worse than wasted.'

'And mine?' said Rachel. 'Spirits and the sea!'

'You've nothing to regret' said Hewet. 'I'd give anything now—When you talked about women the other day I should have told you. That's why I'm called Monk. I am not chaste. I've sinned as they call it.'

'Sinned' said Rachel meditatively. 'That's an odd word.'

'A few weeks ago you'd have minded' said Hewet. 'But now you don't.' He searched her face as if they shared everything.

'You've taught me' said Rachel. 'Terence you've taught me to have courage! to love feelings I mean; even when they're partly bad.'[3]

The point is that the direction the 'sin' is coming from is very difficult to locate. Is it that the mourning for the mother has been for an illicit moment discontinued? Is it that the intention to fall where the mother once fell awakens fundamental problems with the past and the future? Is it just the cry of a child for a mother who might comfort her? And

[2] Ibid., pp. 197–8.
[3] Ibid., p. 198.

Terence, who has 'sinned', 'sown his wild oats', as the saying would have gone at that period, is now forced to reassess his 'past life' in front of a 'pure woman', and all the guilt he did not feel before comes flooding over him. Echoes of Ibsen's *Ghosts*, of Kierkegaard's writing about the breakup with Regine (particularly 'The Ancient Tragical Motif' in *Either /Or*) begin to hover as literary prototypes. As in the published form of the novel, so the early drafts maintain the oscillation between certainty/uncertainty, reality/unreality, belief/unbelief, and allow these oscillations to operate just the other side of words, so that words cannot be of much help to the over-verbalised lovers:

'What have we done?' she said dully disengaging herself.
'Are we in love? Are we going to marry each other?'
She looked at him curiously. She noticed that he was dressed in grey flannel, and that a shabby purple tie was lying outside his waistcoat.
'Terence, you're untidy' she said.
'Ever since I was a boy' he answered.
'Now tell me a long story' she sighed, laying her head upon his knee. 'I'll think no more.'

. . . .

They were silent for some time.
'Did I accept you?' she asked suddenly.
'You did.'
'Without telling you that I loved you. I've let you tell me everything. I love you better—'but no comparisons came to her and the sentence ended in his arms.

. . . .

'We shall understand everything Rachel' he cried. 'There'll be nothing too difficult for us in the whole world so long as we have each other!'
While they embraced they heard a faint cry; at first confusing it with the cry of an animal, they paid no attention. Rachel opened her lips to speak again; then the syllables became unmistakable; Hew-et Hew-et! It was a human voice calling them; it was Hirst's voice. Hewet had to answer him.
'And we've only just begun' said Rachel.
'We shall have all our lives' said Hewet, as he helped her up, and straightened her and kissed her.[4]

'Helen', pacing to and fro by the river bank (p. 201), is anxious: Where can Terence and Rachel have got to? The jungle is a dangerous place (we are to imagine a jungle full of dangerous beasts in the manner of Douanier Rousseau, I think).

---

[4] Ibid., pp. 198–9, 199, 200–1.

She suddenly realised that she hated the place. She was frightened by something unseen, as a child is frightened . . ..
'At any moment the awful thing may happen' she breathed.

(p. 201)

The 'awful thing' that may happen any moment is, of course, that
Terence and Rachel may get engaged, or commit themselves, thus
deserting 'society'. When she sees them emerging from the forest, she
realises immediately that she is right. The point is that this probable
event has been awaited *as* something 'awful'.

'Helen', in fact, whoever she is, and surely she must owe much to
Vanessa, is immediately engaged in a jealousy which she can neither
express nor entirely repress. In the succeeding chapter, the erotic
investment in the relation between Rachel and Helen is made clear
enough:

Helen felt Rachel springing beside her.
She went ahead, and called back over her shoulder to Helen, 'It's like wading
out to sea!'
She left behind her a trail of whitened grass, like a track in water. Without
thinking of her forty years, Helen cried 'Spring on! I'm after you!' whereupon
Rachel took longer leaps and at last ran. Helen pursued her. She plucked tufts of
feathery blades and cast them at her. They outdistanced the others. Suddenly
Rachel stopped and opened her arms so that Helen rushed into them and
tumbled her over onto the ground. 'Oh Helen Helen!' she could hear Rachel
gasping as she rolled her, 'Don't! For God's sake! Stop! I'll tell you a secret! I'm
going to be married!'
Helen paused with one hand upon Rachel's throat holding her head down
among the grasses.
'You think I didn't know that!' she cried.
For some seconds she did nothing but roll Rachel over and over, knocking her
down when she tried to get up; stuffing grass into her mouth; finally laying her
absolutely flat upon the ground, her arms out on either side of her, her hat off,
her hair [*307*: E20/11] down.
'Own yourself beaten' she panted. 'Beg my pardon, and say you worship me!'
Rachel saw Helen's head hanging over her, very large against the sky.
'I love Terence better!' she exclaimed.
'Terence' Helen exclaimed.
She sat clasping her knees and looking down upon Rachel who still lay with
her head on the grass staring in to the sky.
'Are you happy?' she asked.
'Infinitely!' Rachel breathed, and turning round was clasped in Helen's arms.
'I had to tell you' she murmured.
'And if you hadn't, I knew' said Helen.
'He's unlike any one I've ever seen' said Rachel. 'He understands.' Lost in her
knowledge of Terence, which she could not impart, she said no more.

The inevitable jealousy crossed Helen's mind as she saw Rachel pass almost visibly away into communion with someone else. 'I've never told you, but you know I love you, my darling,' she said, flushing as she spoke. 'Sometimes,' the words were spoken with Rachel pressed to her—'you're so like Theresa, and I loved her.'
'Why did she die?' said Rachel. 'Or do people die?'
They sat opposite each other, with a sprinkling of long feathery blades between them.
'The great thing is love' said Helen. They were both pressed [308: E20/12] by the sense that the others were coming near.[5]

The Fall and the kiss between Rachel and Terence is balanced, thus, only a chapter later, by a Fall and a 'kiss' between Rachel and 'Helen'. It is the kiss itself which 'signs and seals'. Realising that she is not going to be able to give Rachel a kiss under these new circumstances of clarification, 'Helen' 'stuffs grass into her mouth' as a kind of metonymic substitution. She follows this up by an action leading to submission: 'Own yourself beaten'. Having failed at erotics, she will overpower by a little sadism. A balance is adjusted somewhere. Rachel, being thus demanded, refuses: 'I love Terence better'. This leads to an exchange of confidences which could only be exchanged between women. But death is right there in the communication, and the love of woman for woman, which somehow seems to transcend the brute masculinity of 'vegetable love'.

In the switchover between Chapters 24 and 25, it is made to appear as if there is an actual rivalry between the young Rachel and her 'Aunt' Helen for the affections of the desirable Terence Hewet, yet that is immediately subverted by the suggestion that the real flow of passion is between the two women themselves. Indeed, the passion may not be anything like simple in nature. Louise DeSalvo suggests that, in the version of *The Voyage Out* that was completed by the beginning of 1913, 'all overt references to Rachel's homosexual love for Helen were eradicated. . . . Helen's overt sadism was pushed underground—instead of overtly victimizing Rachel, she is largely unaware of her envy' (Louise DeSalvo, *Virginia Woolf's First Voyage: A Novel in the Making* [Rowman & Littlefield 1980], p. 102). Louise DeSalvo is suggesting a wide and sometimes contradictory set of values which the relationship of the two women could have covered. In various 'excisions', DeSalvo argues, including the excision of 'the overt sadism of Helen', Woolf 'had removed the most significant and the most personal threads of meaning from her novel' (p. 102). Instead of variation and re-thinking for writerly purposes, a whole tactic of evasion and covering-up seems to be emerging.

[5] Ibid., pp. 208–9.

Stephen Trombley, too, when he comes to examine the various drafts of the love scene in the jungle, leans upon an analysis of Mitchell Leaska which has a similar suggestion to make.

As Leaska points out, the versions become successively more obscure as they are re-written; until, in the end, we are left with the baffling passage which is given in the published version. It would appear that earlier versions, in Virginia's view, gave too much away, that she re-wrote them in order to play certain elements down. She did not succeed in hiding the fact that something very peculiar was afoot, and that it was of central importance.[6]

The Derridan device of 'supplement' has never been more guiltily in evidence. The role of the woman called 'Helen' has to bear a series of shifting significations, as with every re-writing the meaning of the passage about the first kiss on the jungle floor is more deliberately and more sophisticatedly occluded. In *Melymbrosia* the strain is too great, and there is another Forster-esque anacoluthon. Rachel and Terence have declared their love for each other and have assured each other verbally that they now think they are, or that they must be considered happy, when suddenly the writerly control snaps. The strain is too great and Rachel breaks all apart with an intrusion which is quite 'uncanny': 'O Terence', she cried suddenly. 'The dead! My mother is dead!'

Likewise, in the published form, *The Voyage Out*, sudden and brutal intervention from the public world of Others shatters an intimate mood built up with such difficulty over a long period of seclusion. It seems that it is imperative for the novelist to break into, to break up, to destroy a narrative whose physicality she no longer feels able to control:

Voices crying behind them never reached them through the waters in which they were now sunk. The repetition of Hewet's name in short, dissevered syllables was to them the crack of a dry branch or the laughter of a bird. The grasses and breezes sounding and murmuring all round them, they never noticed that the swishing of the grasses grew louder and louder, and did not cease with the lapse of the breeze. A hand dropped abrupt as iron on Rachel's shoulder; it might have been a bolt from heaven. She fell beneath it, and the grass whipped across her eyes and filled her mouth and ears. Through the waving stems she saw a figure, large and shapeless against the sky. Helen was upon her.

(*The Voyage Out*, pp. 287–8)

Almost identical, is it not, with Forster's

He saw radiant joy in her face, he saw the flowers beat against her dress in blue

[6] Stephen Trombley, '*All That Summer She Was Mad*' (Continuum 1982), p. 246.

waves. The bushes above them closed. He stepped quickly forward and kissed her.

Before she could speak, almost before she could feel, a voice called, 'Lucy! Lucy! Lucy!' The silence of life had been broken by Miss Bartlett, who stood brown against the view.

(*A Room with a View*, p. 89)

It appears clearly that Virginia Woolf was striving to malidentify the obvious situation which she appears to be describing, and that she wanted to avoid making too clear something which it was in her own interests to repress. So we have a very interesting play of the signifier here. What seems to happen on the page is that Helen, from being an auntly figure about 40 years of age, merges into an erotic figure transmitting female desire, and thus displaces the suggestion that a satisfying relationship could ever have been achieved between Terence and Rachel, a man and a woman, in the first place. That a satisfying relationship between the sexes is possible is one of the knowledges which *The Voyage Out* wishes to repress, and we recall that it is in order that there should be no physical consummation of the engagement between Rachel and Terence that Rachel dies at the end of the novel. Terence is in fact deeply relieved that no consummation is now necessary. This is probably the reason why the kiss that finally takes place on the jungle floor seems to be between two parties who are *not* available to each other, Helen and Terence.

Helen was upon her, rolled this way and that, now seeing only forests of green, and now the high blue heaven; she was speechless and almost without sense. At last she lay still, all the grasses shaken round her and before her by her panting. Over her loomed two great heads, the heads of a man a woman, the heads of Terence and Helen.

Both were flushed, both laughing, and the lips were moving; they came together and kissed in the air above her. Broken fragments of speech came down to her on the ground. She thought she heard them speak of love and then of marriage. Raising herself and sitting up, she too realized Helen's soft body, the strong and hospitable arms, and happiness swelling and breaking in one vast wave.

(p. 288)

The return to the 'real world', as in the Forster passage, is accompanied by a terrifying sense that something has happened which forms a break with all previous experience, and has given a quite new meaning to people previously known. Indeed, they appear at first as unknown.

. . . . happiness swelling and breaking in one vast wave. When this fell away, and the grasses once more lay low, and the sky became horizontal, and the earth rolled out flat on each side, and the trees stood upright, whe was the first to perceive a little row of human figures standing patiently in the distance. For the moment she could not remember who they were.

'Who are they?', she asked, and then recollected.

(p. 288)

The device is pure Forster. It happens again and again. In Forster the technique could be called the mystical-queer, or the uncanny-obscure. One thinks of the baby that weeps and yet makes no sound in *Where Angels Fear to Tread*; the sudden death of Gerald and the astonishing five-part hinting about the fraternal relationship which haunts the 'Rings' section of *The Longest Journey*; the strange, ultraterrestrial influence of Mrs Wilcox in *Howards End*; and pre-eminently, of course, though much later, the always deferred explanation of what 'really' happened in the Marabar Caves in *A Passage to India*. Forster seems to insist again and again that there is really 'no' explanation for some of life's most mystical passages, or rites of passage, and that any attempt to define them merely aggravates the theological difficulty of speech in the face of their reality.

Virginia Woolf, I believe, learnt a great deal from Forster about the tactics of displacement and substitution, about the tactic of the mystical-queer, about eroding the surface of a text ('hollowing out the text') until it becomes progressively more opaque, about swerve, closure and anacoluthon, and about the technique of forcing the text, by textual means, to repress and hide its own pristine intentions. I think she learnt so much from Forster because the conditions of their own embodiment were so similar.

I have said that 'embodiment' is 'the way one's own body is perceived from the inside, by the living subjectivity, as opposed to what is perceived from the outside, by a world of casual passers-by'. The world of embodiment is therefore a priori closed off from our inspection for the greater part of the time. But where the living subjectivity is a writer, and where he or she has documented at thousands of pages' length what it feels like to be inside that particular body, we are entitled to use the testimony of the texts to speculate upon how it felt to inhabit the body of the writer. The novels, in other words, inform us of much that we could not otherwise know.

It would appear from the novels that Forster's sense of his embodiment had significant similarities with Virginia Woolf's own. Both found it easier to deal with desire in their fiction by studying the effect of it upon the female sex, and locating the 'motor' realities of it, largely unanalysed and unappreciated, in the male sex. Because of this unusual but highly developed transformational ability, both were in a high degree possessed of what Virginia Woolf was later to call 'the androgynous mind'. Both offer us characters in their novels who are, by virtue of their special talents for empathy, 'androgynous': in For-ster's fiction Mrs Moore, in *A Passage to India*; and Mrs Wilcox in *Howards End*; in Woolf's fiction 'Helen' (whoever she is) in *The Voyage Out*; Mrs Hilbery in *Night and Day*; Mrs Ramsay in *To the Lighthouse*; and Mrs Swithin in *Between the Acts*.

In her famous passage on 'androgyny' in *A Room of One's Own*, Virginia Woolf doesn't mention Forster, though she could well have had him in mind. She cites Coleridge and Shakespeare, Keats, Sterne, Cowper and Lamb as possessors of this precious essence, and of course one great Modernist stands out a mile as an example. 'In our time, Proust was wholly androgynous, if not perhaps a little too much of a woman. But that failing is too rare for one to complain of it, since without some mixture of the kind the intellect seems to predominate and the other faculties of the mind harden and become barren.' The strange, expensive dialectical courage that it takes to pen such a passage must surely owe a great deal to Forster's instruction, and indeed must surely refer, in its didactic intention, at least in part to him.

The novelistic technique which most efficiently reduces desire to a merely textual condition, in Forster's work, is the choice of men from other races and from other classes as the promoters of desire. It is Gino the plebeian Italian who so moves first Lilia and then Miss Abbott in *Where Angels Fear to Tread*; in *A Room with a View* it is the plain-minded Italian carriage-lad who conducts Lucy Honeychurch to her fatal meet-ing with George Emerson, and it seems for all the world as if, for Forster, George Emerson emerges from some Gorky-like 'lower depths'; in *Howards End* it is the frankly lower-class Leonard Bast who manages to produce passion in Helen Schlegel; later, of course, it is to be an Indian, Dr Aziz, who manages to transform the repressed Miss Quested.

The Forsterian dilemma, in other words, is shifted through geogra-phical space and time into another dimension than the embodied one. Lucy Honeychurch's sad reflection as she enters the Piazza Signoria— 'The world is certainly full of lovely things, if only I could come across them. Nothing ever happens to me'—is negated in the fiction by the sudden irruption of semi-natural, semi-pagan forces, all of which are only available on a Voyage Out. The experience of desire, though, is submitted to by a series of Forsterian heroines as coming from 'out there', from some unknown, undefined and undefinable male force, frightening and exhilarating at the same time.

This situation is remarkably similar in Virginia Woolf's early fiction. Her heroines are submitted again and again to male desire, male violence, without ever quite knowing what can be coming next. The passionate kiss from Richard Dalloway is experienced, by Rachel, as a kind of attack, even a kind of rape. She has hallucinations all night as a result. Because desire is so much a male prerogative, it is hardly allowed to surface at all during the first two novels, and the electric storm which accompanies the death of Rachel at the end of *The Voyage Out* is, for all its fine writing, a crude evasion of a technical problem that Woolf could not in fact solve. The theme of sexual desire is evaded again in *Jacob's Room*, and it is not until *Mrs Dalloway* that Woolf finally admits that she cannot understand male desire at all except through the medium of words and from a mediated distance:

> yet she could not resist sometimes yielding to the charm of a woman, not a girl, of a woman confessing, as to her they often did, some scrape, some folly. And . . . she did undoubtedly then feel what men felt. Only for a moment; but it was enough. It was a sudden revelation . . . . Then, for that moment, she had seen an illumination; a match burning in a crocus; an inner meaning almost expressed. But the close withdrew; the hard softened. it was over—the moment.
>
> (*Mrs Dalloway*, p. 30)

The pattern begins to look like this. Forster, writing only in an honorary sense as a man, displaces desire by depicting it as coming from another race or from another class, i.e., as an alien force, and each time chooses a woman to take the full brunt of it. Virginia Woolf, writing from a point of view which was from the beginning a feminist one, displaces desire, just as Forster does, by depicting it as a function of male aggression, but, in a kind of two-tier system of perception, also sees male desire as a violation of some sort, a premature or abrupt intrusion upon female rights and privacies, i.e., as an alien force, which most commonly takes the form of an intellectualistic attack upon female sensibility. The line of intellectual lovers who threaten female self-sufficiency runs from St. John Hirst in *The Voyage Out*, who owes so much to Lytton Strachey, through to Mr Ramsay in *To the Lighthouse*, who owes so much to her father. It is always a woman who has to be at the receiving and interpreting end of these male obsessions.

Forster's strangely ambivalent transformation and displacement, whereby he chooses to trace the effect of male desire upon female sensibility, is thus ideally consonant with Woolf's own purposes, and so she is able to adopt Forster's stance, and his device, as it stands, without needing any transformation of her own. There is surely no other novelist writing between 1905 and 1910 from whom Virginia Woolf could have learnt so much, in such a directly assimilable form, which was directly relevant to her own situation and to her own as yet partly unconscious purposes.

Without the early novels of E. M. Forster we might now remember

Virginia Woolf as the author of two talented descriptions of adolescence and the trials of engagement in what was still, in effect, late Victorian England. But Forster twice over made her into a writer: once by what he wrote for her and once, in 1919, by telling her what he really thought of what she had written for him.

Virginia Woolf's Diary and the Forbidding of 'The Soul' (with a Comment by Professor Quentin Bell and a Rejoinder)

The cox and box publication of Virginia Woolf's *Letters* and her *Diary* was an exhilarating experience, and the sheer wealth of material suddenly made available was for that time sufficient. But the rapidity of their combined appearance may have served to hide a very remarkable rhetorical difference between the two sets of texts. The *Letters* are in very strong contrast to the *Diary*. The *Letters* afford us that view of Virginia Woolf that we had every reason to expect—the scintillating wit, literary hostess and trenchant observer of 'men, manners and opinions'. But the *Diary*. Do we come away from it with anything like the same sense of enlightenment?

The *Diary* is a most surprising and a most disconcerting experience. Draw back a little from it. Let us try and focus on what makes it so unusual. Is it that it is not fulfilling the sorts of expectations we usually bring to a literary diary of this kind? And if so, why? Why is it, if the reader peruses the fifty or so pages around any one of the important personal or literary turning points, that a deliberate reticence seems to be maintained on just these very matters? So often, just at those points in Virginia Woolf's life where one would expect the *Diary* to be of the greatest value in shedding light on what was going on in the conscious and even the unconscious mind, there is a kind of artificially contrived black hole, a refusal, a denial. And for this reason it becomes clear that the *Diary* does not belong immediately and obviously to the main tradition of the diary in our literature, but to some other, more modern, genre of the diary. We might think of it as the 'Modernist' diary or as the 'post-Kafka' diary, though the terms do not matter. It is a diary-form which chooses, anyway, to generate mystery and to keep silence. It becomes apparent that the *Diary* is being used for a very special *purpose*.

This is more apparent, perhaps, to someone reading with an eye to the 'biography' of Virginia Woolf than to someone who knows either nothing about her personal life at all or who knows the novels only in literary isolation. But it will become apparent to any reader in time. The repression of the *Diary* is massive. Since I began to read it to see whether it afforded either evidence for or evidence against a biographical speculation of my own, this level of repression struck me more forcibly than it may strike others, but the result was that I found virtually nothing to the purpose. Except in fleeting glances, and then not in the place, or time, or tone or context in which one would expect them, there are no clues to some of the most important issues in her personal life. On the most important and worrying issues, the *Diary* is silent, and is determined, obviously, to be silent.

The published form of the *Diary* begins in 1915. But there are diaries, notebooks, memoirs for earlier periods. These are in the Berg collection of the New York Public Library, and Quentin Bell cites many passages from them in the early part of his famous biography.

These entries (from 1895, 1896, 1897 and early 1898) *are* highly informative in the way one expects diaries to be. They reflect her state of health, her moods, her reading, the preparations for Stella Duckworth's marriage to Jack Hills in April 1897, and her anxiety and sensitivity about accidents in the streets. Although the *Diary* as published now begins in 1915, the lesser and fragmentary diaries of Virginia Woolf's adolescence and young adulthood deserve publishing as well, and I understand that Louise DeSalvo and Mitchell Leaska are in the process of preparing a form of them.

But this *Ur*-diary has a disturbing relationship to the *Diary* as published from 1915. It throws into relief even more strongly the refusal of the post-1915 Virginia Woolf to comment on what she was to call 'the soul'. It makes plain, too, that Virginia Stephen, when she was writing her first memoirs and sketches, *did* regard the diary form (as one naturally does) as a place where one can pour out one's vexations and exaltations in the privacy of an intimate but silent companion, 'dear Diary'. But the fact that she *did* so regard the diary form makes her later use of the form all the more stubborn and austere.

There is no diary of any kind for 1913, when Virginia suffered the first major breakdown of that period of her life which began with her marriage to Leonard Woolf the preceding August. But the mental collapse of 1915 falls within the period when Virginia Woolf had resumed the habit of keeping a diary, and it is puzzling that there is no hint of approaching crisis in the entries preceding the collapse of February 1915; nor is there any direct comment upon that collapse when, two and a half years later, the diary resumes.

This is perfectly amazing, and it seems to me to subvert the contentions of those who assert that if a diary for a certain date exists, then one only has to go and 'look it up' to find out what Virginia Woolf was actually feeling at that time of her life. In fact the reverse seems to be true. One may well go to the *Diary* for information, and hunt about, but more often than not one will find a carefully organized 'gap' in the text, or else a quite deliberate failure to represent anything at all. The last entry before the collapse of 1915, for instance, presents merely this sort of comment:

We both went up to London this afternoon; L. to the Library, and I to ramble about the West End, picking up clothes. I really am in rags. It is very amusing. With age too one's less afraid of the superb shop women . . ..
I bought a ten and eleven penny blue dress, in which I sit at this moment.

(*Diary* Vol I, p. 35)

There then follow three blank sheets. There is next the heading '1917' and the following editorial note:

The last entry made by Virginia Woolf in 1915 was that of 15th February; on the 17th she had an appointment with the dentist, and she and Leonard went to Farringdon Street about a printing press. The next day she had a headache, and from then onwards, with increasingly sleepless nights and restless aching days, she slid inexorably into madness.

Whatever it was she slid into, 'madness' or other, there is nothing in the diary to enlighten us about it. The next entry is dated Friday, 3 August 1917; that is to say, almost exactly two and a half years since the last entry. Whatever one's evaluation of what has happened in the meantime, one is certainly expecting some sort of comment from V.W. herself. But there is none whatsoever. The first entry runs:

Friday 3 August
Came to Asheham. Walked out from Lewes. Stopped raining for the first time since Sunday. Men mending the wall and roof at Asheham. Will has dug up bed in front, leaving only one dahlia. Bees in attic chimney.

(p. 39)

If this should be viewed as some sort of exception, it should be noted that, for months, the entries are no longer than six, eight or ten lines.

The editor, Olivier Bell, tells us, 'The Asheham Diary is a small note-book; the date is written on the verso pages, opposite the text on the recto, each day's entry ruled off with a line across the page.' 'Ruled off' in more than one sense, for the six-, eight- or ten-line diary entry was obviously all that was permitted to the convalescent. She was allowed a little literary exercise, so to speak, but a limit was set. Hence it is not surprising if the entries are themselves of a triviality which more befits a schoolgirl than the authoress of *The Voyage Out* (as she already was at that time).

This pattern of extreme formal triviality is maintained for months. Her observation is painfully literal: she writes of mushrooms and blackberries, caterpillars and picnics. It is not until the new diary is begun on Monday, 8 October 1917, that what we recognize as the authentic 'voice' of V.W. is heard for the first time. The depressed and miserable, plain, meagre, bare and bored style of early 1915 gives way to that great gap of two and a half years, and that gives way to entries that are obviously controlled by medical advice, so that it is only in 1917 that we finally hear the voice that we know (as readers of fiction) to be the mature voice of *The Voyage Out*. Why is this?

One clue is perhaps offered by the opening lines of the entry for 8 October 1917 itself. She writes:

> Hogarth House
> Paradise Road
> Richmond
> Oct. 1917

Monday 8 October
This attempt at a diary is begun on an impulse given by the discovery in a wooden box in my cupboard of an old volume, kept in 1915, and still able to make us laugh at Walter Lamb. This therefore will follow that plan—written after tea, written in discreetly. . . .

(p. 55)

It is true that there is a reference to a meeting with Walter Lamb in the entry for 15 February 1915, but it is not terribly amusing, and the idea that finding *that* entry should have been sufficiently funny for a renewed attempt at a diary points to a deliberate holding away from herself of V.W's own consciousness of what had happened in the meantime.

It is *as if* she has deliberately *decided* on a policy for the diary, and that policy is to be one of organized triviality and superficiality. The diary for 1915 was 'still able to make us laugh at Walter Lamb'. Very well then, *let there be a diary* in which, every day after tea, something can be written down which makes us laugh.

Not by any means a bad reason for writing a diary, but, for a major writer of our time, a very remarkable one. The diary is conceived (or rather, after the immense gap since February 1915) it is *reconceived*, as a therapy. Not, either, a bad reason for writing a diary, but again, given the person involved, a very remarkable one.

This policy of scribbling a few lines after tea, for relaxation, was to be kept to for years, until the demands of writing novels in the morning changed the role of the diary in her writing economy. In March 1922 she writes 'The book dwindles, now that I draw my stream off in the morning' (*Diary* Vol II, p. 170). So she implies that, if her mind is fully engaged in writing fiction, the role of the diary decreases proportionately.

That the diary is conceived as a pastime, a way to make time pass, as an amusement where nothing too serious is to be mentioned, has the consequence I have already hinted at. If one looks at the diary during any period when it was in fact being kept regularly, but a period in which we know from other sources that V.W. was undergoing considerable mental stress, one will find that no mention of the matter has been allowed to get past the censorship of the criterion imposed, that old criterion of 1917, that entries should be 'written after tea, written indiscreetly', and written to make us laugh. The really large issues of V.W's work and life are precluded, almost by fiat, from being treated at length or in depth in the diary.

One can check this proposal by considering the actual quantity of the diary as published by Leonard Woolf in 1953 as *A Writer's Diary*, and comparing it to the sheer mass of the '26 volumes of diary' he refers to as his source, and which have now appeared in print.

Leonard Woolf writes, in his Preface to *A Writer's Diary*:

I have been carefully through the 26 volumes of diary and have extracted and now publish in this volume practically everything which referred to her own writing. . . . The reader must remember that what is printed in this volume is only a very small portion of the diaries and that the extracts were embedded in a mass of matter unconnected with V.W's writing.

This seems a perhaps unnecessarily restricted view of the relation of fiction to life—is anything 'unconnected' in that sense?—but it reinforces the point that I am making. The proportion of the diary which is *explicitly* about writing, art, fiction, method and so on is remarkably small in relationship to the diary as a whole.

Whether or not this lifelong habit of confining mental work to fiction or reviews, and amusement and relaxation to the diary, was an unconscious survival long after the necessity for it had passed, or was an existential decision of Virginia Woolf's own, I do not know. But the question of what constitutes the deliberate aim in writing a diary cannot but pose, by indirection, the question of what sorts of material are (perhaps not 'deliberately') to be suppressed or to be repressed.

This leads necessarily to a re-examination of the function and role of time in the diary. I have suggested that the diary was written originally as a pastime, became a therapy and finally emerged into being a pastime again. But it was also a device for *making time pass*, in a willed and deliberate way. It was not just whiling away the time, it was annihilating time, destroying time. It was written to use time up.

Wednesday 17 August 1921
   To while away the time till L. comes in, from London, Fergusson, office, &c, I may as well scribble.
Thursday 18 August 1921
   Nothing to record; only an intolerable fit of the fidgets to write away. Here I am chained to my rock: forced to do nothing; doomed to let every worry, spite, irritation and obsession scratch & claw & come again. This is to say that I may not walk, & must not work. . . . (13 lines)
   There! I've written out half my irritation.

(*Diary* Vol II, pp.132–3)

One can actually watch time passing ('time passes'!) in the body of the text, as a dialectic is deliberately set up between outer or 'clock' time and time as it is experienced as an inner state.

Sunday 11 December [1921]
   Yes, I ought to be doing the beds; but Leonard insists upon doing them himself. Perhaps that's Lottie on the stairs? Ought I to go out and scold her for not staying in bed? Is the hot water on? Well, it will soon be time to go out & eat a plate of meat in the restaurant in the passage. In other words, both the servants have German measles, & for three days we have been servants instead of masters.
   Excuse this scrawl therefore;—surely that is Lottie washing up?

Here it would have seemed far more natural to go out onto the landing and discover whether it was indeed Lottie on the stairs or washing up, but, in a kind of curious duplicate of time and action, V.W. writes out a temporal equivalent for events in the world. They are not events, but they stand for events. Writing them out puts them at a distance, and anything that puts life at a distance, its intolerable tedium, is a relief and a therapy. Objective time, the time of the clock, goes by too slowly to be endured. Very well then, inner time has to be created to combat it. The *Diary* is the device through which this transformation of outer time into inner time is made both practicable and then easy.

The process can be observed in a slightly earlier entry, written in the evening of Thursday, 15 September 1921.

It is the loveliest of evenings—still; the smoke going up straight in the quarry; the white horse & strawberry coloured horse feeding close together; the women coming out of their cottages for no reason, & standing looking. . . .

There is one woman of genius among the cows. She has decided to leave the herd & eat the branches on the fallen tree. She now has one disciple. The rest utterly condemn. She is a Roger Fry. I heard from Roger the other day, all in a hubblebubble about Mary's sneering pin-pricking article. He is so angry that he can talk of nothing else, (the cow has 2 disciples). We must go on doing what we like in the desert, Roger says, & let Murry climb the heights, as he certainly will.

The birds are moving about like nets full of fish; they turn sideways and vanish; sideways again, & become full of black spots.

(pp. 138–9)

In this entry one can actually measure the time taken to write it. The time taken for the cow to move off, to be observed, to be joined by one disciple, then by two, is literally written into the text as V.W's mind continues to play around the idea of Roger Fry and his loneliness. The writer's eyes travel back and forth between the observed world and the world of the page, and the time of the world is fed scrupulously into the literary temporality and mood.

Or is it vice versa? Does the time of the text impose itself upon the time of the cows, the women, the birds, as the writer deliberately grinds objective time to pieces with her nib?

One thing is certain, the *Diary* records the battle between private time and public time, and for the most part private time is very lonely and very uncomfortable. Quite apart from the endless recital of physical ailments, depressions, tiredness, toothache, enforced rest and so on, there is a kind of continual restlessness, a sense of being chained up, shut off, removed from the current of life, imprisoned. It reads, very often, like a prison journal, where the days in the cell pass intolerably slowly and the diary is written to stave off the worst excesses of loneliness and frustration. The entry I have already quoted from 18 August 1921 seems to give the essence of it.

No one in the whole of Sussex is so miserable as I am; or so conscious of an infinite capacity of enjoyment hoarded in me, could I use it.

(p. 133)

In the novels the situation is different. If the novels present an internalized series of time-flows, the time involved is *also* public time. The chiming of Big Ben in *Mrs Dalloway*, for instance, enforces the public time of the world, as the various time consciousnesses of her characters are examined for significance. But the *Diary* contains no Big Ben. The only objective or public time events which occur are meals. The exclamation, 'Dinner!' (p. 263) which one can find scattered here and there in the *Diary* is the only fixed outside event of the day. All the rest is private time, inwardness. And V.W. obviously feels the moment when dinner is served as a release; she calibrates the time between the moving nib and the sound of the dinner bell, and reacts to its actual incursion into her private world with excited relief.

Perhaps it is because private time is so painfully slow that V.W. treats the *Diary* also as a *period-measuring* device. She is very careful and punctilious with regard to opening and closing the diary at the beginning and the end of a year. It would seem that, for her, to open a diary on 1 January and close it after Christmas means a 'hold' on objective time of which she was very glad. Otherwise, one cannot see why the periodicity of the diary should be so accentuated. There seems to be almost a moral quality to her involvement with starting and closing the diary punctually: she apologizes to herself, or excuses herself, if she comes early or late to the job, or if she has (which she sometimes does for reasons of economy) to start a new year in an old book.

Sunday 2 January 1921
> The first time I've written 1921. And it shouldn't be written here—should be written on the first page of a new book—but we're just back from Monk's, & I can't settle to anything. . . .
>
> (p. 85)

Sometimes the diary for a year is ended with a kind of dramatic resonance. The end of 1917, for instance:

> So we come to the end of the year, & any attempt to sum it up is beyond me, or even to cast a final glance at the evening paper with news from Russia, which has just come in and drawn L. to remark
> 'A very interesting state of things—'
> 'And what's going to happen?'
> 'No human being can fortell that.'
>
> (*Diary* Vol I, p. 95)

Ending a year in such an emphatic way was, I feel, a way of mastering time, of making it conform to some recognized norms. A year finishes (with all its stress and failure) and a year opens (with all its promise and possible success). Virginia Woolf was anxious to 'place' time historically, so that it could not always 'place' her by referring her to the endless sea of inner time as the ultimate reality.

So valuable did she find the *Diary* as a means of imposing public form on private temporality that on occasion she even *re-wrote* a *Diary* entry. There is an example of this at the beginning of 1919. The arrival of a new year, the opening of a new volume of the *Diary* (this once again preceded by the full postal address, which fixes her coordinates of identity in space) is an event which merits a good deal of care and attention.

Monday 20 January (revised version – for first version see Appendix 2, p. 325)

I mean to copy this out when I can buy a book, so I omit the flourishes proper to the new year. . . . One hour's writing daily is my allowance for the next few weeks; & having hoarded it this morning, I may spend part of it now, since L. is out, & I am much behindhand with the month of January.

(p. 233)

If indeed 'one hour's writing daily' was her allowance, it is strange that she should have spent that precious ('hoarded') time in revising and copying entries which, on her own admission in this very entry, are informal and more or less miscellaneous ('I note however that this diary writing does not count as writing, since I have just re-read my year's diary & am much struck by the rapid haphazard gallop at which it swings along, sometimes indeed jerking almost intolerably over the cobbles.'). It is to be noted that she has had time to re-read the whole of last year's diary, and then had time to re-write the versions for 20, 22 and 24 January. But there is not the slightest difference that I can see in literary quality between the first form and the later form, so the re-reading and the re-writing must, once again, have been undertaken in the cause of filling in time.

Again, that phrase 'Since L. is out' has its significance. One of the reasons why private time in the *Diary* is felt as being so remorselessly endless is that Leonard Woolf is 'felt' as being out of the house most of the time. Even when V.W. explicitly mentions that he is storing apples or mowing the lawn, he is felt as pursuing his own interests or running a parallel life, and so V.W. takes up her pen and begins to write the *Diary*.

Leonard's absence is indeed a very noticeable feature of V.W's private writings. The early letters of 1914–15 are often written *to* Leonard Woolf, who is away on lecture tours or visiting friends. V.W. herself is at Asheham, convalescing. One repeated convention of the *Diary* is that, in the absence of Leonard, Virginia Woolf addresses herself rhetorically through the device of the *Diary*. This convention increases the sense of continual loneliness.

The diary is thus a kind of literary counter-subject, but one which never answers back except through the mode of being re-read (and V.W. does indeed take advantage of that property of the *Diary*). This creation of a literary counter-subject may be one of the reasons why the *Diary* is scattered with reported conversations, queries, questions, exclamation marks and other syntactically enlivening devices.

On occasions it appears (quite inadvertently) that V.W. literally does not know whether L.W. is in the house at all, or where he is if he is away. There is an amazing example of this in 1921. A brilliant account of a party at which V.W. had had an intimate and amusing conversation with Bertrand Russell is followed by this:

> & got home & drank cocoa in the kitchen; & at 7:30 this morning traced a smell of shag in the house and found L. smoking his pipe by the kitchen fire, having come back safe.

> (*Diary* Vol II, p. 148)

Leonard, it transpires, had been on a lecture tour in the North of England. He had got back some time, and sat himself by the fire to smoke. It was thus that V.W. traced his presence in the house. Their lives seem to have been lived along entirely separate lines, except where they agreed to act together by going to a party or a concert, a lecture or a dinner.

The day as represented in the *Diary* is two days, Leonard's (working in London, editing, running the Press) and Virginia's (sitting at home, writing her diary, thinking, convalescing). This total independence of their two lives is felt, in the diary, as rather menacing. It started, obviously, before the 1915 collapse:

> We both went up to London this afternoon; L. to the Library, and I to ramble about the West End, picking up clothes.

> (*Diary* Vol I, p. 35)

It continued after the collapse:

> L. up to Labour conference in London. Fine day again. Alix & I to hills for blackberries.

> (p. 41)

And it was still firmly in place as a method of living in 1918:

> On Friday I went to Hippodrome, to see life; L. seeing a different variety of it at the 17 Club.

> (p. 144)

The *Diary* sadly or resignedly sets up these two curves of time and activity through the day, and the formula 'Leonard did this, I did that' is very common. In view of the convalescence, the empty house, the lack of activity, it is not surprising that time seems to hang so heavy on V.W's hands.

It is perhaps for this reason that an intermediate temporal category, somewhere between clock time and purely internal time, looms so large in the diary and plays so large a part in the therapeutic process it affords, and that is the passing of time as such, as evidenced in the private life and fortune of old friends.

This category of observation occupies, no doubt, the greatest volume of the journal, far outweighing all other kinds of preoccupation. The study of the lives, fortunes, failures, successes, love affairs and break-ups of old friends is detailed and uninterrupted. This must be because it fulfils two functions, two therapeutic functions, at once. Not only does it amuse and 'cause us to laugh' but it also represents a continuity of identity through a life experienced as largely inchoate and threatened by dissolution of self. V.W. feels her own identity at risk, but *others* are solidly there and have histories through time, which is very reassuring. So the recounting of what would appear to be gossip very often has an ulterior motive. In a sea of endless inner time, the doings of old friends represent a certain continuity and security.

Indeed, sometimes this is explicit in the text:

Friday 25 November [1921]
> Last weekend we spent at Tidmarsh. We must have talked out 12 hours, I suppose—& I remember so little: for with old, worn, creased, shabby, intimate friends, it runs so easily; no rapids, or waterfalls; room for everything; & no damned brilliance.
>
> (*Diary* Vol II, p.145)

'Old, worn, creased, shabby, intimate friends'—this gives one a sudden insight into the nature of passing time as V. W. experienced it, for the hand that penned this entry was only thirty-nine years old.

Friends are sharply contrasted with acquaintances or people who have been met on a single occassion. There the criticism is razor sharp and death usually instantaneous.

> Witham's elaborately literary get-up is a fair index of his mind. He is what the self-taught working man thinks genius should be; & yet so unassuming and homely that its more amusing than repulsive.
>
> (*Diary* Vol I, p. 113)

Friends provide continuity. The doctrine of G. E. Moore on the preciousness of certain experienced states of consciousness runs through V.W's reference to friendship as a kind of absorbed conviction. Moore wrote, at the end of *Principia Ethica*:

> By far the most valuable things which we know or can imagine, are certain states of consciousness, which may be roughly described as the pleasures of human intercourse and the enjoyment of beautiful objects.

This it is which gives to certain recorded conversations a kind of philosophical depth which is not only due to the fact that the interlocutor, on one occasion, is Bertrand Russell.

> So Bertie Russell was attentive, & we struck out like swimmers who knew their waters. One is old enough to cut the trimmings & get to the point. Bertie is a

fervid egoist—which helps matters. And then, what a pleasure,—this mind on springs. I got as much out of him as I could carry.

(*Diary* Vol II, pp., 146–7)

Old friends not only establish secure identity through time, they are a means of asserting extremely pronounced value judgments which also reassure. V.W. has often been called a snob, and indeed once enquired of herself at essay length whether she was one. Inevitably and interesting is the reason why. The values she most snobbishly admired were those that confirmed her in her own identity. Good breeding, intelligence, privilege, open-mindedness, unconventionality, achievement, these were her positives. In them, and in the affirmation of them, she could feel she existed securely. If others were like this, and she was, then she could feel the pleasant sensation of having values which were shared by a powerful group.

These values are asserted again and again in the discourse of the journal. But other values are repressed. The long lament on childlessness of 2 January 1923, and envy for the children of her sister Vanessa, is accompanied by a deliberate repression of her own feeling of bereftness.

Wednesday 7 February [1923]
Nessa's wedding day. Reflections suppressed. I must describe Cambridge.

(p. 230)

As if aware of her own double intention, she writes only ten days later:

How it would interest me if this diary were ever to become a real diary: something in which I could see changes, trace moods developing; but then I should have to speak of the soul, & did I not banish the soul when I began?

(p. 234)

This is a key entry, for it makes explicit the direction and purpose of the *Diary* from the beginning, the quality which is so puzzling to the reader. V.W's *Diary* departs radically from the convention, long honoured in the use, of intimate record, while retaining many of the traditional devices at a merely formal level. It appears to be self-expression, while in fact deliberately eschewing what V.W. calls 'the soul'. It appears to be the direct conveyance of subjective impression, while in fact carefully keeping the tone guarded, amusing, relaxed. It appears to be obeying the convention of the single subject, 'I', which addresses its diary, while in fact reading most often as a dialogue or polylogue of a variety of selves, all of which are at least partly alienated from, or hostile to, each other.

I have tried to show two things about the normal make-up of the diary entry. It is a therapy, and its aim is to construct a time-scheme which has the effect of shortening outer or objective time. Both of these aims militate against any direct examination of subjective states, for that implies work and effort which would lengthen time, not shorten it. 'But then I should have to speak of the soul, and did I not banish the soul when I began?'

To which convention, then, does the *Diary* really belong? It seems, in the end, impossible to decide. Virginia Woolf has subverted the expectations of the common reader by writing the diary in two parallel styles, two opposed rhetorics. The first one might call the style of false intimacy, the second the style of excluded subjectivity. Common reading of the *Diary* is baffled and harassed, for it operates betwixt and between the two rhetorics and cannot really penetrate either of them in a continuous way.

A diary is usually read for two sorts of information, and the reader hopes to come away with new knowledge on one or both of them. Either the reader seeks information on the inner life of a historical personage of some intrinsic importance, or else seeks an understanding of the period in which such a personage lived. Pepys's diary, Swift's *Journal to Stella* stand as obvious examples of the second form of understanding, and V.W's *Diary* too offers a brilliant sketch of the social group in which the Woolfs lived. But in these two historical cases one also gets to know Pepys and Swift as men, as personalities. True, both have their mysteries, and these are scrupulously guarded. But V.W. systematically seeks to defeat this sort of personal assimilation by any potential reader.

I think the clue to the status of the *Diary* may well lie in the novels. V.W. seems (curiously enough) to have been sufficiently convinced by the received tradition on the status and nature of fiction to believe that she was more 'protected' when she was writing fiction than when she was writing her diary. She seems to have trusted the 'public' utterances enough to consider her own subjective world better conveyed in them than in a diary. This no doubt shows, from a new angle and a quite unsuspected one, how much she believed in art as reality. Almost incredible though it may seem, V.W. appears to have believed that, in an 'encoded' form like fiction, reality as art would be more or less 'invisible'. For a long time, too, her novels were read in accordance with just such a convention of illegibility.

So the discourse of the *Diary* has to be conpared not with the 'objectivity', but with the public subjectivity of the novels. Whenever V.W. felt that she was preserving anonymity through the process of fictional transformation, she wrote freely. But she never realized how transparent, in one obvious sense, her fictions are, and the reading public deliberately followed her in a willed blindness.

The New Criticism of the '40s and '50s made a dogma of what was then but a fashionable assumption, but V.W. herself would have drawn a line, doubtless, between what she experienced in her life (say, the mental breakdown of 1913) and what she later wrote up as 'art' (say, *Mrs Dalloway*). But, although fiction should obviously be treated as autonomous, there is nothing in the nature of things to forbid a free man from enquiring into its subjective or existential origin. The line between experience and fiction, between subjectivity and public objectivity, was in V.W's case largely nonexistent, and, had she realized this, she would doubtless have prevaricated infinitely more than she does in her novels.

The *Diary* offers itself, then, as a modified and guarded objectivity, while the novels are necessarily read as public subjectivity. But this public subjectivity is obviously thought of, by V.W. herself, as an objectivity, and therefore it is and remains a subjectivity of an unsuspected kind, a subjectivity which 'tells' us more than the *Diary* can or will.

There was doubtless a third kind of subjectivity, found mostly in the letters and , I am sure, in the conversation, but that kind of subjectivity is not to be found in the *Diary* (except in reported conversations) because it requires an addressee. A letter to Vita Sackville-West, written in a moment of high infatuation, will do as an illustration.

The poor little Mole [i.e., herself, Virginia] died half an hour after you left: came up to snuggle: found no warmth: and so heaved once, and sighed, and was dead. Would you like the pelt kept for you? It was all very warm and cosy so long as you were here—odd that driven and hunted as you are, you should yet be to me like a sunny patch on a hot bank. God—I'm angry that your time should be frittered and tittered like this. Nothing is more fidgetting and exasperating; and why should it be *you* of all people?

(*Letters*, Vol. 3, p. 440, 22 November 1927)

That particular subjective tone, often adopted with Vanessa, Leonard and other intimates, is not to be found in the *Diary*, because the person addressed has a real existence in time and space and is obviously very 'present' to the writer of the letter. But in the timeless waste of the *Diary*, dialogue with the Other is recorded mainly to distract, to record, to analyze or to vent spleen.

There is one recurring feature of the *Diary* which V.W. could not, however, fully control, and that has to do with the splitness of the writer herself. Other diarists may address their diary as an equal or as a superior, but for the greater part V.W. seems to address herself in her diary as an intimate friend whom she knows too well to take entirely seriously. She can be impatient, irritated, caustic, censorious, harsh, unforgiving, just as she can be witty, penetrating, observant, analytic. But she addresses this other 'Virginia' as an alter ego perceived as such.

Very often the style of the *Diary* is more like a conversation with an alienated other than with herself.

As a result of this split and hostile attitude to the 'other' Virginia Woolf (perceived, perhaps, as 'the writer, Virginia Woolf'), she is aware that she can at any moment redeploy the diary as strategy.

I think I shall initiate a new convention for this book—beginning each day on a new page—my habit in writing serious literature. Certainly, I have room to waste a little paper in this year's book. As for the soul; why did I say I would leave it out? I forget. And the truth is, one can't write directly about the soul. Looked at, it vanishes: but look at the ceiling, at Grizzle, at the cheaper beasts in the Zoo which are exposed to walkers in Regents Park, & the soul slips in. It slipped in this afternoon. I will write that, I said, staring at the bison: answering L. absent-mindedly; but what was I going to write?

(27 February 1926)

It would seem as if the *Diary* is Virginia Woolf's longest and most ambitious novel. It was certainly perceived as a literary construct right from the beginning, when in those unpublished memorials and note-books the young Virginia Stephen set herself literary 'essays' on various correct subjects. She uses the tonality of *The Spectator* sometimes, there is not a little of Dr Johnson in his most sententious vein. The mood is often that of the eighteenth century, and the sentiments are correct. A very serious young woman—and a *writer*. She has a lot to say about Greek, she is reading Aristotle and writing reviews. The task of self-education was seriously undertaken, and the pen was run through a faulty phase.

It would seem as if this early relationship to the diary form was never seriously questioned or modified, and that this early self-training in literary distancing was carefully maintained in later years. Just as the earliest unpublished diaries are exercises of stylized emotion, so the *Diary* from 1915 onwards is the greatest novel that Virginia Woolf ever wrote. It is longer than the others, and has far more details and clues about the central character. But that character, as established in the discourse of the *Diary*, is fictitious, and remained so until the end.

QUENTIN BELL COMMENTS AS FOLLOWS.

I rather doubt whether our readers can be expected to digest the tough yet tenuous disputation which is the usual fare of Woolf scholars. But even if they are, I, for one, cannot serve them. When Dr Poole ventures into categories of time or pursues that indefinable commodity, Virginia's 'soul', I dare not follow him. Nevertheless, in his very interesting article, he does make some remarks which a biographer of Virginia Woolf is bound to examine as best he may.

In writing my biography I found all the diaries useful, but the
1915–41 diaries were my major source. They told me a great deal about
Virginia's daily life, her marriage, her friendships, her art, her thought
and indeed her whole life. Where I could check the *Diary* from other
sources I found her surprisingly accurate, and this impression has been
fully confirmed by the editor of the *Diaries*.

Now if Dr Poole be right, I have been deluded. I had no business to
be enlightened by a diary the form of which 'chooses anyway to
generate mystery and to keep silence'. 'The repression of the *Diary*', Dr
Poole continues, 'is massive . . .'. He who seeks for information . . .
'more often than not will find a carefully organized gap in the text, or
else a quite deliberate failure to represent anything at all'. These are
harsh statements and I can only repeat that they do not correspond
with my own experiences. I would remark in passing that perhaps Dr
Poole is too modest, and at the same time too severe, to observe that
this evidence of *choice* and *organization* must be apparent from the text.
The critic must have been wonderfully perceptive to know so much of
the writer's presumably secret intentions, and the writer amazingly
communicative.

With exemplary candour Dr Poole admits at the outset that in
reading the diaries he was looking for evidence that might support 'a
biographical speculation' of his own. I am not much astonished to find
that he 'found nothing to the purpose'. With the best will and all the
honesty in the world it would be hard to accept the evidence of so
provoking a witness. To this it may be objected that I too may be
prejudiced inasmuch as I came to the *Diaries* with a personal knowledge and an affection for Virginia. But I do honestly believe that any
impartial critic would agree that there is not a scrap of evidence to show
that the author of the diaries intended to deceive the reader.

Having said so much I must in fairness add that it seems to me that
Dr Poole does show that the *Diaries* fail to provide him with the kind of
information which he wanted to find. This does not imply that there
has been 'massive repression', because after all we don't know whether
there was anything to repress. It should also be said that some of his
strictures are less severe than the ordinary reader might suppose.
When, in his conclusion, he describes the *Diaries* as an 'ambitious
novel' it may appear that he is using a polite euphemism: this is a
fiction, *videlicet* a falsehood. No one who had the pleasure of hearing
him at the Cambridge centennial Woolf symposium will suppose this.
On that occasion he asserted that any literary production by a novelist
was in effect a novel. Holding this opinion he had but to prove that the
Diaries were the work of Virginia Woolf and that she was a novelist,
propositions which are unlikely to be disputed, and for him the *Diaries*

must be a novel. But here again, I must admit, Dr Poole enters areas of discussion which are beyond me.

A REJOINDER TO PROFESSOR BELL:

When the editor of the *Charleston Newsletter* told me that Professor Quentin Bell was writing some comments on my observations about the *Diary* of Virginia Woolf, I must admit I had a moment of trepidation. For he and I have had our famous disagreements in the past. But I had not expected to read his comments with quite so much pleasure as I did, for in few words Professor Bell has opened up a matter of great intrinsic interest, and one which happens to be at the very centre of debate in literary theory right now.

I must start, though, with a gesture of self-defence, for even the austere Hobbes, having stripped us of all other rights, allows us to keep *this* one! I did not write that I 'was looking for evidence that might support a biographical speculation of [my] own'. I wrote that 'I began to read [the *Diary*] to see whether it afforded either evidence for or evidence against a biographical speculation of my own'. I think that must be conceded to be quite an important difference.

The 'biographical speculation', as everyone will be aware, was the suggestion in *The Unknown Virginia Woolf* (Cambridge University Press 1978) that, in our present state of ignorance, nothing is to be gained by asserting, as Professor Bell had done in his famous biography, that Virginia Woolf had from time to time been 'mad' or 'insane'. I find these two words useless, especially when applied to a genius.

What I was looking for in reading the *Diary* was evidence about Virginia Woolf's own view about her periodic depresions. I thought she must have had a very interesting and incisive personal vocabulary to describe these shattering events in her life; but no! She says remarkably little about this important matter and there is, I believe, an observable refusal to discuss the matter at all.

She had, as I document in my essay, a doctrine or theory that she had to keep what she called 'the soul' out of the *Diary*. This being so, and the question of periodic illness and depression doubtless coming in under the general area of 'the soul', it is not surprising if she keeps 'the soul' out of the *Diary* very effectively. Without hunting after arcane entities, it is noticeable that around this area of repressed tension, where a frank personal assessment of her own state of mind might have been *expected*, where it would be natural for there to *be* such an assessment, there is a blank.

Professor Bell holds a noble and antique view of things, which I am proud to share, according to which the true is opposed to the false.

Without such a distinction we could not think at all. But it is striking that when Professor Bell says that I contend that the *Diary* is 'a fiction, *videlicet* a falsehood' he introduces the notion of the false where I never did. I have never claimed that the *Diary* is a falsehood, merely that it is a fiction. At that Cambridge celebration which Professor Bell mentions in his closing paragraph, I said, 'the *Diary* as constituted is very near to being a fictional work. It might even be her most interesting novel. If that is so, and if the *Diary* relates to the novels in some such way as Kierkegaard's *Journal* relates to his "indirect communications", then we stand before an enormous, complex structure which belongs almost entirely to the future. It seems to me that it is a good thing to have' (*Virginia Woolf: A Centenary Perspective*, ed. Eric Warner [Macmillan 1984], p. 161).

It is clear from this that I regard the *Diary* as 'true' in a larger cultural context. To say, as Professor Bell does, that 'there is not a scrap of evidence to show that the author of the diaries intended to deceive the reader' is to assume the equation: false = intention to deceive (mislead). But I nowhere use the word false, nor do I suggest any intention to deceive.

When I suggest that the *Diary* is a fiction, I am not referring to any one particular matter at all, but to the necessarily 'literary' or 'fictional' status of *any* diary, *any* autobiography. It is only recently that we have become aware of how deeply compromised an autobiographical work can be. It was Jacques Derrida's essay on the *Confessions* of Rousseau which set this particular ball rolling. Montaigne may have done his best to present himself as he was, but, as Lionel Trilling has argued, sincerity and authenticity become more difficult with the Romantic age, and in Rousseau there is a definite exculpatory intent which, as Paul de Man has demonstrated in a well-known essay, falsifies key passages of the *Confessions* till we cannot really tell what *is* going on! Rousseau's autobiography establishes that any diary is a particular form of fiction or self-fictionalizing. An entire sub-section of literary theory is now studying the problems of veracity and self-deception, presentation and self-betrayal in the autobiographical forms. And that form of literary theory called 'deconstruction', of which Jacques Derrida is the founder, has shown the extent to which a text seems to be not entirely congruent with its author's intentions. Just as the dream, as Freud told us, condenses and displaces in order to outwit the repressing censor, so the literary text, instinct with its own kind of memory and intention, can occlude or forget, suppress or refuse certain kinds of contents it ought to have, and in doing so leaves those significant *gaps*. Very often a text tells us a different story from the one the author intended to tell us. Very often it tells us *more* than the author intended, and it does so by its blanks, its omissions, its refusals, and it is never more treacher-

ous to its own plainly intended sense than when it repeats details about
what ought to be insignificant (Derrida's *petit supplément*) or when it
fails to report what is obviously required of it at that juncture.

It is to this entire wave of literary theory, fascinating in its implications, that I refer when I say that the *Diary* is a fiction. If Virginia Woolf
omits much that one might expect to find in a diary, that is part of what
has come to be called, following Fredric Jameson, its 'textual unconscious'. The diary knows far more than the diarist does. The diary tells
its *own* story!

The *Diary* is not a fiction in the sense that it is false. It is a fiction in
the sense that it shows us a picture of Virginia Woolf as she wanted to
view herself, or as she wanted herself to be viewed. Neither of these
wishes makes the *Diary* false, it merely makes of it a fiction of a certain
kind, a kind which overlaps very often with 'reality'—if anyone is
brave enough to attempt a definition of *that*!

But of truth itself, the truth that Professor Bell considers he com-
mands when he opens the pages of Virginia Woolf's *Diary*, I fear there
is very little, in that pure sense, to be had. But the richer sense one can
now attribute to 'fiction' is perhaps not so bad an exchange for it?

Bibliographical note

As stated in the opening pages of this study, my primary materials have been the novels of Virginia Woolf, together with *A Writer's Diary* (1953) and *The Collected Essays* edited by Leonard Woolf, all published by the Hogarth Press.

Most important too have been the two major biographical accounts we have to date of Virginia's work and health. Pride of place must go to Leonard Woolf's five-volume autobiography, *Sowing* (1960), *Growing* (1961), *Beginning Again* (1964), *Downhill All the Way* (1967) and *The Journey not the Arrival Matters* (1969) published by the Hogarth Press.

The second is Professor Quentin Bell's *Virginia Woolf: A Biography*, volume I: *Virginia Stephen 1882–1912*; volume II: *Mrs Woolf 1912–1941* (Hogarth Press 1972).

But Leonard Woolf's own early novels came to supply a great deal of evidence which we cannot gather from his autobiography, *The Village in the Jungle* (Edward Arnold 1913) and *The Wise Virgins* (Edward Arnold 1914).

Supplementary biographical detail has been furnished by George Spater and Ian Parsons, *A Marriage of True Minds, An Intimate Portrait of Leonard and Virginia Woolf* (Jonathan Cape and Hogarth Press 1977); by Nigel Nicolson, *Portrait of a Marriage* (Weidenfeld and Nicolson 1973); by Gerald Brenan, *Personal Record 1920–72* (Jonathan Cape 1974) and the thirteenth chapter of his *South from Granada* (Hamish Hamilton 1974). Dora Carrington's *Letters* have also been relevant (*Carrington: Letters and Extracts from her Diaries*), chosen and with an introduction by David Garnett (Jonathan Cape 1970).

For the character and thought of Sir Leslie Stephen, I have drawn my own conclusions from reading his own works, but have been indebted to Noel Gilroy Annan's *Leslie Stephen: His Thought and Character in Relation to his Time* (MacGibbon & Kee 1951), and am especially grateful for the lapidary clarity of his chapters 'Cambridge Rationalism', 'Leslie

Stephen Loses his Faith', 'Agnosticism', 'The Moral Society' and 'Literary Criticism'.

The appearance of previously unpublished autobiographical materials from the Sussex University Library, the Monks House Collection and the Berg Collection, in *Virginia Woolf: Moments of Being*, edited with an introduction and notes by Jeanne Schulkind (Sussex University Press 1976), was an event of great importance in the formation of my book. In these pages, in Virginia's own hand, we have the account of the influence of Gerald and George Duckworth, with dates, which clinched my case. Once it is generally realised what Jeanne Schulkind's collection contains, the whole course of writing on Virginia Woolf will take on a completely new direction.

As this book was being written, the first three volumes of *The Letters of Virginia Woolf*[1] and the first volume of *The Diary of Virginia Woolf*[2] were published. They have all been relevant, and contributed much further evidence for the theory advanced here. The fact that the editors all accept Quentin Bell's interpretation of Virginia Woolf as canonical, and that this interpretation is taken to be final, is a very noticeable feature in all of them.

Also during the composition of the preceding pages appeared a massive compendium from Professor S. P. Rosenbaum of Toronto University, *The Bloomsbury Group, A Collection of Memoirs, Commentary and Criticism* (Croom Helm 1975). It contains useful material, but does not offer itself as interpretation of Virginia Woolf's work as such. It is nevertheless the best compendium of its kind I know.

The status, nature and very existence of 'Bloomsbury' has not concerned me at all, except insofar as a certain pervasive rationalism, coupled with a certain destructive or reductive verbalism, pervaded conversations in its milieu. I have adduced Brenan on this as my best evidence, and any book of G. E. Moore's will illustrate my point. But the tone of abrasive rationalism lives on in Michael Holroyd's *Lytton Strachey and the Bloomsbury Group: His Work Their Influence* (Penguin Books 1971), which perpetuates in its own hostile way the myth of Virginia's 'insanity' ('She can be, and has been, put down as a textbook example of a leptosome whose neurosis was schizophrenic though, most probably, her condition was that of a manic depressive').

Indeed, most of the contemporary accounts of 'Bloomsbury' continue

---

[1] Edited by Nigel Nicolson with the assistance of Joanne Trautmann (Hogarth Press 1975, 1976, 1977). 1888–1912: *The Flight of the Mind*; 1913–1922: *The Question of Things Happening*; 1923–1928: *A Change of Perspective*.

[2] 1915–1919, introduced by Quentin Bell and edited by Anne Olivier Bell (Hogarth Press 1977).

to celebrate its Hobbesian 'state of nature' quality without its talent. The sheerly destructive side of it is rarely mentioned, except in something like Frank Swinnerton's sarcastic account of it in *The Georgian Literary Scene*. A recent publication—*Recollections of Virginia Woolf*, edited by Joan-Russell Noble, with an introduction by Michael Holroyd (where the mad, zany Virginia Woolf is again presented) is typical enough. In joking their way through a composite crucifixion of Virginia Woolf, the various participants refuse utterly to admit to that perfected mockery which 'Bloomsbury' rationalism excelled in. Just how destructive, how spiritually murderous much of its scintillating conversation could be is implicitly denied throughout. And Virginia is placed at some point within, but not of, 'Bloomsbury', where her actual tragic dilemma is discounted.

Of critical works on Virginia Woolf there is now an enormous library, but few critics approach or dare to consider her main achievement: the establishment of a new mode of discourse, a new mode of rationality, a new form of deduction and integration in writing her novels. She is rarely, that is to say, considered as philosophically important, although she obviously follows a phenomenological course of enquiry in her writing. Harvena Richter's *The Inward Voyage* (Princeton 1970) is an exception. Herbert Marder's *Feminism and Art* (University of Chicago Press 1968) attempts to solve the basic problem by the concept of 'the androgynous mind', but as I have said in these pages, I do not think there is any such thing in nature. At least Marder shows what a real threat rationalism in a pure state represents to the intuitive mind at work. Further reflection along Marder's lines is to be found in James Naremore's *The World Without a Self* (Yale University Press 1973), Nancy Topping Bazin's *Virginia Woolf and the Androgynous Vision* (Rutgers University Press 1973) and Alice Van Buren Kelley's *Virginia Woolf: Fact and Vision* (University of Chicago Press 1973). Technically adept is Allen McLaurin's difficult but rewarding *Virginia Woolf: The Echoes Enslaved* (Cambridge University Press 1973), which, like Rosenbaum's *Bloomsbury Group*, is an excellent source book.

Fascinating on the parent-child relationship in the nineteenth century is *James and John Stuart Mill, Father and Son in the Nineteenth Century* by Bruce Mazlish (Hutchinson 1975). From there it is only a step to J. S. Mill's *Autobiography*, and from there but a pace to Edmund Gosse's *Father and Son*. Reading that, one is beginning to understand the achievement of Virginia Woolf.

BIBLIOGRAPHICAL NOTE (CONTINUED) (1989)

Since the publication of *The Unknown Virginia Woolf* in 1978, the last three volumes of *The Letters of Virginia Woolf* have been published, as well as four more volumes of *The Diary* (editors and publisher as above).

Further documentation of the Bloomsbury milieu has been forth-coming in the form of Frances Partridge, *Memories* (Robin Clark 1982); Frances Spalding, *Vanessa Bell* (Weidenfeld & Nicolson 1983); Angelica Garnett, *Deceived with Kindness: A Bloomsbury Childhood* (Chatto and Windus, Hogarth Press 1984); Lyndall Gordon, *Virginia Woolf, A Writer's Life* (Oxford U.P. 1984); Claire Tomalin, *Katharine Mansfield, A Secret Life* (Viking 1987); Diane F. Gillespie and Elizabeth Steele (eds), *Julia Duckworth Stephen: Stories for Children, Essays for Adults* (Syracuse University Press 1987); Diane Filby Gillespie, *The Sisters' Arts: The Writing and Painting of Virginia Woolf and Vanessa Bell* (Syracuse University Press 1988).

Further information of the background of Virginia Woolf's alleged 'madness' has been provided in a fully documented book by Stephen Trombley, *'All That Summer She was Mad': Virginia Woolf and Her Doctors* (Junction Books 1981; and [with a different subtitle] Continuum Publishing Company 1982). This study is particularly interesting in throwing into relief the beliefs of the doctors who treated Virginia Woolf, on such subjects as art. Stephen Trombley has more recently published a second study of the mental set and presuppositions of the doctors of the early twentieth century in *The Right to Reproduce: A History of Coercive Sterilisation* (Weidenfeld & Nicolson 1988). The biographical account by Lyndall Gordon (see above) disagrees with me in footnotes while silently absorbing my conclusions into the body of her text; the same is true of Mark Spilka's *Virginia Woolf's Quarrel with Grieving* (University of Nebraska Press 1980), which was preceded by a long review essay, 'New Life in the Works: Some Recent Woolf Studies' in *Novel* (Winter 1979) p. 169ff. My work and Stephen Trombley's also influenced Shirley Panken, *Virginia Woolf and the 'Lust of Creation': A Psychoanalytic Exploration* (State University of New York Press 1987); and Betty Kushen, *Virginia Woolf and the Nature of Communion* (The Raynor Press 1985). Shirley Panken is ticked off by Harvena Richter (*Virginia Woolf Miscellany* No 29, Fall 1987 p. 4) for following 'the generally discredited book by Stephen Trombley, "*All That Summer She was Mad*"', though it remains an open question how any book can be 'generally discredited' which has never been answered, far less refuted.

On the theme specifically of 'madness' in the period of *Mrs Dalloway*, and in particular how 'mad' soldiers suffering on the front or returning from the war may have been treated by the 'nerve-specialists' of the time, a work of very exceptional interest has appeared in the form of *The Female Malady: Women, Madness and English Culture 1830–1980* by Elaine Showalter (Pantheon Books 1985; Virago Press 1987). Elaine Showalter lists Stephen Trombley's work in her bibliography, but not (in a way that grows progressively more predictable) mine.

Meanwhile the physico-neurologico-chemico-determinist-behavioural persuasion continues to argue a case that no one has ever seriously disputed, so obvious is it that the body plays some part in the determinations of the mind. But Thomas C. Caramagno's 'Manic-Depressive Psychosis and Critical Approaches to Virginia Woolf's Life and Work' (*Proceedings of the Modern Language Association* 103, No 1, January 1988, pp. 10–23) hits an all-time low in this manner, advancing an argument on Virginia Woolf's 'madness' so crude and reductive as to become its own parody. Gently invited, in a recent response by Mark Hussey, to modify the raw pre-conceptuality of his case (*P.M.L.A.* 104, No 1, January 1989, p. 75), Professor Caramagno just charges past with a series of half-comprehensible titbits of Stephen family lore which are meant to show that manic-depressive illness is hereditary: 'Accordingly we may hypothesize that (Sir) Leslie inherited non-X-linked genes from his father. . . . The missing X-linked gene. . . . came from either his mother, Jane Venn, or Virginia's mother, the depressive Julia, augmenting the Stephen family genetic code already evident in J. K.'s manias and Sir James's depressions' (pp. 76–7). And this is from a man who deplores other people's 'hypothesizing'.

The chemico-reductivist model of thinking has recently been challenged (in a serious, scientific way) by Steven Rose, R. C. Lewontin and Leon J. Kamin in *Not in Our Genes* (Pelican Books 1984), but it is doubtful whether this intelligent and trenchant enquiry into working hypotheses will make any headway against the chemico-reductivism which is so fashionable at the moment.

A significant addition to our knowledge of Virginia Woolf's working methods and attitudes of mind has been made by Louise A. DeSalvo, first in her study *Virginia Woolf's First Voyage: A Novel in the Making* (Rowman and Littlefield 1980) and then in her edition of *Melymbrosia by Virginia Woolf: An Early Version of the Voyage Out* (The New York Public Library 1982). Louise DeSalvo earns our gratitude a third time for editing, along with Mitchell A. Leaska, *The Letters of Vita Sackville-West to Virginia Woolf* (Hutchinson & Co. 1984). Needless to say, this collection of letters fully bears out my contention in *The Unknown Virginia Woolf*. Her most recent book, *Virginia Woolf: The Impact of Childhood Sexual Abuse on Her Life and Work* (Beacon Press, 1989) shows to what an extent the proposals of *The Unknown Virginia Woolf*, irreceivable at the time, have become orthodoxy. Its subtitle simply assumes as an established fact what I was contending for in 1978 against such entrenched resistance.

It is a matter of pleasure to record the appearance of Mark Hussey's *The Singing of the Real World: The Philosophy of Virginia Woolf's Fiction* (Ohio State University Press 1986). This book sets out explicitly from the premises and preoccupations of Maurice Merleau-Ponty and seriously engages with the philosophical and theological dimension of her work. Carolyn Heilbrun was quick to perceive the implications in a review in *Journal of English and Germanic Philology*, Vol. 87 (3), July 1988, pp. 460–462: 'He views Woolf's writing not as linear or chronological, but as an ever more complex circling around in her search for an answer to that failure of faith that religion cannot assuage.' That is a sufficient theme for our time, and the most profitable thing that Woolf scholarship could do for the next decade is to follow up the implications of Mark Hussey's study.

Index